THE MANGA GUIDE™ TO DATABASES

THE MANGA GUIDE™ TO
DATABASES

MANA TAKAHASHI
SHOKO AZUMA
TREND-PRO CO., LTD.

Ohmsha

no starch
press

The Manga Guide to Databases is a translation of the Japanese original, *Manga de Wakaru Database*, published by Ohmsha, Ltd. of Tokyo, Japan, © 2004 by Mana Takahashi and TREND-PRO Co., Ltd.

This English edition is co-published by No Starch Press, Inc. and Ohmsha, Ltd.

11 10 09 08   1 2 3 4 5 6 7 8 9

ISBN-10: 1-59327-190-5
ISBN-13: 978-1-59327-190-9

FIBER USED IN THIS PRODUCT LINE MEETS THE SOURCING REQUIREMENTS OF THE SFI PROGRAM
WWW.SFIPROGRAM.ORG
SFI CERTIFIED SOURCING

Publisher: William Pollock
Author: Mana Takahashi
Illustrator: Shoko Azuma
Producer: TREND-PRO Co., Ltd.
Production Editor: Megan Dunchak
Developmental Editor: Tyler Ortman
Technical Reviewers: Baron Schwartz and Peter MacIntyre
Compositor: Riley Hoffman
Proofreader: Cristina Chan
Indexer: Sarah Schott

For information on book distributors or translations from the English edition, please contact No Starch Press, Inc.
No Starch Press, Inc.
555 De Haro Street, Suite 250, San Francisco, CA 94107
phone: 415.863.9900; fax: 415.863.9950; info@nostarch.com; http://www.nostarch.com/

Library of Congress Cataloging-in-Publication Data

Takahashi, Mana.
The Manga guide to databases / Mana Takahashi, Shoko Azuma, and Trend-pro Co. -- 1st ed.
p. cm.
Includes index.
ISBN-13: 978-1-59327-190-9
ISBN-10: 1-59327-190-5
1. Database management--Comic books, strips, etc. 2. Database management--Caricatures and cartoons. 3. SQL (Computer program language)--Comic books, strips, etc. 4. SQL (Computer program language)--Caricatures and cartoons. I. Azuma, Shoko, 1974- II. Trend-pro Co. III. Title.
QA76.9.D3T34 2009
005.75'65--dc22

2008046159

Contents

4
LET'S LEARN ABOUT SQL!

5
LET'S OPERATE A DATABASE!

PREFACE

Databases are a crucial part of nearly all computer-based business systems. Some readers of this book may be considering introducing databases into their routine work. Others may have to actually develop real database-based business systems. The database is the technology that supports these systems behind the scenes, and its true nature is difficult to understand.

This book is designed so that readers will be able to learn the basics about databases through a manga story. At the end of each chapter, practice exercises are provided for confirmation and expanding the knowledge you've obtained. Each chapter is designed so that readers can gain an understanding of database technology while confirming how much they understand the contents.

The structure of this book is as follows.

Chapter 1 describes why we use databases. Why is a database necessary? What kind of difficulties will you have if you do not use a database? You will learn the background information that using a database requires.

Chapter 2 provides basic terminology. You'll learn about various database models and other terms relating to databases.

Chapter 3 explains how to design a database, specifically, a relational database, the most common kind.

Chapter 4 covers SQL, a language used to manage relational databases. Using SQL allows you to easily manage your data.

Chapter 5 explains the structure of the database system. Since a database is a system through which many people share data, you will learn how it can do so safely.

Chapter 6 provides descriptions of database applications. You'll learn how Web-based and other types of database systems are used.

This book was published thanks to the joint efforts of many people: Shoko Azuma for cartoons, TREND-PRO for production, and Ohmsha for planning, editing, and marketing. I extend my deep gratitude to all those concerned.

I hope that this book is helpful to all readers.

MANA TAKAHASHI

1
What Is a Database?

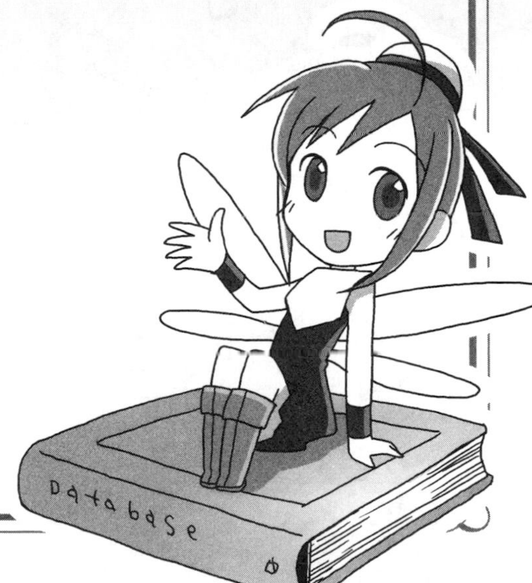
Database

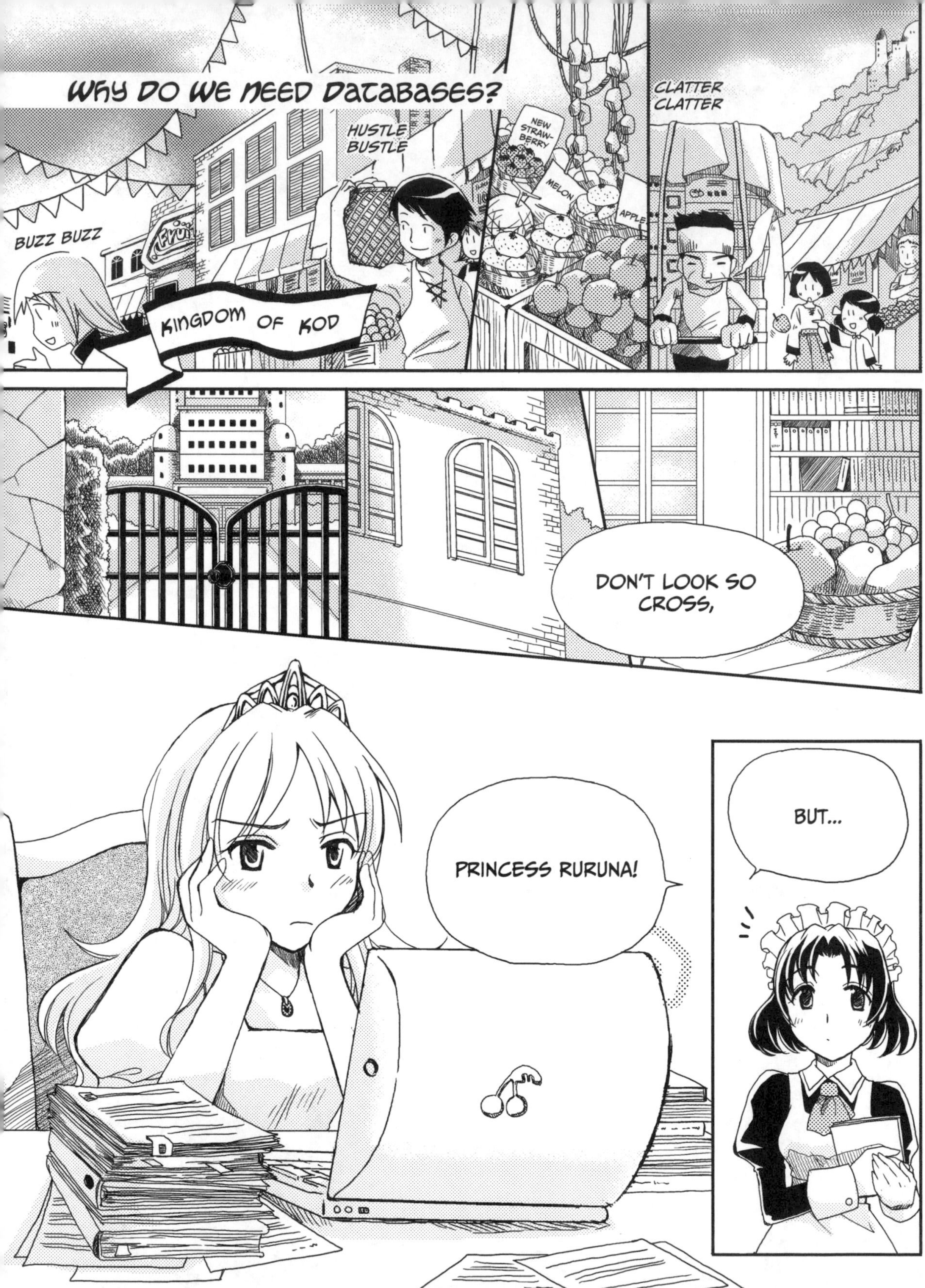
WHY DO WE NEED DATABASES?
BUZZ BUZZ
HUSTLE BUSTLE
KINGDOM OF KOD
NEW STRAW-BERRY
MELON
APPLE
CLATTER CLATTER
DON'T LOOK SO CROSS,
PRINCESS RURUNA!
BUT...

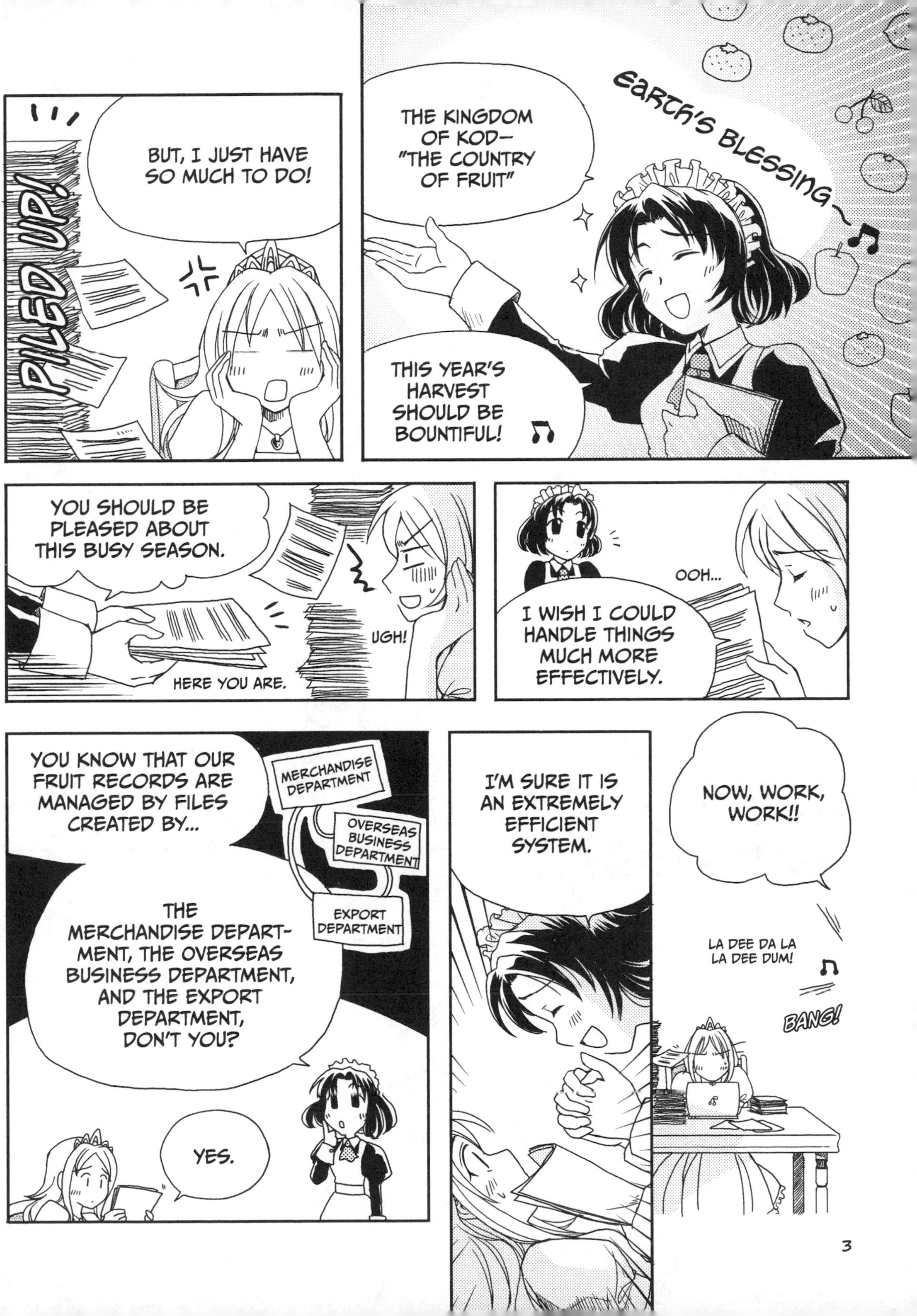
PILED UP!
BUT, I JUST HAVE SO MUCH TO DO!
THE KINGDOM OF KOD—"THE COUNTRY OF FRUIT"
EARTH'S BLESSING~
THIS YEAR'S HARVEST SHOULD BE BOUNTIFUL!
YOU SHOULD BE PLEASED ABOUT THIS BUSY SEASON.
UGH!
HERE YOU ARE.
OOH...
I WISH I COULD HANDLE THINGS MUCH MORE EFFECTIVELY.
YOU KNOW THAT OUR FRUIT RECORDS ARE MANAGED BY FILES CREATED BY...
MERCHANDISE DEPARTMENT
OVERSEAS BUSINESS DEPARTMENT
EXPORT DEPARTMENT
THE MERCHANDISE DEPARTMENT, THE OVERSEAS BUSINESS DEPARTMENT, AND THE EXPORT DEPARTMENT, DON'T YOU?
YES.
I'M SURE IT IS AN EXTREMELY EFFICIENT SYSTEM.
NOW, WORK, WORK!!
LA DEE DA LA LA DEE DUM!
BANG!

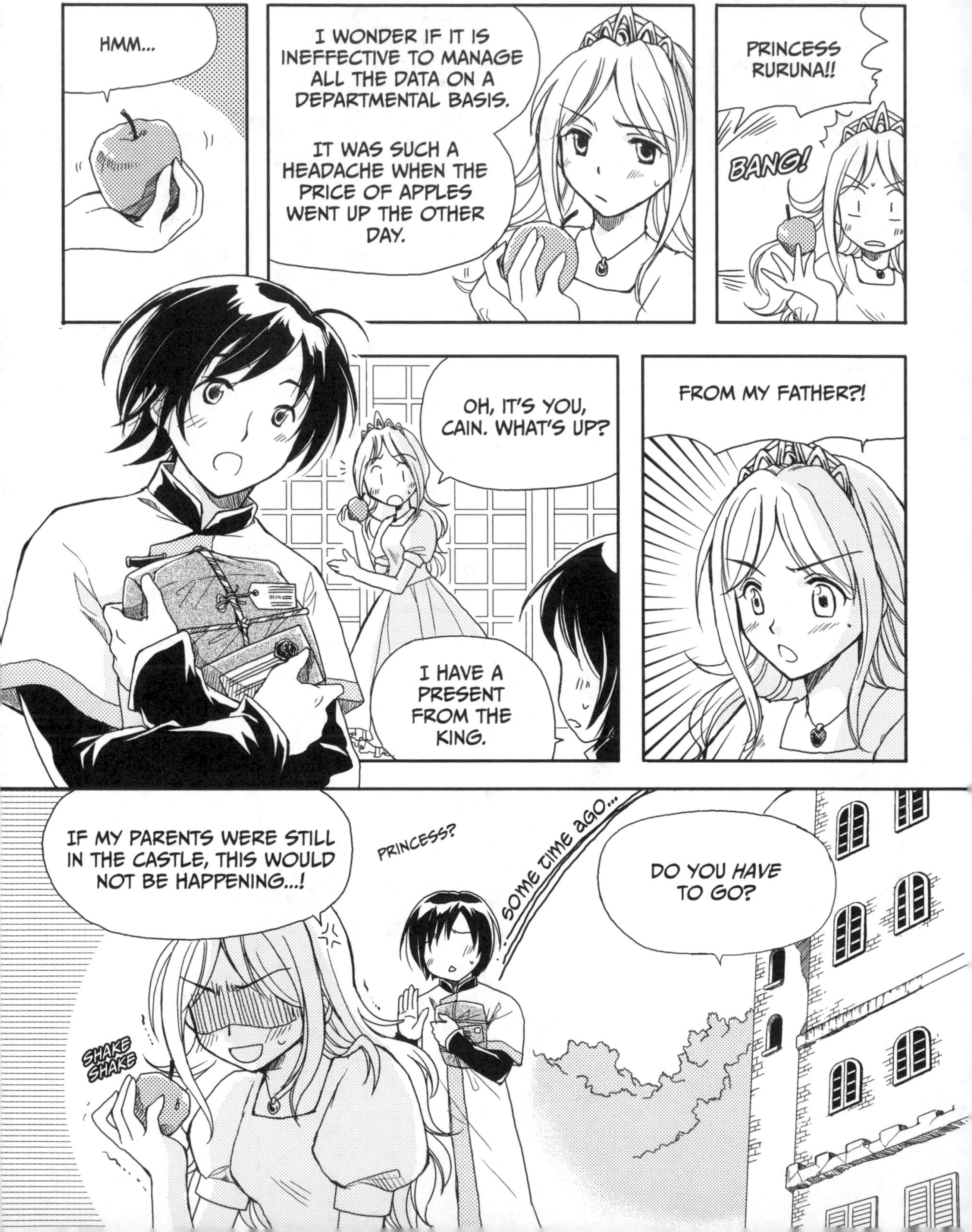
HMM...
I WONDER IF IT IS INEFFECTIVE TO MANAGE ALL THE DATA ON A DEPARTMENTAL BASIS.
IT WAS SUCH A HEADACHE WHEN THE PRICE OF APPLES WENT UP THE OTHER DAY.
PRINCESS RURUNA!!
BANG!
OH, IT'S YOU, CAIN. WHAT'S UP?
I HAVE A PRESENT FROM THE KING.
FROM MY FATHER?!
IF MY PARENTS WERE STILL IN THE CASTLE, THIS WOULD NOT BE HAPPENING...!
PRINCESS?
SOME TIME AGO...
DO YOU HAVE TO GO?
SHAKE SHAKE

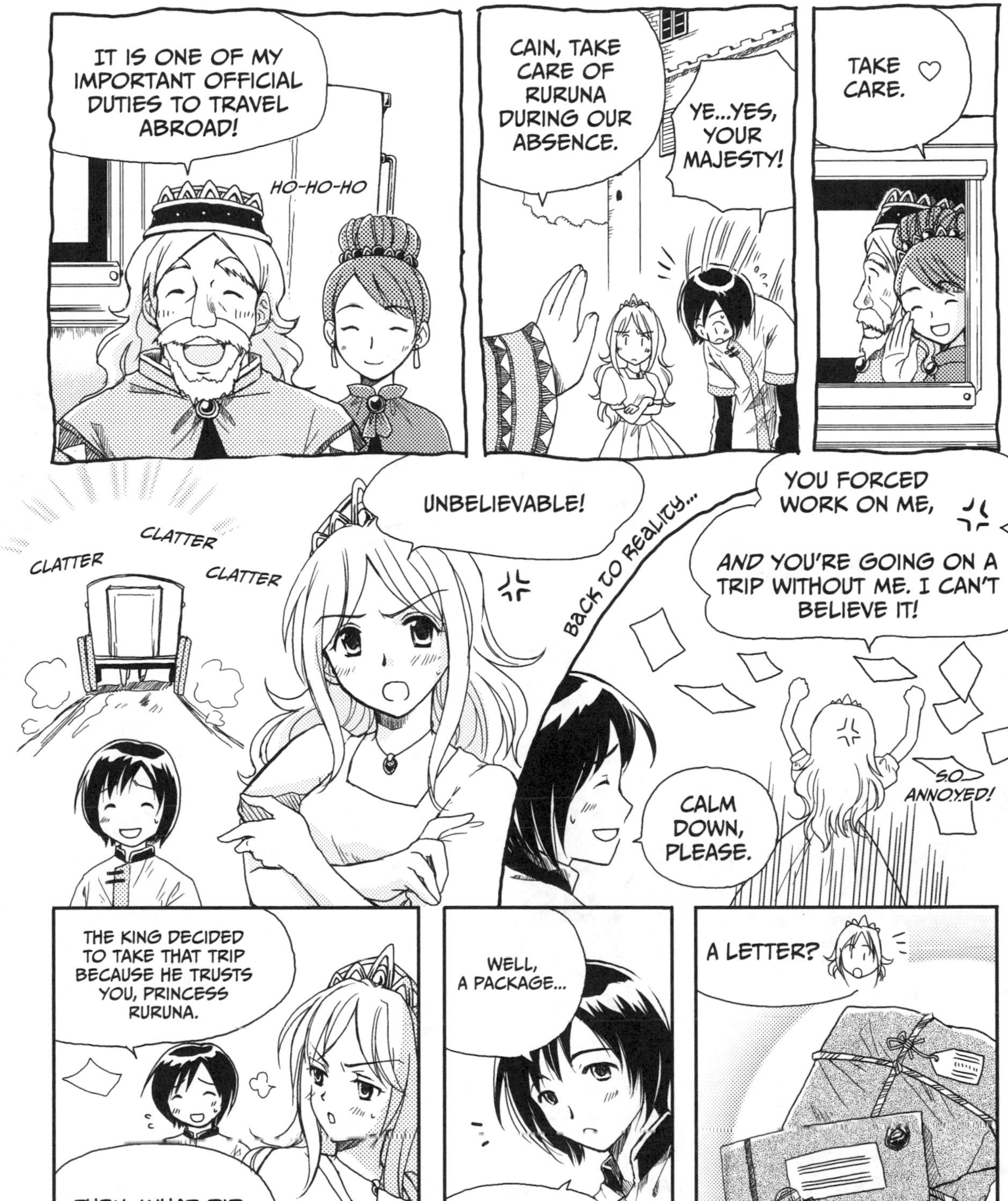
IT IS ONE OF MY IMPORTANT OFFICIAL DUTIES TO TRAVEL ABROAD!
HO-HO-HO
CAIN, TAKE CARE OF RURUNA DURING OUR ABSENCE.
YE...YES, YOUR MAJESTY!
TAKE CARE. ♡
CLATTER
CLATTER
CLATTER
UNBELIEVABLE!
BACK TO REALITY...
YOU FORCED WORK ON ME,
AND YOU'RE GOING ON A TRIP WITHOUT ME. I CAN'T BELIEVE IT!
SO ANNOYED!
CALM DOWN, PLEASE.
THE KING DECIDED TO TAKE THAT TRIP BECAUSE HE TRUSTS YOU, PRINCESS RURUNA.
THEN, WHAT DID HE SEND ME?
WELL, A PACKAGE...
AND A LETTER.
A LETTER?

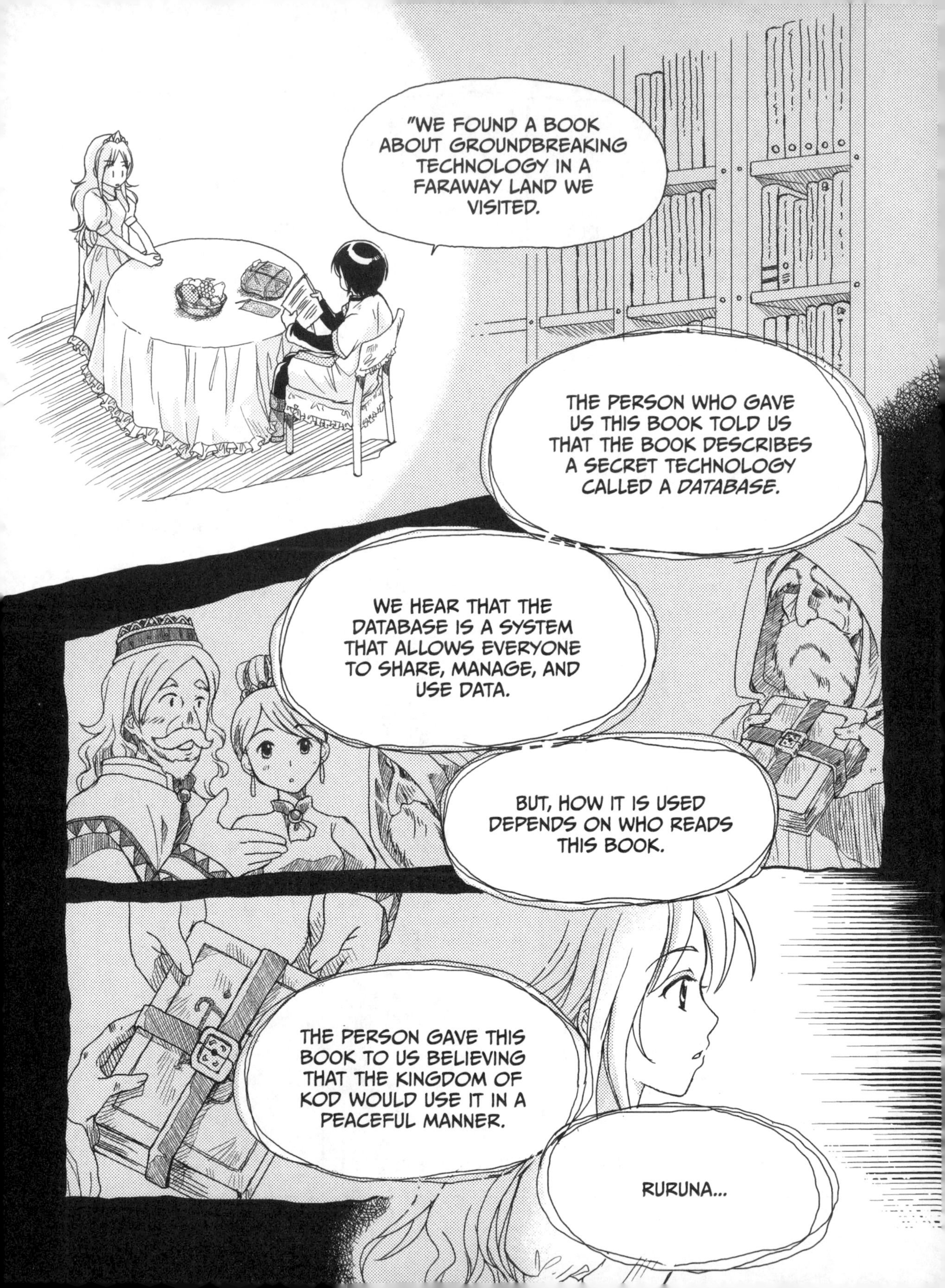
"WE FOUND A BOOK ABOUT GROUNDBREAKING TECHNOLOGY IN A FARAWAY LAND WE VISITED.
THE PERSON WHO GAVE US THIS BOOK TOLD US THAT THE BOOK DESCRIBES A SECRET TECHNOLOGY CALLED A *DATABASE*.
WE HEAR THAT THE DATABASE IS A SYSTEM THAT ALLOWS EVERYONE TO SHARE, MANAGE, AND USE DATA.
BUT, HOW IT IS USED DEPENDS ON WHO READS THIS BOOK.
THE PERSON GAVE THIS BOOK TO US BELIEVING THAT THE KINGDOM OF KOD WOULD USE IT IN A PEACEFUL MANNER.
RURUNA...

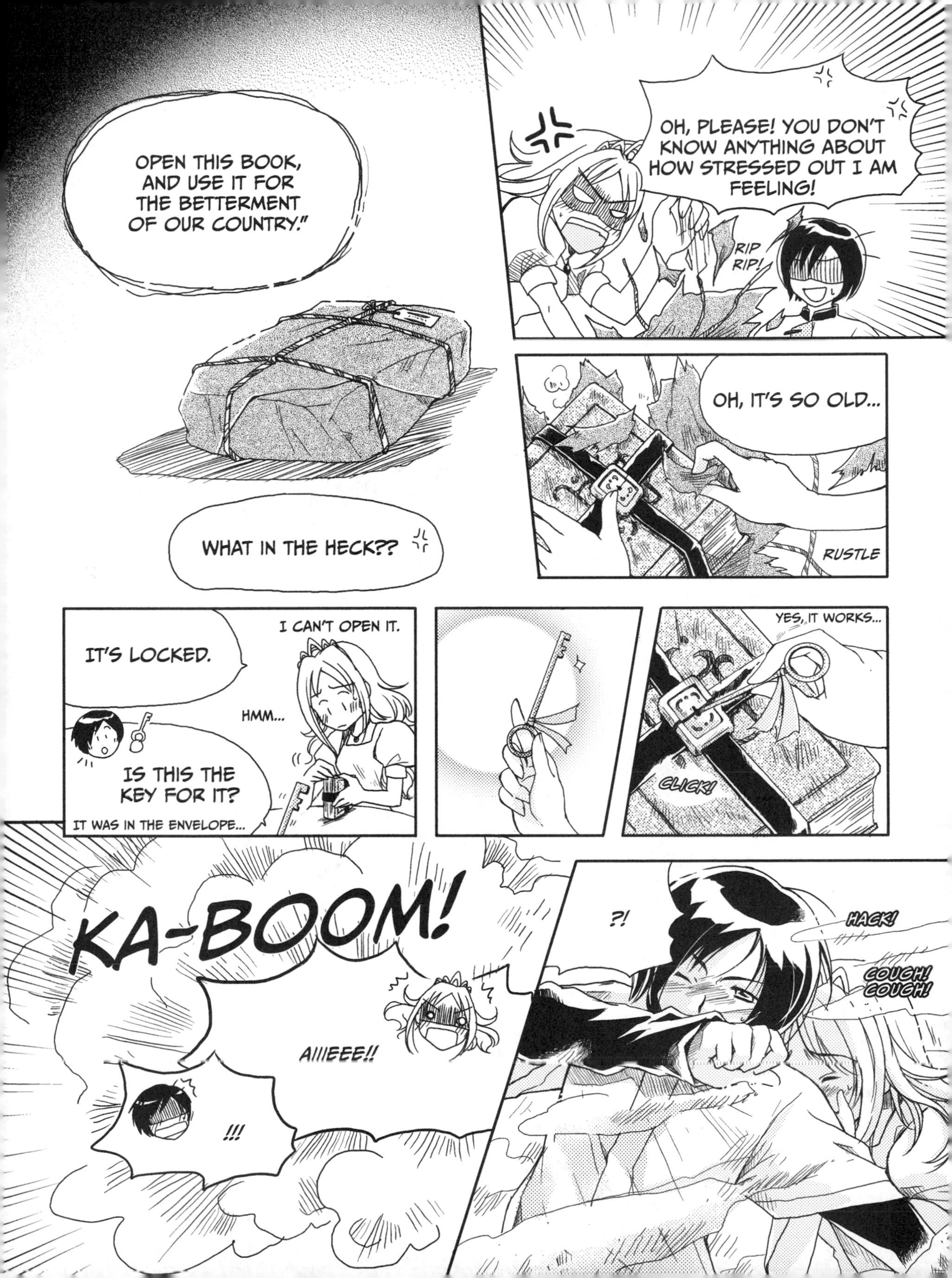
OPEN THIS BOOK, AND USE IT FOR THE BETTERMENT OF OUR COUNTRY."
WHAT IN THE HECK??
OH, PLEASE! YOU DON'T KNOW ANYTHING ABOUT HOW STRESSED OUT I AM FEELING!
RIP RIP!
OH, IT'S SO OLD...
RUSTLE
IT'S LOCKED.
I CAN'T OPEN IT.
HMM...
IS THIS THE KEY FOR IT?
IT WAS IN THE ENVELOPE...
YES, IT WORKS...
CLICK!
KA-BOOM!
AIIIEEE!!
!!!
?!
HACK!
COUGH! COUGH!

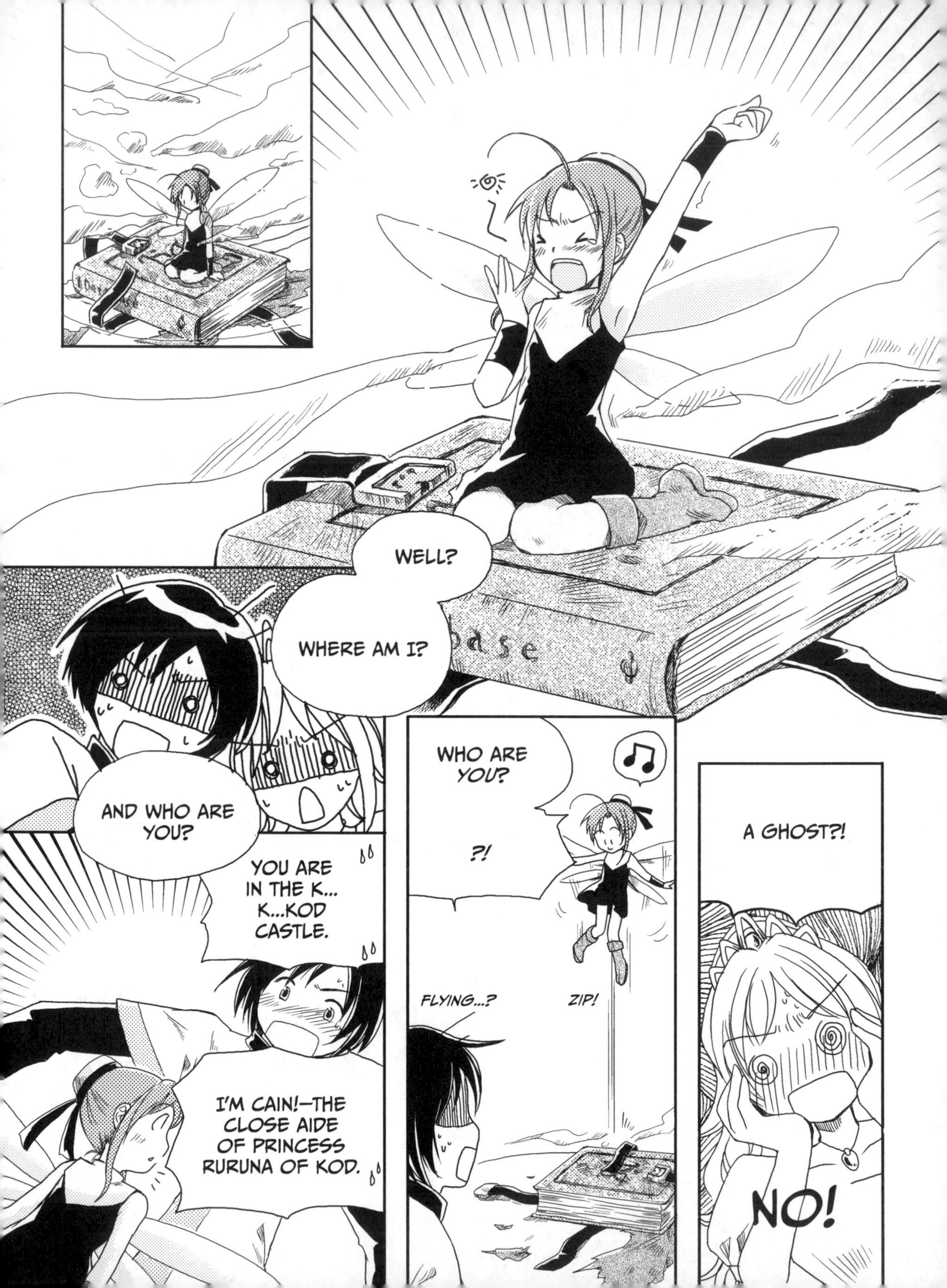
WELL?
WHERE AM I?
AND WHO ARE YOU?
YOU ARE IN THE K... K...KOD CASTLE.
I'M CAIN!—THE CLOSE AIDE OF PRINCESS RURUNA OF KOD.
WHO ARE YOU?
?!
FLYING...?
ZIP!
A GHOST?!
NO!

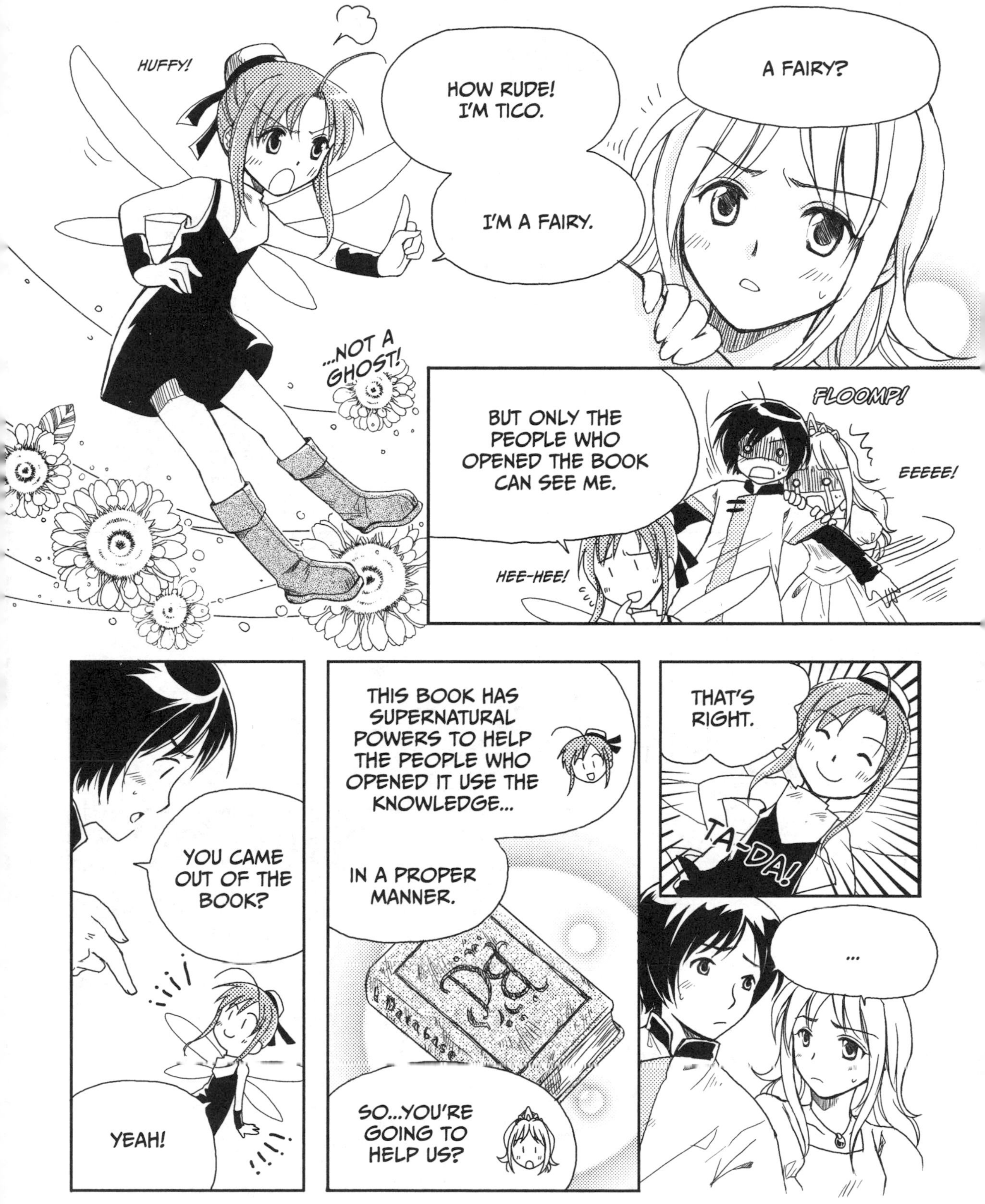
HUFFY!
HOW RUDE! I'M TICO.
I'M A FAIRY.
...NOT A GHOST!
A FAIRY?
BUT ONLY THE PEOPLE WHO OPENED THE BOOK CAN SEE ME.
FLOOMP!
EEEEE!
HEE-HEE!
YOU CAME OUT OF THE BOOK?
YEAH!
THIS BOOK HAS SUPERNATURAL POWERS TO HELP THE PEOPLE WHO OPENED IT USE THE KNOWLEDGE...
IN A PROPER MANNER.
Database
SO...YOU'RE GOING TO HELP US?
THAT'S RIGHT.
TA-DA!
...

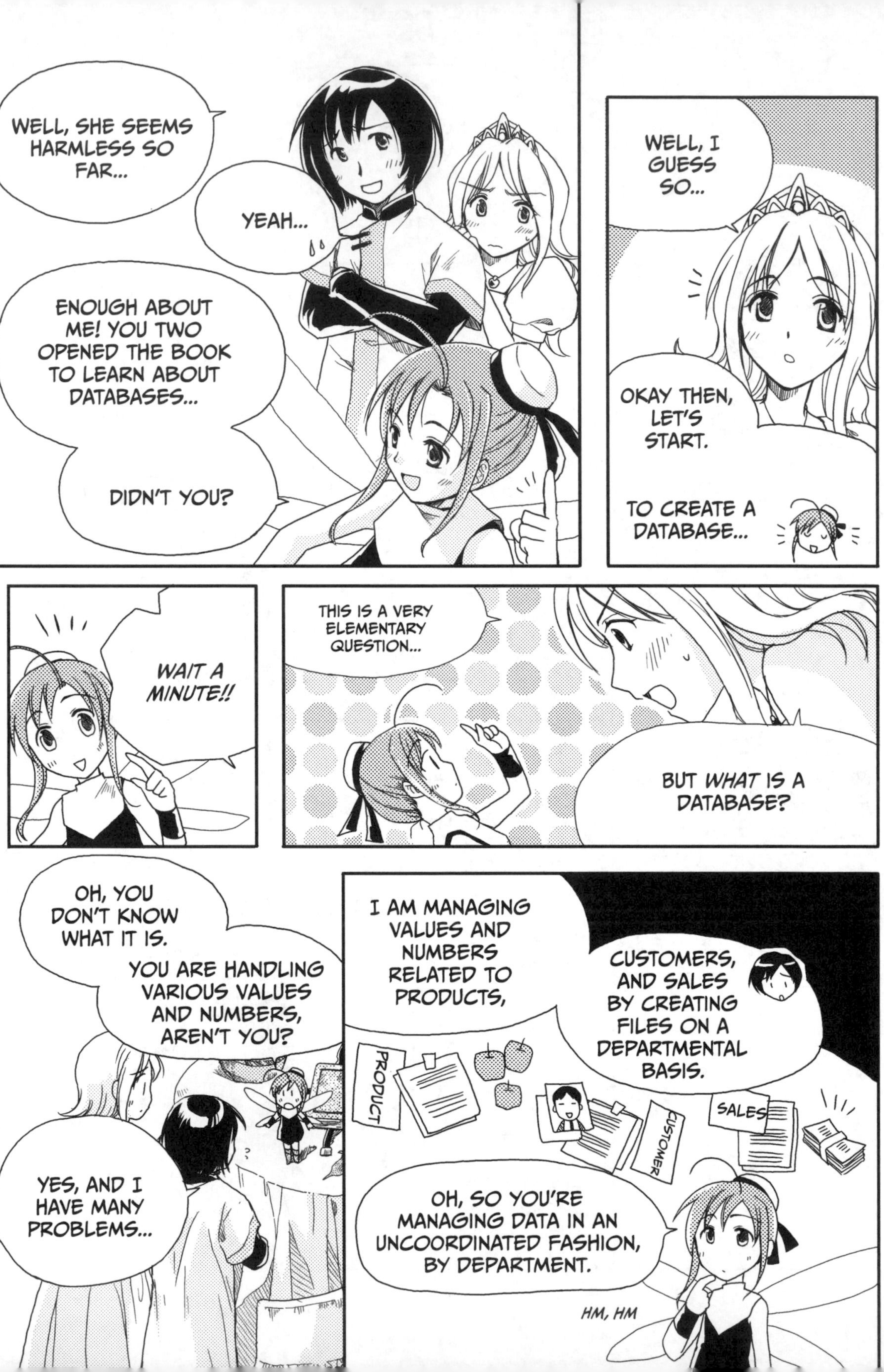
WELL, SHE SEEMS HARMLESS SO FAR...
YEAH...
ENOUGH ABOUT ME! YOU TWO OPENED THE BOOK TO LEARN ABOUT DATABASES...
DIDN'T YOU?
WELL, I GUESS SO...
OKAY THEN, LET'S START.
TO CREATE A DATABASE...
WAIT A MINUTE!!
THIS IS A VERY ELEMENTARY QUESTION...
BUT *WHAT* IS A DATABASE?
OH, YOU DON'T KNOW WHAT IT IS.
YOU ARE HANDLING VARIOUS VALUES AND NUMBERS, AREN'T YOU?
YES, AND I HAVE MANY PROBLEMS...
I AM MANAGING VALUES AND NUMBERS RELATED TO PRODUCTS,
CUSTOMERS, AND SALES BY CREATING FILES ON A DEPARTMENTAL BASIS.
PRODUCT
CUSTOMER
SALES
OH, SO YOU'RE MANAGING DATA IN AN UNCOORDINATED FASHION, BY DEPARTMENT.
HM, HM

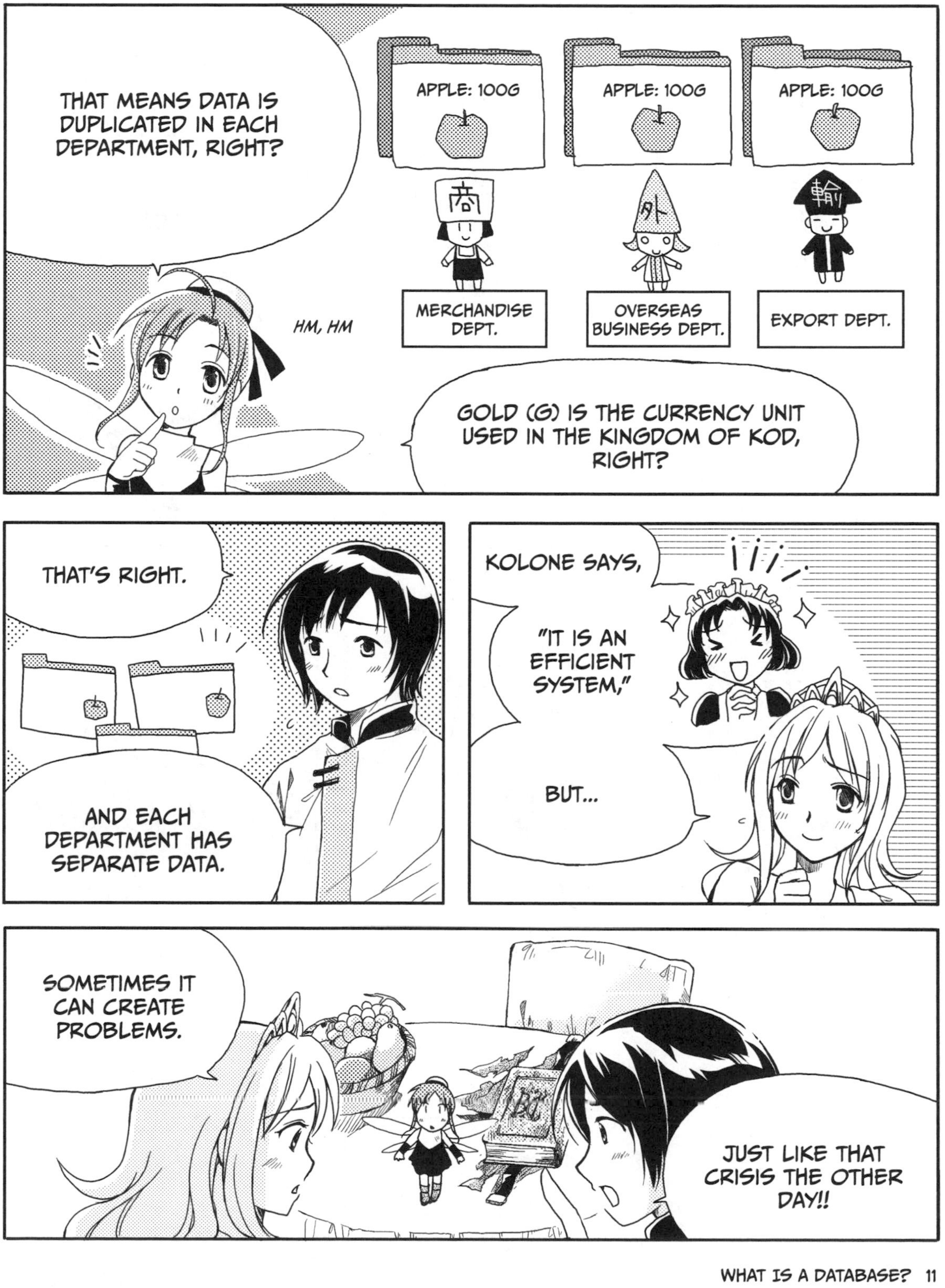
THAT MEANS DATA IS DUPLICATED IN EACH DEPARTMENT, RIGHT?
APPLE: 100G
APPLE: 100G
APPLE: 100G
商
外
輸
HM, HM
MERCHANDISE DEPT.
OVERSEAS BUSINESS DEPT.
EXPORT DEPT.
GOLD (G) IS THE CURRENCY UNIT USED IN THE KINGDOM OF KOD, RIGHT?
THAT'S RIGHT.
AND EACH DEPARTMENT HAS SEPARATE DATA.
KOLONE SAYS,
"IT IS AN EFFICIENT SYSTEM,"
BUT...
SOMETIMES IT CAN CREATE PROBLEMS.
JUST LIKE THAT CRISIS THE OTHER DAY!!

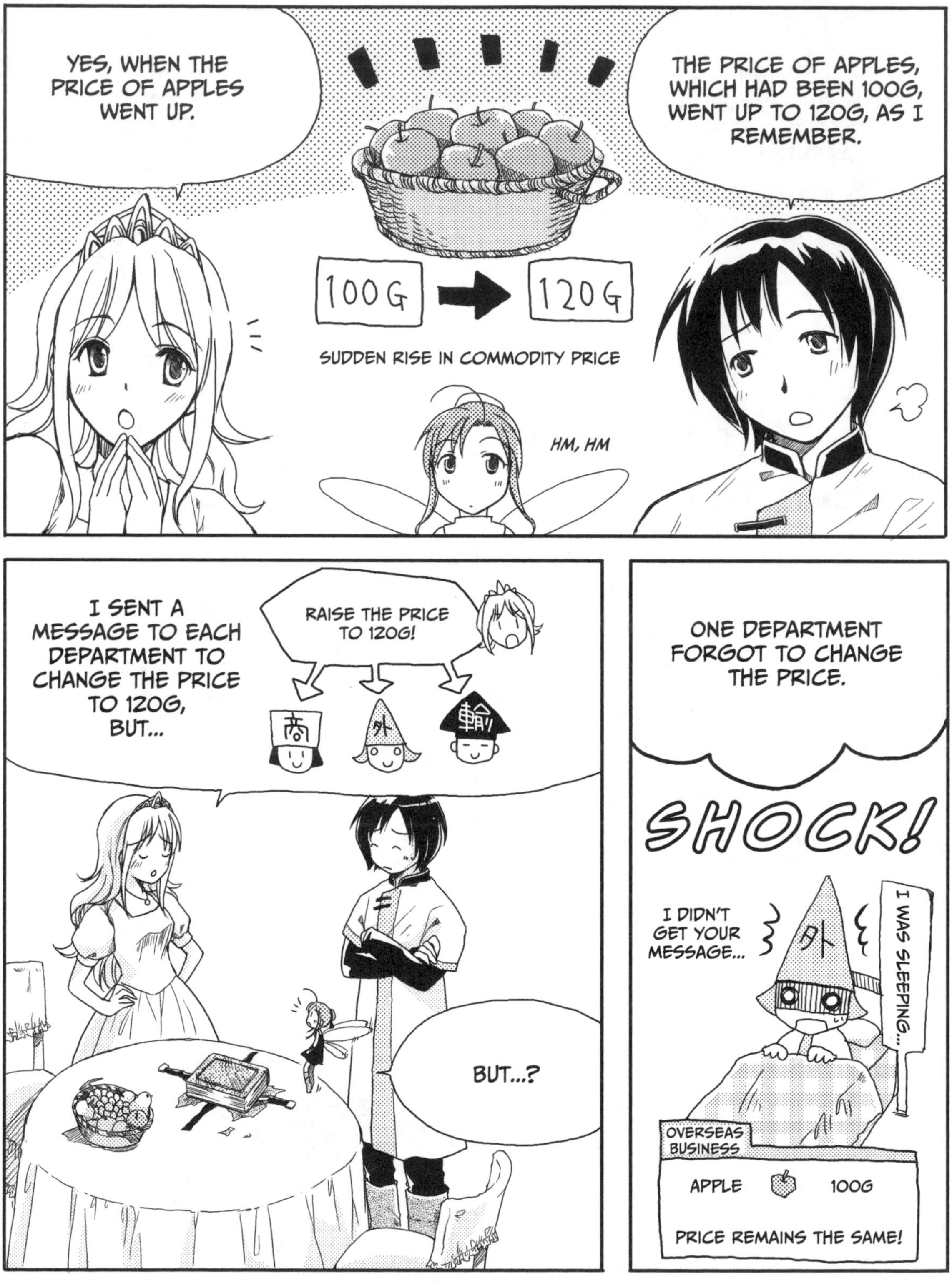
YES, WHEN THE PRICE OF APPLES WENT UP.
THE PRICE OF APPLES, WHICH HAD BEEN 100G, WENT UP TO 120G, AS I REMEMBER.
100G
120G
SUDDEN RISE IN COMMODITY PRICE
HM, HM
I SENT A MESSAGE TO EACH DEPARTMENT TO CHANGE THE PRICE TO 120G, BUT...
RAISE THE PRICE TO 120G!
商
外
輸
BUT...?
ONE DEPARTMENT FORGOT TO CHANGE THE PRICE.
SHOCK!
I DIDN'T GET YOUR MESSAGE...
外
I WAS SLEEPING...
OVERSEAS BUSINESS
APPLE
100G
PRICE REMAINS THE SAME!

NOT ONLY THAT...

UGH, I SHUDDER AT THE MEMORY OF IT...

ANOTHER DEPARTMENT CHANGED THE PRICE TO 300G BY MISTAKE.

CHAOS!

APPLE: 120G

APPLE: 100G

APPLE: 300G

IS THAT RIGHT?

THAT'S STRANGE...

WHY...?

SOMETHING'S WRONG!

MERCHANDISE DEPT.

OVERSEAS BUSINESS DEPT.

EXPORT DEPT.

THE DATA IN RESPECTIVE DEPARTMENTS CONFLICTS, DOESN'T IT?

SIGH

THAT'S RIGHT.

IT WAS PARTICULARLY HARD FOR CAIN! HE HAD TO RUN AROUND THE KINGDOM...

AND CORRECT ALL THE ERRORS.

YEAH...

APPLE 120G

THE PRICE OF APPLES IS NOT CORRECT...

FIX THE PRICE, PLEASE!

OH, GEE.

STILL A BIT TIRED...

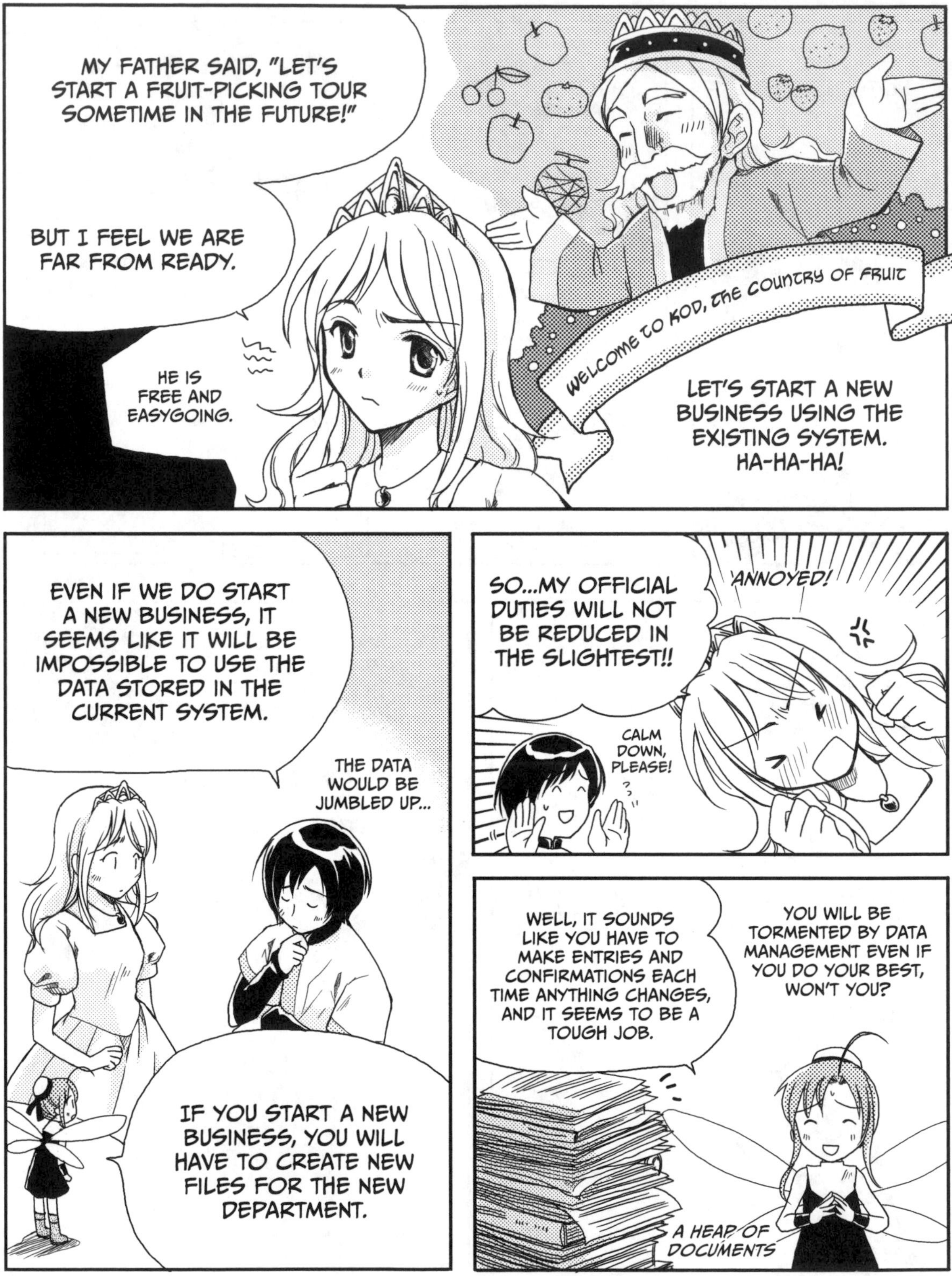
MY FATHER SAID, "LET'S START A FRUIT-PICKING TOUR SOMETIME IN THE FUTURE!"
BUT I FEEL WE ARE FAR FROM READY.
HE IS FREE AND EASYGOING.
WELCOME TO KOD, THE COUNTRY OF FRUIT
LET'S START A NEW BUSINESS USING THE EXISTING SYSTEM. HA-HA-HA!
EVEN IF WE DO START A NEW BUSINESS, IT SEEMS LIKE IT WILL BE IMPOSSIBLE TO USE THE DATA STORED IN THE CURRENT SYSTEM.
THE DATA WOULD BE JUMBLED UP...
IF YOU START A NEW BUSINESS, YOU WILL HAVE TO CREATE NEW FILES FOR THE NEW DEPARTMENT.
SO...MY OFFICIAL DUTIES WILL NOT BE REDUCED IN THE SLIGHTEST!!
ANNOYED!
CALM DOWN, PLEASE!
WELL, IT SOUNDS LIKE YOU HAVE TO MAKE ENTRIES AND CONFIRMATIONS EACH TIME ANYTHING CHANGES, AND IT SEEMS TO BE A TOUGH JOB.
YOU WILL BE TORMENTED BY DATA MANAGEMENT EVEN IF YOU DO YOUR BEST, WON'T YOU?
A HEAP OF DOCUMENTS

A SYSTEM IN WHICH DATA IS SHARED BY EVERYONE IS CALLED A DATABASE.

IF YOU USED ONE, YOU WOULD NOT HAVE TO KEEP USELESS DATA.

INSIGHT!

IS IT TRUE?

YOU MEAN WE CAN HAVE A MUCH MORE EFFICIENT SYSTEM THAN THE CURRENT ONE?

IT SOUNDS LIKE IT IS WORTH STUDYING, DOESN'T IT?

YEAH!

YOU KNOW SO MUCH...

CAN'T *YOU* JUST DO IT?

......

HEE HEE

I DO NOT HAVE A PHYSICAL BODY, SO I CAN'T USE COMPUTERS IN THE REAL WORLD.

I'M SORRY.

I SEE.

BUT IN GRATITUDE FOR BRINGING ME OUT OF THE BOOK...

I WILL TEACH YOU EVERYTHING. BUT YOU MUST DO YOUR BEST!

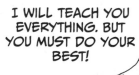

FOR ME *AND* MY COUNTRY...

I'M GOING FOR IT!

OH, PRINCESS!

WHAT'S UP IN THE KINGDOM?

The Kingdom of Kod currently uses a file-based system to manage its data. But it seems that the current system has a few problems. What are they, in particular? Let's look at the system in detail.

The Kingdom currently has three departments: the Merchandise Department, the Overseas Business Department, and the Export Department. The Merchandise Department keeps track of all fruit produced in the country, the Overseas Business Department manages the foreign countries that are the Kingdom's business partners, and the Export Department keeps records of the amount of fruit the Kingdom exports.

PRINCESS RURUNA
商
MERCHANDISE DEPARTMENT
外
OVERSEAS BUSINESS DEPARTMENT
輸
EXPORT DEPARTMENT

DATA IS DUPLICATED

Princess Ruruna isn't satisfied with the current system. But why not? Each department in the Kingdom manages data independently. For example, the Merchandise Department and the Export Department each create files to manage fruit data. Therefore, data is duplicated needlessly across the departments. Each department must enter the data, store the data, then print receipts for confirmation, all of which is a waste. In addition, data trapped in one particular department is never shared effectively with the other departments.

PRINCESS RURUNA
Data is duplicated.
MERCHANDISE DEPT.
OVERSEAS BUSINESS DEPT.
EXPORT DEPT.

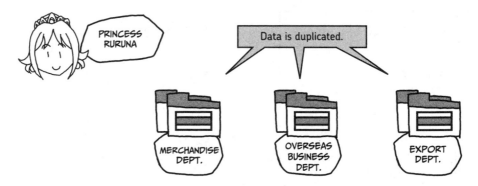

But that's not all. The system also creates problems when someone needs to change the data. For example, let's assume that the price of apples changes. To deal with this, Princess Ruruna must notify every department individually that the price of apples has changed. Isn't that inconvenient?

PRINCESS RURUNA
The Princess must send a message to each department.
MERCHANDISE DEPT.
OVERSEAS BUSINESS DEPT.
EXPORT DEPT.

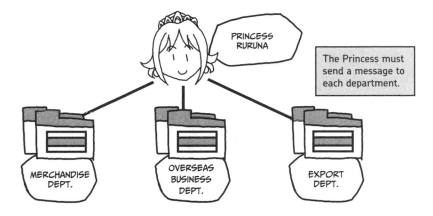

DATA CAN CONFLICT

It may seem easy enough to notify each department that the price of apples has changed, but it can create a new set of problems. Let's say that Princess Ruruna does notify the three departments that the price of apples has changed. However, the Overseas Business Department may forget to change the price, or the Export Department might change the price to 300G instead of 120G. These kinds of errors result in conflicting data between departments, which causes the content of the file systems to differ from the conditions of the real world. What a pain!

CHANGE THE PRICE OF APPLES FROM 100G TO 120G.
PRINCESS RURUNA
This may cause conflicting data.

MERCHANDISE DEPARTMENT

Product name	Unit price	
Melon	800G	
Strawberry	150G	
Apple	*120G*	
Lemon	200G	

OVERSEAS BUSINESS DEPARTMENT

Product name	Unit price	
Melon	800G	
Strawberry	150G	
Apple	*100G*	
Lemon	200G	

EXPORT DEPARTMENT

Product name	Unit price	
Melon	800G	
Strawberry	150G	
Apple	*300G*	
Lemon	200G	

DATA IS DIFFICULT TO UPDATE

The current system not only creates conflicting data, but it also makes it difficult to respond to changes in business. For example, let's say that the King wants to launch a new Tourism Department. When a tour guide conducts a tour of the orchards and discusses the Kingdom's fruit sales, the guide will want to use the most up-to-date sales figures.

But, unfortunately, the current system does not necessarily allow the departments to access each other's data, since the files are kept independently. To manage a new tourism business, Princess Ruruna will have to make copies of all the relevant files for the Tourism Department!

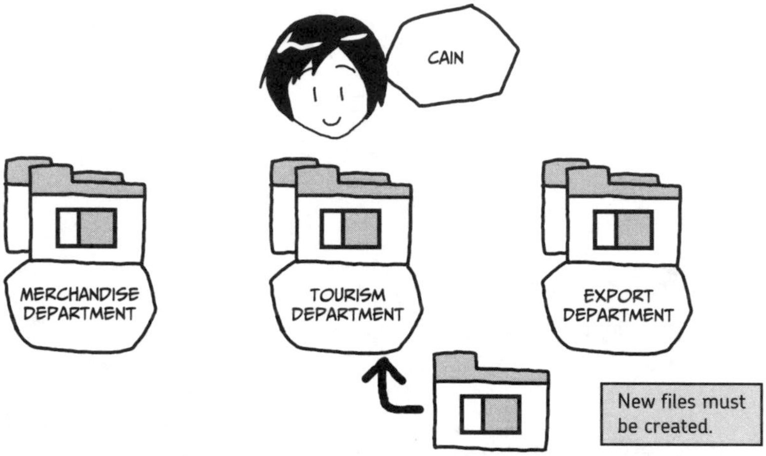
CAIN
MERCHANDISE DEPARTMENT
TOURISM DEPARTMENT
EXPORT DEPARTMENT
New files must be created.

FILE FOR MERCHANDISE DEPT.

Product name	Unit price	
Melon	800G	
Strawberry	150G	
Apple	120G	
Lemon	200G	

FILE FOR TOURISM DEPT.

Product name	Unit price	
Melon	*800G*	
Strawberry	*150G*	
Apple	*120G*	
Lemon	*200G*	

This, in turn, increases the amount of duplicated data created when a new department starts. Considering these weaknesses, the current system is not efficient. It makes it difficult to start new projects and respond to environmental changes.

a Database—That's Our Solution!

Well, why is this system so inefficient? The problems all stem from separate and independent data management. What should Ruruna and Cain do? That's right—they should create a database! They must unify the management of data for the entire Kingdom. I will show you how to do this in the next chapter.

DATABASE
PRINCESS RURUNA
Data is accessible to everyone.
商
MERCHANDISE DEPT.
外
OVERSEAS BUSINESS DEPT.
輸
EXPORT DEPT.

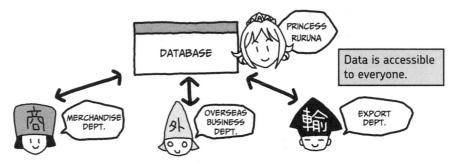

Uniform data management ensures that each department has the correct information, because each department sends a query to a single source of data. What an efficient system it is! It prevents data conflicts, and it also eliminates duplicated data, allowing for easy introduction and integration of new departments.

How to Use a Database

To introduce and operate a database, you must understand its unique challenges. First, the database will be used by many people, so you'll need a way for them to easily input and extract data. It needs to be a method that is easy for everybody to use.

WHAT IS THE PRICE OF APPLES IN G?
DATABASE
PRINCESS RURUNA
WHAT WAS THE SALES VOLUME ON MARCH 5?
商
MERCHANDISE DEPT.
外
OVERSEAS BUSINESS DEPT.
輸
EXPORT DEPT.

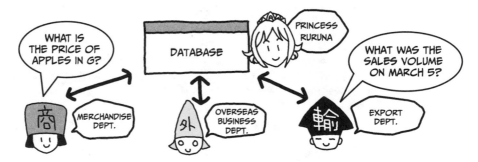

The new system also presents some risks—for example, it may make it possible for users to steal or overwrite important information like salary data, which is confidential and should be protected by an access restriction. Or, for example, only the Export Department should have access to sales data. Setting up database security and permissions is important when designing a system.

I CAN'T ACCESS SALES DATA.
DATABASE
PRINCESS RURUNA
I CAN ACCESS SALES DATA.
商
MERCHANDISE DEPT.
外
OVERSEAS BUSINESS DEPT.
輸
EXPORT DEPT.

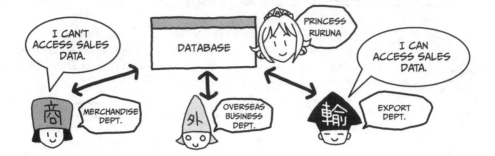

The new system can have other problems, too. The database can be used by many people at one time. Assume that someone in the Overseas Business Department and someone in the Export Department both try to change the name of a fruit at the same time—the former, from *Apple* to *AP*, and the latter, from *Apple* to *APL*. If they do this, what will happen to the product name? For a database that will be used by many people, this kind of problem must be considered.

DATABASE
PRINCESS RURUNA
AP?
APL?
商
MERCHANDISE DEPT.
外
OVERSEAS BUSINESS DEPT.
輸
EXPORT DEPT.

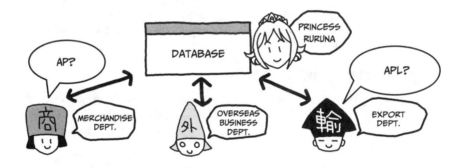

You also need to be careful not to lose any data. Furthermore, the system may go down or a hard disk could fail, causing data to be corrupted. The database must have mechanisms to recover from these common kinds of failures.

DATABASE
We must prepare for failures.

In addition, since the database will hold a large amount of data, you must be able to perform searches at high speeds. The new system must have the power to handle that.

Let's start studying databases together with Princess Ruruna and Cain to learn how to solve these problems. Onward to Chapter 2!

summary

- File-based management can create conflicting data and data duplication.
- A database allows you to share data easily and prevents conflicting and duplicated data.

USING SOFTWARE TO MANAGE DATABASES

The database we are going to study is managed by software called a database management system (DBMS). A DBMS has many useful functions—it allows you to do things like input data into a database, prevent conflicting data, and retrieve a large amount of data at high speed. Thanks to our DBMS, the database can be used by many people simultaneously. In addition, a DBMS can protect the security of the database— for example, it allows the database to operate properly even if a failure occurs. In addition, the DBMS provides an easy-to-use interface between the database and its users. We'll study databases and the functions of a DBMS in the next chapter.

2

WHAT IS A RELATIONAL DATABASE?

DATABASE TERMS

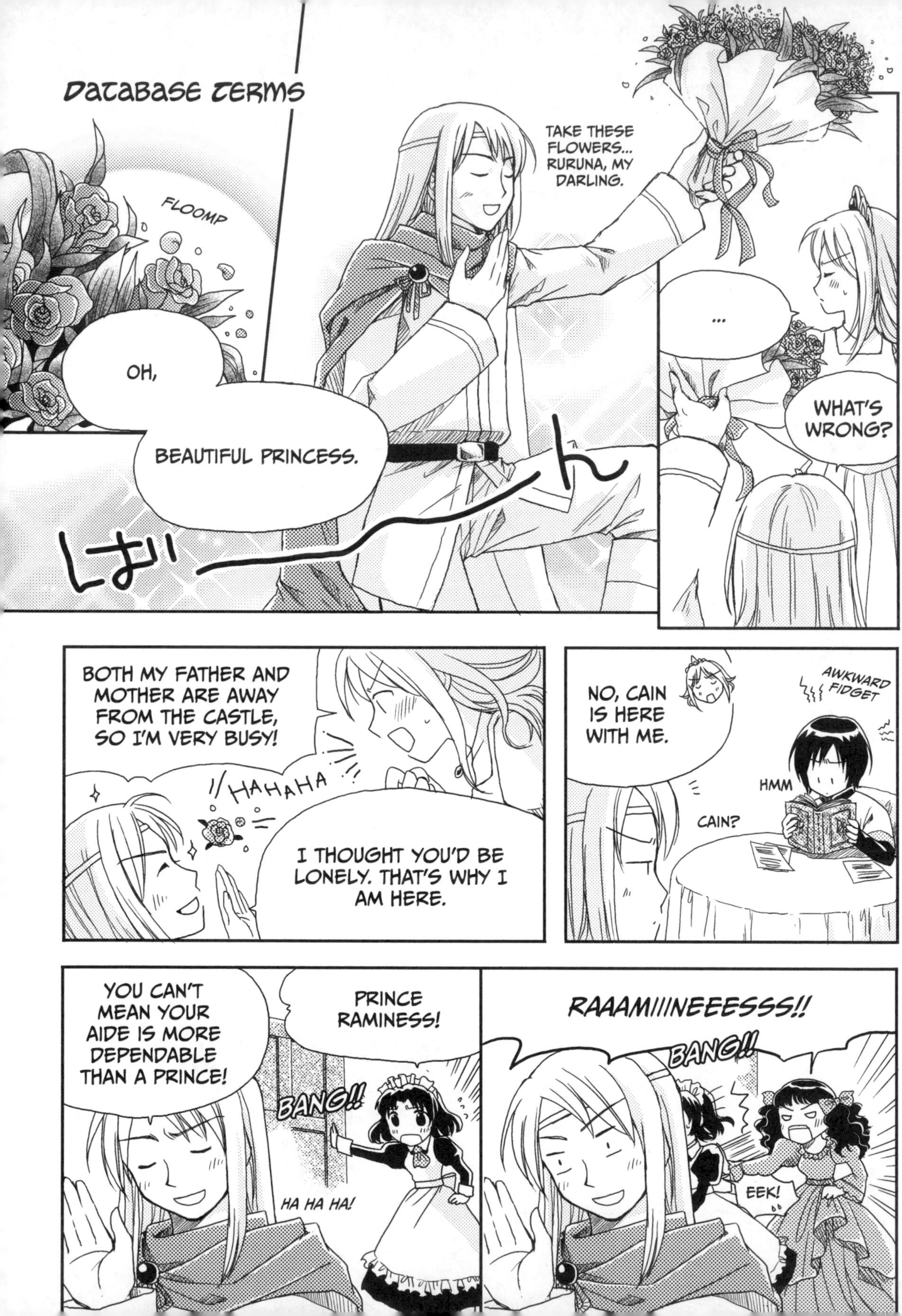
FLOOMP
OH,
BEAUTIFUL PRINCESS.
TAKE THESE FLOWERS... RURUNA, MY DARLING.
しおーーーん
...
WHAT'S WRONG?
BOTH MY FATHER AND MOTHER ARE AWAY FROM THE CASTLE, SO I'M VERY BUSY!
HAHAHA
I THOUGHT YOU'D BE LONELY. THAT'S WHY I AM HERE.
NO, CAIN IS HERE WITH ME.
AWKWARD FIDGET
HMM
CAIN?
YOU CAN'T MEAN YOUR AIDE IS MORE DEPENDABLE THAN A PRINCE!
PRINCE RAMINESS!
BANG!!
HA HA HA!
RAAAMIIIINEEEESSS!!
BANG!!
EEK!

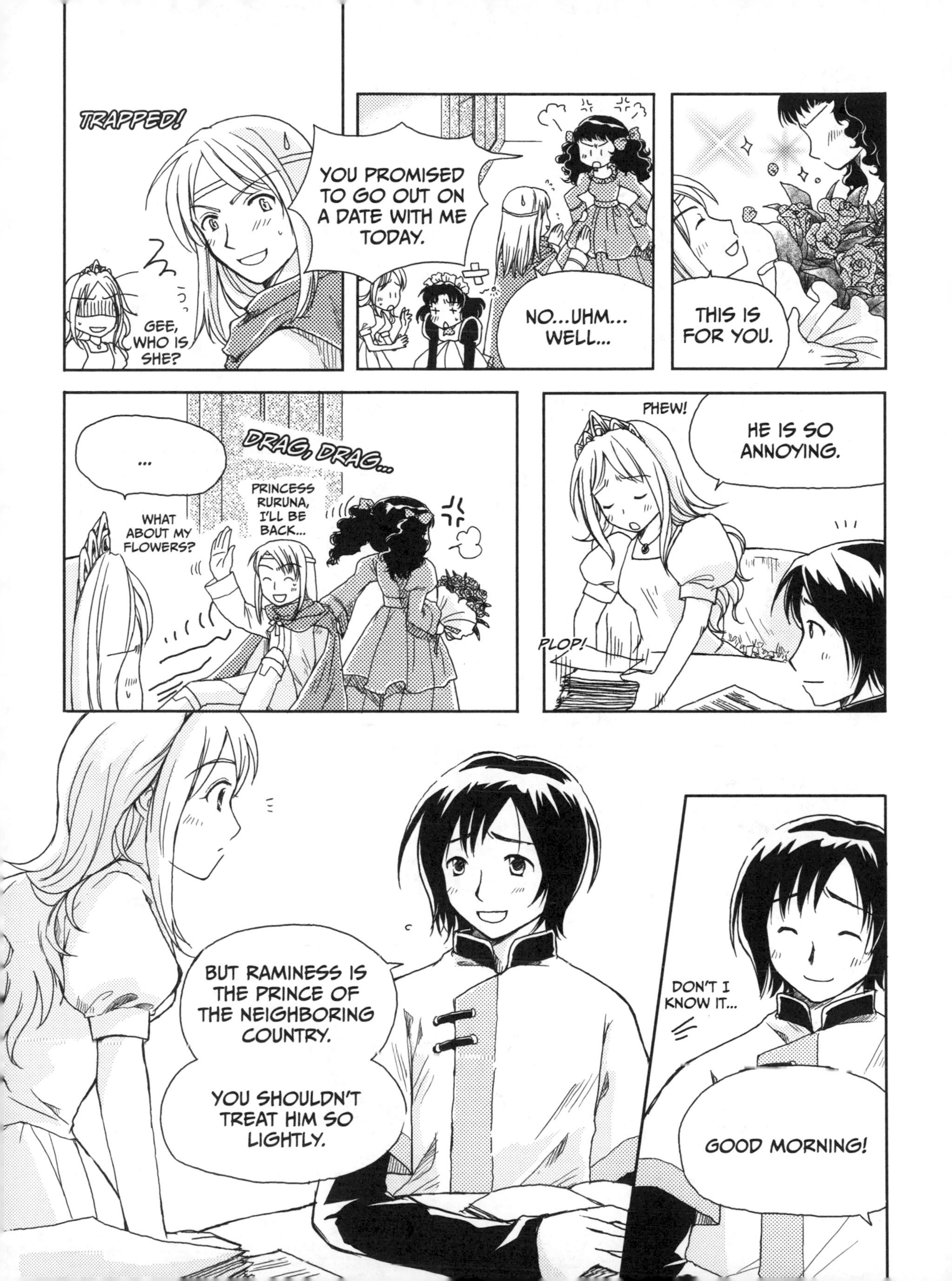
TRAPPED!
GEE, WHO IS SHE?
YOU PROMISED TO GO OUT ON A DATE WITH ME TODAY.
NO...UHM... WELL...
THIS IS FOR YOU.
...
WHAT ABOUT MY FLOWERS?
DRAG, DRAG...
PRINCESS RURUNA, I'LL BE BACK...
PHEW!
HE IS SO ANNOYING.
PLOP!
BUT RAMINESS IS THE PRINCE OF THE NEIGHBORING COUNTRY.
YOU SHOULDN'T TREAT HIM SO LIGHTLY.
DON'T I KNOW IT...
GOOD MORNING!

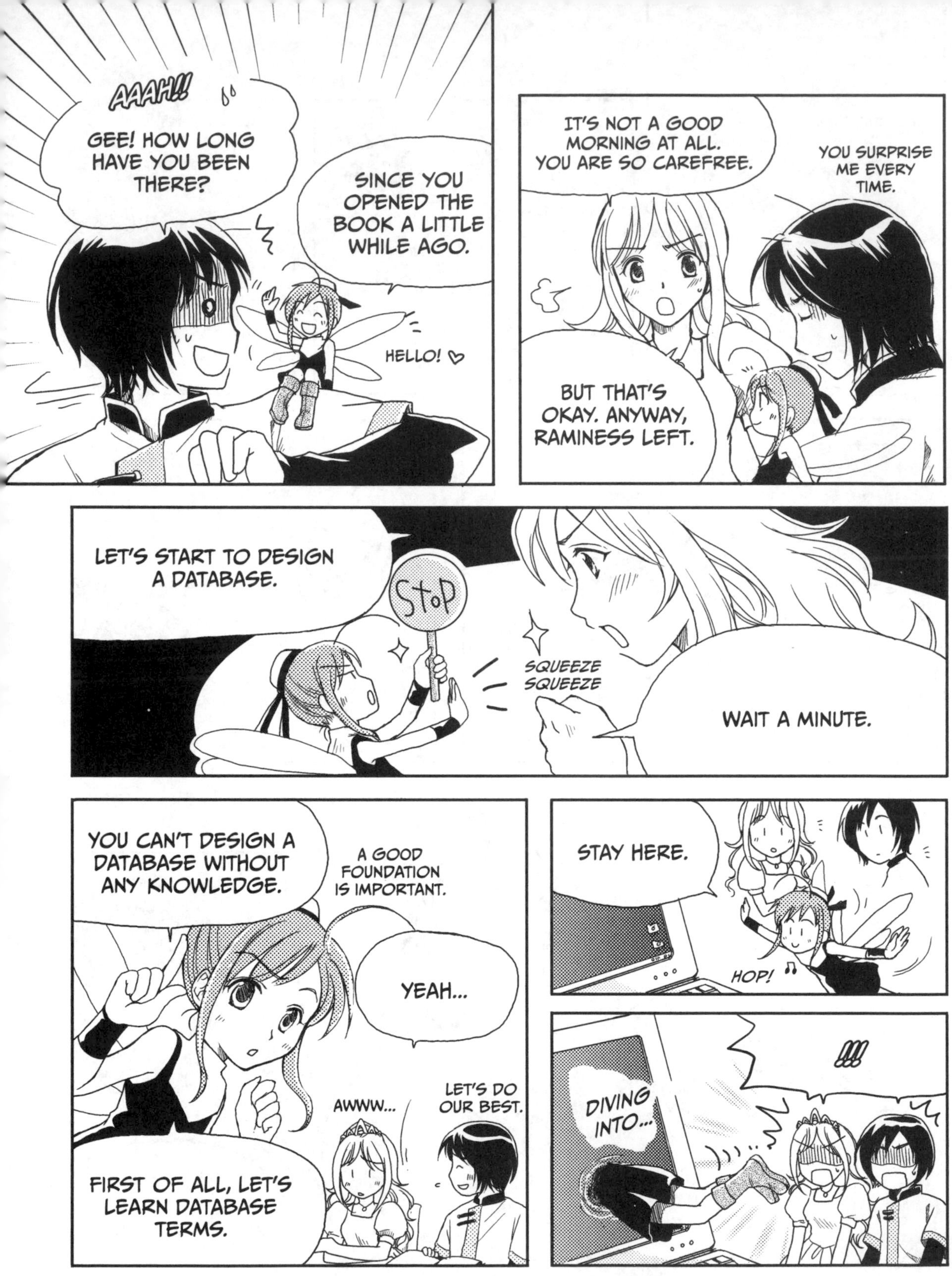
AAAH!!
GEE! HOW LONG HAVE YOU BEEN THERE?
SINCE YOU OPENED THE BOOK A LITTLE WHILE AGO.
HELLO!
IT'S NOT A GOOD MORNING AT ALL. YOU ARE SO CAREFREE.
YOU SURPRISE ME EVERY TIME.
BUT THAT'S OKAY. ANYWAY, RAMINESS LEFT.
LET'S START TO DESIGN A DATABASE.
StoP
SQUEEZE SQUEEZE
WAIT A MINUTE.
YOU CAN'T DESIGN A DATABASE WITHOUT ANY KNOWLEDGE.
A GOOD FOUNDATION IS IMPORTANT.
YEAH...
AWWW...
LET'S DO OUR BEST.
FIRST OF ALL, LET'S LEARN DATABASE TERMS.
STAY HERE.
HOP!
!!!
DIVING INTO...

WHAT?

WRIGGLE WRIGGLE

ZZZ

ZZZ

WHAT DID YOU SAY?

N...NO, NOTHING...

SHE WENT INTO THE LAPTOP..!

AND PULLED SOMETHING OUT...

?

THIS IS ONE OF THE FILES YOU ARE USING.

UH-HUH.

PRODUCT CODE	PRODUCT NAME	UNIT PRICE	REMARKS
101	MELON	800G	WITH SEEDS
102	STRAWBERRY	150G	
103	APPLE	120G	
104	LEMON	200G	
201	CHESTNUT	100G	
202	PERSIMMON	160G	

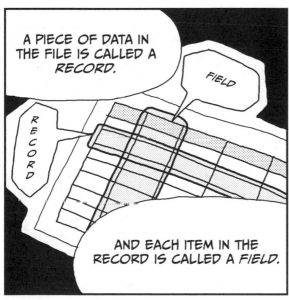

A PIECE OF DATA IN THE FILE IS CALLED A *RECORD*.

FIELD

RECORD

AND EACH ITEM IN THE RECORD IS CALLED A *FIELD*.

ONE PRODUCT IS ONE RECORD, RIGHT?

UH-HUH.

THEN THE *PRODUCT CODE, PRODUCT NAME, UNIT PRICE,* AND *REMARKS* ARE FIELDS, CORRECT?

EACH RECORD CONTAINS FIELDS OF THE SAME TYPE.

RECORD

I SEE.

PRODUCT CODE	PRODUCT NAME	UNIT PRICE	REMARKS
101	MELON	800G	WITH SEEDS
102	STRAWBERRY	150G	
103	APPLE	120G	
104	LEMON	200G	SOUR
201	CHESTNUT	100G	WITH BUR
202	PERSIMMON	160G	
301	PEACH	130G	
302	KIWI	200G	VALUABLE

FIELD

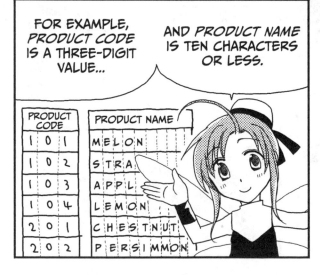

FOR EXAMPLE, *PRODUCT CODE* IS A THREE-DIGIT VALUE...

AND *PRODUCT NAME* IS TEN CHARACTERS OR LESS.

PRODUCT CODE
101
102
103
104
201
202

PRODUCT NAME
M E L O N
S T R A
A P P L
L E M O N
C H E S T N U T
P E R S I M M O N

THEN, NEXT, LET'S THINK ABOUT THE PRODUCT CODE IN A LITTLE MORE DETAIL.

PRODUCT CODE
101
102
103
104
201
202
301
302

HERE!

HMMM... RECORD... FIELD... MUTTER... MUTTER...

CAIN?

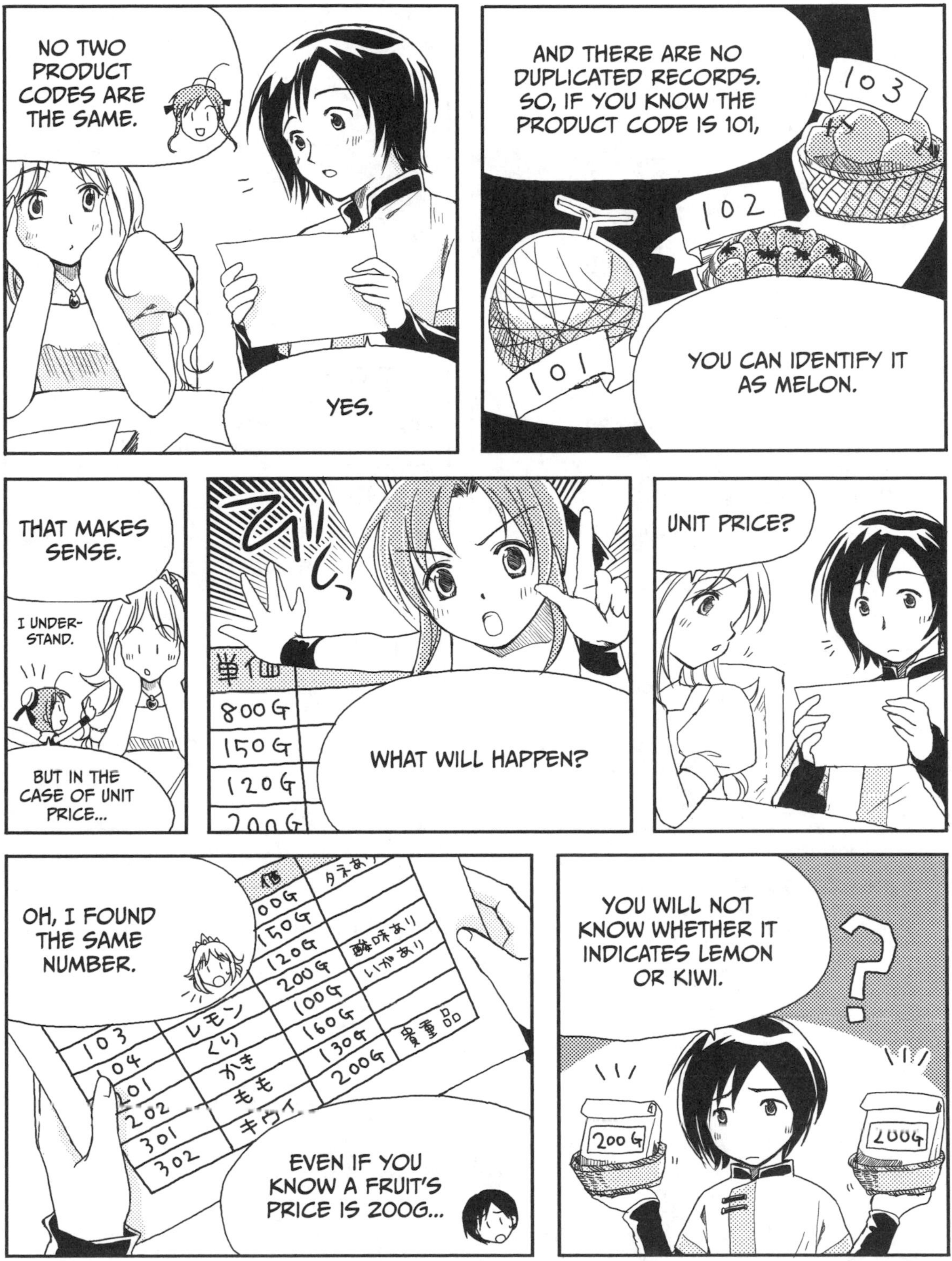
NO TWO PRODUCT CODES ARE THE SAME.
YES.
AND THERE ARE NO DUPLICATED RECORDS. SO, IF YOU KNOW THE PRODUCT CODE IS 101,
103
102
101
YOU CAN IDENTIFY IT AS MELON.
THAT MAKES SENSE.
I UNDER-STAND.
BUT IN THE CASE OF UNIT PRICE...
単価
800G
150G
120G
WHAT WILL HAPPEN?
UNIT PRICE?
OH, I FOUND THE SAME NUMBER.
EVEN IF YOU KNOW A FRUIT'S PRICE IS 200G...
YOU WILL NOT KNOW WHETHER IT INDICATES LEMON OR KIWI.
200G
200G

SO WE CAN IDENTIFY DATA WITH ITS PRODUCT CODE, BUT NOT WITH ITS UNIT PRICE.

EXACTLY.

IN THE DATABASE WORLD, SUCH A FIELD...

IS CALLED *UNIQUE*.

PRODUCT CODE IS UNIQUE

UNIQUE?

OTHER PEOPLE OFTEN SAY THAT ABOUT MY FATHER...

UMMMM...

HA, HA, HA, KING KOD IS UNIQUE. MWAHAHA

IT MEANS THE ONE AND ONLY.

ONE!

ONLY!

IT HAS A SPECIFIC MEANING, YOU KNOW.

THEN, NEXT, LET'S THINK ABOUT *REMARKS*.

REMARKS?

REMARKS ARE REMARKS, AREN'T THEY?

CHARACTER-ISTICS LIKE THIS...

PERSON	REMARKS
RURUNA	BLONDE ACTIVE
CAIN	BRUNET RELAXED

RELAXED?

TAKE A LOOK FROM THE POINT OF VIEW OF A DATABASE.

SOME VALUES UNDER REMARKS HAVE NO ENTRIES, RIGHT?

I SEE YOUR POINT...

	REMARKS
G	WITH SEEDS
0 G	
120 G	
200 G	SOUR
00 G	WITH BUR

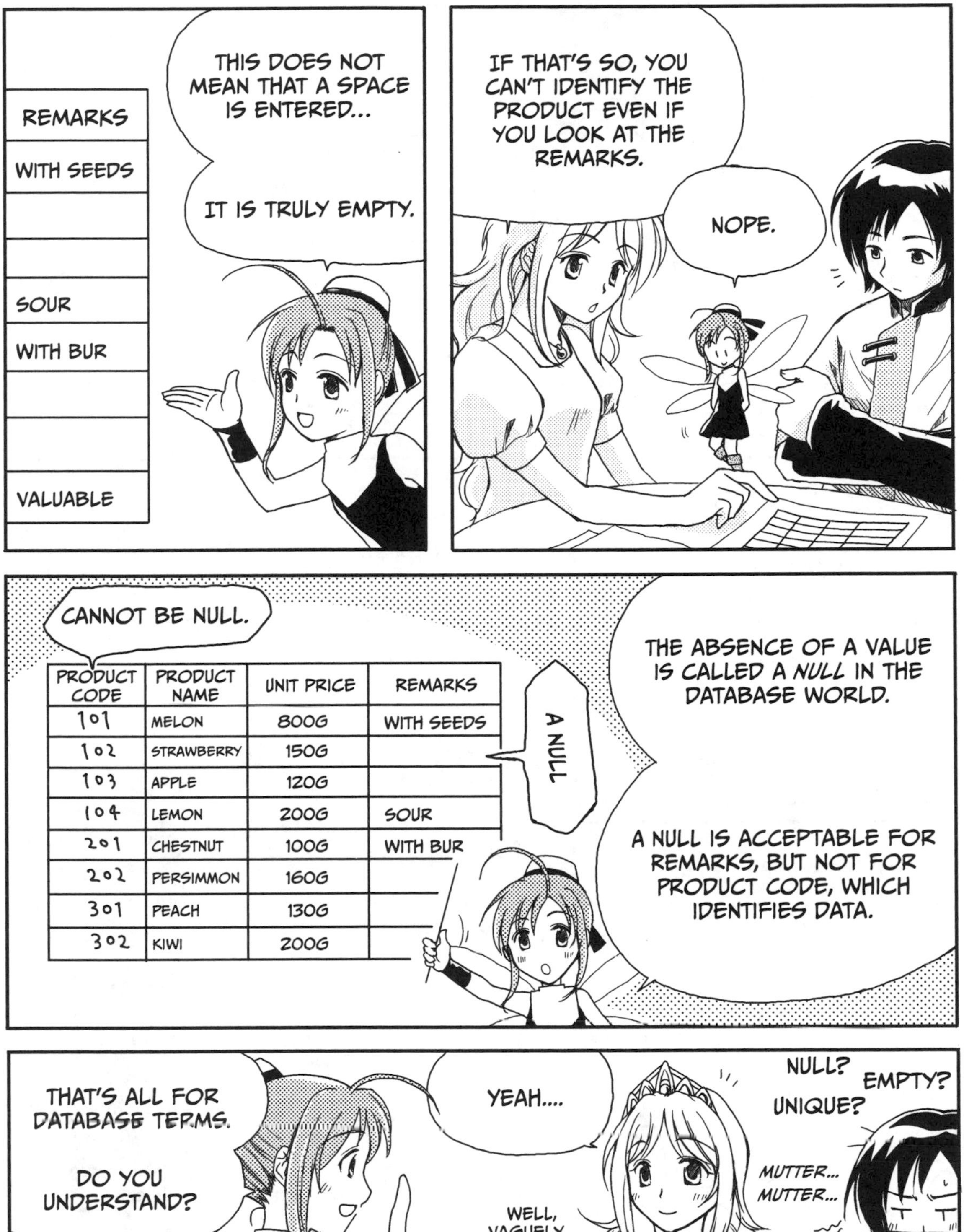
REMARKS
WITH SEEDS
SOUR
WITH BUR
VALUABLE
THIS DOES NOT MEAN THAT A SPACE IS ENTERED...
IT IS TRULY EMPTY.
IF THAT'S SO, YOU CAN'T IDENTIFY THE PRODUCT EVEN IF YOU LOOK AT THE REMARKS.
NOPE.
CANNOT BE NULL.

PRODUCT CODE	PRODUCT NAME	UNIT PRICE	REMARKS
101	MELON	800G	WITH SEEDS
102	STRAWBERRY	150G	
103	APPLE	120G	
104	LEMON	200G	SOUR
201	CHESTNUT	100G	WITH BUR
202	PERSIMMON	160G	
301	PEACH	130G	
302	KIWI	200G	

A NULL
THE ABSENCE OF A VALUE IS CALLED A *NULL* IN THE DATABASE WORLD.
A NULL IS ACCEPTABLE FOR REMARKS, BUT NOT FOR PRODUCT CODE, WHICH IDENTIFIES DATA.
THAT'S ALL FOR DATABASE TERMS.
DO YOU UNDERSTAND?
YEAH....
WELL, VAGUELY...
NULL?
EMPTY?
UNIQUE?
MUTTER... MUTTER...

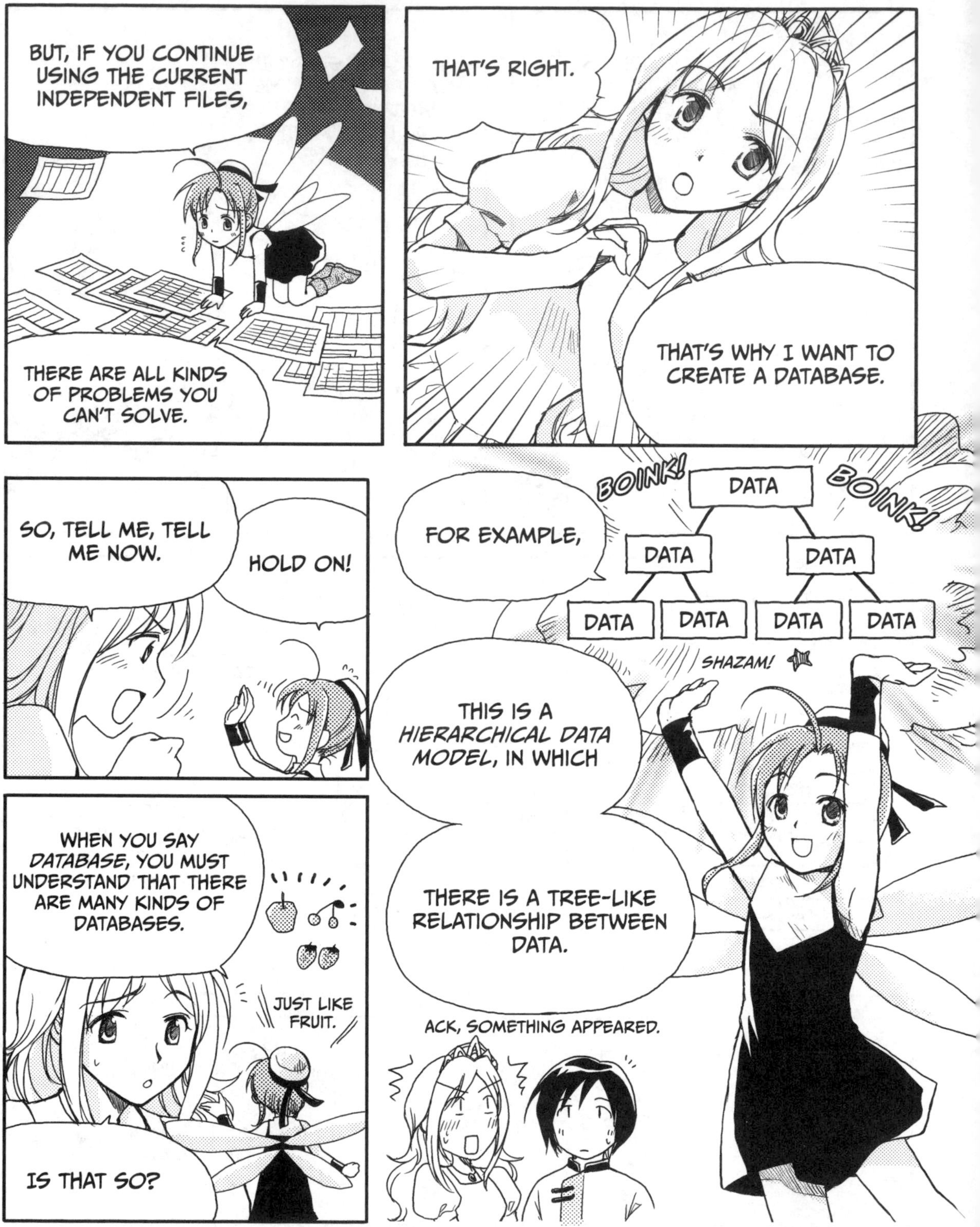
BUT, IF YOU CONTINUE USING THE CURRENT INDEPENDENT FILES,
THERE ARE ALL KINDS OF PROBLEMS YOU CAN'T SOLVE.
THAT'S RIGHT.
THAT'S WHY I WANT TO CREATE A DATABASE.
SO, TELL ME, TELL ME NOW.
HOLD ON!
WHEN YOU SAY *DATABASE*, YOU MUST UNDERSTAND THAT THERE ARE MANY KINDS OF DATABASES.
JUST LIKE FRUIT.
IS THAT SO?
FOR EXAMPLE,
BOINK!
DATA
BOINK!
DATA
DATA
DATA
DATA
DATA
DATA
SHAZAM!
THIS IS A *HIERARCHICAL DATA MODEL*, IN WHICH
THERE IS A TREE-LIKE RELATIONSHIP BETWEEN DATA.
ACK, SOMETHING APPEARED.

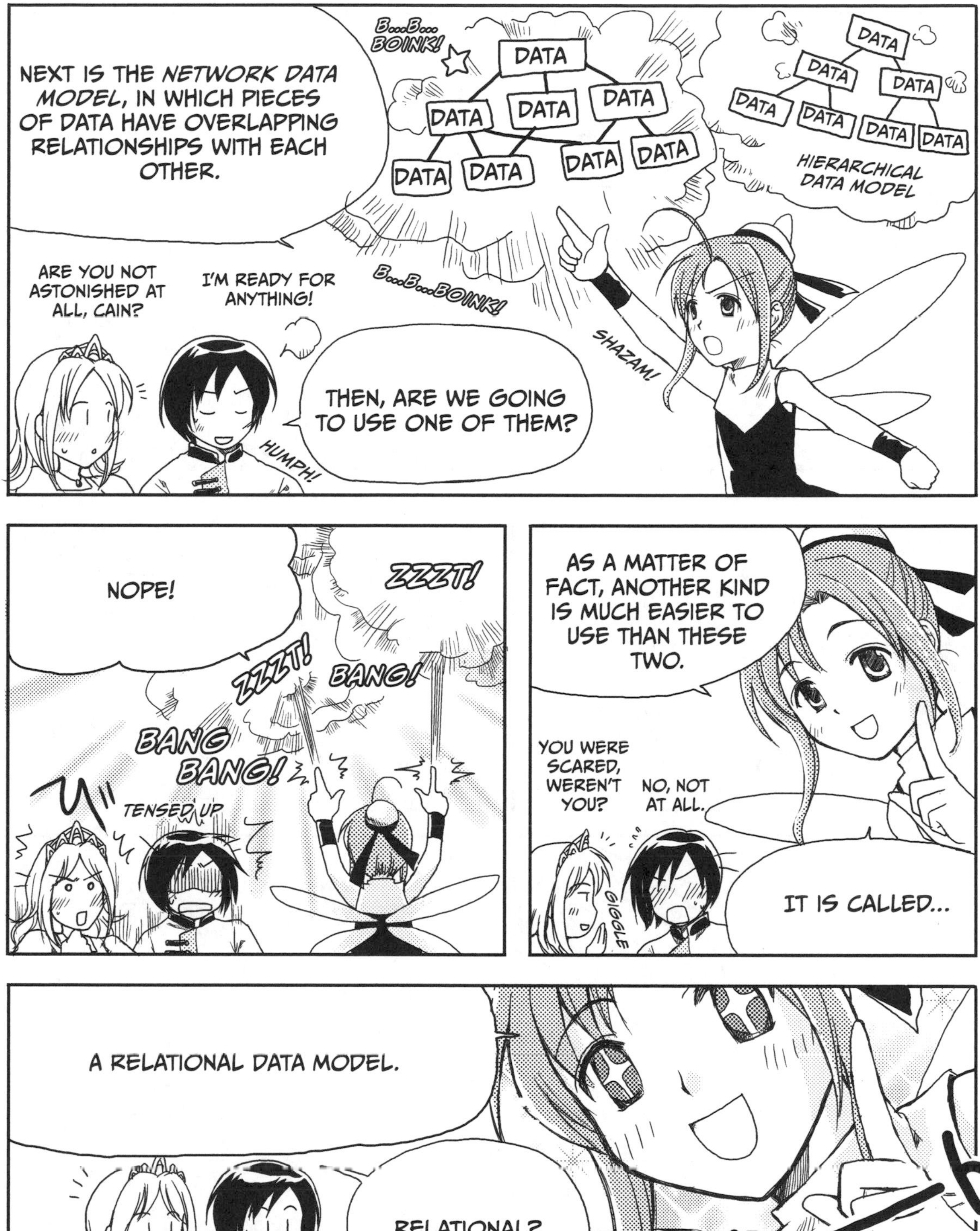
NEXT IS THE *NETWORK DATA MODEL*, IN WHICH PIECES OF DATA HAVE OVERLAPPING RELATIONSHIPS WITH EACH OTHER.
B...B... BOINK!
DATA
DATA
DATA
DATA
DATA
DATA
DATA
DATA
DATA
DATA
DATA
DATA
DATA
DATA
DATA
DATA
HIERARCHICAL DATA MODEL
B...B...BOINK!
SHAZAM!
ARE YOU NOT ASTONISHED AT ALL, CAIN?
I'M READY FOR ANYTHING!
HUMPH!
THEN, ARE WE GOING TO USE ONE OF THEM?
NOPE!
ZZZT!
ZZZT!
BANG!
BANG BANG!
TENSED UP
AS A MATTER OF FACT, ANOTHER KIND IS MUCH EASIER TO USE THAN THESE TWO.
YOU WERE SCARED, WEREN'T YOU?
NO, NOT AT ALL.
GIGGLE
IT IS CALLED...
A RELATIONAL DATA MODEL.
RELATIONAL?

Relational Databases

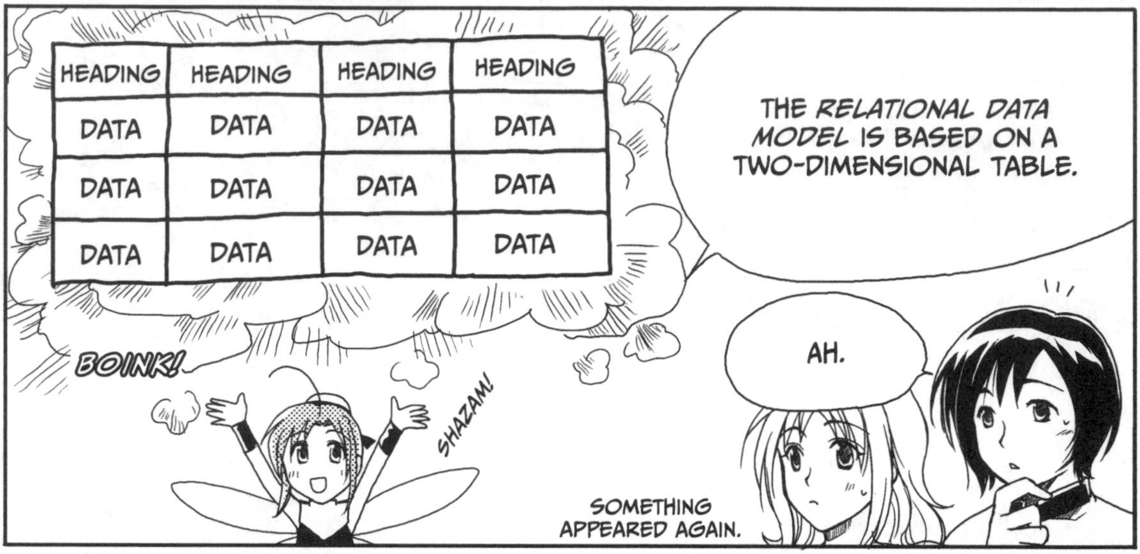
HEADING HEADING HEADING HEADING
DATA DATA DATA DATA
DATA DATA DATA DATA
DATA DATA DATA DATA
BOINK!
SHAZAM!
THE *RELATIONAL DATA MODEL* IS BASED ON A TWO-DIMENSIONAL TABLE.
AH.
SOMETHING APPEARED AGAIN.

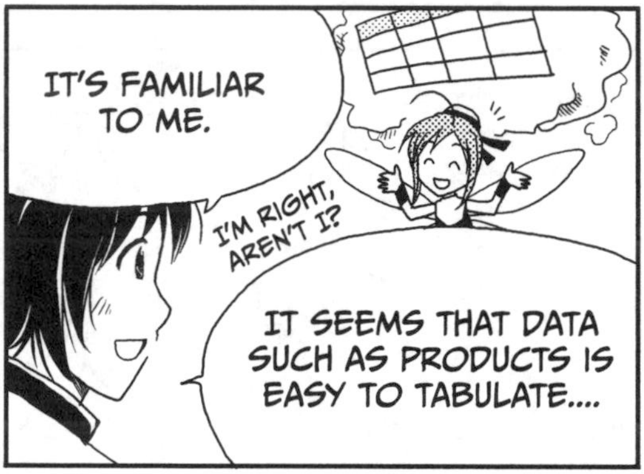
IT'S FAMILIAR TO ME.
I'M RIGHT, AREN'T I?
IT SEEMS THAT DATA SUCH AS PRODUCTS IS EASY TO TABULATE....

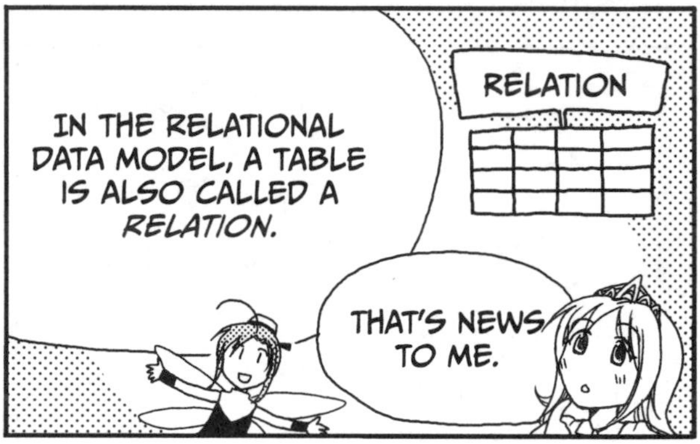
IN THE RELATIONAL DATA MODEL, A TABLE IS ALSO CALLED A *RELATION*.
RELATION
THAT'S NEWS TO ME.

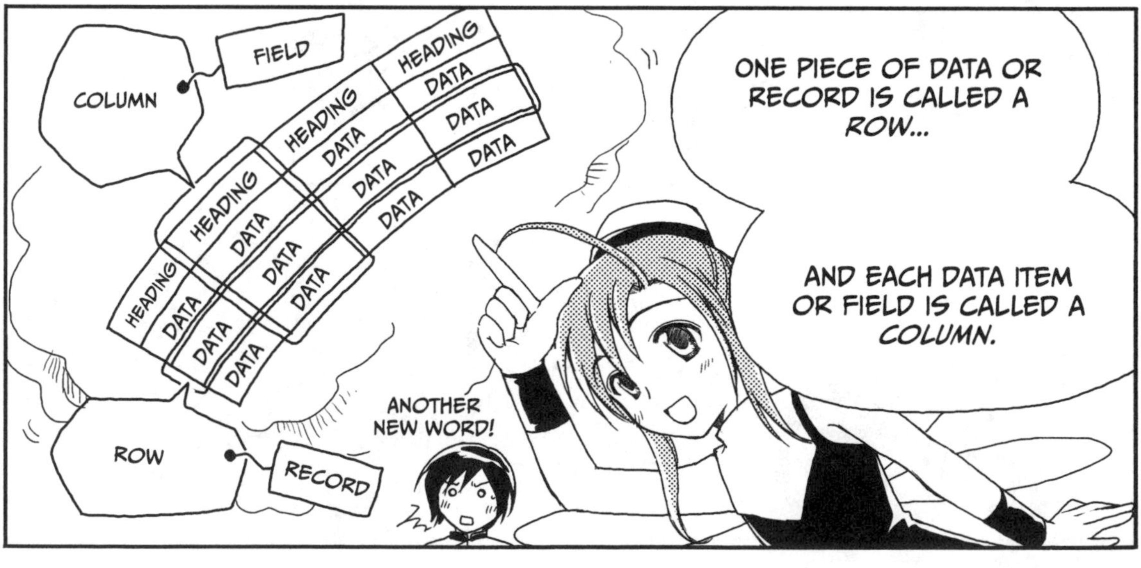
FIELD
COLUMN
HEADING HEADING HEADING HEADING
DATA DATA DATA DATA
DATA DATA DATA DATA
DATA DATA DATA DATA
ONE PIECE OF DATA OR RECORD IS CALLED A *ROW*...
AND EACH DATA ITEM OR FIELD IS CALLED A *COLUMN*.
ROW
RECORD
ANOTHER NEW WORD!

IN ADDITION, A FIELD IS SOMETIMES GIVEN AN IMPORTANT ROLE IN THE DATABASE.

THIS SPECIAL FIELD IS CALLED A *KEY*.

KEY

IMPORTANT ROLE?

YES. FOR EXAMPLE,

THE PRODUCT CODE IN THE FILE YOU SAW A LITTLE WHILE AGO.

THE FIELD SERVES AN IMPORTANT ROLE: TO IDENTIFY DATA.

THIS CODE IS CALLED A *PRIMARY KEY*.

I DIDN'T KNOW THERE WERE SO MANY TERMS.

PRIMARY KEY

PROD. CODE
101
102
103
104
201
202
301
302

WELL, I'M FAMILIAR WITH TABLES.

IT IS EASY TO UNDERSTAND IF YOU CAN PROCESS DATA USING A TABLE.

THIS IS ONE MERIT OF THE RELATIONAL DATA MODEL.

EVEN PEOPLE WHO DO NOT KNOW MUCH ABOUT DATABASES CAN PROCESS DATA.

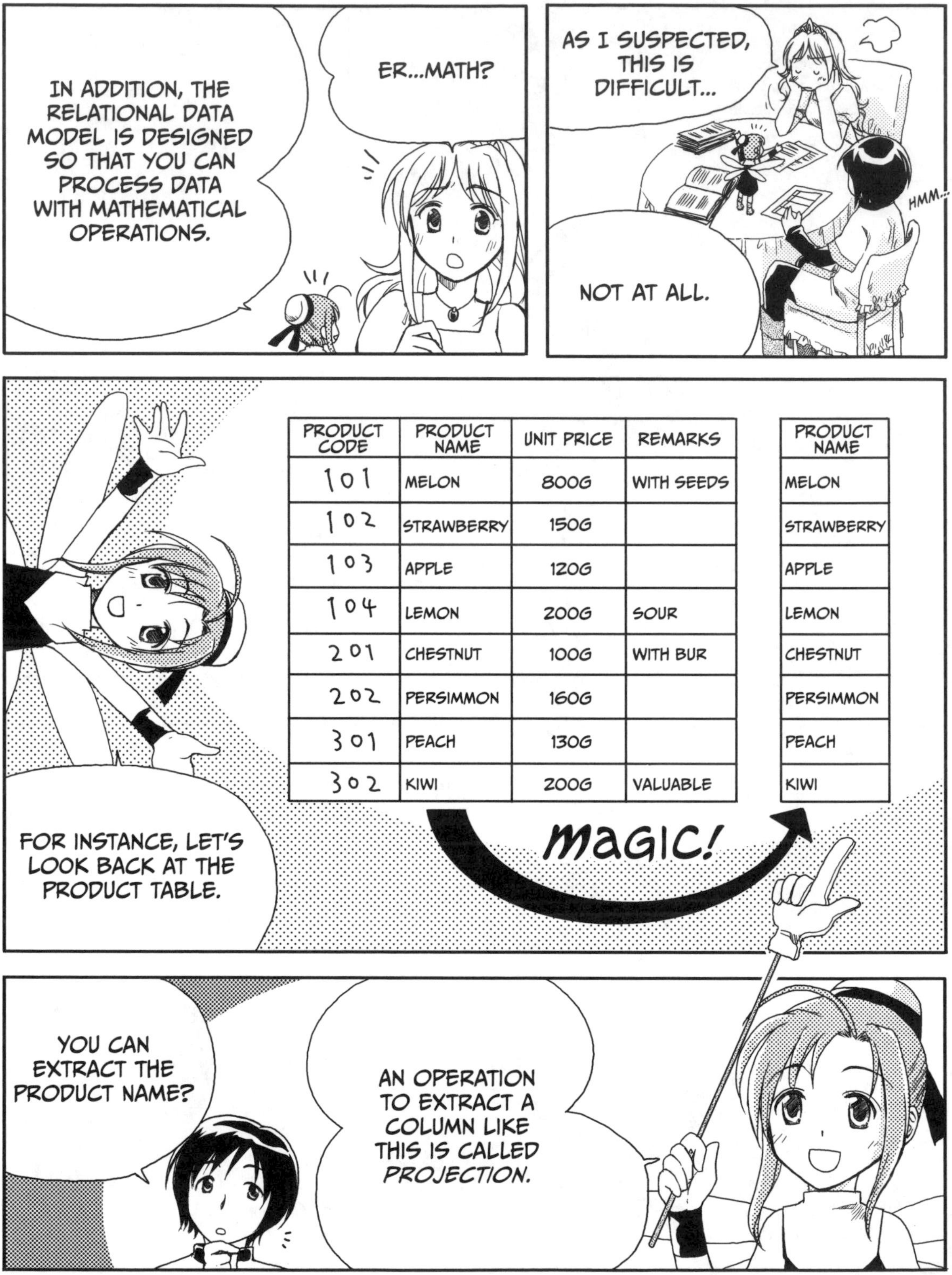
IN ADDITION, THE RELATIONAL DATA MODEL IS DESIGNED SO THAT YOU CAN PROCESS DATA WITH MATHEMATICAL OPERATIONS.
ER...MATH?
AS I SUSPECTED, THIS IS DIFFICULT...
HMM...
NOT AT ALL.
FOR INSTANCE, LET'S LOOK BACK AT THE PRODUCT TABLE.

PRODUCT CODE	PRODUCT NAME	UNIT PRICE	REMARKS
101	MELON	800G	WITH SEEDS
102	STRAWBERRY	150G	
103	APPLE	120G	
104	LEMON	200G	SOUR
201	CHESTNUT	100G	WITH BUR
202	PERSIMMON	160G	
301	PEACH	130G	
302	KIWI	200G	VALUABLE

MAGIC!

PRODUCT NAME
MELON
STRAWBERRY
APPLE
LEMON
CHESTNUT
PERSIMMON
PEACH
KIWI

YOU CAN EXTRACT THE PRODUCT NAME?
AN OPERATION TO EXTRACT A COLUMN LIKE THIS IS CALLED *PROJECTION*.

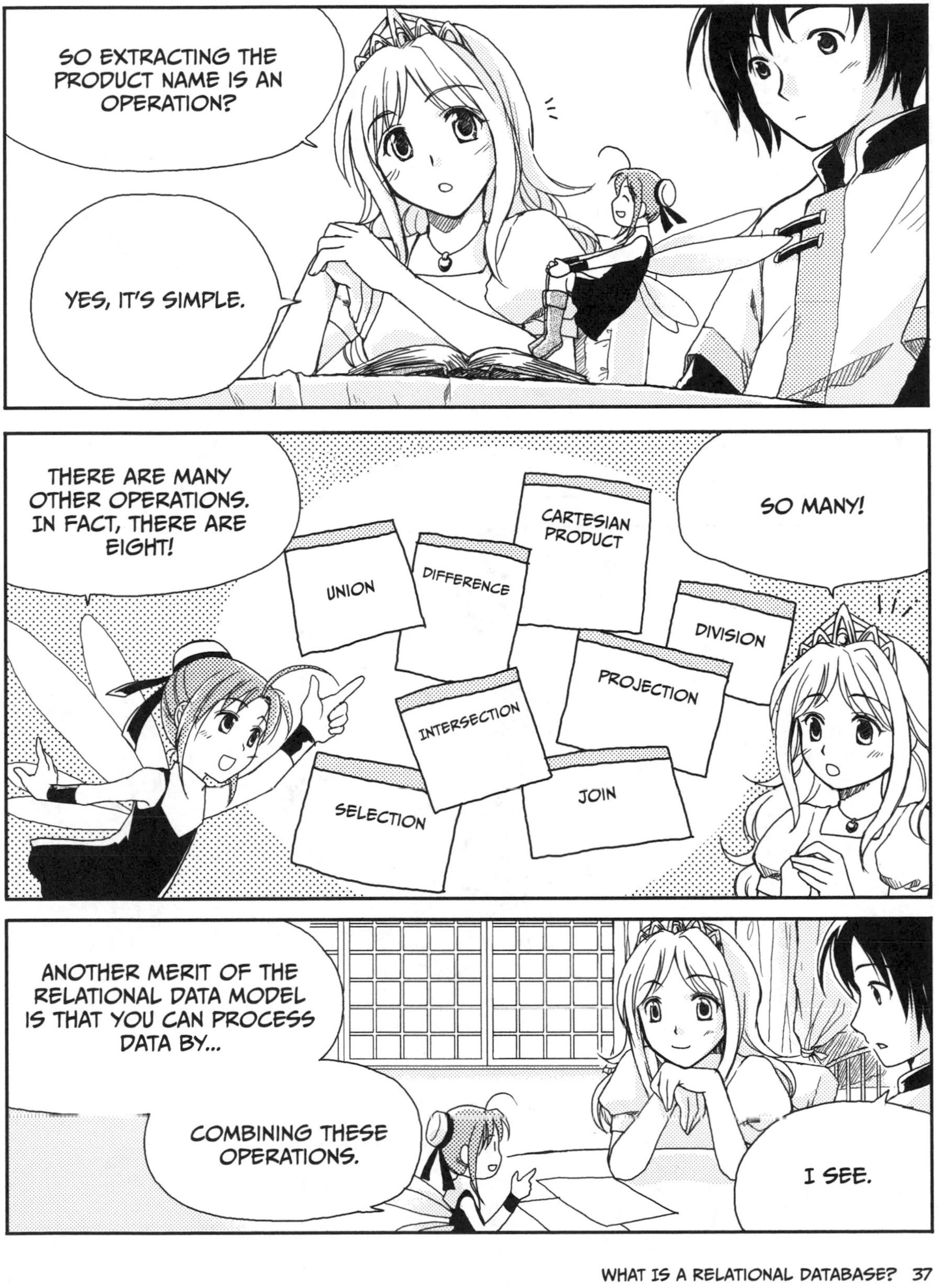
SO EXTRACTING THE PRODUCT NAME IS AN OPERATION?
YES, IT'S SIMPLE.
THERE ARE MANY OTHER OPERATIONS. IN FACT, THERE ARE EIGHT!
UNION
DIFFERENCE
CARTESIAN PRODUCT
DIVISION
PROJECTION
INTERSECTION
SELECTION
JOIN
SO MANY!
ANOTHER MERIT OF THE RELATIONAL DATA MODEL IS THAT YOU CAN PROCESS DATA BY...
COMBINING THESE OPERATIONS.
I SEE.

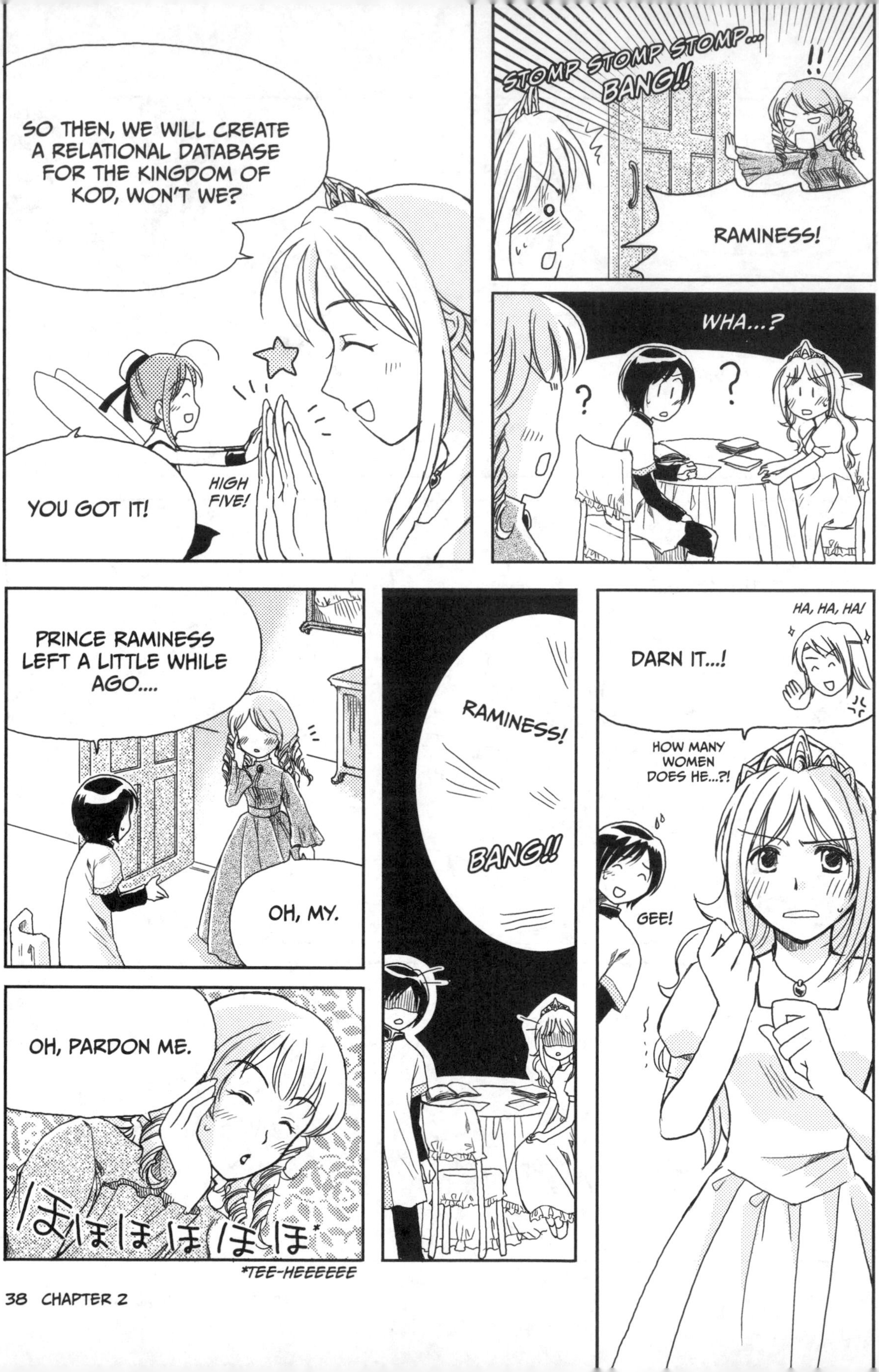
SO THEN, WE WILL CREATE A RELATIONAL DATABASE FOR THE KINGDOM OF KOD, WON'T WE?
YOU GOT IT!
HIGH FIVE!
STOMP STOMP STOMP... BANG!!
!!
RAMINESS!
WHA...?
?
?
PRINCE RAMINESS LEFT A LITTLE WHILE AGO....
OH, MY.
OH, PARDON ME.
ほほほほほほ*
*TEE-HEEEEEE
RAMINESS!
BANG!!
HA, HA, HA!
DARN IT...!
HOW MANY WOMEN DOES HE...?!
GEE!

Types of Data Models

When you use the term *database*, what kind of database do you mean? There are many types available for data management. The data association and operation methods that a database uses is called its *data model*. There are three commonly used data models.

As I described to Ruruna and Cain, the first type is the hierarchical data model. In the *hierarchical data model*, child data has only one piece of parent data. The second type is the network data model. Unlike the hierarchical data model, in the *network data model*, child data can have multiple pieces of parent data.

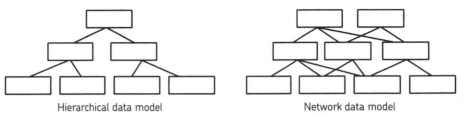

Hierarchical data model   Network data model

To use either of these models, you must manage data by keeping the physical location and the order of data in mind. Therefore, it is difficult to perform a flexible and high-speed search of your data if you use a hierarchical or network data model.

The third type of model is the relational data model. A *relational* database processes data using the easy-to-understand concept of a table. Let's discuss this model in more detail.

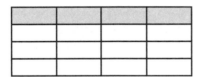

Relational data model

Data Extraction Operations

How is data extracted in a relational database? You can process and extract data in a relational database by performing stringently defined mathematical operations. There are eight main operations that you can use, and they fall into two categories—set operations and relational operations.

SET OPERATIONS

The union, difference, intersection, and Cartesian product operations are called *set operations*. These operations work upon one or more sets of rows to produce a new set of rows. In short, they determine which rows from the input appear in the output. Let's look at some examples using Product Table 1 and Product Table 2.

PRODUCT TABLE 1

Product name	Unit price
Melon	800G
Strawberry	150G
Apple	120G
Lemon	200G

PRODUCT TABLE 2

Product name	Unit price
Melon	800G
Strawberry	150G
Chestnut	100G
Persimmon	350G

UNION

Carrying out the *union* operation allows you to extract all products included in Product Table 1 and Product Table 2. The result is below.

Product name	Unit price
Melon	800G
Strawberry	150G
Apple	120G
Lemon	200G
Chestnut	100G
Persimmon	350G

Performing a union operation extracts all rows in the two tables and combines them. The following figure shows what the data from the two tables looks like once a union operation has been performed. All rows in Product Table 1 and Product Table 2 have been extracted.

PRODUCT TABLE 1
PRODUCT TABLE 2
Apple
Lemon
Melon
Strawberry
Chestnut
Persimmon

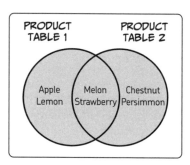

DIFFERENCE

Difference is an operation that extracts rows from just *one* of the tables. For example, a difference operation can extract all of the products from the first table that are not included in the second. The results depend on which table contains rows to extract, and which table has rows to exclude.

Product name	Unit price
Apple	120G
Lemon	200G

Product name	Unit price
Chestnut	100G
Persimmon	350G

PRODUCT TABLE 1
PRODUCT TABLE 2
Apple
Lemon
Melon
Strawberry
Chestnut
Persimmon

PRODUCT TABLE 1
PRODUCT TABLE 2
Apple
Lemon
Melon
Strawberry
Chestnut
Persimmon

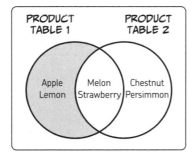

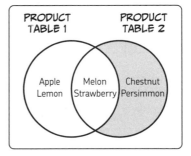

INTERSECTION

You can also extract products that are included in *both* Product Table 1 and Product Table 2. This operation is called an *intersection* operation. Here is the result of the intersection of Product Tables 1 and 2.

Product name	Unit price
Melon	800G
Strawberry	150G

PRODUCT TABLE 1
PRODUCT TABLE 2
Apple
Lemon
Melon
Strawberry
Chestnut
Persimmon

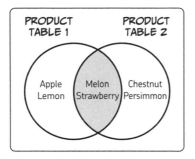

CARTESIAN PRODUCT

The *Cartesian product* operation is a method that combines all rows in the two tables. Let's look at the Product and Export Destination Tables below.

The Cartesian product operation combines all rows in the two tables. In this example, it resulted in 3 × 3 = 9 rows. Notice that the column names (or fields) in these two tables are not the same—unlike our previous examples.

PRODUCT TABLE

Product code	Product name	Unit price
101	Melon	800G
102	Strawberry	150G
103	Apple	120G

EXPORT DESTINATION TABLE

Export dest. code	Export dest. name
12	The Kingdom of Minanmi
23	Alpha Empire
25	The Kingdom of Ritol

3 rows

CARTESIAN PRODUCT

Product code	Product name	Unit price	Export dest. code	Export dest. name
101	Melon	800G	12	The Kingdom of Minanmi
101	Melon	800G	23	Alpha Empire
101	Melon	800G	25	The Kingdom of Ritol
102	Strawberry	150G	12	The Kingdom of Minanmi
102	Strawberry	150G	23	Alpha Empire
102	Strawberry	150G	25	The Kingdom of Ritol
103	Apple	120G	12	The Kingdom of Minanmi
103	Apple	120G	23	Alpha Empire
103	Apple	120G	25	The Kingdom of Ritol

3 x 3 = 9 rows

RELATIONAL OPERATIONS

A relational database is designed so that data can be extracted by set operations and relational operations. Let's look at the other four operations specific to a relational database, called *relational operations*—projection, selection, join, and division.

PROJECTION

Projection is an operation that extracts columns from a table. In the example shown here, this operation is used to extract only product names included in the Product Table.

Product name
Melon
Strawberry
Apple
Lemon

Think of projection as extracting "vertically," as shown below.

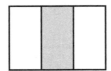

SELECTION

The *selection* operation extracts two rows from a table.

Product name	Unit price
Melon	800G
Strawberry	150G

Selection is like projection, but it extracts rows instead of columns. Selection extracts data "horizontally."

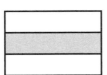

JOIN

The *join* operation is a very powerful one. This operation literally refers to the work of joining tables. Let's look at the tables below as an example.

PRODUCT TABLE

Product code	Product name	Unit price
101	Melon	800G
102	Strawberry	150G
103	Apple	120G
104	Lemon	200G

SALES TABLE

Date	Product code	Quantity
11/1	102	1,100
11/1	101	300
11/5	103	1,700
11/8	101	500

The Product Code columns in these two tables represent the same information. On November 1st, 1,100 strawberries (product code 102) were sold. The Sales Table does not include the product name, but it does include the product code. In other words, the Sales Table allows you to understand which product was sold by making reference to the product code, which is the *primary key* in the Product Table. The product code in the Sales Table is a *foreign key*. Joining the two tables so that the foreign key refers to the primary key results in the following table.

Date	Product code	Product name	Unit price	Quantity
11/1	102	Strawberry	150G	1,100
11/1	101	Melon	800G	300
11/5	103	Apple	120G	1,700
11/8	101	Melon	800G	500

This creates a new dynamic table of sales data, including date, product code, product name, unit price, and quantity. The figure below shows a join—the shaded area represents a column that appears in both original tables.

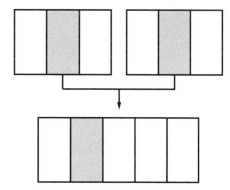

DIVISION

Finally, let's look at division. *Division* is an operation that extracts the rows whose column values match those in the second table, but only returns columns that don't exist in the second table. Let's look at an example.

SALES TABLE

Export dest. code	Export dest. name	Date
12	The Kingdom of Minanmi	3/5
12	The Kingdom of Minanmi	3/10
23	Alpha Empire	3/5
25	The Kingdom of Ritol	3/21
30	The Kingdom of Sazanna	3/25

EXPORT DESTINATION TABLE

Export dest. code	Export dest. name
12	The Kingdom of Minanmi
23	Alpha Empire

Dividing the Sales Table by the Export Destination Table results in the following table. This allows you to find the dates when fruit was exported to both the Alpha Empire and the Kingdom of Minanmi.

Date
3/5

QUESTIONS

Now, let's answer some questions to see how well you understand relational databases. The answers are on page 48.

Q1

What do you call the key referring to a column in a different table in a relational database?

Q2

The following table displays information about books. Which item can you use as a primary key? The ISBN is the International Standard Book Number, a unique identifying number given to every published book. Some books may have the same title.

ISBN	Book name	Author name	Publication date	Price

Q3

What do you call the operation used here to extract data?

Export dest. code	Export dest. name
12	The Kingdom of Minanmi
23	Alpha Empire
25	The Kingdom of Ritol
30	The Kingdom of Sazanna

→

Export dest. code	Export dest. name
25	The Kingdom of Ritol

Q4

What do you call the operation used here to extract data?

Export dest. code	Export dest. name
12	The Kingdom of Minanmi
23	Alpha Empire
25	The Kingdom of Ritol
30	The Kingdom of Sazanna

Export dest. code	Export dest. name
15	The Kingdom of Paronu
22	The Kingdom of Tokanta
31	The Kingdom of Taharu
33	The Kingdom of Mariyon

Export dest. code	Export dest. name
12	The Kingdom of Minanmi
15	The Kingdom of Paronu
22	The Kingdom of Tokanta
23	Alpha Empire
25	The Kingdom of Ritol
30	The Kingdom of Sazanna
31	The Kingdom of Taharu
33	The Kingdom of Mariyon

Q5

What do you call the operation used here to extract data?

Export dest. code	Export dest. name
12	The Kingdom of Minanmi
23	Alpha Empire
25	The Kingdom of Ritol
30	The Kingdom of Sazanna

Export dest. code	Date
12	3/1
23	3/1
12	3/3
30	3/5
12	3/6
25	3/10

Export dest. code	Date	Export dest. name
12	3/1	The Kingdom of Minanmi
23	3/1	Alpha Empire
12	3/3	The Kingdom of Minanmi
30	3/5	The Kingdom of Sazanna
12	3/6	The Kingdom of Minanmi
25	3/10	The Kingdom of Ritol

The Relational Database Prevails!

In a relational database, you can use eight different operations to extract data. The extracted results are tabulated. If you combine the operations explained in this section, you can extract data for any purpose. For example, you can use the name and price of a product to create gross sales aggregate data for it. Relational databases are popular because they're easy to understand and provide flexible data processing.

Summary

- One row of data is called a *record*, and each column is called a *field*.
- A column that can be used to identify data is called a *primary key*.
- In a relational database, you can process data using the concept of a table.
- In a relational database, you can process data based on mathematical operations.

Answers

Q1 Foreign key

Q2 ISBN

Q3 Selection

Q4 Union

Q5 Join

3
LET'S DESIGN A DATABASE!

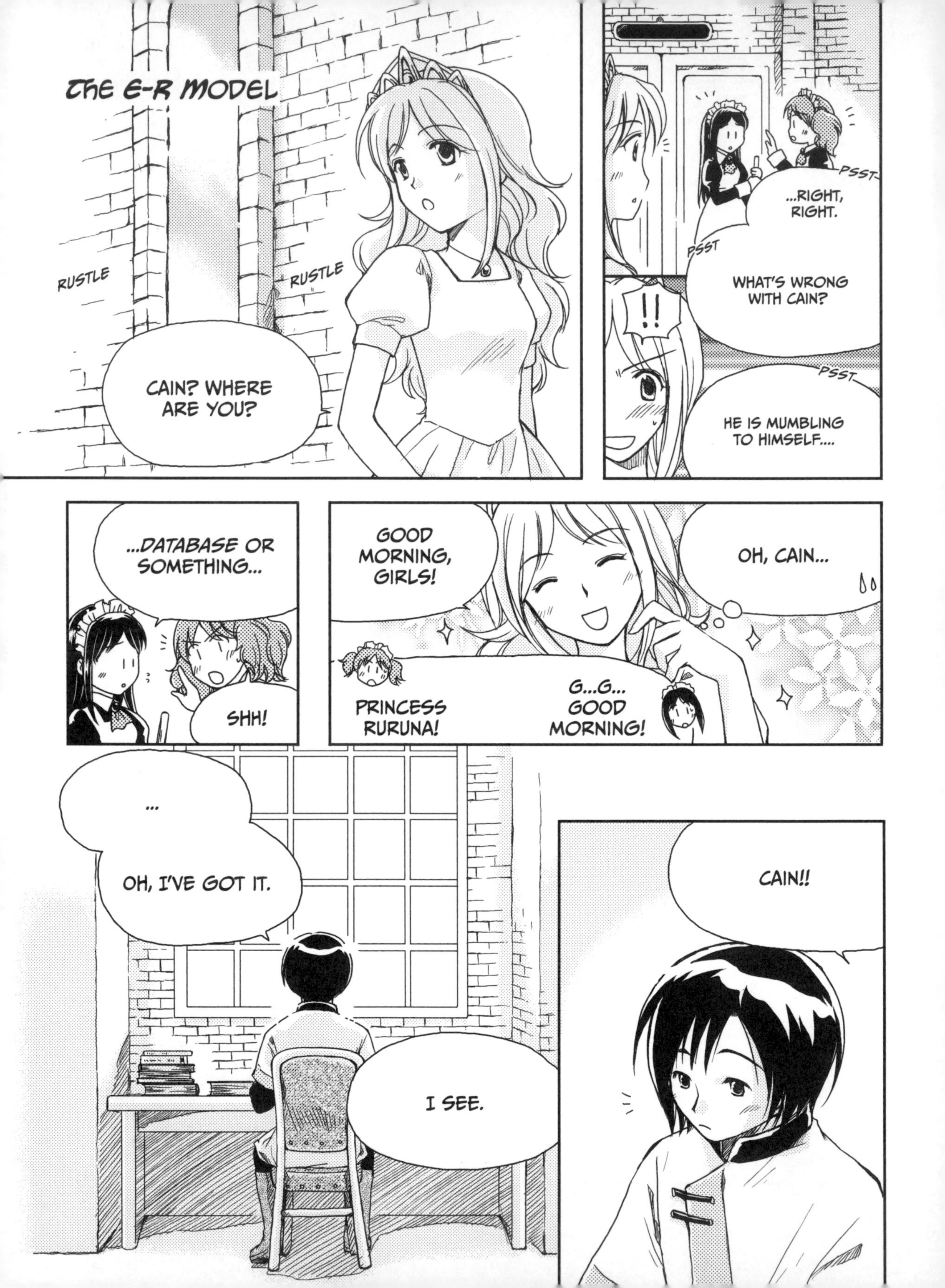
THE E-R MODEL
RUSTLE
RUSTLE
CAIN? WHERE ARE YOU?
PSST
...RIGHT, RIGHT.
PSST
WHAT'S WRONG WITH CAIN?
!!
PSST
HE IS MUMBLING TO HIMSELF....
...DATABASE OR SOMETHING...
SHH!
GOOD MORNING, GIRLS!
OH, CAIN...
PRINCESS RURUNA!
G...G... GOOD MORNING!
...
OH, I'VE GOT IT.
I SEE.
CAIN!!

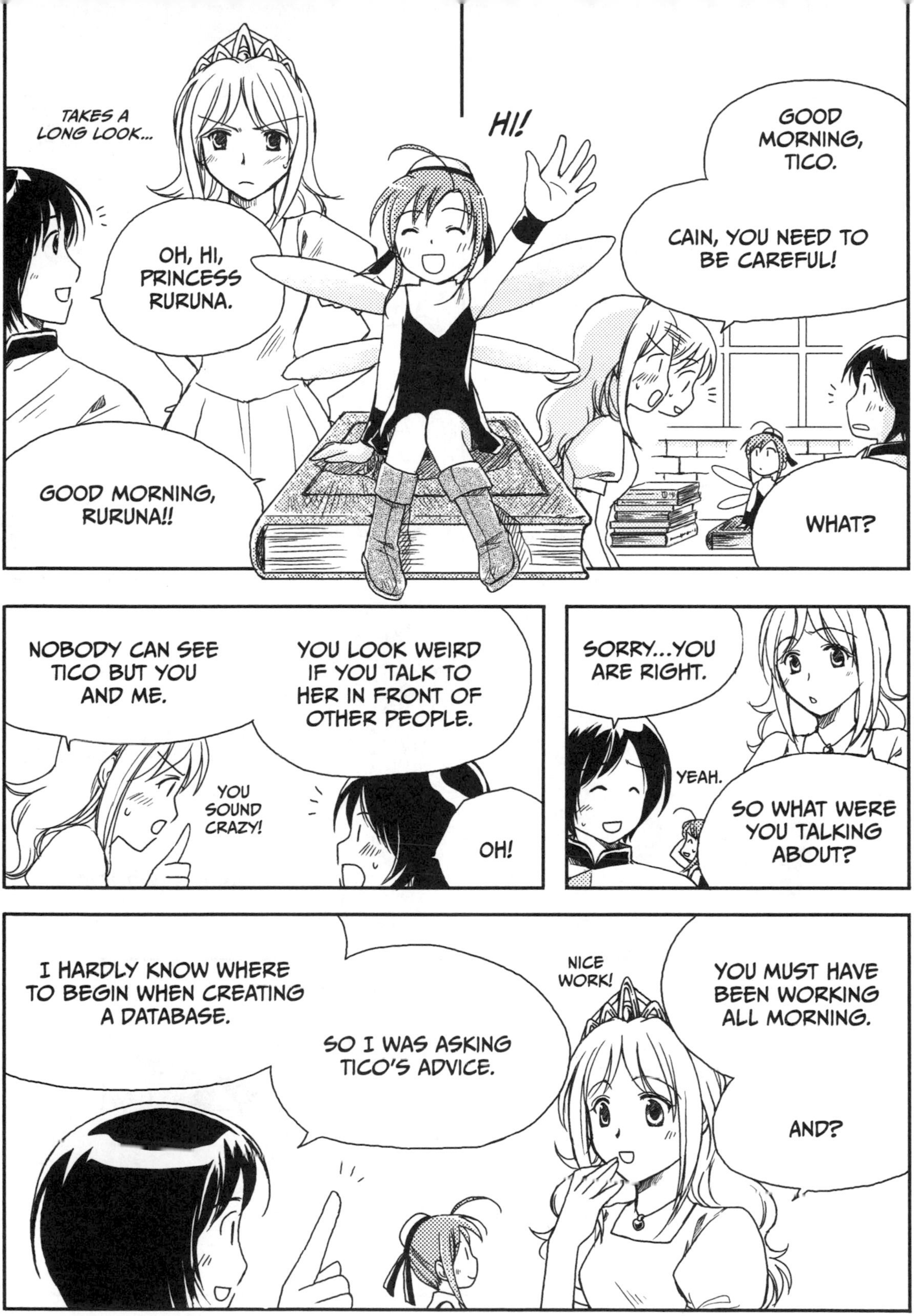
TAKES A LONG LOOK...
OH, HI, PRINCESS RURUNA.
HI!
GOOD MORNING, RURUNA!!
GOOD MORNING, TICO.
CAIN, YOU NEED TO BE CAREFUL!
WHAT?
NOBODY CAN SEE TICO BUT YOU AND ME.
YOU LOOK WEIRD IF YOU TALK TO HER IN FRONT OF OTHER PEOPLE.
YOU SOUND CRAZY!
OH!
SORRY...YOU ARE RIGHT.
YEAH.
SO WHAT WERE YOU TALKING ABOUT?
I HARDLY KNOW WHERE TO BEGIN WHEN CREATING A DATABASE.
SO I WAS ASKING TICO'S ADVICE.
NICE WORK!
YOU MUST HAVE BEEN WORKING ALL MORNING.
AND?

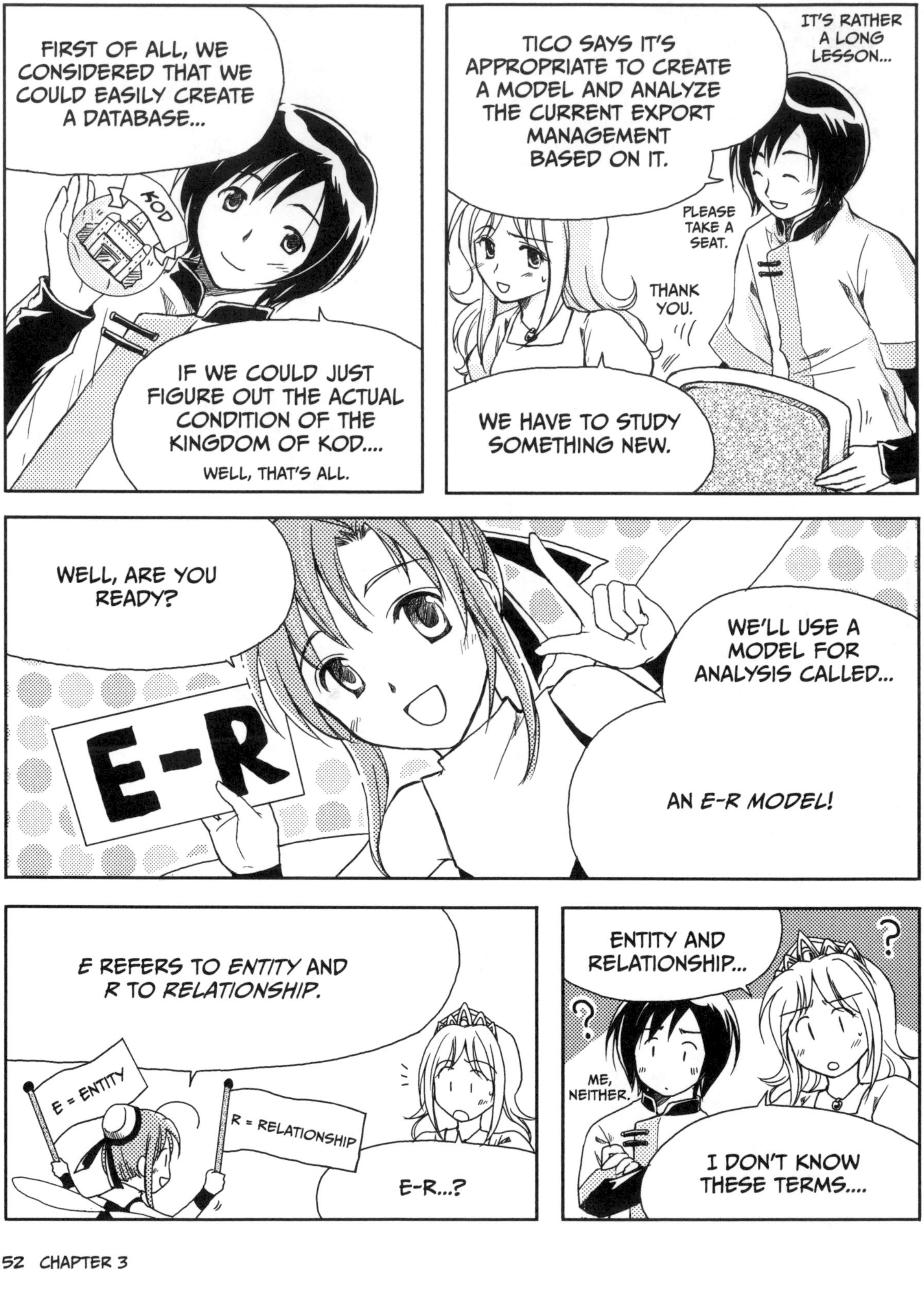
FIRST OF ALL, WE CONSIDERED THAT WE COULD EASILY CREATE A DATABASE...
KOD
IF WE COULD JUST FIGURE OUT THE ACTUAL CONDITION OF THE KINGDOM OF KOD....
WELL, THAT'S ALL.
TICO SAYS IT'S APPROPRIATE TO CREATE A MODEL AND ANALYZE THE CURRENT EXPORT MANAGEMENT BASED ON IT.
IT'S RATHER A LONG LESSON...
PLEASE TAKE A SEAT.
THANK YOU.
WE HAVE TO STUDY SOMETHING NEW.
WELL, ARE YOU READY?
E-R
WE'LL USE A MODEL FOR ANALYSIS CALLED...
AN E-R MODEL!
E REFERS TO ENTITY AND R TO RELATIONSHIP.
E = ENTITY
R = RELATIONSHIP
E-R...?
ENTITY AND RELATIONSHIP...
ME, NEITHER.
I DON'T KNOW THESE TERMS....

IN THE E-R MODEL, YOU CONSIDER THE ACTUAL WORLD USING THE CONCEPTS OF ENTITY AND RELATIONSHIP.

I'LL CLARIFY THAT A BIT...

PLUNK!!

PLUNK!!

ENTITY REFERS TO A RECOGNIZABLE OBJECT IN THE ACTUAL WORLD.

FOR EXAMPLE, WHEN EXPORTING FRUIT TO OTHER COUNTRIES, *FRUIT* AND *EXPORT DESTINATION* CAN BE CONSIDERED ENTITIES.

SQUEAK!

SQUEAK

SQUEAK SQUEAK

SQUEEEAK

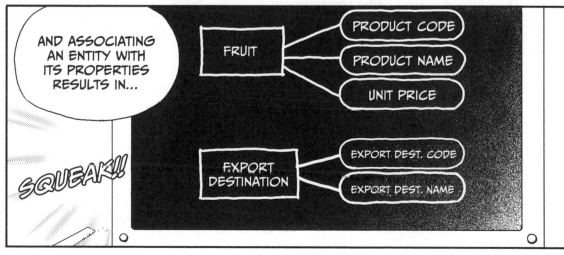

AND ASSOCIATING AN ENTITY WITH ITS PROPERTIES RESULTS IN...

FRUIT
- PRODUCT CODE
- PRODUCT NAME
- UNIT PRICE

EXPORT DESTINATION
- EXPORT. DEST. CODE
- EXPORT. DEST. NAME

SQUEAK!!

YOU HAVE ANALYZED FRUIT AND EXPORT DESTINATIONS.

THEN, WHAT IS A *RELATIONSHIP?*

IT REFERS TO HOW ENTITIES RELATE TO EACH OTHER.

FOR INSTANCE...

FRUIT AND EXPORT DESTINATION ARE ASSOCIATED WITH EACH OTHER BECAUSE YOU SELL FRUIT TO EXPORT DESTINATIONS.

FRUIT

EXPORT DESTINATION

SO WE CAN CONSIDER SALES TO BE THE RELATIONSHIP.

FRUIT

SALES

SQUEEEEAK!!

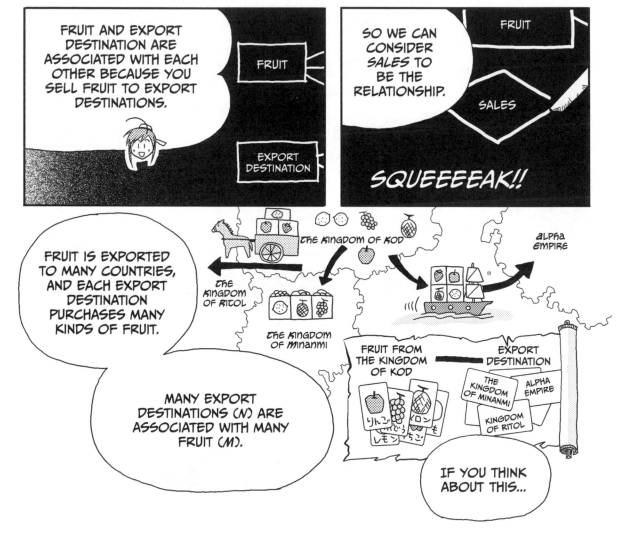

FRUIT IS EXPORTED TO MANY COUNTRIES, AND EACH EXPORT DESTINATION PURCHASES MANY KINDS OF FRUIT.

MANY EXPORT DESTINATIONS (N) ARE ASSOCIATED WITH MANY FRUIT (M).

THE KINGDOM OF KOD

ALPHA EMPIRE

THE KINGDOM OF RITOL

THE KINGDOM OF MINANMI

FRUIT FROM THE KINGDOM OF KOD

EXPORT DESTINATION

THE KINGDOM OF MINANMI

ALPHA EMPIRE

KINGDOM OF RITOL

IF YOU THINK ABOUT THIS...

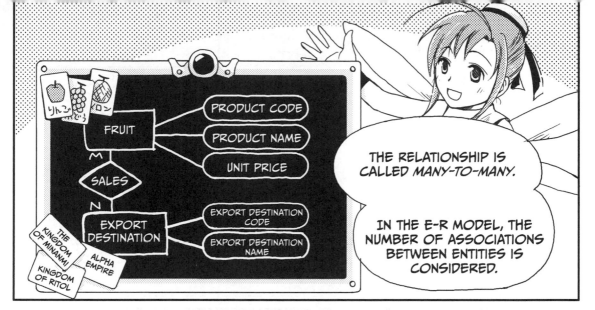

りんご
FRUIT
PRODUCT CODE
PRODUCT NAME
UNIT PRICE
M
SALES
N
EXPORT DESTINATION
EXPORT DESTINATION CODE
EXPORT DESTINATION NAME
THE KINGDOM OF MINANMI
ALPHA EMPIRE
KINGDOM OF RITOL
THE RELATIONSHIP IS CALLED *MANY-TO-MANY.*
IN THE E-R MODEL, THE NUMBER OF ASSOCIATIONS BETWEEN ENTITIES IS CONSIDERED.
WELL THEN, IF CAIN SELLS JUST ONE KIND OF FRUIT TO VARIOUS FAMILIES,
ONLY APPLES
CAIN-BRAND APPLES
ONLY APPLES
ONLY APPLES
WHY ME?
THEN THE RELATIONSHIP IS *ONE-TO-MANY?*
CAIN-BRAND APPLE
FRUIT
SALES
THOMAS'S FAMILY
GEORGE'S FAMILY
MALHO'S FAMILY
EXPORT DESTINATION
BINGO!
THAT'S RIGHT!
AND THEREFORE, THIS IS THE ACTUAL CONDITION OF THE KINGDOM OF KOD.
THE E-R MODEL SHOWS US THE ACTUAL CONDITION, DOESN'T IT?
FRUIT
PRODUCT CODE
PRODUCT NAME
UNIT PRICE
M
SALES
N
EXPORT DESTINATION
EXPORT DESTINATION CODE
EXPORT DESTINATION NAME
YEAH!
THIS IS HOW THE KINGDOM OF KOD'S EXPORT BUSINESS WORKS!

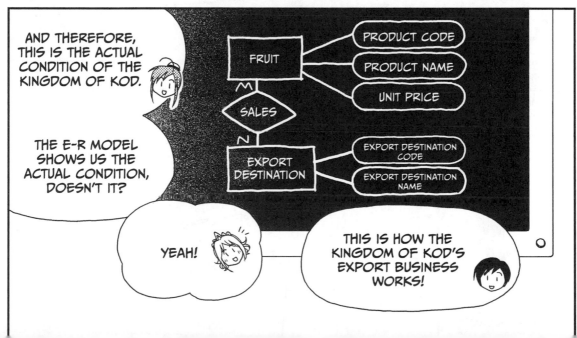

Normalizing a Table

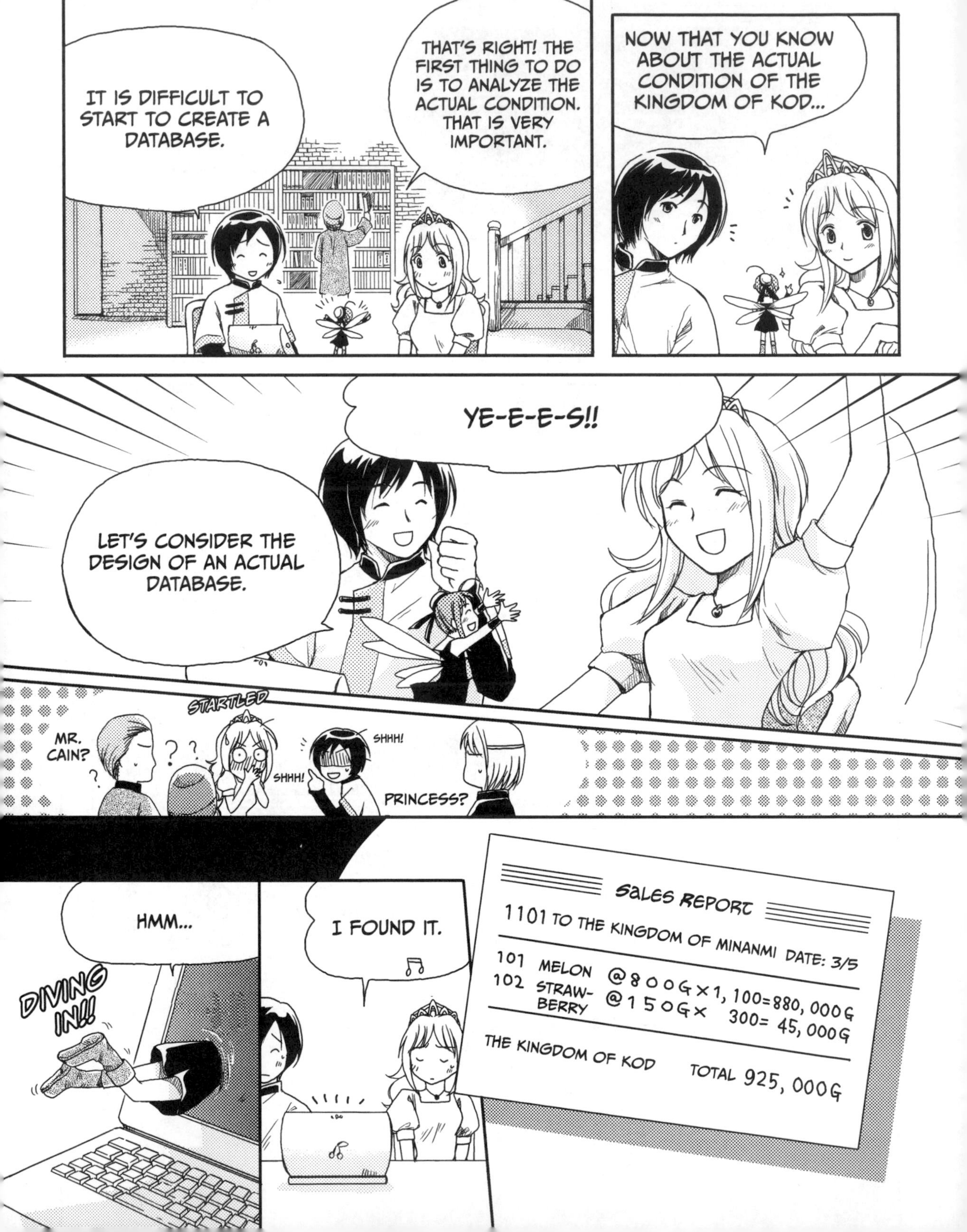

IT IS DIFFICULT TO START TO CREATE A DATABASE.
THAT'S RIGHT! THE FIRST THING TO DO IS TO ANALYZE THE ACTUAL CONDITION. THAT IS VERY IMPORTANT.
NOW THAT YOU KNOW ABOUT THE ACTUAL CONDITION OF THE KINGDOM OF KOD...
LET'S CONSIDER THE DESIGN OF AN ACTUAL DATABASE.
YE-E-E-S!!
STARTLED
MR. CAIN?
? ? ?
SHHH!
SHHH!
PRINCESS?
HMM...
DIVING IN!!
I FOUND IT. ♫
SALES REPORT
1101 TO THE KINGDOM OF MINANMI DATE: 3/5
101 MELON @800G×1,100=880,000G
102 STRAW-BERRY @150G× 300= 45,000G
THE KINGDOM OF KOD TOTAL 925,000G

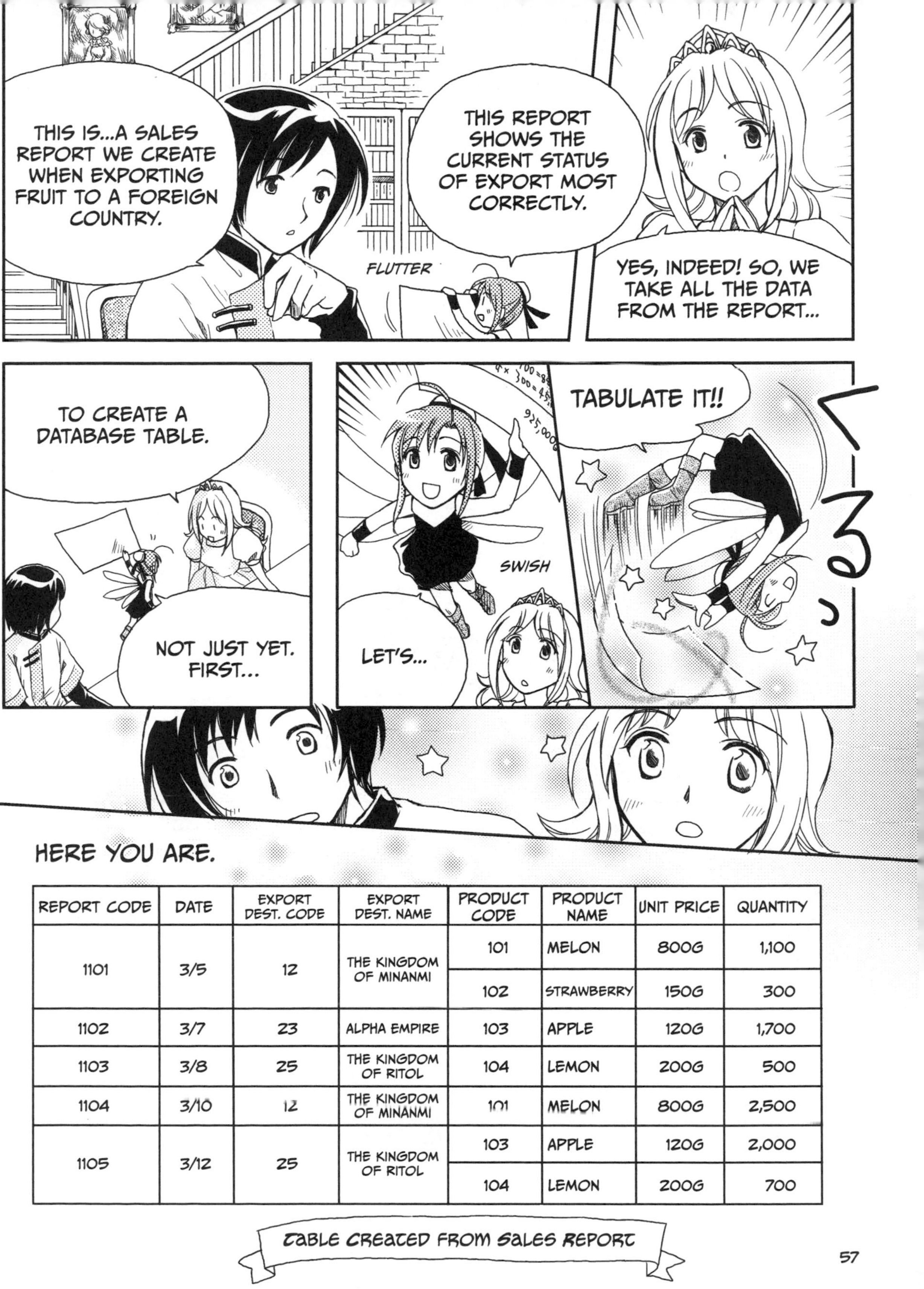
THIS IS...A SALES REPORT WE CREATE WHEN EXPORTING FRUIT TO A FOREIGN COUNTRY.
THIS REPORT SHOWS THE CURRENT STATUS OF EXPORT MOST CORRECTLY.
FLUTTER
YES, INDEED! SO, WE TAKE ALL THE DATA FROM THE REPORT...
TO CREATE A DATABASE TABLE.
NOT JUST YET. FIRST...
LET'S...
SWISH
TABULATE IT!!
HERE YOU ARE.

REPORT CODE	DATE	EXPORT DEST. CODE	EXPORT DEST. NAME	PRODUCT CODE	PRODUCT NAME	UNIT PRICE	QUANTITY
1101	3/5	12	THE KINGDOM OF MINANMI	101	MELON	800G	1,100
				102	STRAWBERRY	150G	300
1102	3/7	23	ALPHA EMPIRE	103	APPLE	120G	1,700
1103	3/8	25	THE KINGDOM OF RITOL	104	LEMON	200G	500
1104	3/10	12	THE KINGDOM OF MINANMI	101	MELON	800G	2,500
1105	3/12	25	THE KINGDOM OF RITOL	103	APPLE	120G	2,000
				104	LEMON	200G	700

TABLE CREATED FROM SALES REPORT

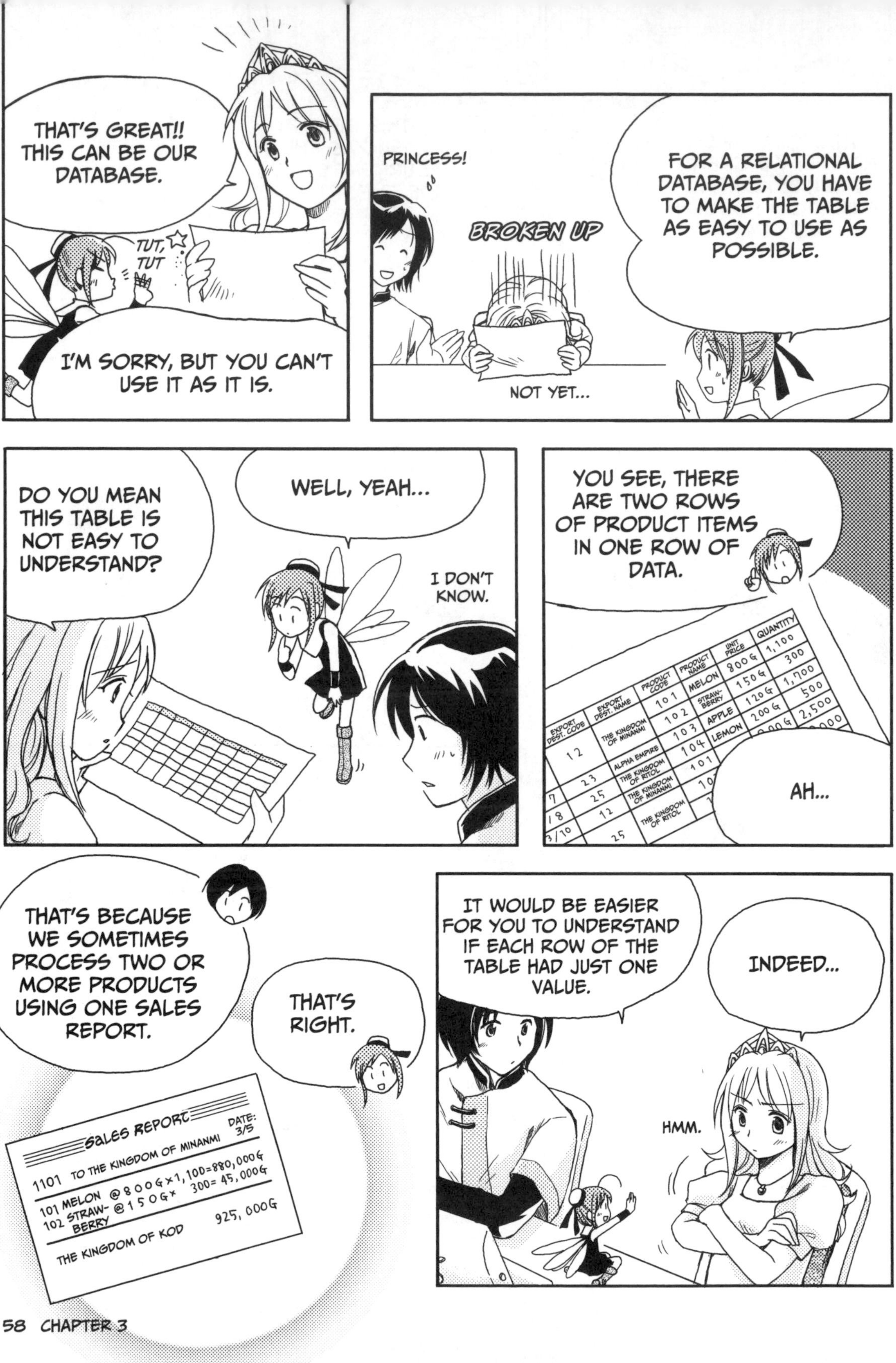
THAT'S GREAT!! THIS CAN BE OUR DATABASE.
TUT, TUT
I'M SORRY, BUT YOU CAN'T USE IT AS IT IS.
PRINCESS!
BROKEN UP
NOT YET...
FOR A RELATIONAL DATABASE, YOU HAVE TO MAKE THE TABLE AS EASY TO USE AS POSSIBLE.
DO YOU MEAN THIS TABLE IS NOT EASY TO UNDERSTAND?
WELL, YEAH...
I DON'T KNOW.
YOU SEE, THERE ARE TWO ROWS OF PRODUCT ITEMS IN ONE ROW OF DATA.
EXPORT DEST. CODE
EXPORT DEST. NAME
PRODUCT CODE
PRODUCT NAME
UNIT PRICE
QUANTITY
AH...
THAT'S BECAUSE WE SOMETIMES PROCESS TWO OR MORE PRODUCTS USING ONE SALES REPORT.
THAT'S RIGHT.
SALES REPORT
DATE: 3/5
1101 TO THE KINGDOM OF MINANMI
101 MELON @800G×1,100=880,000G
102 STRAWBERRY @150G× 300= 45,000G
925,000G
THE KINGDOM OF KOD
IT WOULD BE EASIER FOR YOU TO UNDERSTAND IF EACH ROW OF THE TABLE HAD JUST ONE VALUE.
INDEED...
HMM.

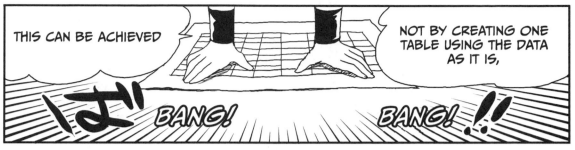

THIS CAN BE ACHIEVED

NOT BY CREATING ONE TABLE USING THE DATA AS IT IS,

BANG!

BANG!

BUT BY DIVIDING IT INTO MULTIPLE TABLES!

SHAZAM!!

LIKE THIS!!

AH, I SEE!

BUT THIS IS MUCH MORE DIFFICULT THAN THE SINGLE TABLE....

IT MAY LOOK COMPLICATED,

BUT IT IS IMPORTANT TO MANAGE DATA CORRECTLY AND COMPATIBLY.

AND IT'S OUR JOB.

MUMBLE MUMBLE

FIGURE OUT THE ACTUAL CONDITION...

USING AN E-R MODEL....

UH-HUH.

WHAT?! I WAS JUST THINKING...

CAIN, WHAT'S THE MATTER WITH YOU?

YOU MUMBLE ALOUD QUITE OFTEN.

ASSUME WE WANT TO RAISE THE UNIT PRICE OF MELON BY 20G.

20G UP

IF YOU USE THIS TABLE AS IT IS,

YOU HAVE TO FIND ALL ROWS FOR MELON AND CORRECT THE UNIT PRICE.

IT'S HERE!

820G

800G

150G

HERE, TOO...

820G

20G

BUT, IF YOU HAVE A TABLE RELATING ONLY TO PRODUCTS,

YOU CAN CORRECT THE PRICE IN JUST ONE PLACE—ONE ROW IN THE PRODUCT TABLE.

ONLY HERE!!

EASY!

820G

PRODUCT TABLE	
MELON	800 G
STRAWBERRY	150 G
APPLE	120 G
LEMON	200 G

NO CONFLICT WILL OCCUR, EVEN IF YOU FORGET TO CORRECT ANY OTHER ROWS!! ISN'T THAT GREAT?

YOU KNOW, USING A SINGLE TABLE MAKES IT EASY TO FORGET TO CORRECT DATA.

HUH...

DIVIDING THE TABLE TO PREVENT DATA CONFLICTS LIKE THIS FROM OCCURRING...

I SEE. VIEWED IN THIS LIGHT, IT IS INCONVENIENT.

IS CALLED NORMALIZATION.

NORMALIZATION, NORMALIZATION

MUMBLING, AGAIN?

HISS

YES, THIS IS IMPORTANT!

SO, WHAT AM I SUPPOSED TO DO?

FIRST OF ALL...

LET'S TRY CHANGING IT SO THAT ONE ROW HAS ONE VALUE.

REPEATED DATA IS A CLUE THAT ROWS HAVE TO BE DIVIDED.

SO, I'LL DIVIDE IT INTO...

ONE TABLE WITH DATE, EXPORT DESTINATION CODE, AND EXPORT DESTINATION NAME...

AND ANOTHER TABLE WITH PRODUCT CODE, PRODUCT NAME, UNIT PRICE, AND QUANTITY.

SALES TABLE (FIRST NORMAL FORM (1))

REPORT CODE	DATE	EXPORT DEST. CODE	EXPORT DEST. NAME
1101	3/5	12	THE KINGDOM OF MINANMI
1102	3/7	23	ALPHA EMPIRE
1103	3/8	25	THE KINGDOM OF RITOL
1104	3/10	12	THE KINGDOM OF MINANMI
1105	3/12	25	THE KINGDOM OF RITOL

SALES TABLE (FIRST NORMAL FORM (2))

REPORT CODE	PRODUCT CODE	PRODUCT NAME	UNIT PRICE	QUANTITY
1101	101	MELON	800G	1,100
1101	102	STRAWBERRY	150G	300
1102	103	APPLE	120G	1,700
1103	104	LEMON	200G	500
1104	101	MELON	800G	2,300
1105	103	APPLE	120G	2,000
1105	104	LEMON	200G	700

BUT THE REPORT CODE IS PROVIDED IN BOTH TABLES, ISN'T IT?

HUH.

YES, THAT WAY YOU CAN IDENTIFY IF THERE IS AN ASSOCIATION BETWEEN THE TWO TABLES.

THE TABLE THAT RESULTS FROM A DIVISION LIKE THIS IS CALLED THE *FIRST NORMAL FORM*.

FIRST NORMAL FORM, FIRST NORMAL FORM

STOP MUMBLING!

THE TABLE THAT HAS ROWS WITH TWO OR MORE VALUES BEFORE IT IS DIVIDED IS CALLED THE *UNNORMALIZED FORM*.

IT MEANS THAT THE FIRST NORMAL FORM IS CREATED BY DIVIDING THE UNNORMALIZED FORM.

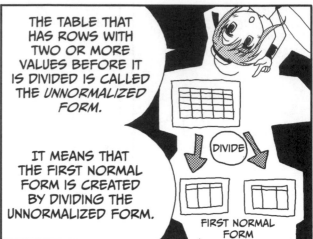

DIVIDE

FIRST NORMAL FORM

LET'S SEE...

WAIT A MINUTE.

THESE ARE THE "FIRST NORMAL FORMS." DOES THAT MEAN THERE ARE THE "SECOND" AND "THIRD" NORMAL FORMS, TOO?

BINGO!

THE FIRST NORMAL FORM CANNOT BE USED AS A RELATIONAL DATABASE TABLE AS IT IS.

HANG IN THERE!

AH, I SEE...

COME ON!!

IT'S A LONG WAY!!

FIRST NORMAL FORM

MT. RELATIONAL DATABASE

STUMBLE STUMBLE

WELL THEN, LOOK AT THE FIRST NORMAL FORM (2) FIRST.

HERE YOU ARE.

IT'S THE SALES STATEMENT TABLE.

REPORT CODE	PRODUCT CODE	PRODUCT NAME	UNIT PRICE	QUANTITY
1101	101	MELON	800G	1,100
1101	102	STRAW-BERRY	150G	300

SALES STATEMENT TABLE (FIRST NORMAL FORM (1))

YOU CAN'T MANAGE PRODUCTS WITH THIS TABLE YET.

AIEE!! WHY?

IF YOU RECEIVE MANDARIN ORANGES,

YOU CAN'T ADD THEM TO THIS TABLE IF THEY HAVE NOT BEEN SOLD YET.

WHAT DO YOU MEAN?

I'VE GOT IT!

BECAUSE NO SALES HAVE BEEN REPORTED, THE REPORT CODE AND QUANTITY ARE UNKNOWN.

APPLES WITH SALES

REPORT CODE

PRODUCT CODE

PRODUCT NAME

QUANTITY

UNIT PRICE

ORANGES WITHOUT SALES

LACK OF DATA

UNIT PRICE

PRODUCT CODE

PRODUCT NAME

IN TABLE (2), DATA RELATING TO PRODUCTS AND SALES IS MIXED.

GOOD JOB!

SNAP?!

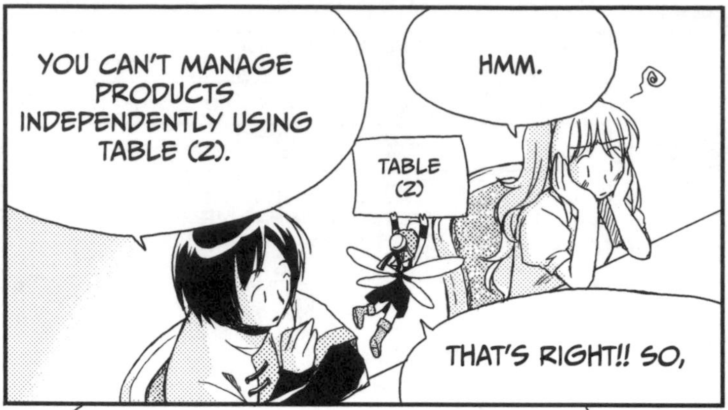
YOU CAN'T MANAGE PRODUCTS INDEPENDENTLY USING TABLE (2).
HMM.
TABLE (2)
THAT'S RIGHT!! SO,

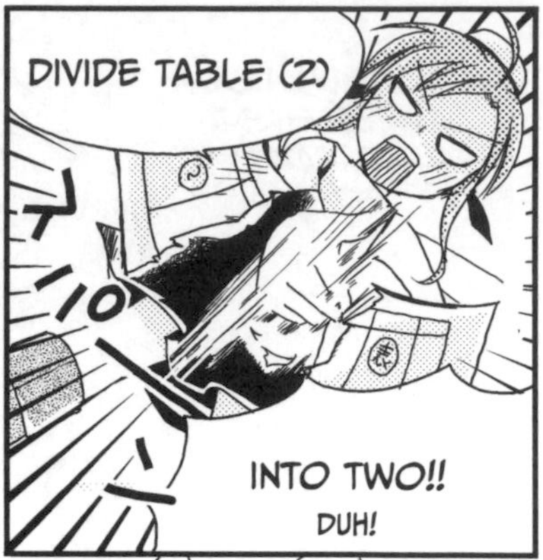
DIVIDE TABLE (2)
INTO TWO!!
DUH!

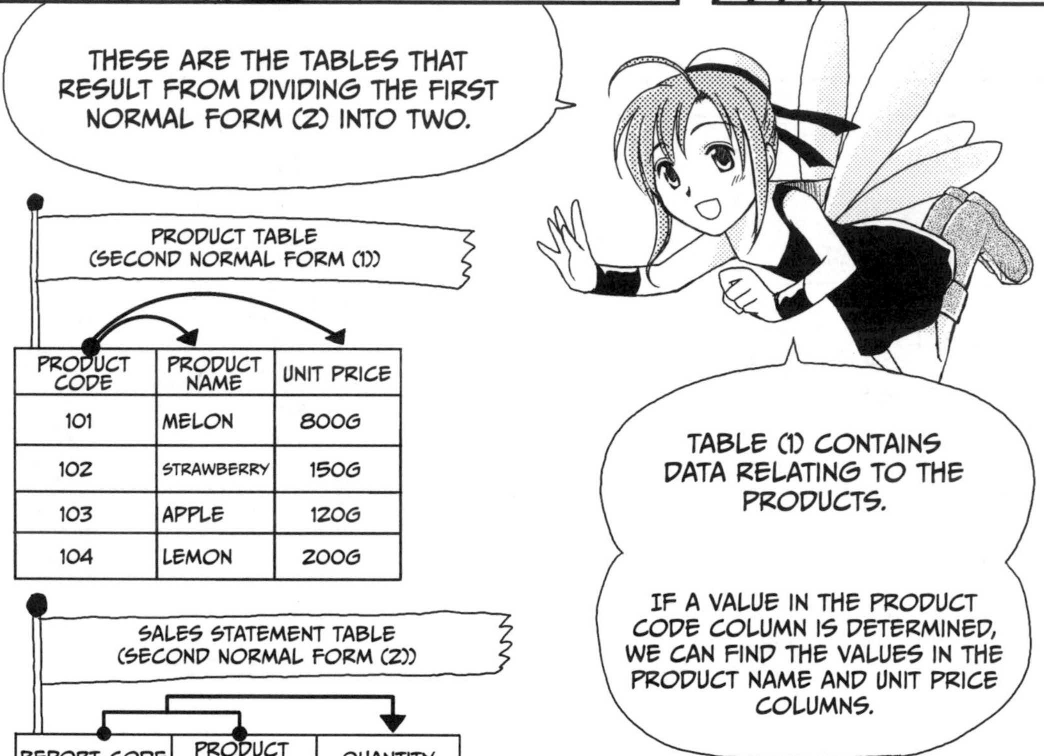
THESE ARE THE TABLES THAT RESULT FROM DIVIDING THE FIRST NORMAL FORM (2) INTO TWO.
TABLE (1) CONTAINS DATA RELATING TO THE PRODUCTS.
IF A VALUE IN THE PRODUCT CODE COLUMN IS DETERMINED, WE CAN FIND THE VALUES IN THE PRODUCT NAME AND UNIT PRICE COLUMNS.

PRODUCT TABLE
(SECOND NORMAL FORM (1))

PRODUCT CODE	PRODUCT NAME	UNIT PRICE
101	MELON	800G
102	STRAWBERRY	150G
103	APPLE	120G
104	LEMON	200G

SALES STATEMENT TABLE
(SECOND NORMAL FORM (2))

REPORT CODE	PRODUCT CODE	QUANTITY
1101	101	1,100
1101	102	300
1102	103	1,700
1103	104	500
1104	101	2,500
1105	103	2,000
1105	104	700

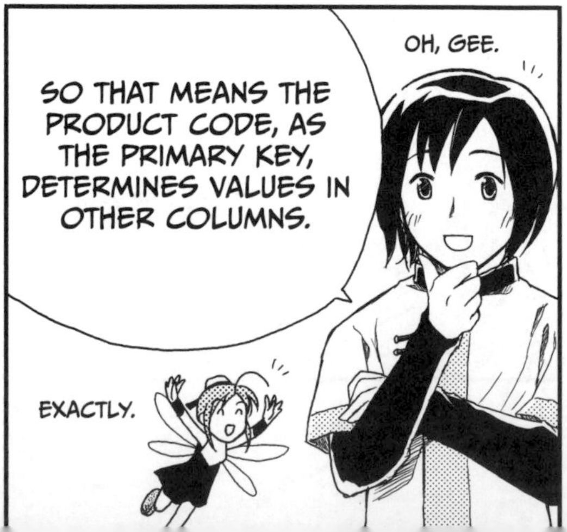
OH, GEE.
SO THAT MEANS THE PRODUCT CODE, AS THE PRIMARY KEY, DETERMINES VALUES IN OTHER COLUMNS.
EXACTLY.

FOR DATA RELATING TO SALES STATEMENT ITEMS IN TABLE (2),

AND IN THIS TABLE, THE PRIMARY KEY DETERMINES VALUES IN OTHER COLUMNS.

BUT...

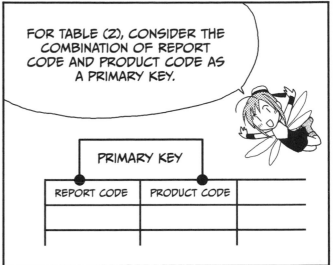

FOR TABLE (2), CONSIDER THE COMBINATION OF REPORT CODE AND PRODUCT CODE AS A PRIMARY KEY.

PRIMARY KEY		
REPORT CODE	PRODUCT CODE	

IN SOME CASES, TWO KINDS OF PRODUCTS SELL AT THE SAME TIME...

IN OTHER CASES, ONE KIND OF PRODUCT SELLS IN DIFFERENT QUANTITIES.

THIS MEANS...

YOU DIVIDE THE TABLE SO THAT WHEN A PRIMARY KEY IS DETERMINED, VALUES IN OTHER COLUMNS ARE DETERMINED.

①

PRODUCT CODE	PRODUCT NAME	UNIT PRICE

PRIMARY KEY

②

REPORT CODE	PRODUCT CODE	QUANTITY

PRIMARY KEY

UNDERSTAND?

I SEE.

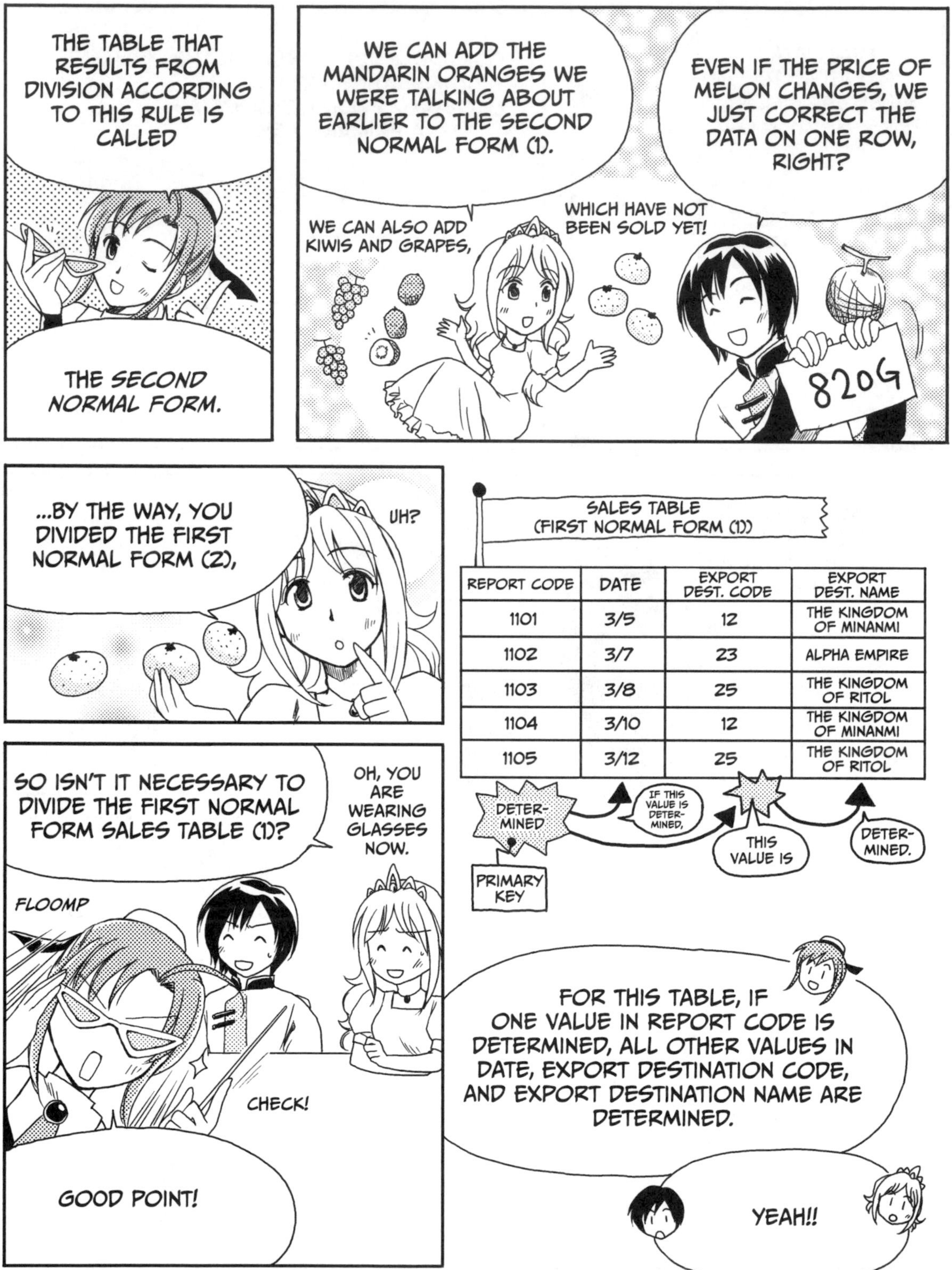
THE TABLE THAT RESULTS FROM DIVISION ACCORDING TO THIS RULE IS CALLED
THE SECOND NORMAL FORM.
WE CAN ADD THE MANDARIN ORANGES WE WERE TALKING ABOUT EARLIER TO THE SECOND NORMAL FORM (1).
WE CAN ALSO ADD KIWIS AND GRAPES,
WHICH HAVE NOT BEEN SOLD YET!
EVEN IF THE PRICE OF MELON CHANGES, WE JUST CORRECT THE DATA ON ONE ROW, RIGHT?
820G
...BY THE WAY, YOU DIVIDED THE FIRST NORMAL FORM (2),
UH?
SALES TABLE (FIRST NORMAL FORM (1))
DETERMINED
PRIMARY KEY
IF THIS VALUE IS DETERMINED,
THIS VALUE IS
DETERMINED.
SO ISN'T IT NECESSARY TO DIVIDE THE FIRST NORMAL FORM SALES TABLE (1)?
OH, YOU ARE WEARING GLASSES NOW.
FLOOMP
CHECK!
GOOD POINT!
FOR THIS TABLE, IF ONE VALUE IN REPORT CODE IS DETERMINED, ALL OTHER VALUES IN DATE, EXPORT DESTINATION CODE, AND EXPORT DESTINATION NAME ARE DETERMINED.
YEAH!!

REPORT CODE	DATE	EXPORT DEST. CODE	EXPORT DEST. NAME
1101	3/5	12	THE KINGDOM OF MINANMI
1102	3/7	23	ALPHA EMPIRE
1103	3/8	25	THE KINGDOM OF RITOL
1104	3/10	12	THE KINGDOM OF MINANMI
1105	3/12	25	THE KINGDOM OF RITOL

WHAT DO YOU CALL A TABLE IN WHICH VALUES IN OTHER COLUMNS ARE DETERMINED WHEN THE PRIMARY KEY IS DETERMINED?

THE SECOND NORMAL FORM!!

SO, THIS TABLE IS A SECOND NORMAL FORM, RIGHT?

SALES TABLE (FIRST NORMAL FORM (1))				SALES TABLE (SECOND NORMAL FORM (3))			
REPORT CODE	DATE	EXPORT DEST. CODE	EXPORT DEST. NAME	REPORT CODE	DATE	EXPORT DEST. CODE	EXPORT DEST. NAME
			THE KINGDOM OF MINANMI				THE KINGDOM OF MINANMI
			ALPHA EMPIRE				ALPHA EMPIRE
			THE KINGDOM OF RITOL				THE KINGDOM OF RITOL

THAT'S RIGHT. YOU CAN CONSIDER THE FIRST NORMAL FORM (1)...

AS THE SECOND NORMAL FORM (3)!

WE HAVE COMPLETED THE FIRST AND SECOND NORMAL FORMS!

NOW, OUR RELATIONAL DATABASE IS COMPLETED!?

THE SECOND NORMAL FORM IS....

EXCITED

SHOCKED

AH

HOLD ON A SECOND...

HANG IN THERE!

NOT YET...

WE'RE ALMOST DONE!!

STEEPER THAN BEFORE

SECOND NORMAL FORM

MT. RELATIONAL DATABASE

YOU CAN FLY, TICO. THAT'S NOT FAIR!

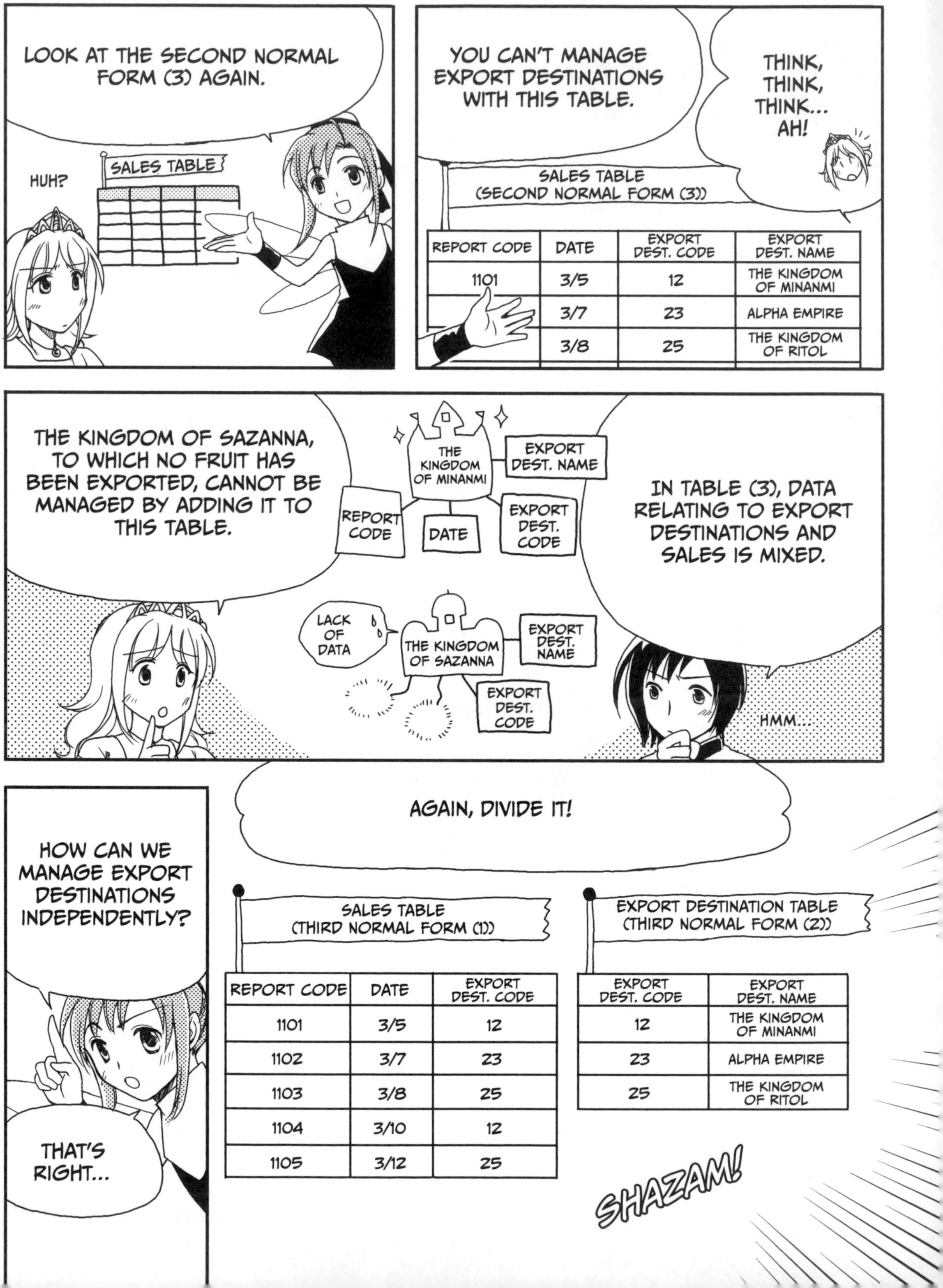
LOOK AT THE SECOND NORMAL FORM (3) AGAIN.
HUH?
SALES TABLE
YOU CAN'T MANAGE EXPORT DESTINATIONS WITH THIS TABLE.
THINK, THINK, THINK... AH!
SALES TABLE (SECOND NORMAL FORM (3))

REPORT CODE	DATE	EXPORT DEST. CODE	EXPORT DEST. NAME
1101	3/5	12	THE KINGDOM OF MINANMI
	3/7	23	ALPHA EMPIRE
	3/8	25	THE KINGDOM OF RITOL

THE KINGDOM OF SAZANNA, TO WHICH NO FRUIT HAS BEEN EXPORTED, CANNOT BE MANAGED BY ADDING IT TO THIS TABLE.
THE KINGDOM OF MINANMI
EXPORT DEST. NAME
REPORT CODE
DATE
EXPORT DEST. CODE
IN TABLE (3), DATA RELATING TO EXPORT DESTINATIONS AND SALES IS MIXED.
LACK OF DATA
THE KINGDOM OF SAZANNA
EXPORT DEST. NAME
EXPORT DEST. CODE
HMM...
HOW CAN WE MANAGE EXPORT DESTINATIONS INDEPENDENTLY?
THAT'S RIGHT...
AGAIN, DIVIDE IT!
SALES TABLE (THIRD NORMAL FORM (1))

REPORT CODE	DATE	EXPORT DEST. CODE
1101	3/5	12
1102	3/7	23
1103	3/8	25
1104	3/10	12
1105	3/12	25

EXPORT DESTINATION TABLE (THIRD NORMAL FORM (2))

EXPORT DEST. CODE	EXPORT DEST. NAME
12	THE KINGDOM OF MINANMI
23	ALPHA EMPIRE
25	THE KINGDOM OF RITOL

SHAZAM!

IN THE SECOND NORMAL FORM (3), EXPORT DESTINATION NAME IS DETERMINED ACCORDING TO REPORT CODE.

YES.

BUT IN FACT, DETERMINATION OF REPORT CODE DETERMINES A VALUE IN EXPORT DESTINATION CODE,

THEREBY DETERMINING EXPORT DESTINATION NAME INDIRECTLY.

REPORT CODE
↓
EXPORT DESTINATION CODE
↓
EXPORT DESTINATION NAME

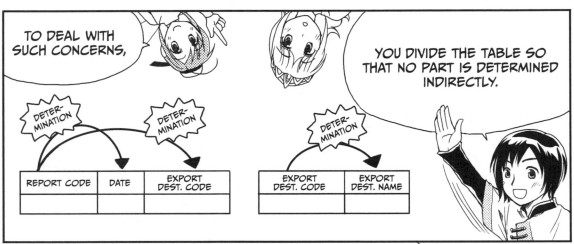

TO DEAL WITH SUCH CONCERNS,

YOU DIVIDE THE TABLE SO THAT NO PART IS DETERMINED INDIRECTLY.

DETER-MINATION

DETER-MINATION

REPORT CODE	DATE	EXPORT DEST. CODE

DETER-MINATION

EXPORT DEST. CODE	EXPORT DEST. NAME

THAT'S RIGHT. A TABLE THAT DOES NOT ALLOW ANY NON-PRIMARY KEY TO DETERMINE VALUES IN OTHER COLUMNS...

IS CALLED THE THIRD NORMAL FORM!!

FINALLY, WE'VE GOTTEN TO THE THIRD NORMAL FORM!!

NOW, YOU CAN MANAGE EVEN THE KINGDOM OF SAZANNA.

BREATHING HARD...

"THIRD" NORMAL FORM

SALES TABLE

REPORT CODE	DATE	EXPORT DEST. CODE
1101	3/5	12
1102	3/7	23
1103	3/8	25
1104	3/10	12
1105	3/12	25

EXPORT DESTINATION TABLE

EXPORT DEST. CODE	EXPORT DESTINATION NAME
12	THE KINGDOM OF MINANMI
23	ALPHA EMPIRE
25	THE KINGDOM OF RITOL

SALES STATEMENT TABLE

REPORT CODE	PRODUCT CODE	QUANTITY
1101	101	1,100
1101	102	300
1102	103	1,700
1103	104	500
1104	101	2,500
1105	103	2,000
1105	104	700

PRODUCT TABLE

PRODUCT CODE	PRODUCT NAME	UNIT PRICE
101	MELON	800G
102	STRAWBERRY	150G
103	APPLE	120G
104	LEMON	200G

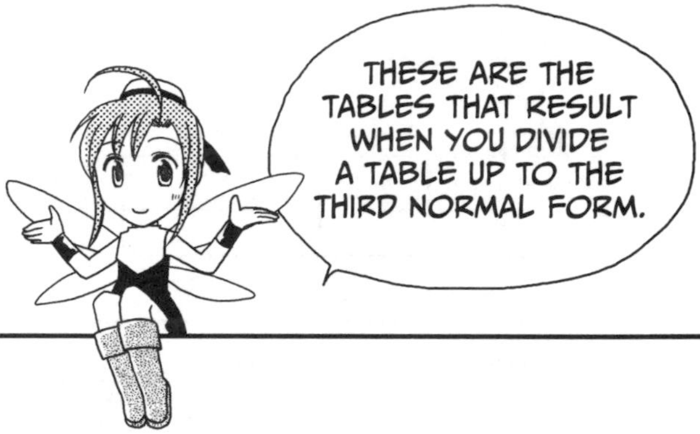
THESE ARE THE TABLES THAT RESULT WHEN YOU DIVIDE A TABLE UP TO THE THIRD NORMAL FORM.

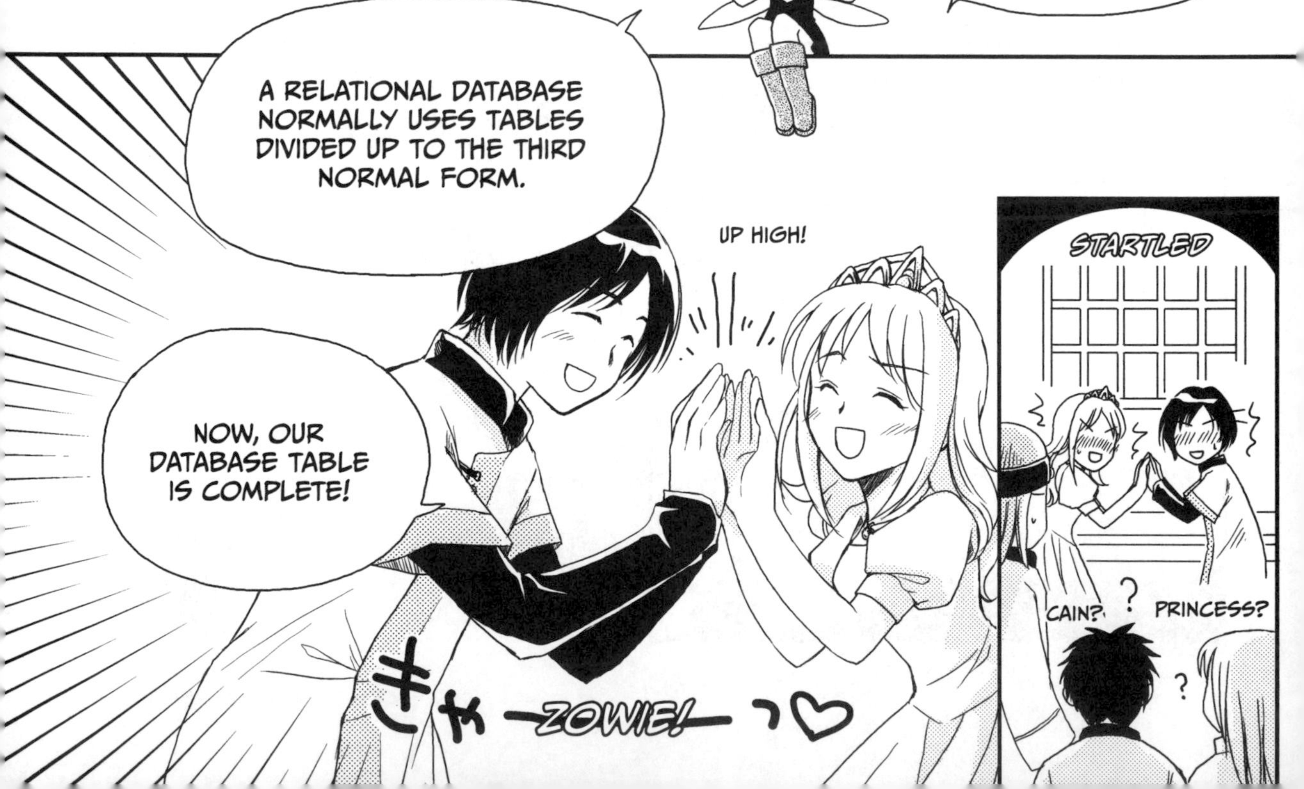
A RELATIONAL DATABASE NORMALLY USES TABLES DIVIDED UP TO THE THIRD NORMAL FORM.
UP HIGH!
NOW, OUR DATABASE TABLE IS COMPLETE!
ZOWIE!
STARTLED
CAIN?
?
PRINCESS?
?

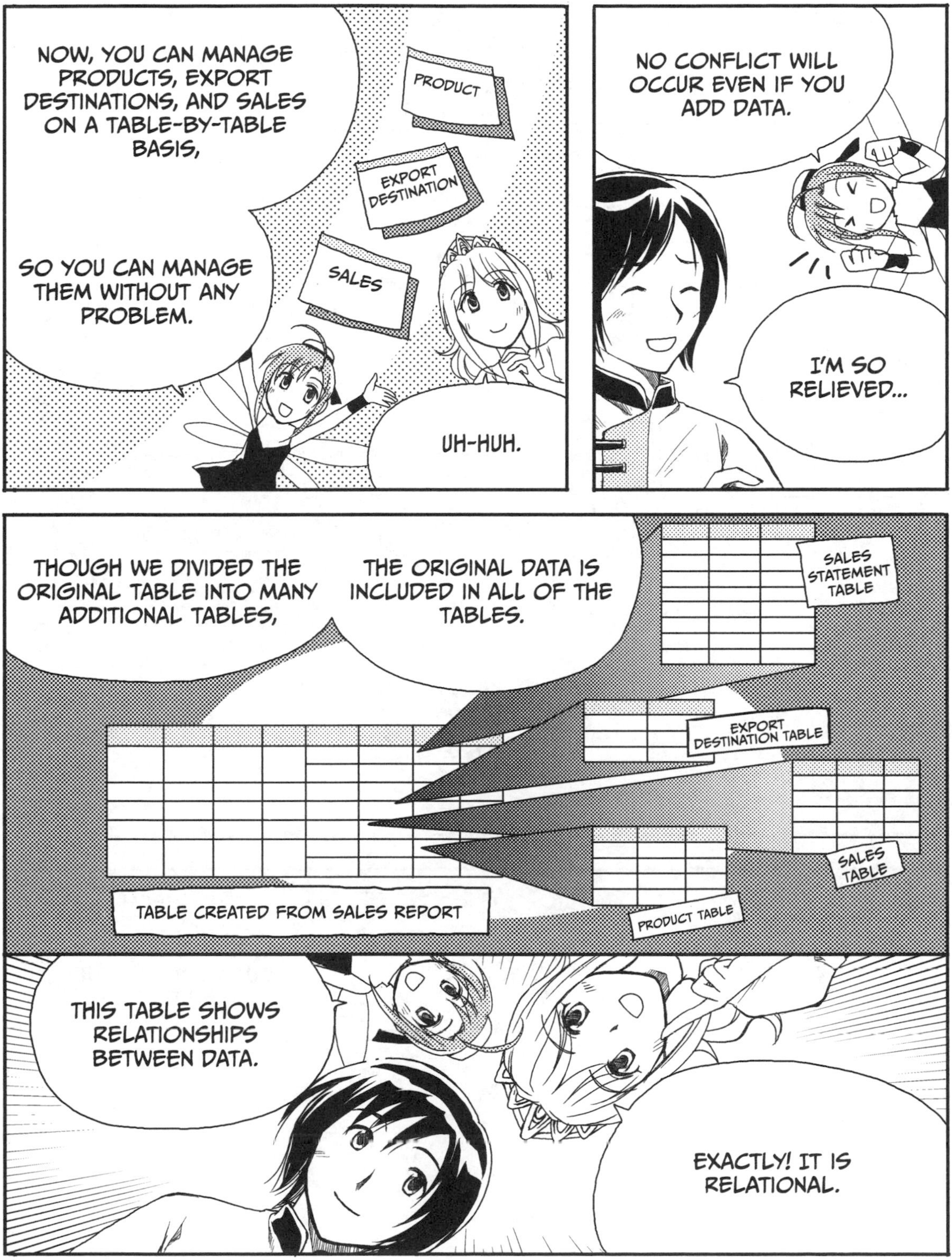
NOW, YOU CAN MANAGE PRODUCTS, EXPORT DESTINATIONS, AND SALES ON A TABLE-BY-TABLE BASIS,
PRODUCT
EXPORT DESTINATION
SALES
SO YOU CAN MANAGE THEM WITHOUT ANY PROBLEM.
UH-HUH.
NO CONFLICT WILL OCCUR EVEN IF YOU ADD DATA.
I'M SO RELIEVED...
THOUGH WE DIVIDED THE ORIGINAL TABLE INTO MANY ADDITIONAL TABLES,
THE ORIGINAL DATA IS INCLUDED IN ALL OF THE TABLES.
SALES STATEMENT TABLE
EXPORT DESTINATION TABLE
SALES TABLE
TABLE CREATED FROM SALES REPORT
PRODUCT TABLE
THIS TABLE SHOWS RELATIONSHIPS BETWEEN DATA.
EXACTLY! IT IS RELATIONAL.

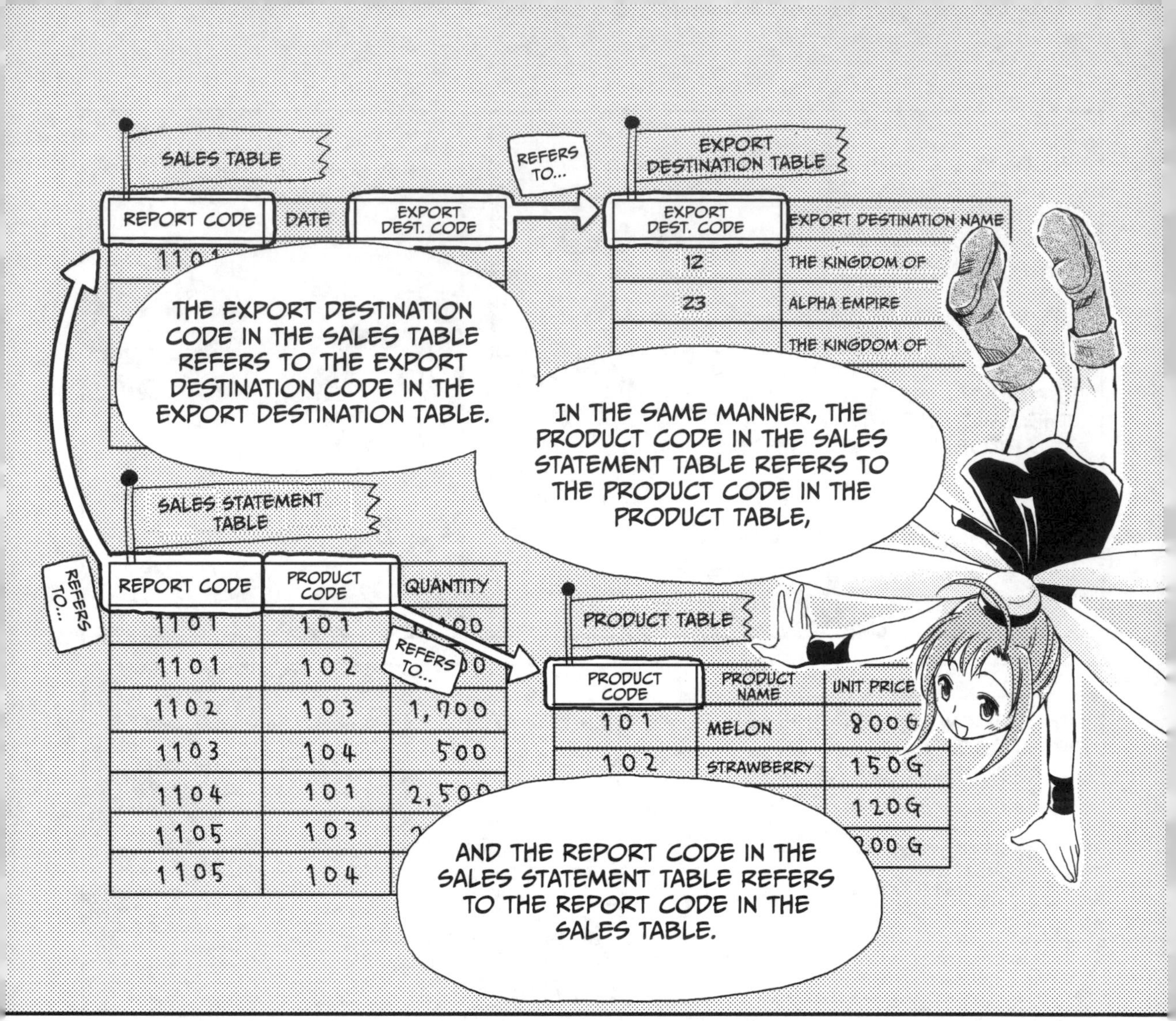
SALES TABLE
REPORT CODE
DATE
EXPORT DEST. CODE
REFERS TO...
EXPORT DESTINATION TABLE
EXPORT DEST. CODE
EXPORT DESTINATION NAME
12
THE KINGDOM OF
23
ALPHA EMPIRE
THE KINGDOM OF
THE EXPORT DESTINATION CODE IN THE SALES TABLE REFERS TO THE EXPORT DESTINATION CODE IN THE EXPORT DESTINATION TABLE.
IN THE SAME MANNER, THE PRODUCT CODE IN THE SALES STATEMENT TABLE REFERS TO THE PRODUCT CODE IN THE PRODUCT TABLE,
SALES STATEMENT TABLE
REFERS TO...
REPORT CODE
PRODUCT CODE
QUANTITY
1101
101
1101
102
1102
103
1,700
1103
104
500
1104
101
1105
103
1105
104
REFERS TO...
PRODUCT TABLE
PRODUCT CODE
PRODUCT NAME
UNIT PRICE
101
MELON
800G
102
STRAWBERRY
150G
120G
AND THE REPORT CODE IN THE SALES STATEMENT TABLE REFERS TO THE REPORT CODE IN THE SALES TABLE.

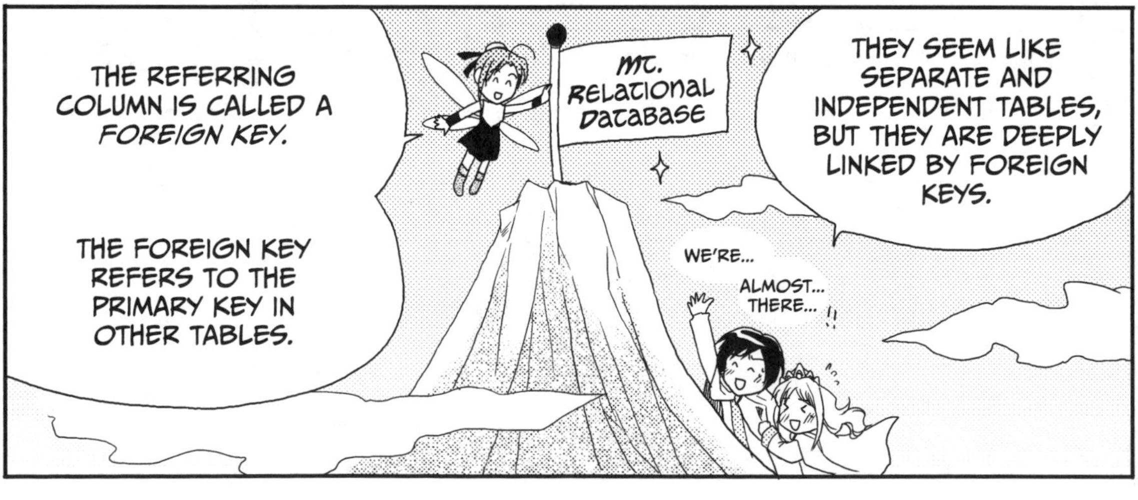
THE REFERRING COLUMN IS CALLED A *FOREIGN KEY*.
THE FOREIGN KEY REFERS TO THE PRIMARY KEY IN OTHER TABLES.
Mt. Relational Database
THEY SEEM LIKE SEPARATE AND INDEPENDENT TABLES, BUT THEY ARE DEEPLY LINKED BY FOREIGN KEYS.
WE'RE...
ALMOST... THERE... !!

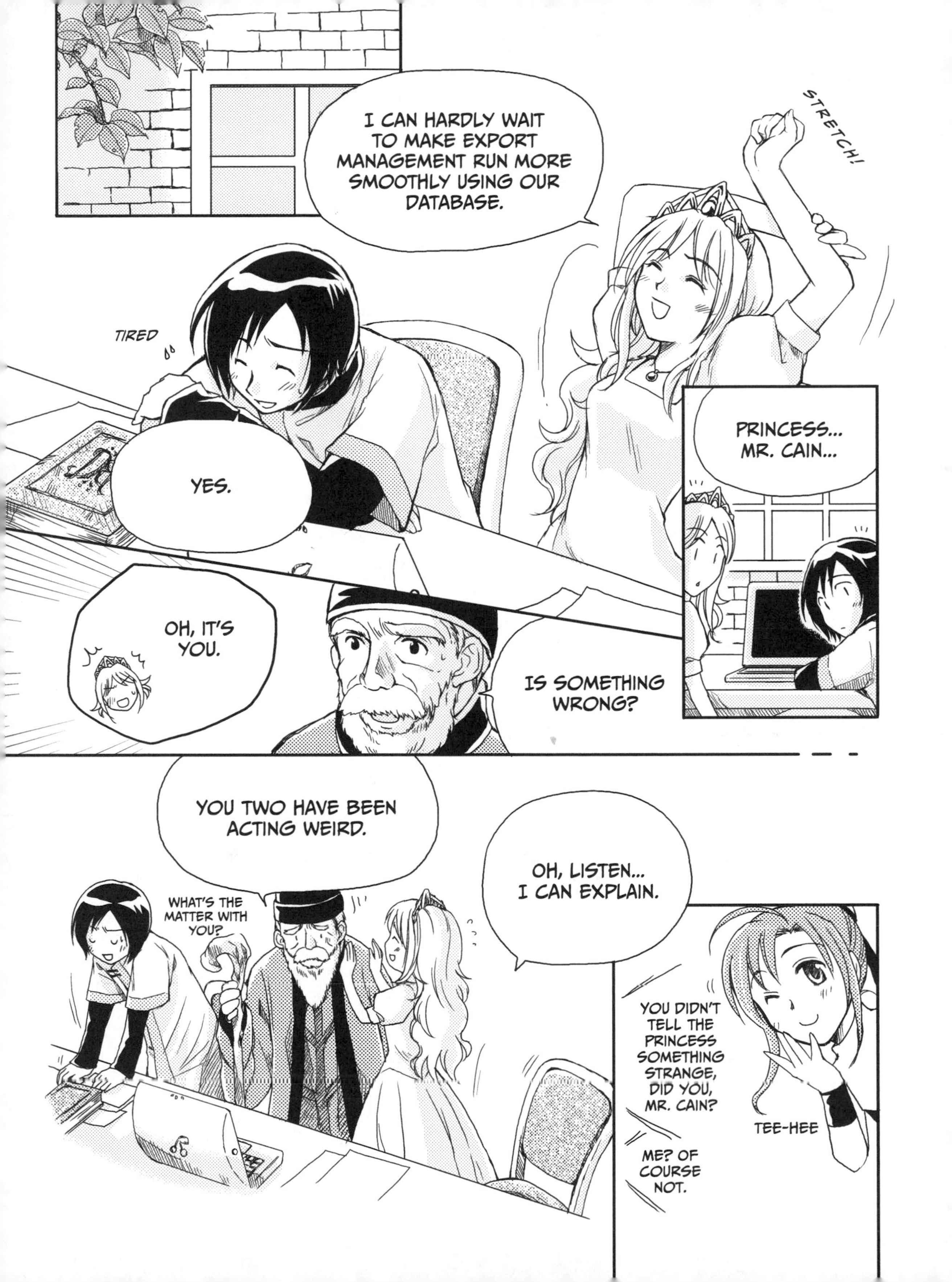
I CAN HARDLY WAIT TO MAKE EXPORT MANAGEMENT RUN MORE SMOOTHLY USING OUR DATABASE.
STRETCH!
TIRED
YES.
PRINCESS... MR. CAIN...
OH, IT'S YOU.
IS SOMETHING WRONG?
YOU TWO HAVE BEEN ACTING WEIRD.
WHAT'S THE MATTER WITH YOU?
OH, LISTEN... I CAN EXPLAIN.
YOU DIDN'T TELL THE PRINCESS SOMETHING STRANGE, DID YOU, MR. CAIN?
TEE-HEE
ME? OF COURSE NOT.

What Is the E-R Model?

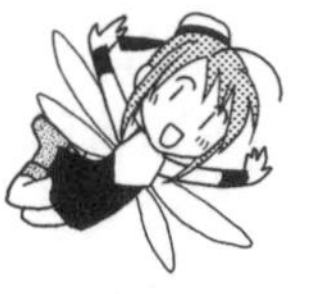

Princess Ruruna and Cain have figured out the actual condition of the Kingdom of Kod using an E-R (entity-relationship) model. When you try to create a database yourself, the first step is to determine the conditions of the data you are trying to model.

Using the E-R model, try to define an entity in your data. An *entity* is a real-world object or "thing," such as *fruit* or *export destination*.

In addition, an E-R model shows the relationship between entities. Princess Ruruna and Cain performed their analysis on the assumption that there was a relationship called *sales* between fruit and export destination. Fruit is exported to multiple export destinations, while each export destination also imports multiple kinds of fruit. For this reason, an analysis was made for the E-R model assuming that there was a relationship called *many-to-many* between fruit and export destinations. M fruit have a relationship with N export destinations. The number of associations between entities is called *cardinality*.

PRODUCT CODE
FRUIT
PRODUCT NAME
M
UNIT PRICE
SALES
QUANTITY
N
EXPORT DESTINATION CODE
EXPORT DESTINATION
EXPORT DESTINATION NAME

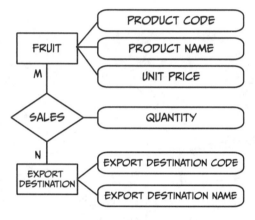

How to Analyze the E-R Model

How would you perform analyses in the cases below? Think about it.

Case 1: One-to-One Relationship

One export destination manages one piece of export history information. This kind of relationship is called a *one-to-one* relationship.

PRINCE RAMINESS
EXPORT DESTINATION INFORMATION
EXPORT DESTINATION
1
MANAGEMENT
1
EXPORT HISTORY

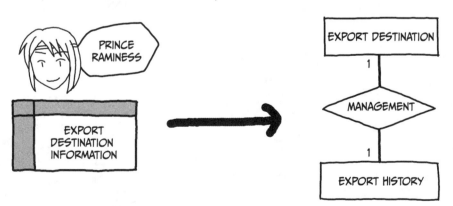

CASE 2: ONE-TO-MANY RELATIONSHIP

Multiple servants serve one princess. The servants do not serve any other princess or even the king.

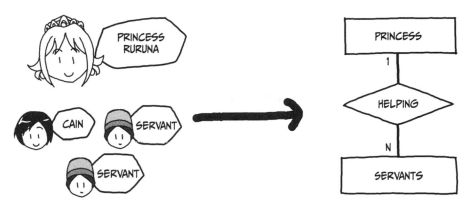

PRINCESS RURUNA
CAIN
SERVANT
SERVANT
PRINCESS
1
HELPING
N
SERVANTS

This kind of relationship is called a *one-to-many* relationship.

CASE 3: MANY-TO-MANY RELATIONSHIP

Fruit is exported to multiple export destinations. The export destinations import multiple kinds of fruit.

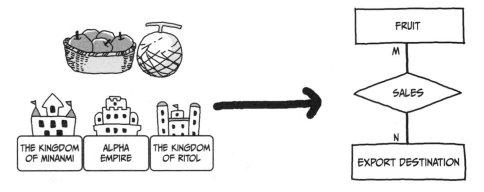

THE KINGDOM OF MINANMI
ALPHA EMPIRE
THE KINGDOM OF RITOL
FRUIT
M
SALES
N
EXPORT DESTINATION

This kind of relationship is called a *many-to-many* relationship.

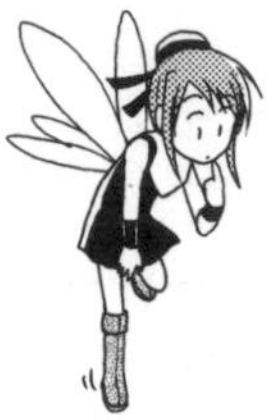

QUESTIONS

How well do you understand the E-R model? Analyze and draw an E-R model for each of the cases below. The answers are on page 82.

Q1

One staff member manages multiple customers. One customer will never be contacted by more than one staff member.

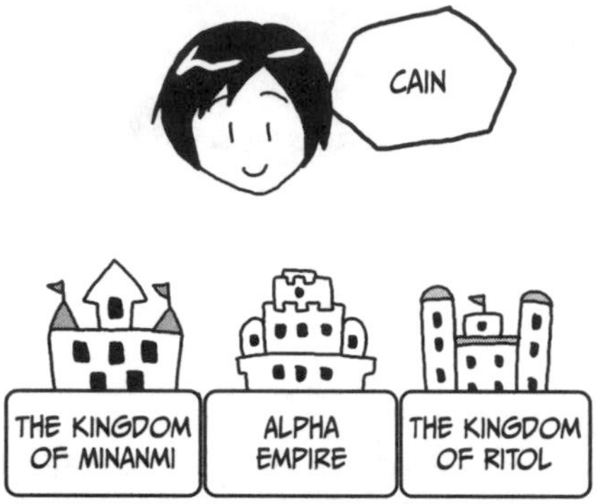

CAIN
THE KINGDOM OF MINANMI
ALPHA EMPIRE
THE KINGDOM OF RITOL

Q2

One person can check out multiple books. Books can be checked out to multiple students at different times.

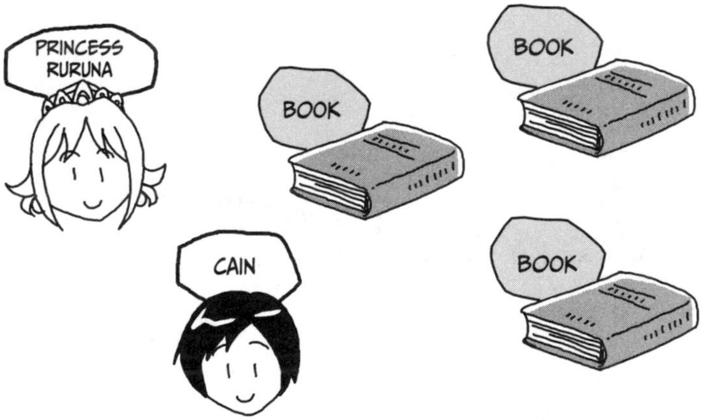

PRINCESS RURUNA
BOOK
BOOK
CAIN
BOOK

Q3

Each student attends multiple lectures. Each lecture is attended by multiple students. One teacher gives multiple lectures. Each lecture is given by one teacher.

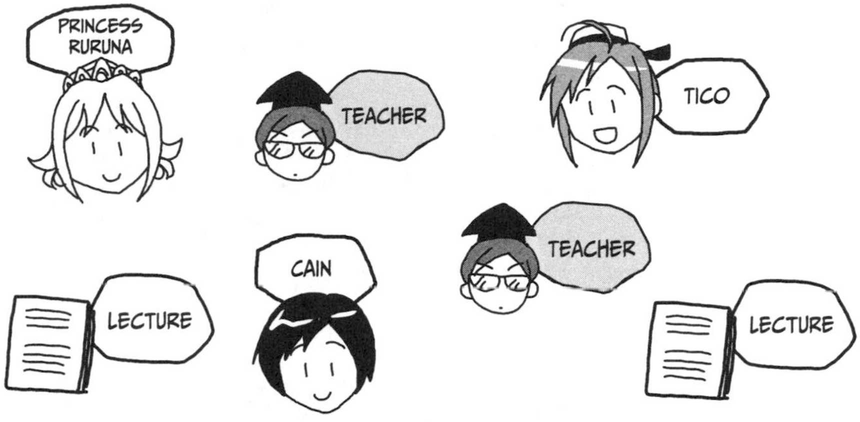
PRINCESS RURUNA
TEACHER
TICO
TEACHER
CAIN
LECTURE
LECTURE

Q4

Each customer can open multiple deposit accounts. Each deposit account is opened by one customer. Each bank manages multiple deposit accounts. Each deposit account is managed by one bank.

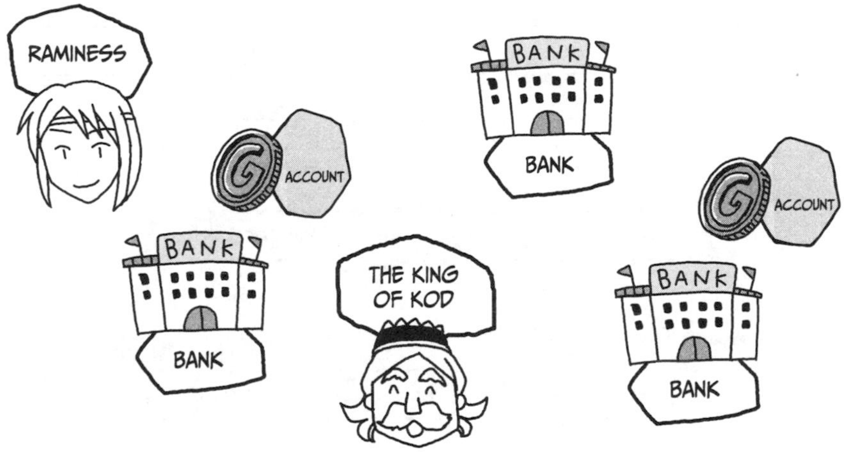
RAMINESS
BANK
BANK
ACCOUNT
ACCOUNT
BANK
BANK
THE KING OF KOD
BANK
BANK

Keep in mind that E-R model-based analysis does not necessarily produce one "correct" result. There can be many ways to logically organize data to reflect real-world conditions.

Normalizing a Table

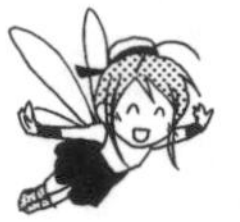

Princess Ruruna and Cain learned about normalization, the process of tabulating data from the real world for a relational database. It is necessary to normalize data in order to properly manage a relational database. Normalization is summarized here (the shaded fields are *primary keys*).

Unnormalized Form

Report code	Date	Export destination code	Export destination name	Product code	Product name	Unit price	Quantity

First Normal Form

Report code	Date	Export destination code	Export destination name

Report code	Product code	Product name	Unit price	Quantity

Second Normal Form

Report code	Date	Export destination code	Export destination name

Report code	Product code	Quantity

Product code	Product name	Unit price

Third Normal Form

Report code	Date	Export destination code

Export destination code	Export destination name

Report code	Product code	Quantity

Product code	Product name	Unit price

The *unnormalized form* is a table in which items that appear more than once have not been removed. We've seen that you cannot manage data well using this kind of table for a relational database. Consequently, you need to divide the table.

The *first normal form* refers to a simple, two-dimensional table resulting from division of the original, unnormalized table. You can consider it to be a table with one item in each cell. The table is divided so that no items will appear more than once.

The *second normal form* refers to a table in which a key that can identify data determines values in other columns. Here, it is the *primary key* that determines values in other columns.

In a relational database, a value is called *functionally dependent* if that value determines values in other columns. In the second normal form, the table is divided so that values in other columns are functionally dependent on the primary key.

In the *third normal form*, a table is divided so that a value is not determined by any non-primary key. In a relational database, a value is called *transitively dependent* if that value determines values in other columns indirectly, which is part of functionally dependent operation. In the third normal form, the table is divided so that transitively dependent values are removed.

QUESTIONS

It is important to be able to design a relational database table for various situations, so let's look at some examples of normalizing tables. Determine how the table was normalized in each of the cases below. The answers are on page 82.

Q5

The following table manages book lending like the example in Q2. To what stage is it normalized?

Lending code	Date	Student code	Student name	Student address	Department	Entrance year

ISBN	Book name	Author name	Publication date	Total page count

Lending code	ISBN	Quantity

Q6

The following table also shows a book lending situation. To what stage is it normalized?

Lending code	Date	Student code

Student code	Student name	Student address	Department	Entrance year

ISBN	Book name	Author name	Publication date	Total page count

Lending code	ISBN	Quantity

Q7

The following table shows monthly sales for each staff member. Each department has multiple staff members. A staff member can only be part of one department. Normalize this table to the third normal form.

Staff member code	Staff member name	Month	Member's sales	Department code	Department name

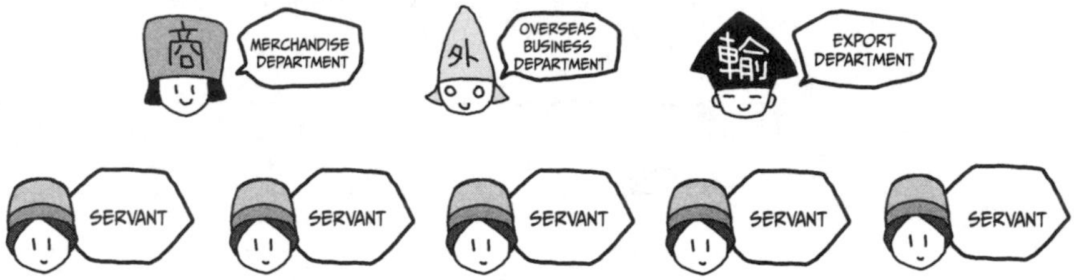
MERCHANDISE DEPARTMENT
OVERSEAS BUSINESS DEPARTMENT
EXPORT DEPARTMENT
SERVANT
SERVANT
SERVANT
SERVANT
SERVANT

Q8

The following table represents an order-receiving system. Normalize it to the third normal form. However, process one customer per order-taking code. You can process multiple products based on one order-taking code. In addition, one order-taking code should correspond to only one representative.

Order-taking code	Date	Customer code	Customer name	Product code	Product name	Unit price	Represen-tative code	Represen-tative name	Quantity

Q9

The following table represents an order-receiving system. Normalize it to the third normal form. Assume that products are classified by product code.

Order-taking code	Date	Customer code	Customer name	Product code	Product name	Unit price	Product classification code	Product classification name	Quantity

STEPS FOR DESIGNING A DATABASE

You have learned how to design a database! However, you have to do more than just that. You need to design a detailed file structure inside the database and devise methods for importing and exporting data. In general, you can divide the whole database design into three parts: conceptual schema, internal schema, and external schema.

The *conceptual schema* refers to a method that models the actual world. Namely, it is a way to determine the logical structure of a database. The conceptual schema is designed taking into consideration an E-R model–based understanding of the actual world and normalization of a table.

The *internal schema* refers to a database viewed from the inside of a computer. Namely, it is a way to determine the physical structure of a database. The internal schema is designed after creating a method to search the database at high speed.

The *external schema* refers to a database as viewed by users or applications. The external schema is designed after creating data required for application programs.

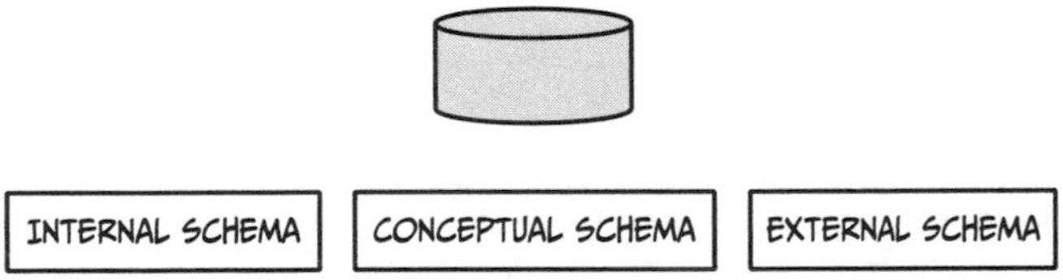
INTERNAL SCHEMA
CONCEPTUAL SCHEMA
EXTERNAL SCHEMA

Princess Ruruna and Cain have designed a database with a focus on the conceptual schema in this chapter. They are in the midst of improving the database.

Now that you've completed the basic design of a database, we'll go straight to using the database in the next chapter.

SUMMARY

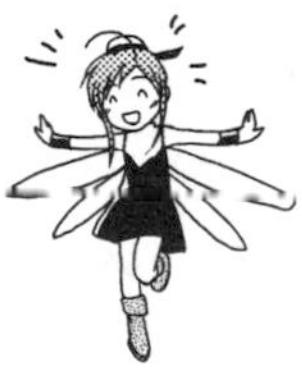

- An *E-R model* is used to analyze entities and relationships.
- Relationships between entities can be one-to-one, one-to-many, and many-to-many.
- The data in a table must be normalized before you can use it to create a relational database.
- The design of a database can be divided into three types: conceptual schema, internal schema, and external schema.

answers

Q1

STAFF MEMBER
1
MANAGING
N
CUSTOMERS

Q2

BOOK
M
LENDING
N
STUDENTS

Q3

STUDENTS
M
ATTENDING
N
LECTURES
M
TEACHING
1
TEACHER

Q4

CUSTOMER
1
OPENING
N
ACCOUNT
M
MANAGEMENT
1
BANK

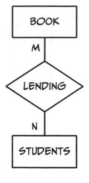

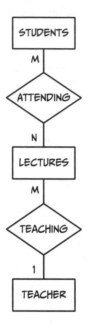

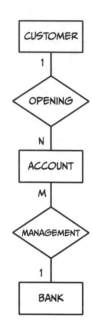

Q5 Second normal form

Q6 Third normal form

Q7

Staff member code	Month	Member's sales

Staff member code	Staff member name	Department code

Department code	Department name

Q8

Order-taking code	Date	Customer code	Representative code

Customer code	Customer name

Order-taking code	Product code	Quantity

Product code	Product name	Unit price

Representative code	Representative name

Q9

Order-taking code	Date	Customer code

Customer code	Customer name

Order-taking code	Product code	Quantity

Product code	Product classification code	Product name	Unit price

Product classification code	Product classification name

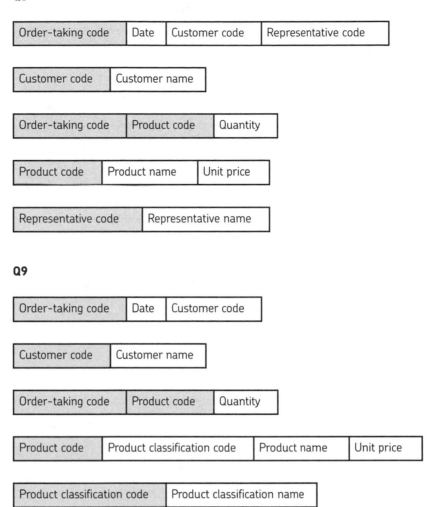

DESIGNING A DATABASE

In this chapter, you learned how to design a relational database. However, there are other database design methods. Usability and efficiency of a database depend on an analysis and design method. Therefore, it is important to create an appropriate database in the design stage.

In the database design stage, you need to perform various tasks in addition to table design. For example, you need to consider a datatype to use in the table. You may also need to specify columns indicating numerical values, currencies, and character strings. In addition, you need to devise a search method so you can carry out fast searches. Sometimes, you must create a design while keeping physical file organization in mind. And you have to control which users can access the database to ensure security. There are many factors you need to think about when designing a database. We'll look at some of these factors in the following chapters.

4

LET'S LEARN ABOUT SQL!

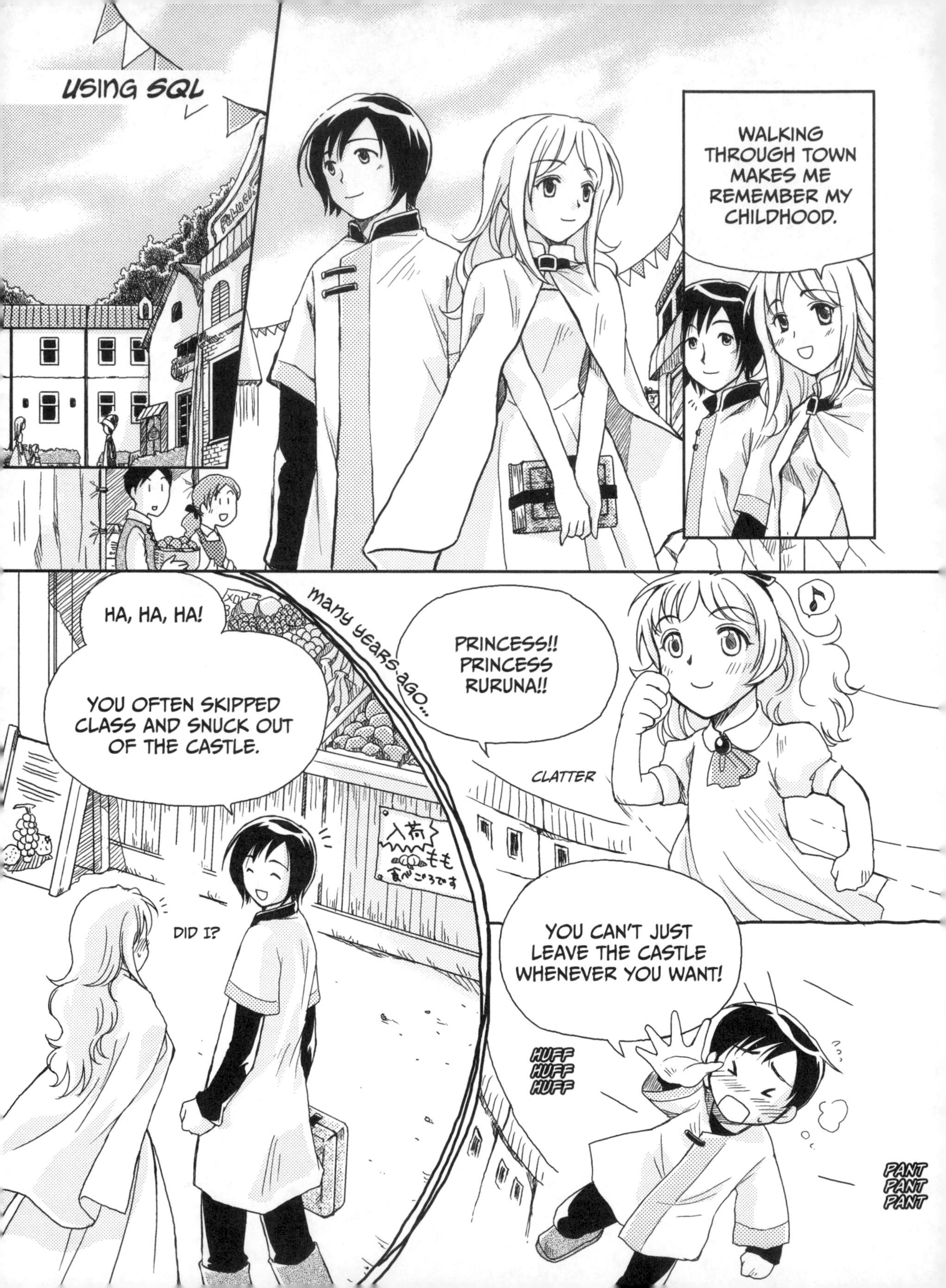
USING SQL
WALKING THROUGH TOWN MAKES ME REMEMBER MY CHILDHOOD.
many years ago...
HA, HA, HA!
YOU OFTEN SKIPPED CLASS AND SNUCK OUT OF THE CASTLE.
入荷 もも 食べごろです
DID I?
PRINCESS!! PRINCESS RURUNA!!
CLATTER
YOU CAN'T JUST LEAVE THE CASTLE WHENEVER YOU WANT!
HUFF HUFF HUFF
PANT PANT PANT

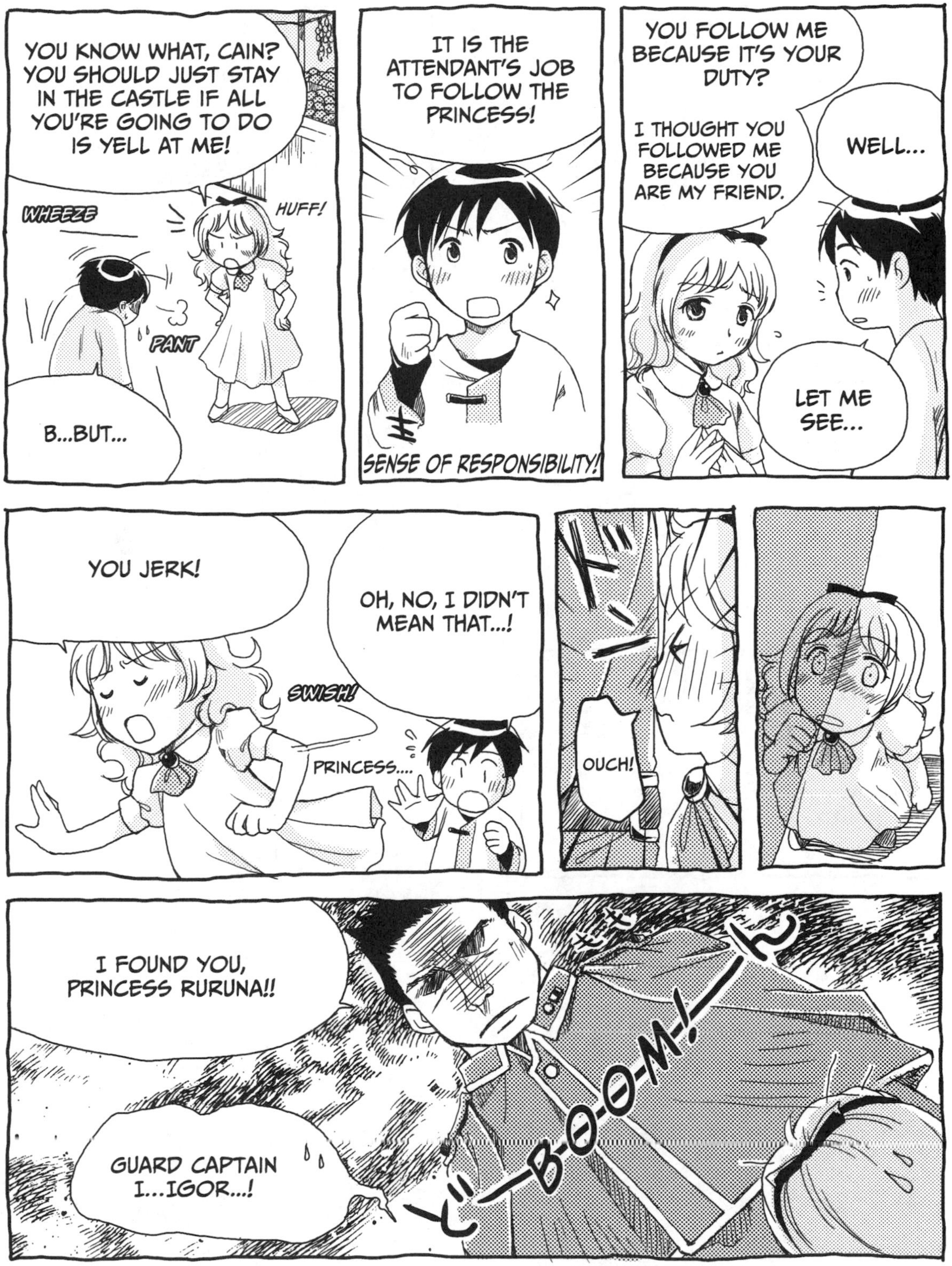
YOU KNOW WHAT, CAIN? YOU SHOULD JUST STAY IN THE CASTLE IF ALL YOU'RE GOING TO DO IS YELL AT ME!
WHEEZE
HUFF!
PANT
B...BUT...
IT IS THE ATTENDANT'S JOB TO FOLLOW THE PRINCESS!
SENSE OF RESPONSIBILITY!
YOU FOLLOW ME BECAUSE IT'S YOUR DUTY?
I THOUGHT YOU FOLLOWED ME BECAUSE YOU ARE MY FRIEND.
WELL...
LET ME SEE...
YOU JERK!
OH, NO, I DIDN'T MEAN THAT...!
SWISH!
PRINCESS....
OUCH!
I FOUND YOU, PRINCESS RURUNA!!
GUARD CAPTAIN I...IGOR...!
B-O-O-M!

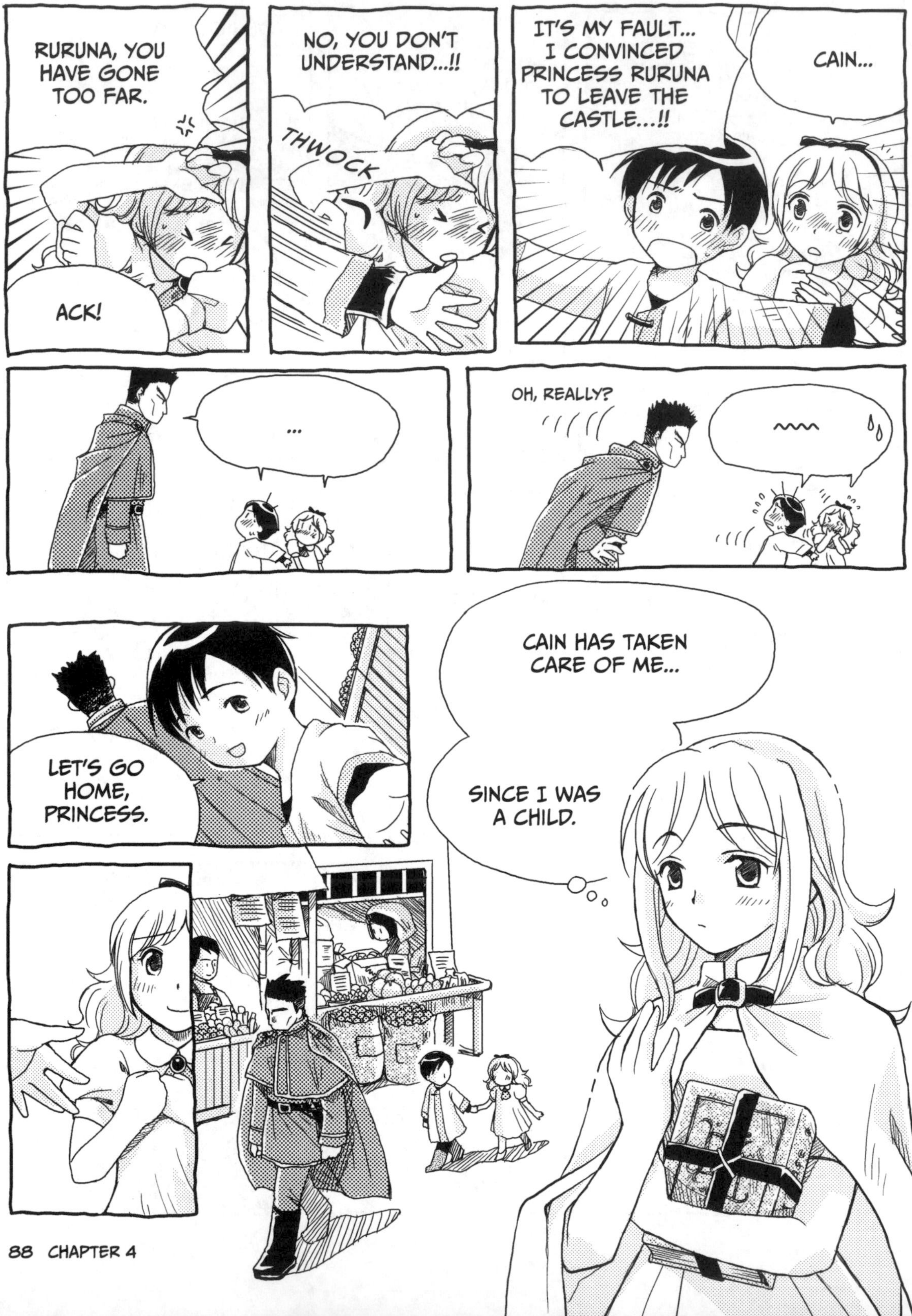
RURUNA, YOU HAVE GONE TOO FAR.
ACK!
NO, YOU DON'T UNDERSTAND...!!
THWOCK
IT'S MY FAULT... I CONVINCED PRINCESS RURUNA TO LEAVE THE CASTLE...!!
CAIN...
...
OH, REALLY?
~~~
LET'S GO HOME, PRINCESS.
CAIN HAS TAKEN CARE OF ME...
SINCE I WAS A CHILD.
~~~

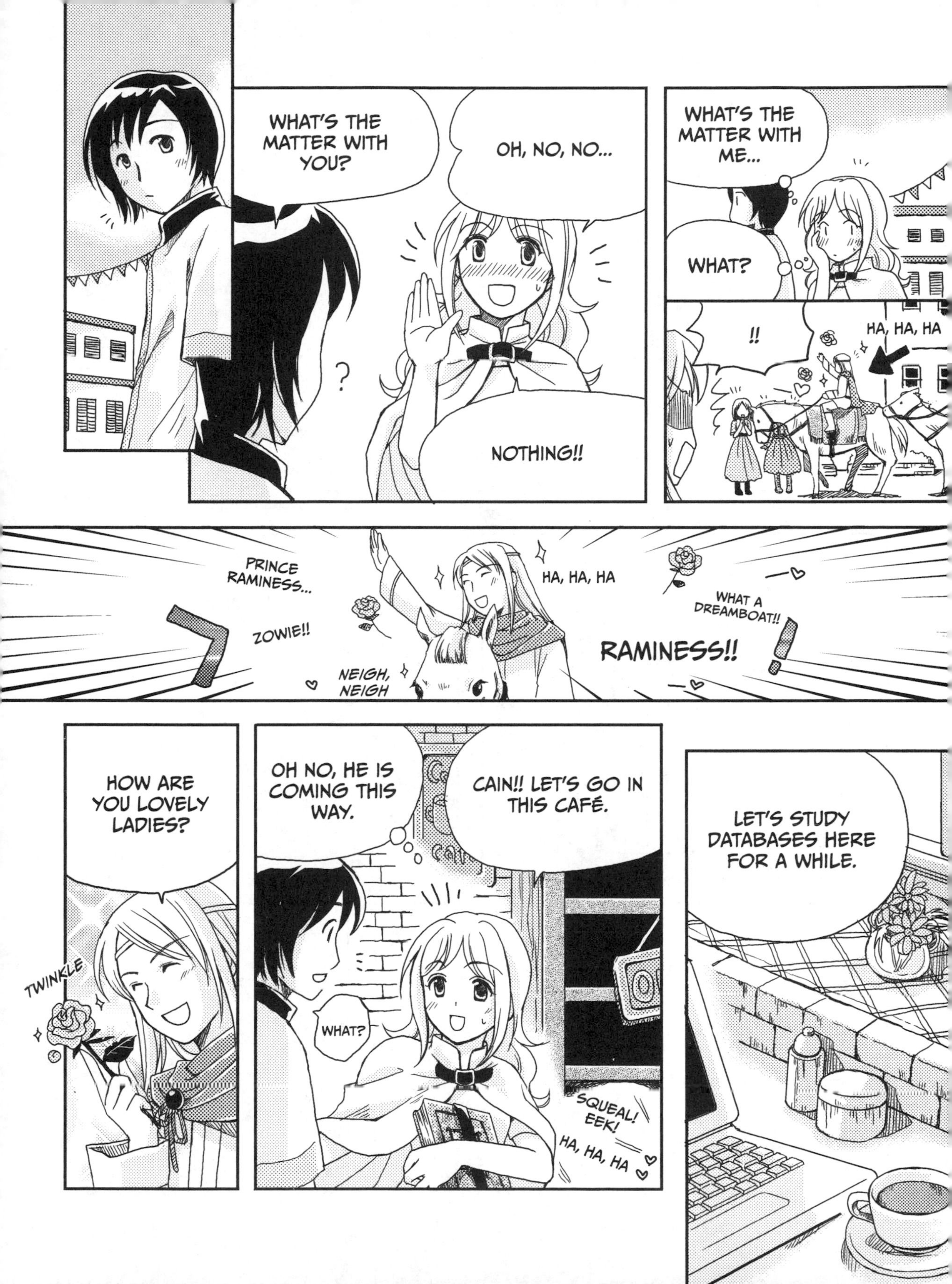
WHAT'S THE MATTER WITH YOU?
OH, NO, NO...
?
NOTHING!!
WHAT'S THE MATTER WITH ME...
WHAT?
!!
HA, HA, HA
PRINCE RAMINESS...
ZOWIE!!
NEIGH, NEIGH
HA, HA, HA
WHAT A DREAMBOAT!!
RAMINESS!!
HOW ARE YOU LOVELY LADIES?
TWINKLE
OH NO, HE IS COMING THIS WAY.
CAIN!! LET'S GO IN THIS CAFÉ.
WHAT?
SQUEAL! EEK!
HA, HA, HA
LET'S STUDY DATABASES HERE FOR A WHILE.

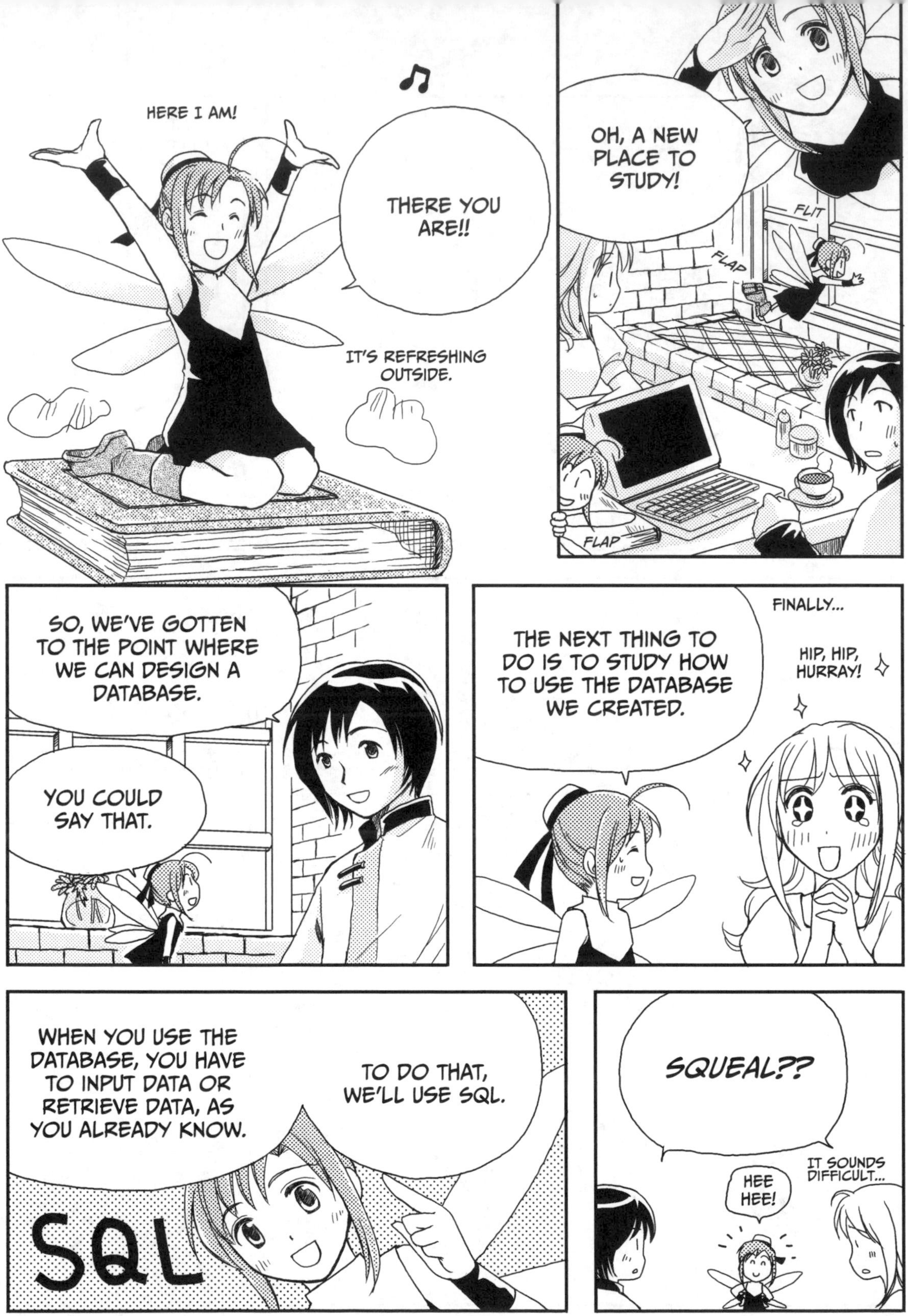
HERE I AM!
♫
THERE YOU ARE!!
IT'S REFRESHING OUTSIDE.
OH, A NEW PLACE TO STUDY!
FLIT
FLAP
FLAP
SO, WE'VE GOTTEN TO THE POINT WHERE WE CAN DESIGN A DATABASE.
YOU COULD SAY THAT.
THE NEXT THING TO DO IS TO STUDY HOW TO USE THE DATABASE WE CREATED.
FINALLY...
HIP, HIP, HURRAY!
WHEN YOU USE THE DATABASE, YOU HAVE TO INPUT DATA OR RETRIEVE DATA, AS YOU ALREADY KNOW.
TO DO THAT, WE'LL USE SQL.
SQL
SQUEAL??
HEE HEE!
IT SOUNDS DIFFICULT...

SWIMMY REGION
FOR EXAMPLE, WHEN YOU HAVE A CONVERSATION IN THE SWIMMY REGION ACROSS THE SEA,
OH, YOU SPEAK SWIMMY LANGUAGE.
SPLISH, SPLASH....
YOU NEED TO SPEAK SWIMMY LANGUAGE.
IN THE SAME MANNER, YOU USE A LANGUAGE CALLED *STRUCTURED QUERY LANGUAGE (SQL)*
TO HAVE A CONVERSATION WITH A DATABASE.
REALLY?
THAT'S GREAT!!
WAIT, WHAT?
THE DATABASE DOES NOT *REALLY* SPEAK, YOU UNDERSTAND?
OF COURSE, I KNOW THAT!

SALES TABLE

REPORT CODE	DATE	EXPORT DESTINATION CODE
1101	3/5	12
1102	3/7	23
1103	3/8	25
1104	3/10	12
1105	3/12	25

EXPORT DESTINATION TABLE

EXPORT DESTINATION CODE	EXPORT DESTINATION NAME
12	THE KINGDOM OF MINANMI
23	ALPHA EMPIRE
25	THE KINGDOM OF RITOL

PRODUCT TABLE

PRODUCT CODE	PRODUCT NAME	UNIT PRICE
101	MELON	800G
102	STRAWBERRY	150G
103	APPLE	120G
104	LEMON	200G

SALES STATEMENT TABLE

REPORT CODE	PRODUCT CODE	QUANTITY
1101	101	1,100
1101	102	300
1102	103	1,700
1103	104	500
1104	101	2,500
1105	103	2,000
1105	104	700

YOU DESIGNED THESE KINDS OF TABLES THE OTHER DAY. REMEMBER?

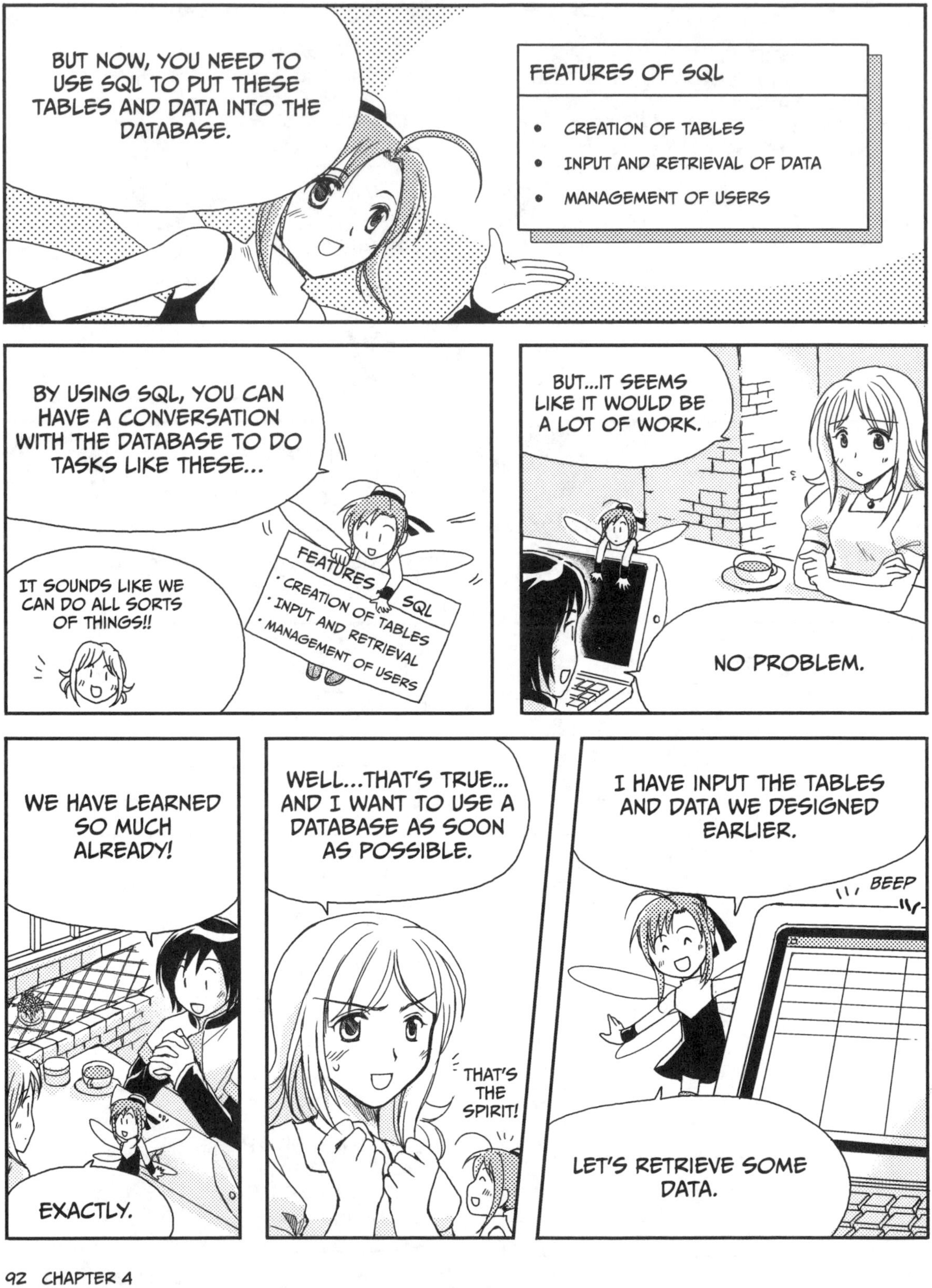
BUT NOW, YOU NEED TO USE SQL TO PUT THESE TABLES AND DATA INTO THE DATABASE.
FEATURES OF SQL
• CREATION OF TABLES
• INPUT AND RETRIEVAL OF DATA
• MANAGEMENT OF USERS
BY USING SQL, YOU CAN HAVE A CONVERSATION WITH THE DATABASE TO DO TASKS LIKE THESE...
FEATURES SQL
· CREATION OF TABLES
· INPUT AND RETRIEVAL
· MANAGEMENT OF USERS
IT SOUNDS LIKE WE CAN DO ALL SORTS OF THINGS!!
BUT...IT SEEMS LIKE IT WOULD BE A LOT OF WORK.
NO PROBLEM.
WE HAVE LEARNED SO MUCH ALREADY!
EXACTLY.
WELL...THAT'S TRUE... AND I WANT TO USE A DATABASE AS SOON AS POSSIBLE.
THAT'S THE SPIRIT!
I HAVE INPUT THE TABLES AND DATA WE DESIGNED EARLIER.
BEEP
LET'S RETRIEVE SOME DATA.

Searching for Data Using a *SELECT* Statement

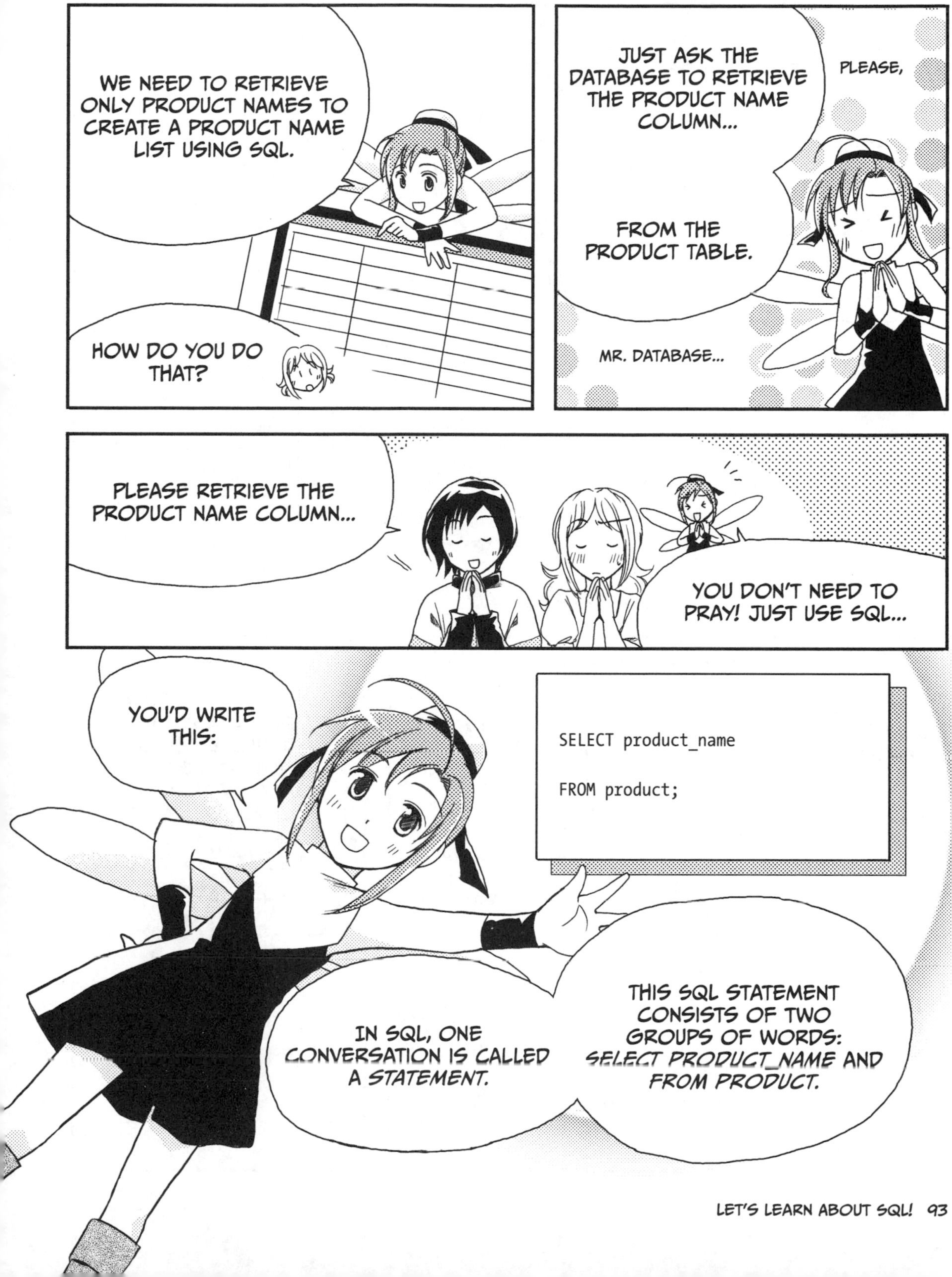
WE NEED TO RETRIEVE ONLY PRODUCT NAMES TO CREATE A PRODUCT NAME LIST USING SQL.
HOW DO YOU DO THAT?
JUST ASK THE DATABASE TO RETRIEVE THE PRODUCT NAME COLUMN...
PLEASE,
FROM THE PRODUCT TABLE.
MR. DATABASE...
PLEASE RETRIEVE THE PRODUCT NAME COLUMN...
YOU DON'T NEED TO PRAY! JUST USE SQL...
YOU'D WRITE THIS:
SELECT product_name
FROM product;
IN SQL, ONE CONVERSATION IS CALLED A *STATEMENT*.
THIS SQL STATEMENT CONSISTS OF TWO GROUPS OF WORDS: *SELECT PRODUCT_NAME* AND *FROM PRODUCT*.

THESE GROUPS OF WORDS ARE CALLED *PHRASES*.

IN SQL, YOU SPECIFY A COLUMN NAME YOU WANT TO RETRIEVE WITH THE SELECT PHRASE AND THE TABLE NAME FROM WHICH YOU WANT TO RETRIEVE IT WITH THE FROM PHRASE.

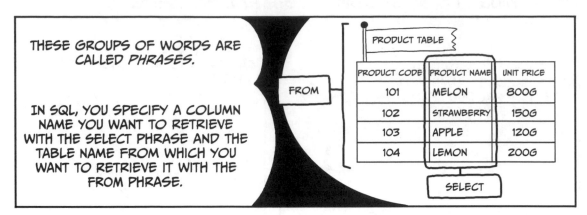

FROM

PRODUCT TABLE

PRODUCT CODE	PRODUCT NAME	UNIT PRICE
101	MELON	800G
102	STRAWBERRY	150G
103	APPLE	120G
104	LEMON	200G

SELECT

HERE IS THE RETRIEVED DATA.

THIS ALLOWS YOU TO RETRIEVE ALL PRODUCT NAMES FROM THE PRODUCT TABLE.

HERE YOU ARE! ♪

PRODUCT NAME
MELON
STRAWBERRY
APPLE
LEMON

WE ARE HAVING A CONVERSATION WITH A DATABASE USING SQL.

THAT'S RIGHT. YOU CAN RETRIEVE NECESSARY DATA BY USING VARIOUS KINDS OF PHRASES.

VARIOUS KINDS... HMM.

WELL THEN, FOR EXAMPLE,

WHAT ABOUT ASKING FOR A LIST OF PRODUCTS WHOSE UNIT PRICE IS GREATER THAN OR EQUAL TO 200G?

GREATER THAN OR EQUAL TO 200G

IN THAT CASE, YOU DON'T WANT ALL THE PRODUCT DATA.

YOU ONLY NEED TO RETRIEVE PRODUCTS WHOSE UNIT PRICE IS GREATER THAN OR EQUAL TO 200G.

YES, OF COURSE.

IN SUCH CASES, YOU SPECIFY CONDITIONS WITH THE WHERE PHRASE.
FOR EXAMPLE,

WHERE

WHERE unit_price>=200

YOU WRITE IT LIKE THIS.

I SEE... BUT...

IT IS INCONVENIENT TO SPECIFY A COLUMN NAME EACH TIME, ISN'T IT?

NO PROBLEM! TO SPECIFY ALL COLUMNS,

IT'S A PAIN!

HMM...

YOU CAN USE *! IT CAN BE SUMMARIZED AS FOLLOWS.

BANG!!

```
SELECT *

FROM product

WHERE unit_price>=200
```

SO,

THIS STATEMENT RETRIEVES ALL THE DATA FROM THE PRODUCT TABLE...

HERE YOU ARE!

PRODUCTS THAT COST 200G OR MORE		
PRODUCT CODE	PRODUCT NAME	UNIT PRICE
101	MELON	800G
104	LEMON	200G

THAT HAS A UNIT PRICE OF GREATER THAN OR EQUAL TO 200G.

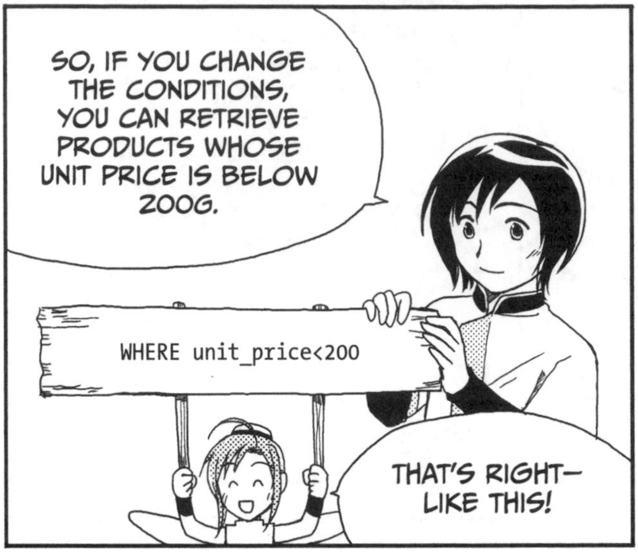
SO, IF YOU CHANGE THE CONDITIONS, YOU CAN RETRIEVE PRODUCTS WHOSE UNIT PRICE IS BELOW 200G.
WHERE unit_price<200
THAT'S RIGHT—LIKE THIS!

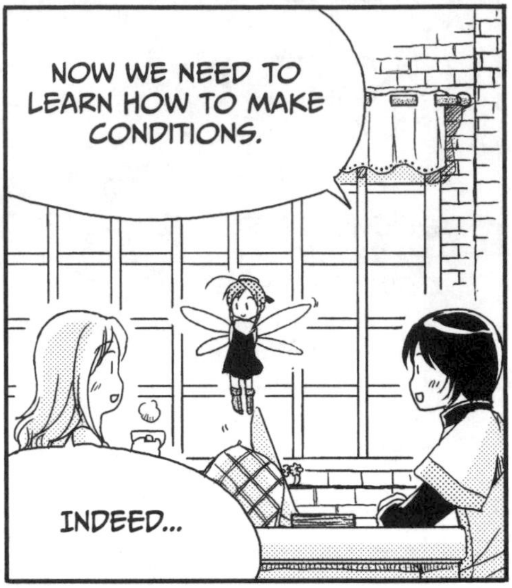
NOW WE NEED TO LEARN HOW TO MAKE CONDITIONS.
INDEED...

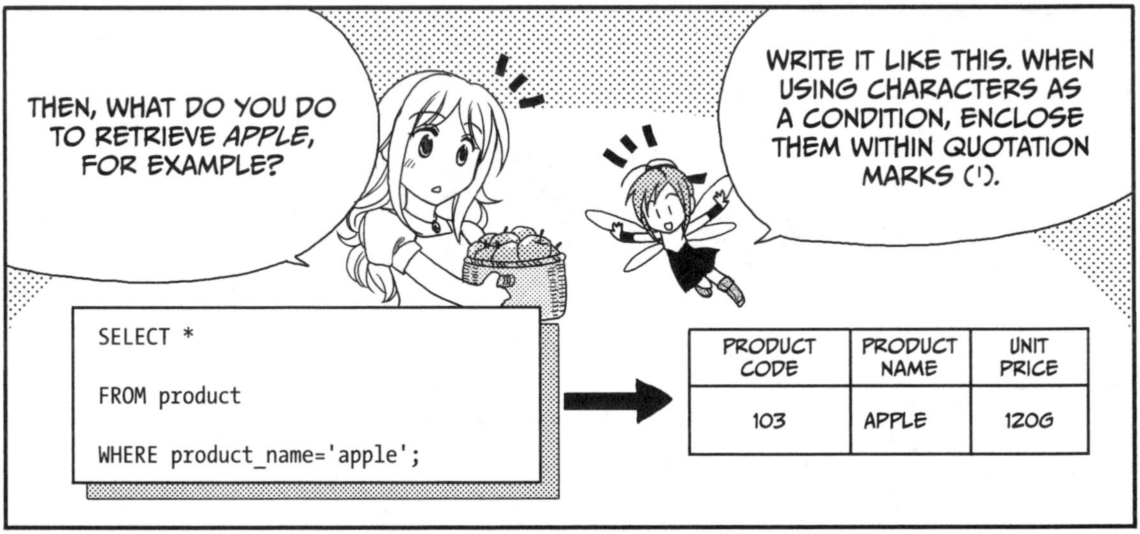
THEN, WHAT DO YOU DO TO RETRIEVE *APPLE*, FOR EXAMPLE?
WRITE IT LIKE THIS. WHEN USING CHARACTERS AS A CONDITION, ENCLOSE THEM WITHIN QUOTATION MARKS (').

```
SELECT *
FROM product
WHERE product_name='apple';
```

PRODUCT CODE	PRODUCT NAME	UNIT PRICE
103	APPLE	120G

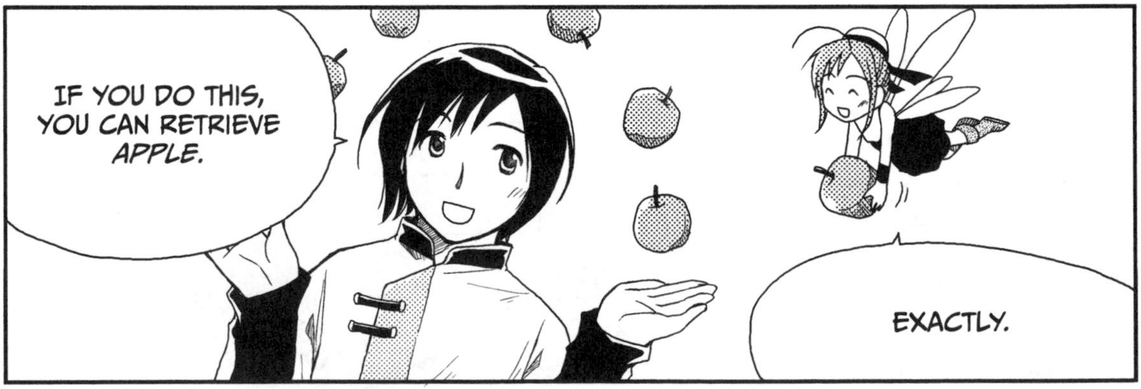
IF YOU DO THIS, YOU CAN RETRIEVE *APPLE*.
EXACTLY.

WHAT ABOUT WHEN YOU AREN'T SURE ABOUT THE PRODUCT NAME?

WHAT DO YOU DO IN THAT CASE?

YOU COMBINE THE WORD *LIKE* WITH A SYMBOL.

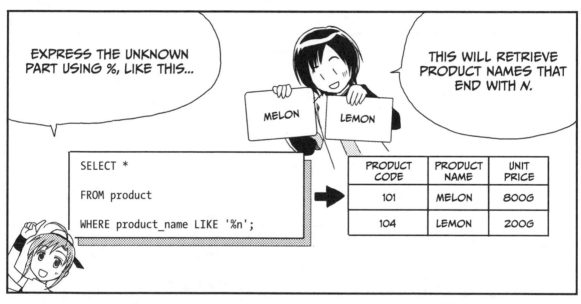

EXPRESS THE UNKNOWN PART USING %, LIKE THIS...

THIS WILL RETRIEVE PRODUCT NAMES THAT END WITH *N*.

MELON

LEMON

```
SELECT *
FROM product
WHERE product_name LIKE '%n';
```

PRODUCT CODE	PRODUCT NAME	UNIT PRICE
101	MELON	800G
104	LEMON	200G

MELON AND *LEMON* ARE RETRIEVED LIKE THAT!

ISN'T IT?

THAT'S CONVENIENT!

USING AGGREGATE FUNCTIONS

YOU CAN ALSO SORT RETRIEVED RESULTS WITH AN *ORDER BY* PHRASE.

TO SORT PRODUCTS IN ORDER OF ASCENDING PRICE, ADD A STATEMENT LIKE *ORDER BY UNIT PRICE.*

YOU CAN FIND OUT INFORMATION ABOUT PRODUCTS BY DOING THIS.

THAT'S GREAT!!

```
SELECT *
FROM product
WHERE product_name LIKE '%n';
ORDER BY unit_price;
```

PRODUCT CODE	PRODUCT NAME	UNIT PRICE
103	APPLE	120G
102	STRAWBERRY	150G

I WANT TO KNOW MORE ABOUT SQL, TICO!

OH, REALLY?

I'M GLAD.

HOW ABOUT THIS ONE?

IN THE SELECT PHRASE, USE *AVG (COLUMN NAME)* TO OBTAIN THE AVERAGE OF EACH ROW.

```
SELECT AVG(unit_price)

FROM product;
```

IT'S AMAZING.

ZZOOP!!

AVERAGE UNIT PRICE
3.175

WE NOW HAVE THE AVERAGE UNIT PRICE OF PRODUCTS.

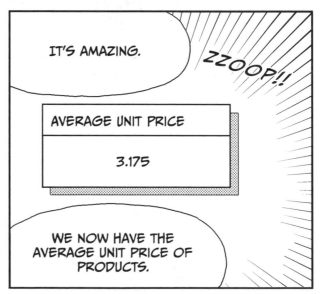

I DIDN'T KNOW THE AVERAGE FRUIT PRICE WAS AT THIS LEVEL...

THERE ARE MANY THINGS I DON'T KNOW ABOUT, EVEN THOUGH THEY ARE HAPPENING IN MY COUNTRY.

AVERAGE UNIT PRICE

3.175

EXACTLY.

SQL ALSO HAS A FUNCTION THAT AGGREGATES THE RETRIEVED DATA VALUES.

ISN'T IT CONVENIENT?

SO YOU CAN GET DATA OTHER THAN THE AVERAGE VALUE?

OF COURSE. FOR EXAMPLE...

THE NUMBER OF ITEMS, SUM, AVERAGE, MAXIMUM VALUE, AND MINIMUM VALUE CAN BE OBTAINED BY SPECIFYING AN AGGREGATE FUNCTION.

AGGREGATE FUNCTIONS IN SQL

Function	Description
COUNT(*)	Obtains the number of rows
COUNT(column_name)	Obtains the number of times the column is not null
COUNT(DISTINCT column_name)	Obtains the number of distinct values in the column
SUM(column_name)	Obtains the sum of the column's values in all rows
AVG(column_name)	Obtains the average of the column's values in all rows
MAX(column_name)	Obtains the maximum value of the column
MIN(column_name)	Obtains the minimum value of the column

LIKE THIS...

WOW!

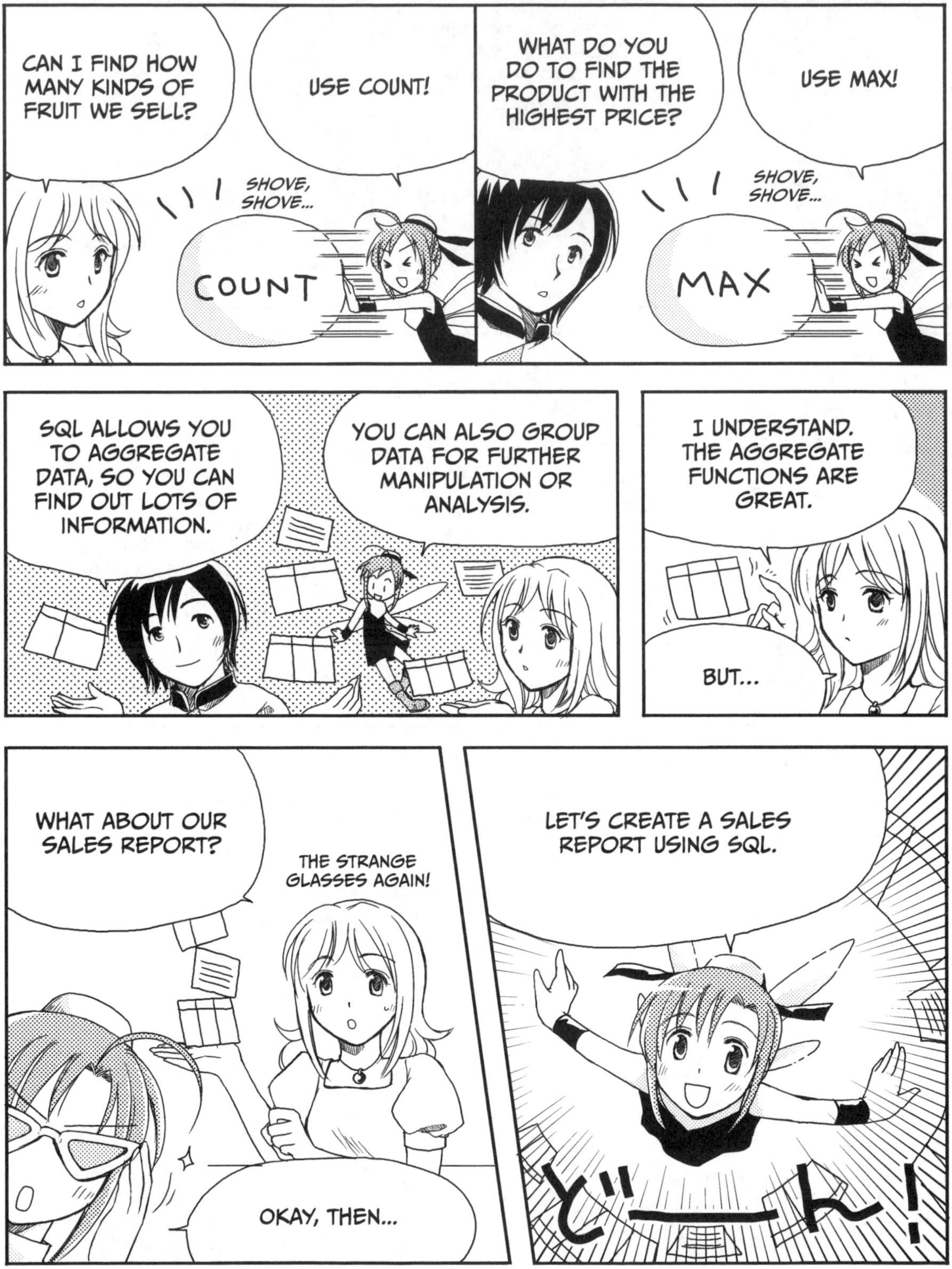
CAN I FIND HOW MANY KINDS OF FRUIT WE SELL?
USE COUNT!
SHOVE, SHOVE...
COUNT
WHAT DO YOU DO TO FIND THE PRODUCT WITH THE HIGHEST PRICE?
USE MAX!
SHOVE, SHOVE...
MAX
SQL ALLOWS YOU TO AGGREGATE DATA, SO YOU CAN FIND OUT LOTS OF INFORMATION.
YOU CAN ALSO GROUP DATA FOR FURTHER MANIPULATION OR ANALYSIS.
I UNDERSTAND. THE AGGREGATE FUNCTIONS ARE GREAT.
BUT...
WHAT ABOUT OUR SALES REPORT?
THE STRANGE GLASSES AGAIN!
OKAY, THEN...
LET'S CREATE A SALES REPORT USING SQL.
どーーん!

JOINING TABLES

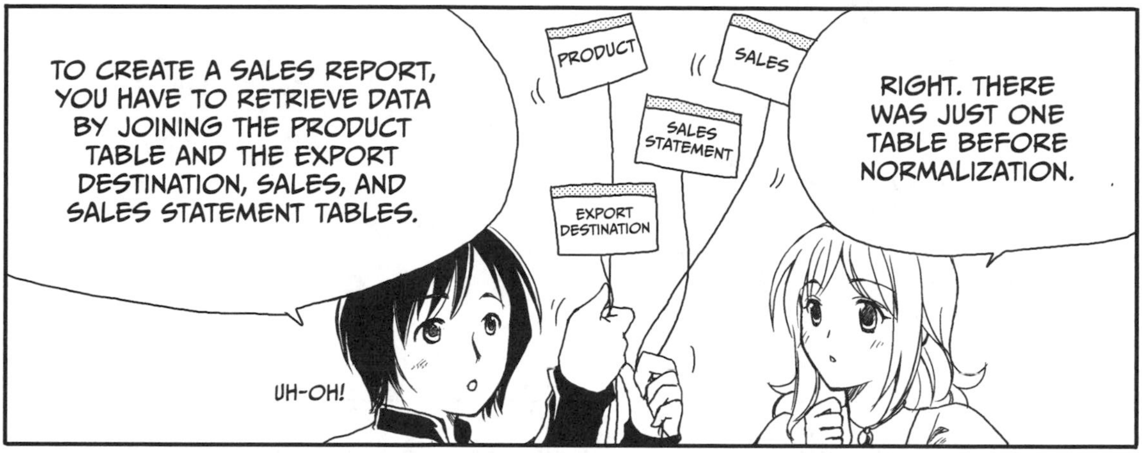
TO CREATE A SALES REPORT, YOU HAVE TO RETRIEVE DATA BY JOINING THE PRODUCT TABLE AND THE EXPORT DESTINATION, SALES, AND SALES STATEMENT TABLES.
PRODUCT
SALES STATEMENT
EXPORT DESTINATION
SALES
UH-OH!
RIGHT. THERE WAS JUST ONE TABLE BEFORE NORMALIZATION.

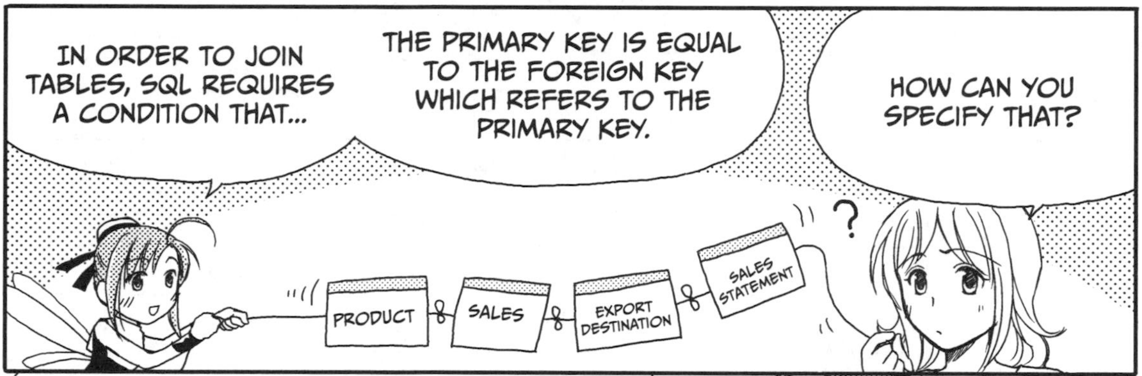
IN ORDER TO JOIN TABLES, SQL REQUIRES A CONDITION THAT...
THE PRIMARY KEY IS EQUAL TO THE FOREIGN KEY WHICH REFERS TO THE PRIMARY KEY.
HOW CAN YOU SPECIFY THAT?
PRODUCT
SALES
EXPORT DESTINATION
SALES STATEMENT
?

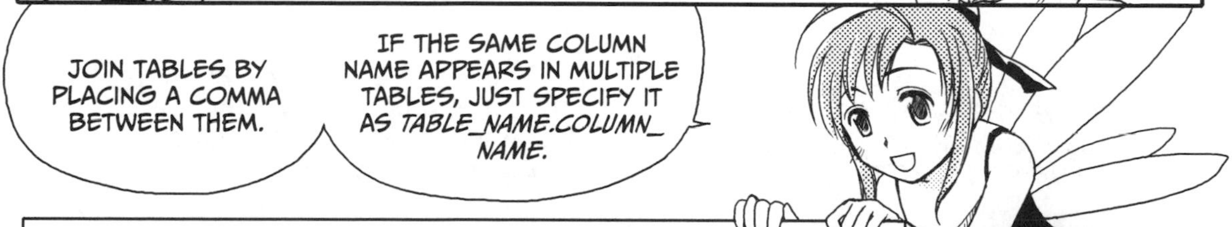
JOIN TABLES BY PLACING A COMMA BETWEEN THEM.
IF THE SAME COLUMN NAME APPEARS IN MULTIPLE TABLES, JUST SPECIFY IT AS *TABLE_NAME.COLUMN_NAME.*

```
SELECT   sales.report_code, date, sales.export_destination_code,
         export_destination_name, sales_statement.product_code,
         product_name, unit_price, export_destination

FROM     sales, sales_statement, product, export_destination

WHERE    sales.report_code = sales_statement.report_code
         AND
         sales_statement.product_code = product.product_code
         AND
         export_destination.export_destination_code =
         sales.export_destination_code
```

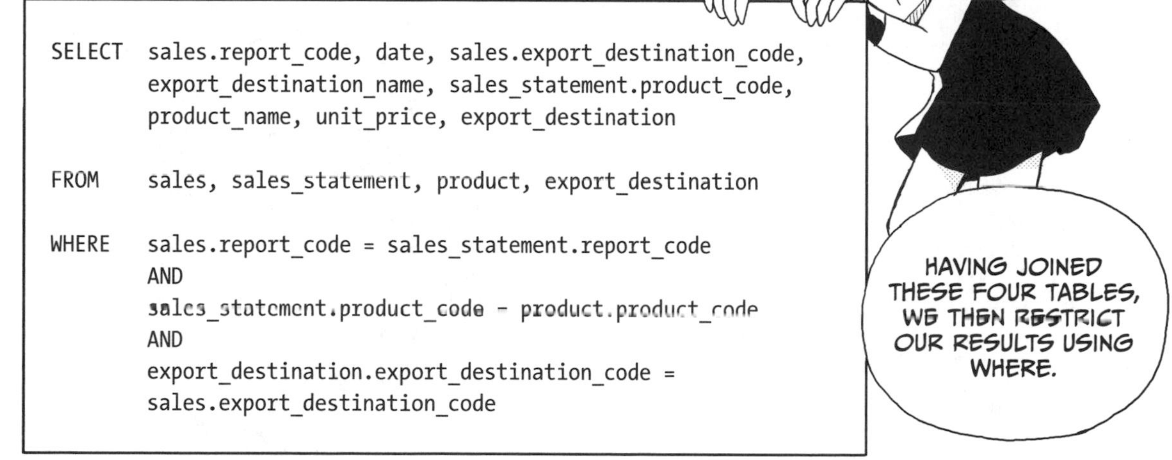
HAVING JOINED THESE FOUR TABLES, WE THEN RESTRICT OUR RESULTS USING WHERE.

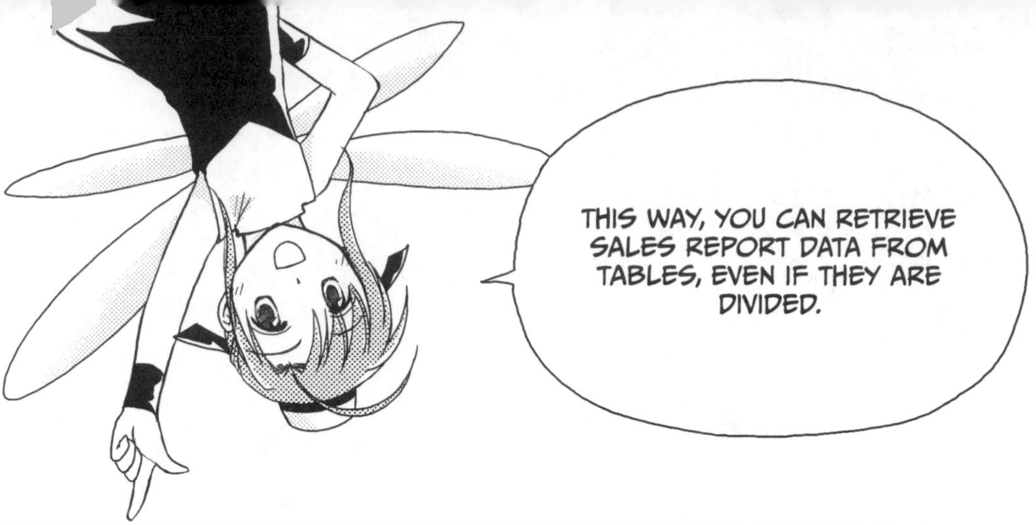
THIS WAY, YOU CAN RETRIEVE SALES REPORT DATA FROM TABLES, EVEN IF THEY ARE DIVIDED.

REPORT CODE	DATE	EXPORT DEST. CODE	EXPORT DEST. NAME	PRODUCT CODE	PRODUCT NAME	UNIT PRICE	QUANTITY
1101	3/5	12	THE KINGDOM OF MINANMI	101	MELON	800G	1,100
1101	3/5	12	THE KINGDOM OF MINANMI	102	STRAWBERRY	150G	300
1102	3/7	23	ALPHA EMPIRE	103	APPLE	120G	1,700
1103	3/8	25	THE KINGDOM OF RITOL	104	LEMON	200G	500
1104	3/10	12	THE KINGDOM OF MINANMI	101	MELON	800G	2,500
1105	3/12	25	THE KINGDOM OF RITOL	103	APPLE	120G	2,000
1105	3/12	25	THE KINGDOM OF RITOL	104	LEMON	200G	700

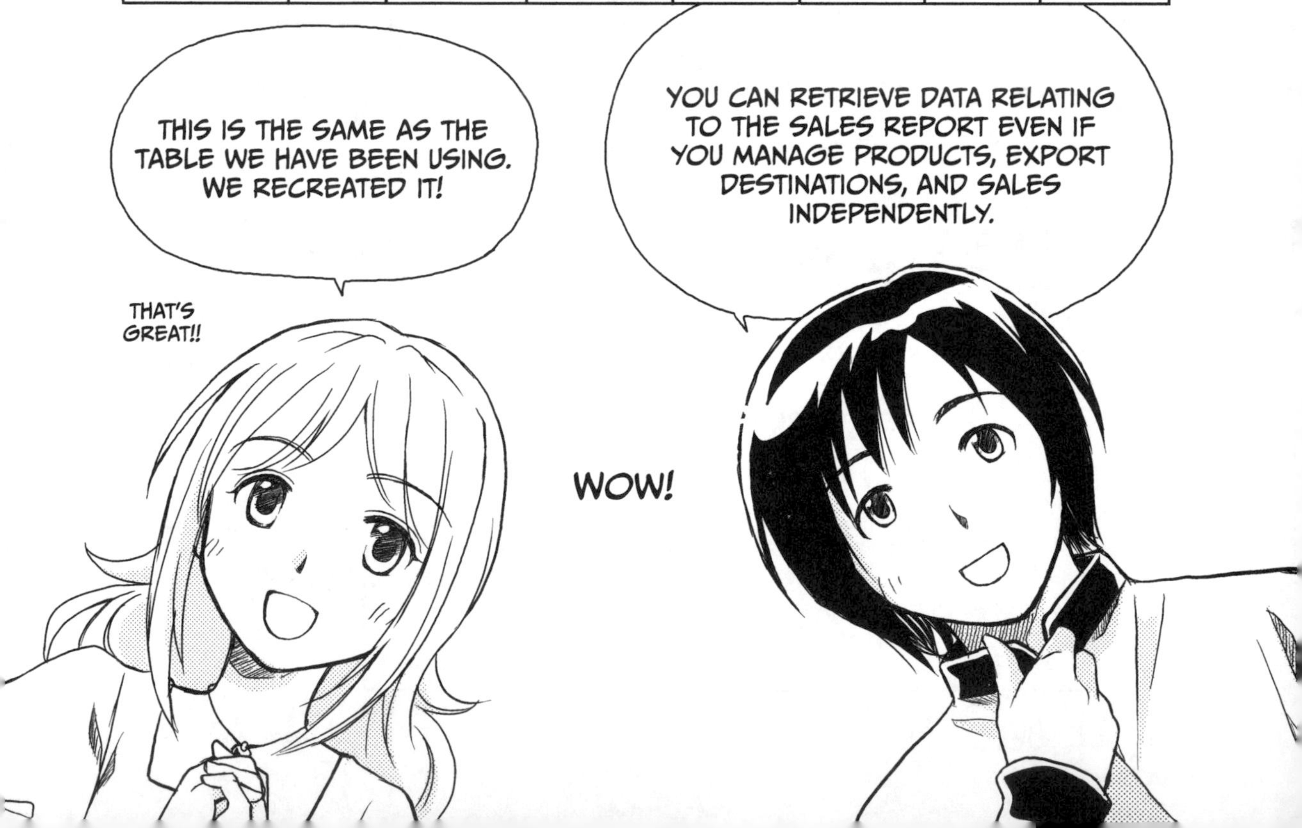
THIS IS THE SAME AS THE TABLE WE HAVE BEEN USING. WE RECREATED IT!
YOU CAN RETRIEVE DATA RELATING TO THE SALES REPORT EVEN IF YOU MANAGE PRODUCTS, EXPORT DESTINATIONS, AND SALES INDEPENDENTLY.
THAT'S GREAT!!
WOW!

CREATING a TABLE

NOW I REMEMBER. YOU MADE THIS TABLE USING SQL, RIGHT TICO?

SO YOU HAVE ALREADY INPUT A TABLE AND DATA, RIGHT?

THAT'S RIGHT.

HOW DID YOU MAKE IT?

CREATE TABLE

YOU USE A *CREATE TABLE* STATEMENT TO MAKE A TABLE.

```
CREATE TABLE product
(
product_code int NOT NULL,
product_name varchar(255),
unit_price int,
PRIMARY KEY(product_code)
);
```

PRODUCT CODE	PRODUCT NAME	UNIT PRICE

YOU MUST SPECIFY THE PRIMARY KEY, AS WELL. I USED THE PRODUCT CODE AS A PRIMARY KEY.*

WE'VE ALSO SET THE DATATYPE OF EACH COLUMN. YOU CAN SEE THAT PRODUCT AND UNIT_PRICE ARE INTEGERS (INT). *VARCHAR* MEANS THAT THE DATABASE EXPECTS TEXT, AND *(255)* LIMITS THE PRODUCT_NAME TO 255 CHARACTERS.

LIKE THIS...

THIS PREVENTS YOU FROM ENTERING INCORRECT VALUES.

* SEE PAGE 115 FOR A COMPLETE EXPLANATION OF CREATE TABLE STATEMENTS.

NOW WE CAN INPUT DATA IN THE TABLE WE CREATED, RIGHT?

PRODUCT CODE	PRODUCT NAME	UNIT PRICE

THAT'S RIGHT.

YOU USE AN *INSERT* STATEMENT TO ADD DATA.

INSERT

```
INSERT INTO product (product_code,product_name,unit_price)

VALUES (101,'melon',800);
```

PRODUCT CODE	PRODUCT NAME	UNIT PRICE
101	MELON	800G

YOU CAN ALSO DELETE (DELETE STATEMENT) AND UPDATE (UPDATE STATEMENT) THE DATA.

AND THE UNIT PRICE OF A PRODUCT CAN BE CORRECTED USING SQL.

MELON WAS INSERTED IN THE PRODUCT TABLE LIKE THIS.

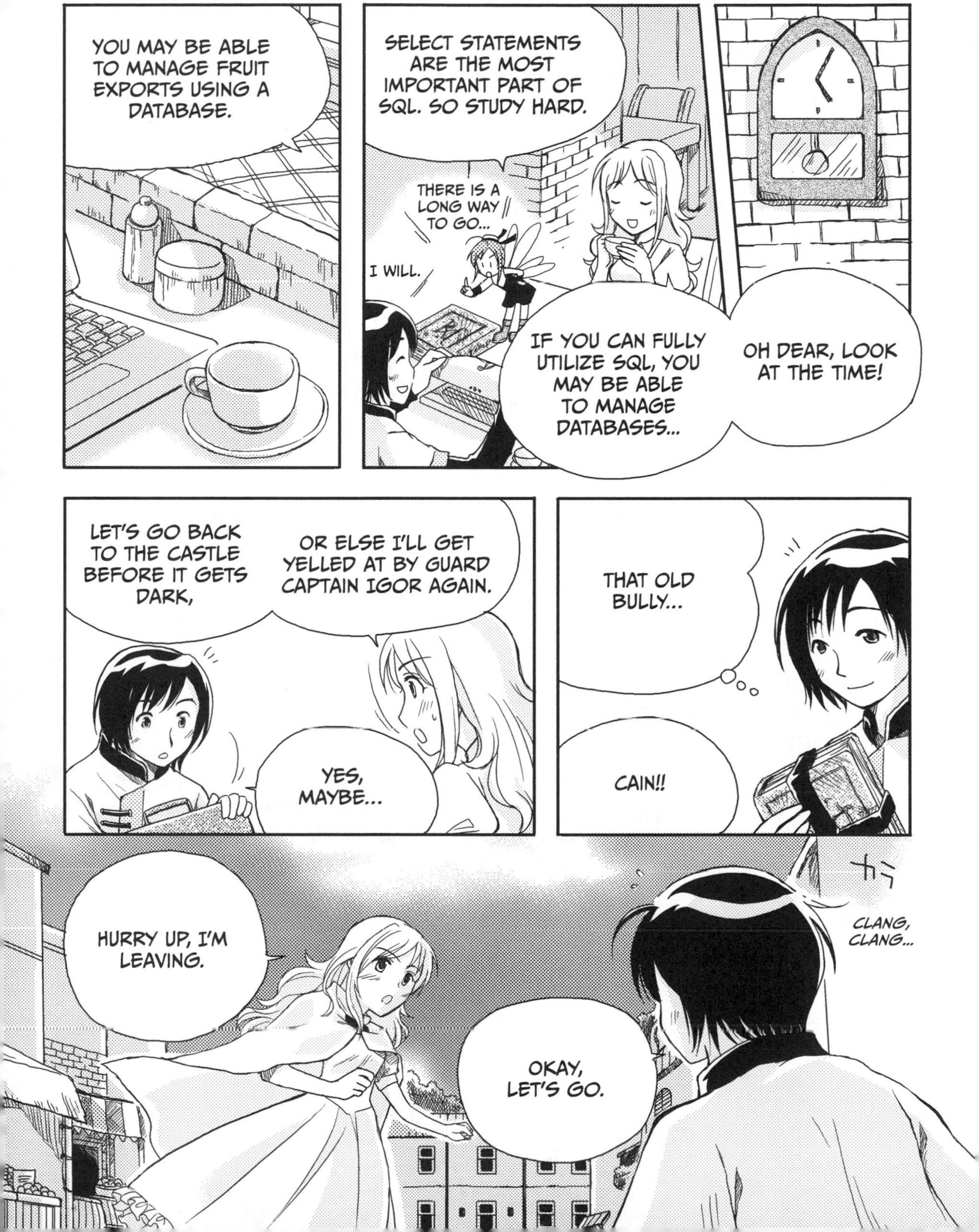
YOU MAY BE ABLE TO MANAGE FRUIT EXPORTS USING A DATABASE.
SELECT STATEMENTS ARE THE MOST IMPORTANT PART OF SQL. SO STUDY HARD.
THERE IS A LONG WAY TO GO...
I WILL.
IF YOU CAN FULLY UTILIZE SQL, YOU MAY BE ABLE TO MANAGE DATABASES...
OH DEAR, LOOK AT THE TIME!
LET'S GO BACK TO THE CASTLE BEFORE IT GETS DARK,
OR ELSE I'LL GET YELLED AT BY GUARD CAPTAIN IGOR AGAIN.
YES, MAYBE...
THAT OLD BULLY...
CAIN!!
HURRY UP, I'M LEAVING.
カラ
CLANG, CLANG...
OKAY, LET'S GO.

SQL OVERVIEW

In this chapter, Princess Ruruna and Cain learned about *SQL*, or *Structured Query Language*, a language used to operate a relational database. SQL's commands can be broken down into three distinct types:

Data Definition Language (DDL)   Creates a table

Data Manipulation Language (DML)   Inputs and retrieves data

Data Control Language (DCL)   Manages user access

SQL has commands that create the framework of a database, and a command that creates a table within a database. You can use this language to change and delete a table as well. The database language that has these functions is called the *Data Definition Language (DDL)*.

SQL also has commands that manipulate data in a database, such as inserting, deleting, and updating data. It also has a command that allows you to search for data. The database language with these functions is called the *Data Manipulation Language (DML)*.

In addition, SQL offers the capability to control a database, so that data conflicts will not occur even if multiple people use the database at the same time. The database language associated with these functions is called the *Data Control Language (DCL)*.

SEARCHING FOR DATA USING A SELECT STATEMENT

Princess Ruruna and Cain started learning SQL by using a basic data search function. SQL searches for data when one *statement* (a combination of phrases) is input. To search for a certain product with a unit price of 200G, for example, you would use the following SQL statement.

```
SELECT *
FROM product
WHERE unit_price=200
```

Create an SQL statement by combining phrases.

A SELECT statement is the most basic SQL statement. It specifies *which column, from which table* (FROM), and *matching which conditions* (WHERE). You can combine these phrases to make intuitive, query-type statements in SQL—even a user unfamiliar with databases can use them to search for data.

CREATING CONDITIONS

Cain said earlier, "Now we need to learn how to make conditions." Let's look at some ways to create conditions using SQL.

COMPARISON OPERATORS

One way to express conditions is by using *comparison operators* like >= and =. For example, the condition "A is greater than or equal to B" is expressed using >=, and the condition "A is equal to B" is expressed using =. More examples of comparison operators are shown in the table below.

COMPARISON OPERATORS

Comparison operator	Description	Example	Description of example
A = B	A is equal to B.	unit_price=200	Unit price is 200G.
A > B	A is greater than B.	unit_price>200	Unit price is greater than 200G.
A >= B	A is greater than or equal to B.	unit_price>=200	Unit price is greater than or equal to 200G.
A < B	A is less than B.	unit_price<200	Unit price is less than 200G.
A <= B	A is less than or equal to B.	unit_price<=200	Unit price is less than or equal to 200G.
A <> B	A is not equal to B.	unit_price<>200	Unit price is not 200G.

LOGICAL OPERATORS

In some cases, you need to express conditions that are more complex than simple comparisons. You can use *logical operators* (*AND*, *OR*, and *NOT*) to combine operator-based conditions and create more complicated conditions, as shown in the table below.

LOGICAL OPERATORS

Logical operator	Description	Example	Description of example
AND	A and B	Product code >= 200 AND unit price = 100	The product code is greater than or equal to 200 and the unit price is 100G.
OR	A or B	Product code >= 200 OR unit price = 100	The product code is greater than or equal to 200 or the unit price is 100G.
NOT	Not A	NOT unit price = 100	The unit price is not 100G.

PATTERNS

When you don't know exactly what to search for, you can also use pattern matching in conditions by using wildcard characters. When using pattern matching, use characters such as % or _ in a LIKE statement; this will search for a character string that matches the pattern you specify. You can search for a value that corresponds to a partially specified character string using %, which indicates a character string of any length, and _, which specifies only one character.

An example of a query using wild cards is shown below. This example statement searches for a character string that has *n* at the end of the product name.

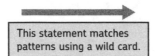

```
SELECT *
FROM product
WHERE product_name LIKE '%n';
```

This statement matches patterns using a wild card.

Product code	Product name	Unit price
101	Melon	800G
104	Lemon	200G

The wild cards you can use in an SQL statement are explained below.

WILD CARDS

Wild card	Description	Example of pattern	Matching character string
%	Matches any number of characters	%n n%	Lemon Melon Nut Navel orange
_	Matches one character	_t t_	it to

SEARCHES

There are also many other search methods. For example, you can specify BETWEEN *X* AND *Y* for a value range. If you specify a range as shown below, you can extract products with unit prices greater than or equal to 150G or less than 200G.

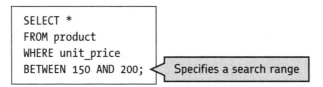

```
SELECT *
FROM product
WHERE unit_price
BETWEEN 150 AND 200;
```

Specifies a search range

In addition, you can specify IS NULL when searching for rows. If you use the search shown below, you can extract products with null unit prices.

```
SELECT *
FROM product
WHERE unit_price is NULL;
```

Searches for a null

QUESTIONS

Now, let's create SQL statements using various kinds of conditions. Let's use the Export Destination Table below (assuming the unit for population is 10,000). Answer the questions below using SQL statements. The answers are on page 119.

EXPORT DESTINATION TABLE

Export destination code	Export destination name	Population
12	The Kingdom of Minanmi	100
23	Alpha Empire	120
25	The Kingdom of Ritol	150
30	The Kingdom of Sazanna	80

Q1

To find countries in which the population is greater than or equal to 1 million, extract the table below.

Export destination code	Export destination name	Population
12	The Kingdom of Minanmi	100
23	Alpha Empire	120
25	The Kingdom of Ritol	150

Q2

To find countries in which the population is less than 1 million, extract the table below.

Export destination code	Export destination name	Population
30	The Kingdom of Sazanna	80

Q3

Find countries in which the export destination code is less than 20 and the population is greater than or equal to 1 million.

Q4

Find countries in which the export destination code is greater than or equal to 30 and the population is greater than 1 million.

Q5

What is the population of the Kingdom of Ritol?

Q6

Find countries whose names contain the letter *n*.

aggregate functions

Princess Ruruna and Cain have learned about various aggregate functions. Aggregate functions are also known as *set functions*. You can use these functions to aggregate information such as maximum and minimum values, number of items, and sum.

If you specify a WHERE phrase along with an aggregate function, you can obtain an aggregated value for just the specified rows. If you specify a phrase like the one shown below, you can figure out the number of products with unit prices greater than or equal to 200G.

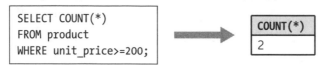

```
SELECT COUNT(*)
FROM product
WHERE unit_price>=200;
```

COUNT(*)
2

AGGREGATING DATA BY GROUPING

If you group data, you can obtain aggregated values easily. For example, if you want to obtain the number of products and average unit price based on district, you can use the grouping function.

To group data, combine the aggregate function and the GROUP BY phrase. Let's use the Product Table shown below.

PRODUCT TABLE

Product code	Product name	Unit price	District
101	Melon	800G	South Sea
102	Strawberry	150G	Middle
103	Apple	120G	North Sea
104	Lemon	200G	South Sea
201	Chestnut	100G	North Sea
202	Persimmon	160G	Middle
301	Peach	130G	South Sea
302	Kiwi	200G	South Sea

To obtain the average unit price for each district in the Product Table, specify the District column and the AVG function for the GROUP BY phrase. This will group data based on district and give you the average unit value of the products in each district.

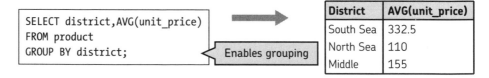

```
SELECT district,AVG(unit_price)
FROM product
GROUP BY district;
```

Enables grouping

District	AVG(unit_price)
South Sea	332.5
North Sea	110
Middle	155

What if you wanted to further restrict your results, based on a particular property of the data? Assume that you want to find products with regional average unit prices greater than or equal to 200G. In this case, do not specify a condition in the WHERE phrase, but use a HAVING phrase instead. This allows you to extract only districts in which the average unit price is greater than or equal to 200G.

```
SELECT district,AVG(unit_price)
FROM product
GROUP BY district;
HAVING AVG(unit_price)>=200;
```

Filters results after being grouped

District	AVG(unit_price)
South Sea	332.5

QUESTIONS

Answer the questions below using this Export Destination Table (assuming the unit for population is 10,000). The answers are on page 120.

EXPORT DESTINATION TABLE

Export destination code	Export destination name	Population	District
12	The Kingdom of Minanmi	100	South Sea
15	The Kingdom of Paronu	200	Middle
22	The Kingdom of Tokanta	160	North Sea
23	Alpha Empire	120	North Sea
25	The Kingdom of Ritol	150	South Sea
30	The Kingdom of Sazanna	80	South Sea
31	The Kingdom of Taharu	240	North Sea
33	The Kingdom of Mariyon	300	Middle

Q7

What is the smallest population?

Q8

What is the largest population?

Q9

What is the total population of all countries included in the Export Destination Table?

Q10

What is the total population of the countries in which the export destination code is greater than 20?

Q11

How many countries are there in which the population is greater than or equal to 1 million?

Q12

How many countries are in the North Sea district?

Q13

Which country in the North Sea district has the largest population?

Q14

What is the total population of every country excluding the Kingdom of Ritol?

Q15

Find the districts in which the average population is greater than or equal to 2 million.

Q16

Find the districts that contain at least three countries.

Searching for Data

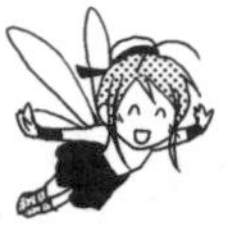

There are more complicated query methods available in SQL, in addition to the ones we've already discussed.

Using a Subquery

For example, you can embed one query in another query. This is called a *subquery*. Let's look at the tables below.

PRODUCT TABLE

Product code	Product name	Unit price
101	Melon	800G
102	Strawberry	150G
103	Apple	120G
104	Lemon	200G

SALES STATEMENT TABLE

Report code	Product code	Quantity
1101	101	1,100
1101	102	300
1102	103	1,700
1103	104	500
1104	101	2,500
1105	103	2,000
1105	104	700

You can use these two tables to search for the names of products for which the sales volume is greater than or equal to 1,000. The following SQL statement will conduct that search.

```
SELECT * FROM product
WHERE product_code IN
(SELECT product_code
FROM sales_statement
WHERE quantity>=1000);
```

This statement contains a subquery.

In this SQL statement, the SELECT statement in parentheses is performed first: The product code in the Sales Statement Table is searched for first, and product codes 101 and 103 are found (as these are the only reports with sales volume greater than 1,000). These product codes are used as a part of the condition for the SELECT statement outside the parentheses. For IN, the condition is satisfied when a row matches any value enclosed within parentheses. Thus, products that correspond to the product codes 101 and 103 will be returned.

In other words, in the case of a subquery, the result of the SELECT statement within parentheses will be sent to the other SELECT statement for searching. The following information will be the result of the whole query.

Product code	Product name	Unit price
101	Melon	800G
103	Apple	120G

USING A CORRELATED SUBQUERY

Let's consider a subquery as being *contained inside* another query. Such a subquery may refer to data from the outer query. This is called a *correlated subquery*. In the query below, the `sales_statement` table in the outer query is temporarily given the new name U so the subquery can refer to it unambiguously. The syntax `U.product_code` indicates which `product_code` column is intended, since there are two sources for that column inside the subquery.

Because the subquery refers to data from the outer query, the subquery is not independent of the outer query as in previous examples. This dependency is called a *correlation*.

❶
```
SELECT *
FROM sales_statement U
```

❷
```
WHERE quantity>
```

❸
```
(SELECT AVG(quantity)
FROM sales_statement
WHERE product_code=U.product_code);
```

Report code	Product code	Quantity
1104	101	2,500
1105	103	2,000
1105	104	700

This query extracts statements with sales volume greater than the product's average.

Let's look at how this correlated subquery is processed. In the correlated subquery, the query outside is implemented first.

❶
```
SELECT *
FROM sales_statement U
```

This result is sent to the query inside to be evaluated row by row. Let's explore the evaluation of the first row, product code 101.

❸
```
(SELECT AVG(quantity)
FROM sales_statement
WHERE product_code=101)
```

The product code for the first row is 101, or melons—the average sales quantity of melons is 1,800. This result is then sent as a condition for the query outside.

❷
```
WHERE quantity>(1,800)
```

This process continues for all rows in the sales statement—steps ❷ and ❸ are performed for all possible product codes. In other words, this query extracts reports in which the sales volume of a fruit is greater than that particular fruit's average sales quantity. Consequently, only the fifth, sixth, and seventh rows of ❶ are extracted.

QUESTIONS

Now, answer the following questions based on the Product Table and the Sales Statement Table. The answers are on page 122.

Q17

Find the sales statement for fruit with unit prices greater than or equal to 300G, and extract the table below.

Report code	Product code	Quantity
1101	101	1,100
1104	101	2,500

Q18

Obtain the average sales volume by product, and find items that have sales volumes that are less than the average.

JOINING TABLES

After conducting an SQL-based search, Princess Ruruna and Cain created a sales report by combining tables. Joining tables by combining columns with the same names is called an *equi join*. For an equi join, rows with the same value are designated as join conditions for joining tables. Joining columns with the same name into one is called a *natural join*.

The join method in which only rows having a common value like equi join are selected is called *inner join*.

In contrast, the join method that keeps all rows of one table and specifies a null for rows not included in another table is called an *outer join*. If you place a table created from an outer join on the right or left of an SQL statement, it is called a *left outer join* or a *right outer join*, depending on which rows are kept.

Left table
Right table
Left outer join
Right outer join

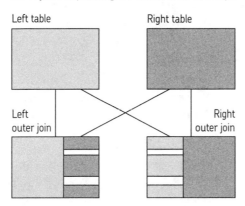

Creating a Table

Finally, Princess Ruruna and Cain learned about the statement syntax that creates a table, CREATE TABLE. The statement syntax inside a CREATE TABLE statement often depends on the particular kind of database you use. An example is shown below.

```
CREATE TABLE product
(
product_code int NOT NULL,
product_name varchar(255),
unit_price int,
PRIMARY KEY(product_code)
);
```

This statement creates a table.

When you create a table, you must specify its column names. Additionally, you can specify a primary key and a foreign key for each column. In this example, the product code is specified as a PRIMARY KEY and product code is not allowed to be null. When creating a table, you may need to include the following specifications.

Constraint	Description
PRIMARY KEY	Sets a primary key
UNIQUE	Should be unique
NOT NULL	Does not accept a NULL value
CHECK	Checks a range
DEFAULT	Sets a default value
FOREIGN KEY REFERENCES	Sets a foreign key

These specifications are called *constraints*. Giving constraints when creating a table helps to prevent data conflicts later on and allows you to correctly manage the database.

INSERTING, UPDATING, OR DELETING ROWS

You can use the INSERT, UPDATE, and DELETE statements to insert, update, or delete data from a table created by the CREATE TABLE statement. Let's insert, update, and delete some data using SQL.

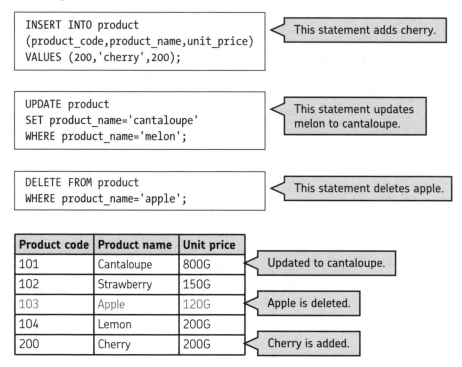

```
INSERT INTO product
(product_code,product_name,unit_price)
VALUES (200,'cherry',200);
```

This statement adds cherry.

```
UPDATE product
SET product_name='cantaloupe'
WHERE product_name='melon';
```

This statement updates melon to cantaloupe.

```
DELETE FROM product
WHERE product_name='apple';
```

This statement deletes apple.

Product code	Product name	Unit price	
101	Cantaloupe	800G	Updated to cantaloupe.
102	Strawberry	150G	
103	Apple	120G	Apple is deleted.
104	Lemon	200G	
200	Cherry	200G	Cherry is added.

When inserting, updating, or deleting a row, you cannot violate the constraints set by the CREATE TABLE statement. If a product with product code 200 already exists, you cannot add cherry, since you cannot add duplicated data as a primary key. When you insert, update, or delete data in a database, you must consider the database's constraints.

CREATING A VIEW

Based on the table you created with the CREATE TABLE statement, you can also create a virtual table that exists only when it is viewed by a user. This is called a *view*. The table from which a view is derived is called a *base table*.

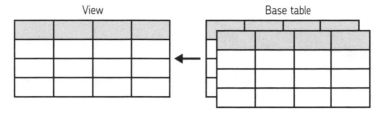

Use the SQL statement shown below to create a view.

```
CREATE VIEW expensive_product
(product_code,product_name,unit_price)
AS SELECT *
FROM product
WHERE unit_price>=200;
```

> This statement creates a view.

The Expensive Product Table is a view based on the Product Table, which is a base table. It was created by extracting data with unit prices greater than or equal to 200G from the Product Table.

EXPENSIVE PRODUCT TABLE

Product code	Product name	Unit price
101	Melon	800G
104	Lemon	200G
202	Persimmon	200G

Once you create the Expensive Product view, you can search for data in it the same way you would search for data in a base table.

```
SELECT *
FROM expensive_product
WHERE unit_price>=500;
```

> Allows the view to be used in the same manner as a base table

It is convenient to create a view when you want to make part of the data in a base table public.

There are also SQL statements for deleting a base table or view. The statement used to delete a base table or view is shown below.

```
DROP VIEW expensive_product;
```

```
DROP TABLE product;
```

QUESTIONS

Create SQL statements for the following questions (assuming the unit for population is 10,000). The answers are on page 123.

Q19

The following Export Destination Table was created using a CREATE TABLE statement. Add the data below.

EXPORT DESTINATION TABLE

Export destination code	Export destination name	Population	District
12	The Kingdom of Minanmi	100	South Sea
15	The Kingdom of Paronu	200	Middle
22	The Kingdom of Tokanta	160	North Sea
23	Alpha Empire	120	North Sea

Q20

From the Export Destination Table in Q19, create a view titled *North Sea Country* that shows countries belonging to the North Sea district.

EXPORT DESTINATION TABLE

Export destination code	Export destination name	Population
22	The Kingdom of Tokanta	160
23	Alpha Empire	120

Q21

Change the population of the Kingdom of Tokanta in the Export Destination Table to 1.5 million.

Q22

In the Export Destination Table, delete all data for the Kingdom of Paronu.

Summary

- You can use SQL functions to define, operate, and control data.
- To search for data, use a SELECT statement.
- To specify a condition, use a WHERE phrase.
- To insert, update, and delete data, use INSERT, UPDATE, and DELETE statements.
- To create a table, use a CREATE TABLE statement.

Answers

Q1

```
SELECT *
FROM export_destination
WHERE population>=100;
```

Q2

```
SELECT *
FROM export_destination
WHERE population<100;
```

Q3

```
SELECT *
FROM export_destination
WHERE export_destination_code<20
AND population>=100;
```

Export destination code	Export destination name	Population
12	The Kingdom of Minanmi	100

Q4

```
SELECT *
FROM export_destination
WHERE export_destination_code>=30
AND population>100;
```

Export destination code	Export destination name	Population
23	Alpha Empire	120
25	The Kingdom of Ritol	150
30	The Kingdom of Sazanna	80

Q5

```
SELECT population
FROM export_destination
WHERE export_destination_name='the Kingdom of Ritol';
```

Population
150

Q6

```
SELECT *
FROM export_destination
WHERE export_destination_name LIKE '%n%';
```

Export destination code	Export destination name	Population
12	The Kingdom of Minanmi	100
30	The Kingdom of Sazanna	80

Q7

```
SELECT MIN(population)
FROM export_destination;
```

MIN(population)
80

Q8

```
SELECT MAX(population)
FROM export_destination;
```

MAX(population)
300

Q9

```
SELECT SUM(population)
FROM export_destination;
```

SUM(population)
1,350

Q10

```
SELECT SUM(population)
FROM export_destination
WHERE export_destination_code>20;
```

SUM(population)
1,050

Q11

```
SELECT COUNT(*)
FROM export_destination
WHERE population>=100;
```

COUNT(*)
7

Q12

```
SELECT COUNT(*)
FROM export_destination
WHERE district='north sea';
```

COUNT(*)
3

Q13

```
SELECT MAX(population)
FROM export_destination
WHERE district='north sea';
```

MAX(population)
240

Q14

```
SELECT SUM(population)
FROM export_destination
WHERE NOT(export_destination_name='the Kingdom of Ritol');
```

SUM(population)
1,200

Q15

```
SELECT district, AVG(population)
FROM export_destination
GROUP BY district
HAVING AVG(population)>=200;
```

District	AVG(population)
Middle	250

Q16

```
SELECT district, COUNT(*)
FROM export_destination
GROUP BY district
HAVING COUNT(*)>=3;
```

District	COUNT(*)
North Sea	3
South Sea	3

Q17

```
SELECT *
FROM sales_statement
WHERE product_code IN
(SELECT product_code
FROM product
WHERE unit_price>=300);
```

Q18

```
SELECT *
FROM sales_statement U
WHERE quantity<
(SELECT AVG(quantity)
FROM sales_statement
WHERE product_code=U.product_code);
```

Report code	Product code	Quantity
1101	101	1,100
1102	103	1,700
1103	104	500

Q19

```
INSERT INTO export_destination(export_destination_
code,export_destination_name,population,district)
VALUES(12,'the Kingdom of Minanmi',100,'south sea');
INSERT INTO export_destination(export_destination_
code,export_destination_name,population,district)
VALUES(15,'the Kingdom of Paronu',200,'middle');
INSERT INTO export_destination(export_destination_
code,export_destination_name,population,district)
VALUES(22,'the Kingdom of Tokanta',160,'north sea');
INSERT INTO export_destination(export_destination_
code,export_destination_name,population,district)
VALUES(23,'Alpha Empire',120,'north sea');
```

Q20

```
CREATE VIEW north_sea_country(export_destination_
code,export_destination_name,population)
AS SELECT export_destination_code,export_destination_name,population
FROM export_destination_name
WHERE district='north sea';
```

Q21

```
UPDATE export_destination
SET population=150
WHERE export_destination_name='the Kingdom of Tokanta';
```

Q22

```
DELETE FROM export_destination
WHERE export_destination_name='the Kingdom of Paronu';
```

STANDARDIZATION OF SQL

SQL is standardized by the International Organization for Standardization (ISO). In Japan, it is standardized by JIS (Japanese Industrial Standards).

Other SQL standards include SQL92, established in 1992, and SQL99, established in 1999. Relational database products are designed so that queries can be made in accordance with these standards.

Some relational database products have their own specifications. Refer to the operation manual for your database product for further information.

5

LET'S OPERATE A DATABASE!

What is a Transaction?

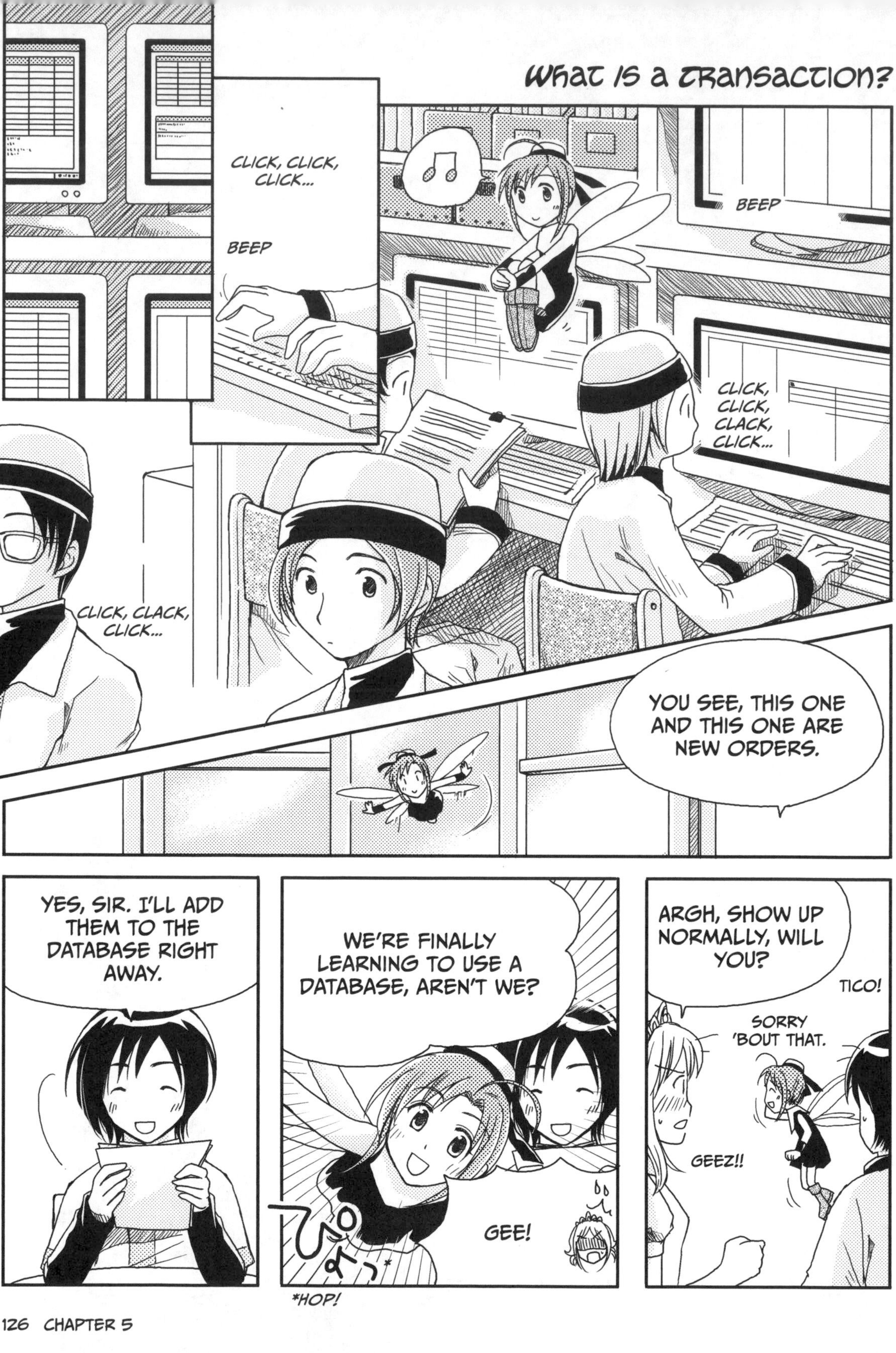

CLICK, CLICK, CLICK...
BEEP
BEEP
CLICK, CLICK, CLACK, CLICK...
CLICK, CLACK, CLICK...
YOU SEE, THIS ONE AND THIS ONE ARE NEW ORDERS.
YES, SIR. I'LL ADD THEM TO THE DATABASE RIGHT AWAY.
WE'RE FINALLY LEARNING TO USE A DATABASE, AREN'T WE?
GEE!
*HOP!
ARGH, SHOW UP NORMALLY, WILL YOU?
TICO!
SORRY 'BOUT THAT.
GEEZ!!

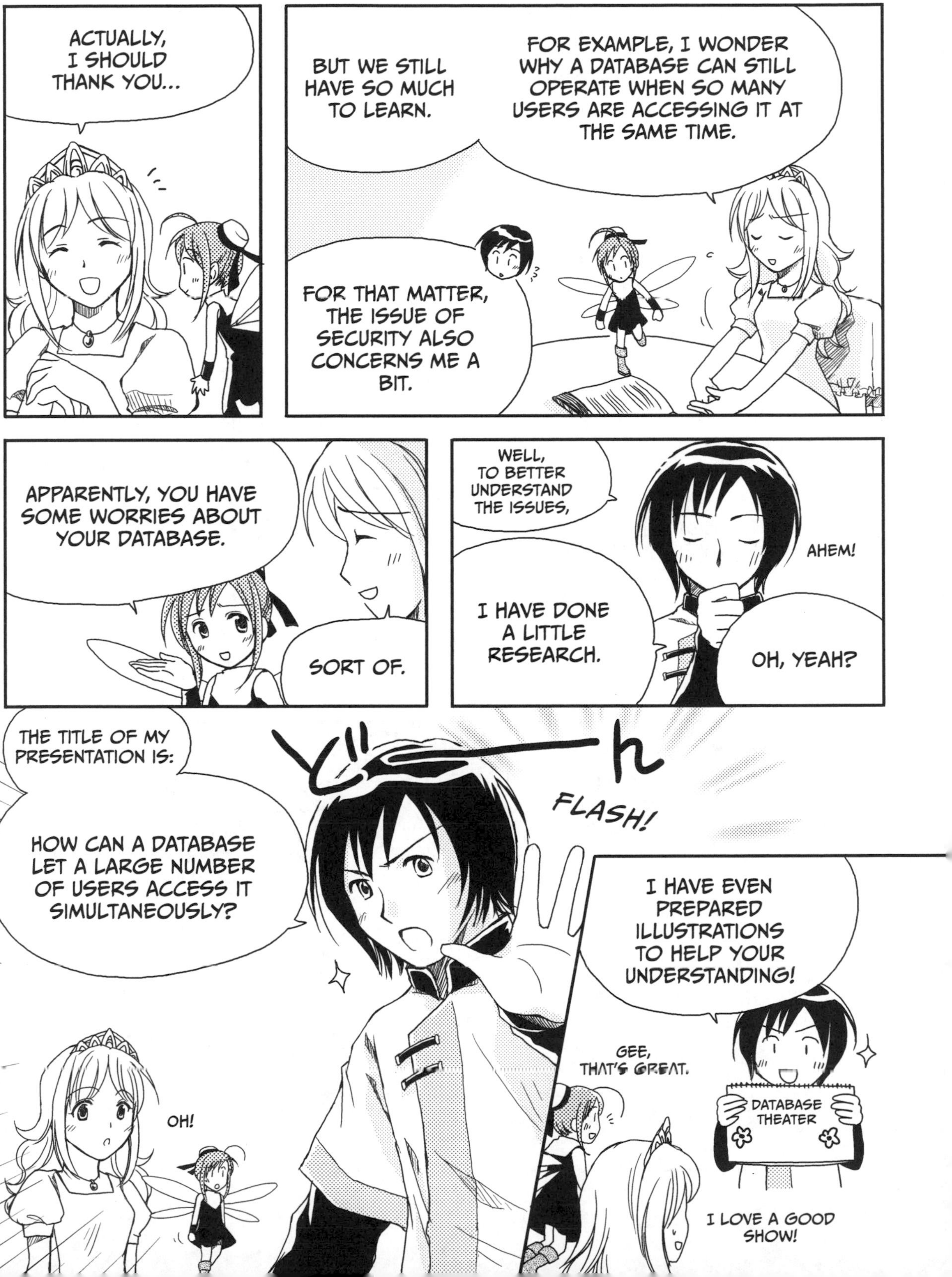
ACTUALLY, I SHOULD THANK YOU...
BUT WE STILL HAVE SO MUCH TO LEARN.
FOR EXAMPLE, I WONDER WHY A DATABASE CAN STILL OPERATE WHEN SO MANY USERS ARE ACCESSING IT AT THE SAME TIME.
FOR THAT MATTER, THE ISSUE OF SECURITY ALSO CONCERNS ME A BIT.
APPARENTLY, YOU HAVE SOME WORRIES ABOUT YOUR DATABASE.
SORT OF.
WELL, TO BETTER UNDERSTAND THE ISSUES,
AHEM!
I HAVE DONE A LITTLE RESEARCH.
OH, YEAH?
THE TITLE OF MY PRESENTATION IS:
HOW CAN A DATABASE LET A LARGE NUMBER OF USERS ACCESS IT SIMULTANEOUSLY?
FLASH!
OH!
I HAVE EVEN PREPARED ILLUSTRATIONS TO HELP YOUR UNDERSTANDING!
GEE, THAT'S GREAT.
DATABASE THEATER
I LOVE A GOOD SHOW!

NOW LET ME BEGIN.

CLAP, CLAP, CLAP

WHOOPEE!

ONE DAY, ANDY AND BECKY ACCESSED THE DATABASE AT THE SAME TIME.

DATABASE

ACCESS

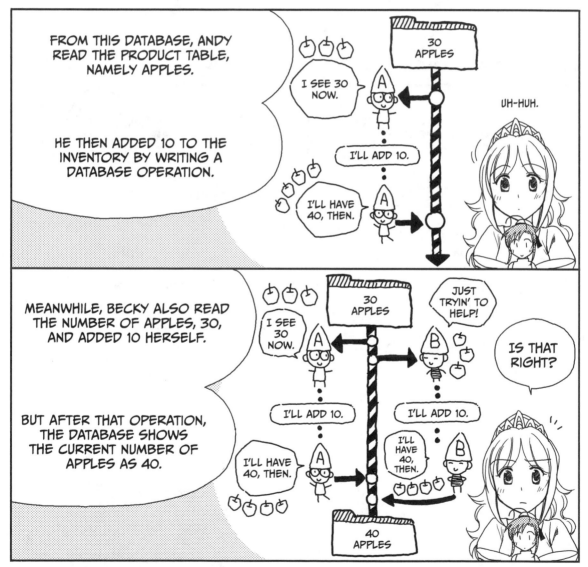

FROM THIS DATABASE, ANDY READ THE PRODUCT TABLE, NAMELY APPLES.

HE THEN ADDED 10 TO THE INVENTORY BY WRITING A DATABASE OPERATION.

30 APPLES

I SEE 30 NOW.

I'LL ADD 10.

I'LL HAVE 40, THEN.

UH-HUH.

MEANWHILE, BECKY ALSO READ THE NUMBER OF APPLES, 30, AND ADDED 10 HERSELF.

BUT AFTER THAT OPERATION, THE DATABASE SHOWS THE CURRENT NUMBER OF APPLES AS 40.

30 APPLES

JUST TRYIN' TO HELP!

IS THAT RIGHT?

I SEE 30 NOW.

I'LL ADD 10.

I'LL ADD 10.

I'LL HAVE 40, THEN.

I'LL HAVE 40, THEN.

40 APPLES

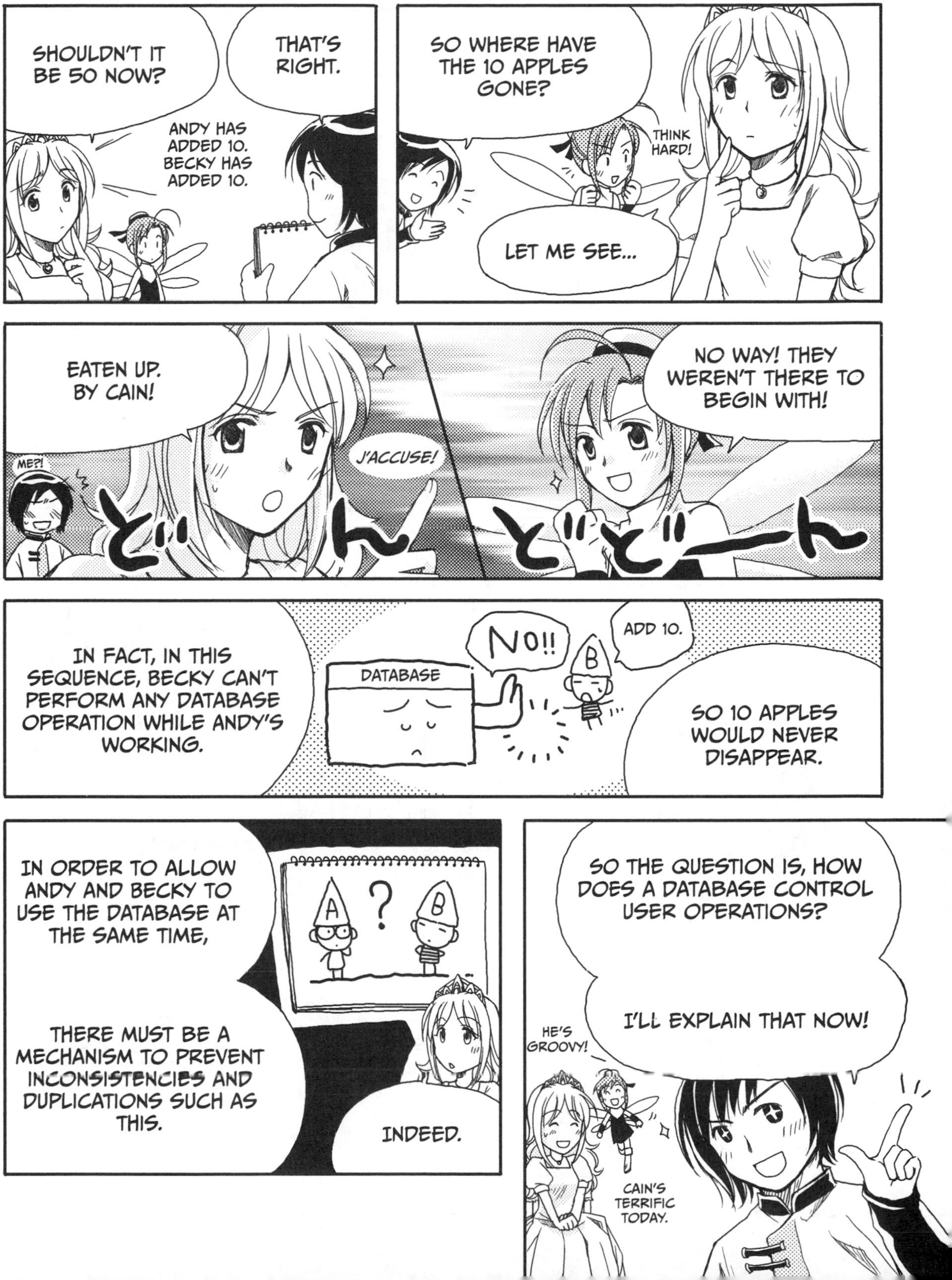
SHOULDN'T IT BE 50 NOW?
THAT'S RIGHT.
ANDY HAS ADDED 10. BECKY HAS ADDED 10.
SO WHERE HAVE THE 10 APPLES GONE?
THINK HARD!
LET ME SEE...
EATEN UP. BY CAIN!
ME?!
J'ACCUSE!
どん
NO WAY! THEY WEREN'T THERE TO BEGIN WITH!
どどーん
IN FACT, IN THIS SEQUENCE, BECKY CAN'T PERFORM ANY DATABASE OPERATION WHILE ANDY'S WORKING.
DATABASE
NO!!
B
ADD 10.
SO 10 APPLES WOULD NEVER DISAPPEAR.
IN ORDER TO ALLOW ANDY AND BECKY TO USE THE DATABASE AT THE SAME TIME,
A
?
B
THERE MUST BE A MECHANISM TO PREVENT INCONSISTENCIES AND DUPLICATIONS SUCH AS THIS.
INDEED.
SO THE QUESTION IS, HOW DOES A DATABASE CONTROL USER OPERATIONS?
I'LL EXPLAIN THAT NOW!
HE'S GROOVY!
CAIN'S TERRIFIC TODAY.

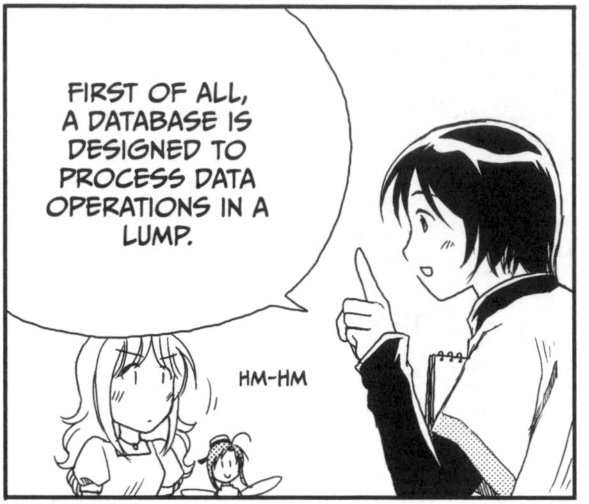
FIRST OF ALL, A DATABASE IS DESIGNED TO PROCESS DATA OPERATIONS IN A LUMP.
HM-HM

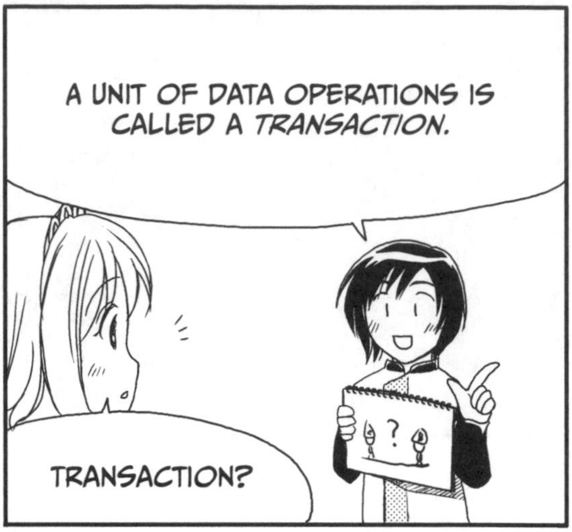
A UNIT OF DATA OPERATIONS IS CALLED A *TRANSACTION*.
TRANSACTION?

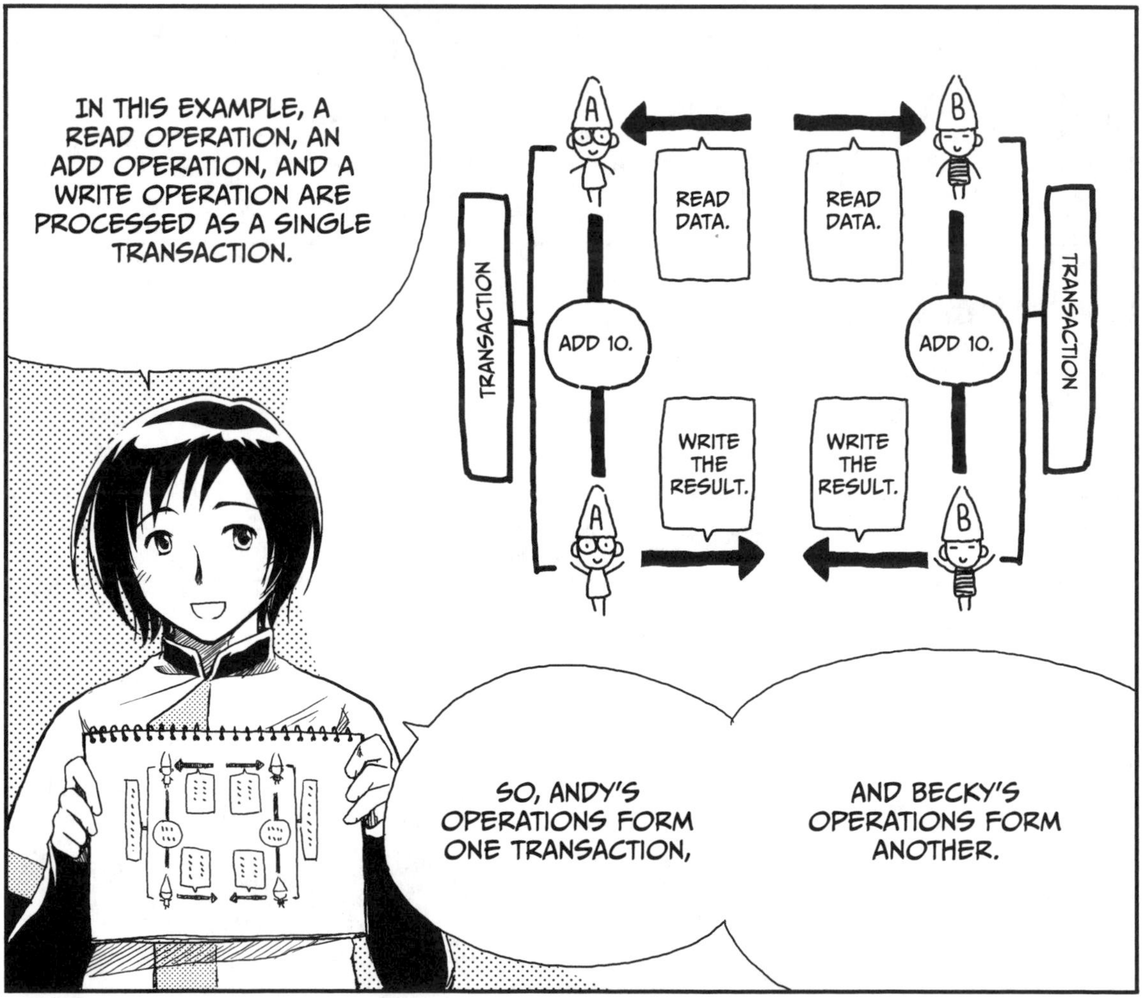
IN THIS EXAMPLE, A READ OPERATION, AN ADD OPERATION, AND A WRITE OPERATION ARE PROCESSED AS A SINGLE TRANSACTION.
A
B
READ DATA.
READ DATA.
TRANSACTION
ADD 10.
ADD 10.
TRANSACTION
WRITE THE RESULT.
WRITE THE RESULT.
A
B
SO, ANDY'S OPERATIONS FORM ONE TRANSACTION,
AND BECKY'S OPERATIONS FORM ANOTHER.

What is a Lock?

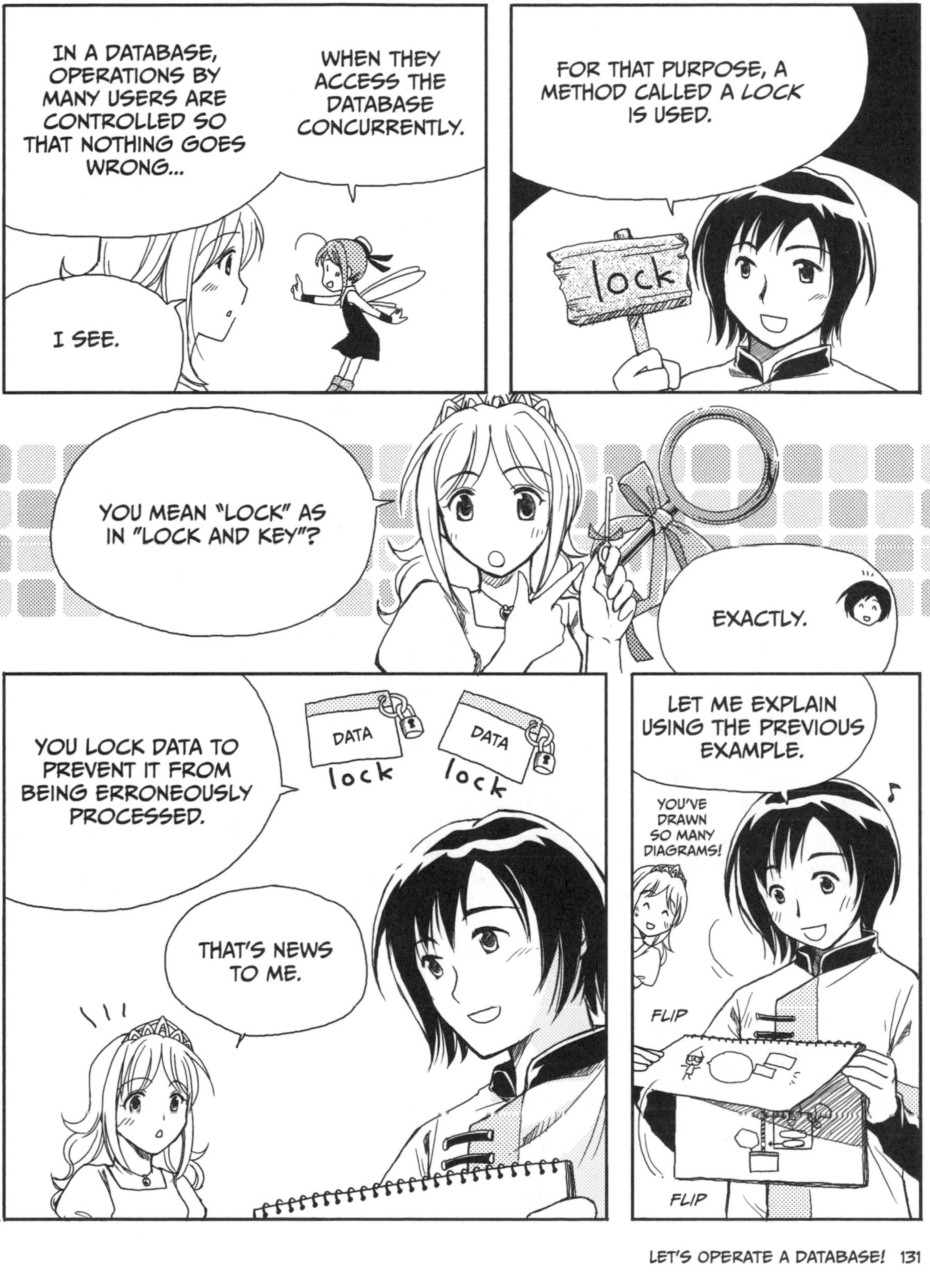

IN A DATABASE, OPERATIONS BY MANY USERS ARE CONTROLLED SO THAT NOTHING GOES WRONG...
WHEN THEY ACCESS THE DATABASE CONCURRENTLY.
I SEE.
FOR THAT PURPOSE, A METHOD CALLED A *LOCK* IS USED.
lock
YOU MEAN "LOCK" AS IN "LOCK AND KEY"?
EXACTLY.
YOU LOCK DATA TO PREVENT IT FROM BEING ERRONEOUSLY PROCESSED.
DATA
lock
DATA
lock
THAT'S NEWS TO ME.
LET ME EXPLAIN USING THE PREVIOUS EXAMPLE.
YOU'VE DRAWN SO MANY DIAGRAMS!
FLIP
FLIP

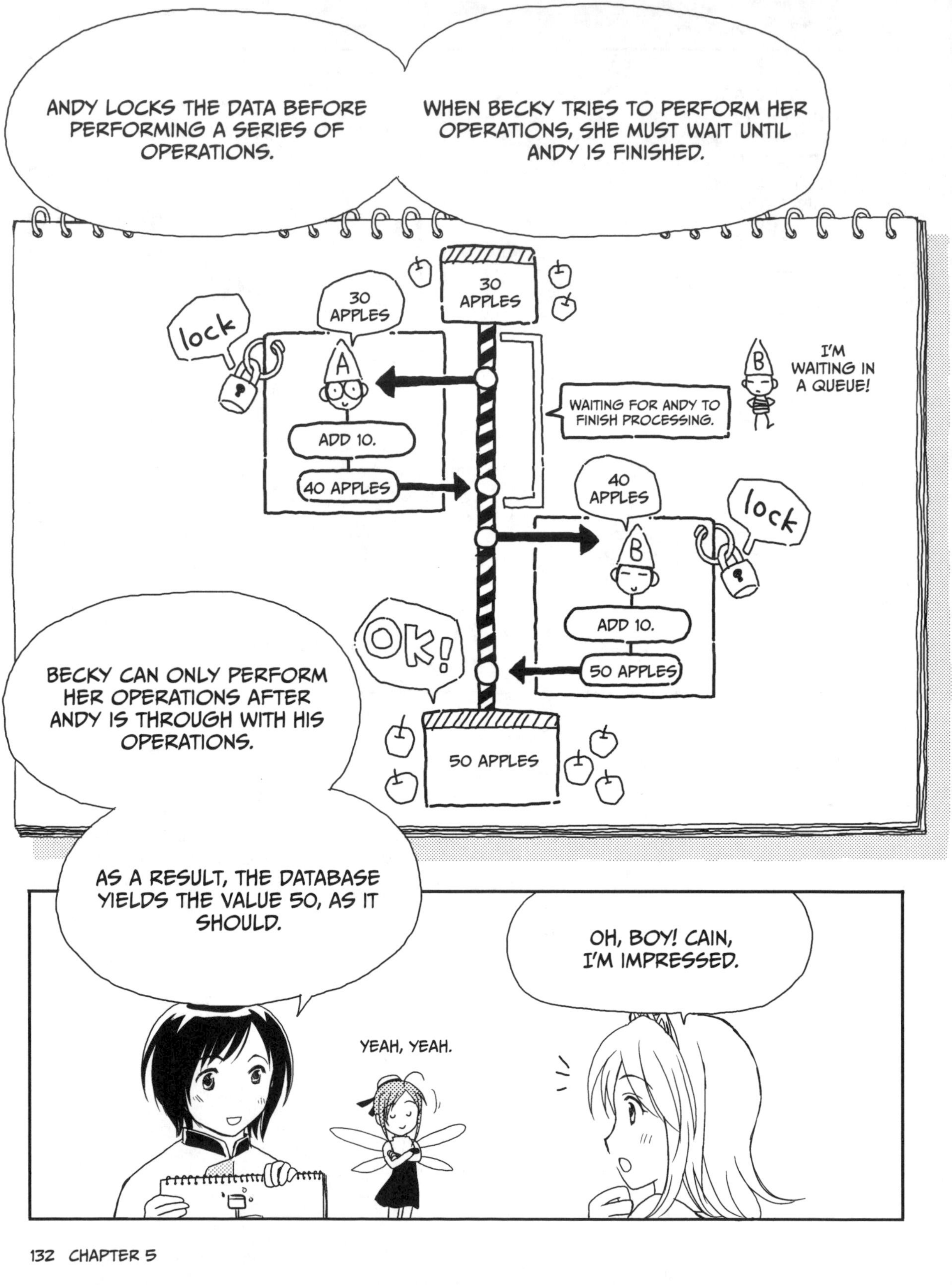
ANDY LOCKS THE DATA BEFORE PERFORMING A SERIES OF OPERATIONS.
WHEN BECKY TRIES TO PERFORM HER OPERATIONS, SHE MUST WAIT UNTIL ANDY IS FINISHED.
30 APPLES
lock
30 APPLES
A
ADD 10.
40 APPLES
B
I'M WAITING IN A QUEUE!
WAITING FOR ANDY TO FINISH PROCESSING.
40 APPLES
lock
B
ADD 10.
50 APPLES
OK!
BECKY CAN ONLY PERFORM HER OPERATIONS AFTER ANDY IS THROUGH WITH HIS OPERATIONS.
50 APPLES
AS A RESULT, THE DATABASE YIELDS THE VALUE 50, AS IT SHOULD.
OH, BOY! CAIN, I'M IMPRESSED.
YEAH, YEAH.

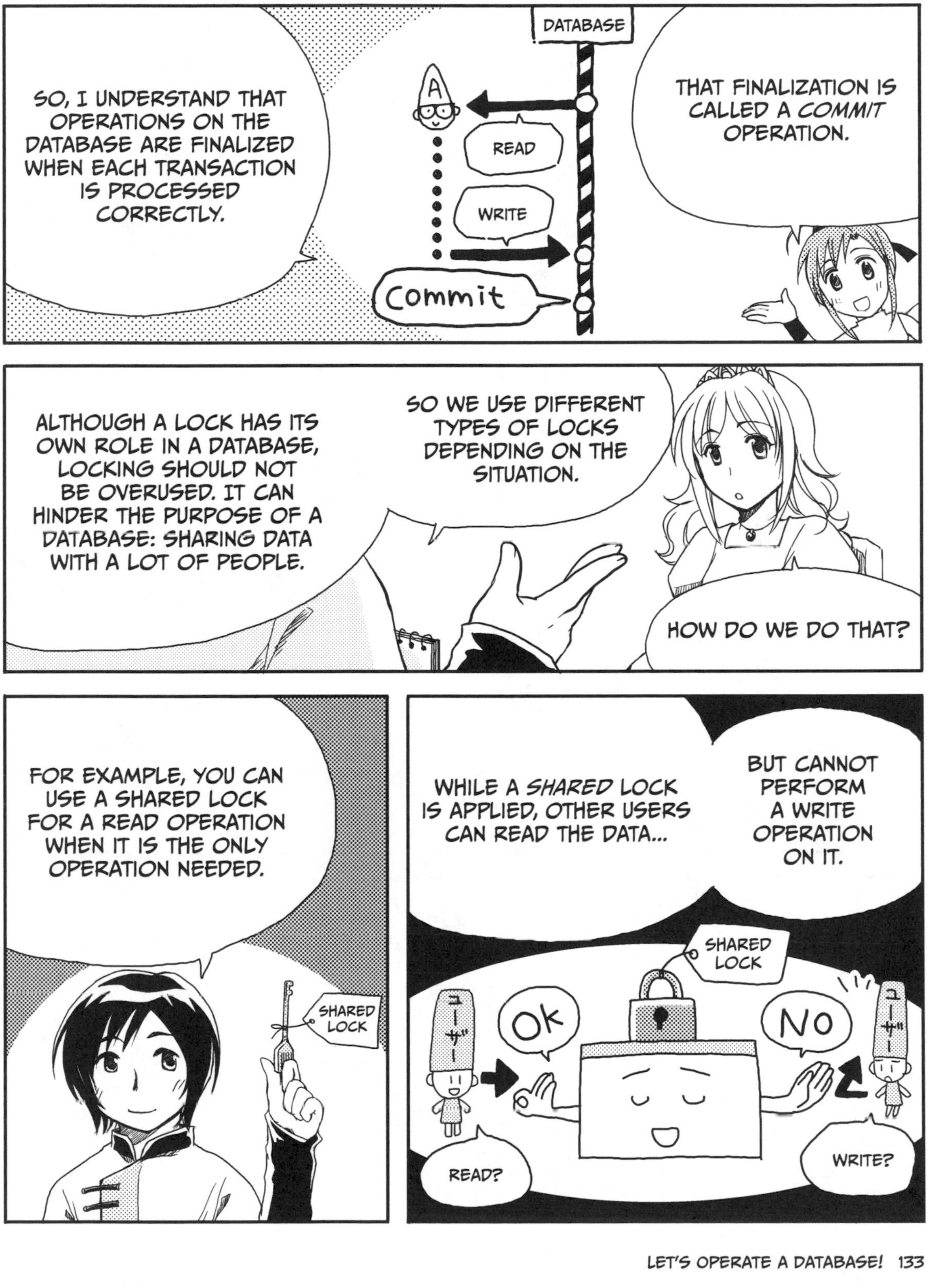
SO, I UNDERSTAND THAT OPERATIONS ON THE DATABASE ARE FINALIZED WHEN EACH TRANSACTION IS PROCESSED CORRECTLY.
DATABASE
A
READ
WRITE
Commit
THAT FINALIZATION IS CALLED A *COMMIT* OPERATION.
ALTHOUGH A LOCK HAS ITS OWN ROLE IN A DATABASE, LOCKING SHOULD NOT BE OVERUSED. IT CAN HINDER THE PURPOSE OF A DATABASE: SHARING DATA WITH A LOT OF PEOPLE.
SO WE USE DIFFERENT TYPES OF LOCKS DEPENDING ON THE SITUATION.
HOW DO WE DO THAT?
FOR EXAMPLE, YOU CAN USE A SHARED LOCK FOR A READ OPERATION WHEN IT IS THE ONLY OPERATION NEEDED.
SHARED LOCK
WHILE A *SHARED* LOCK IS APPLIED, OTHER USERS CAN READ THE DATA...
BUT CANNOT PERFORM A WRITE OPERATION ON IT.
SHARED LOCK
ユーザー
Ok
No
ユーザー
READ?
WRITE?

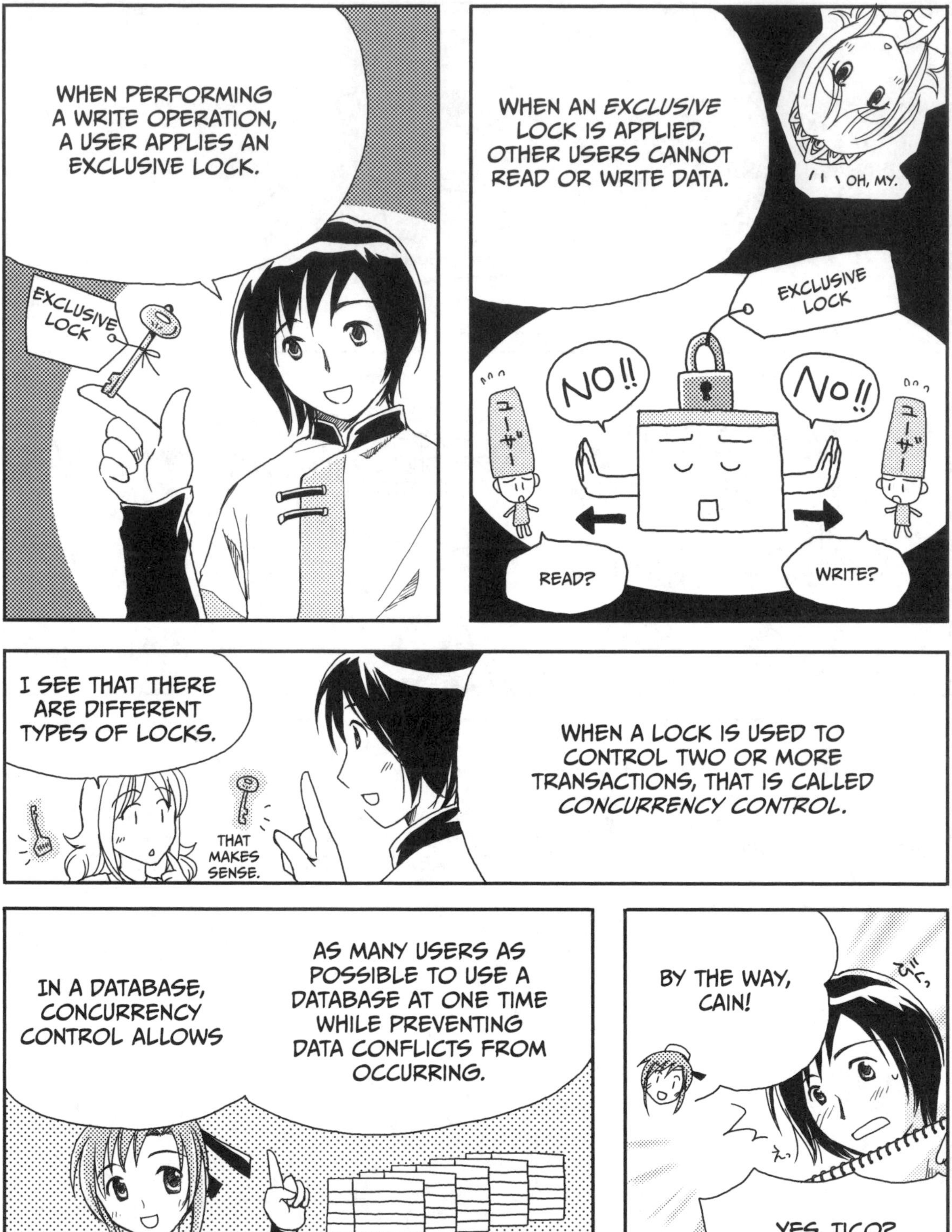
WHEN PERFORMING A WRITE OPERATION, A USER APPLIES AN EXCLUSIVE LOCK.
EXCLUSIVE LOCK
WHEN AN *EXCLUSIVE* LOCK IS APPLIED, OTHER USERS CANNOT READ OR WRITE DATA.
OH, MY.
EXCLUSIVE LOCK
NO!!
ユーザー
No!!
ユーザー
READ?
WRITE?
I SEE THAT THERE ARE DIFFERENT TYPES OF LOCKS.
THAT MAKES SENSE.
WHEN A LOCK IS USED TO CONTROL TWO OR MORE TRANSACTIONS, THAT IS CALLED *CONCURRENCY CONTROL*.
IN A DATABASE, CONCURRENCY CONTROL ALLOWS
AS MANY USERS AS POSSIBLE TO USE A DATABASE AT ONE TIME WHILE PREVENTING DATA CONFLICTS FROM OCCURRING.
BY THE WAY, CAIN!
えっ
YES, TICO?

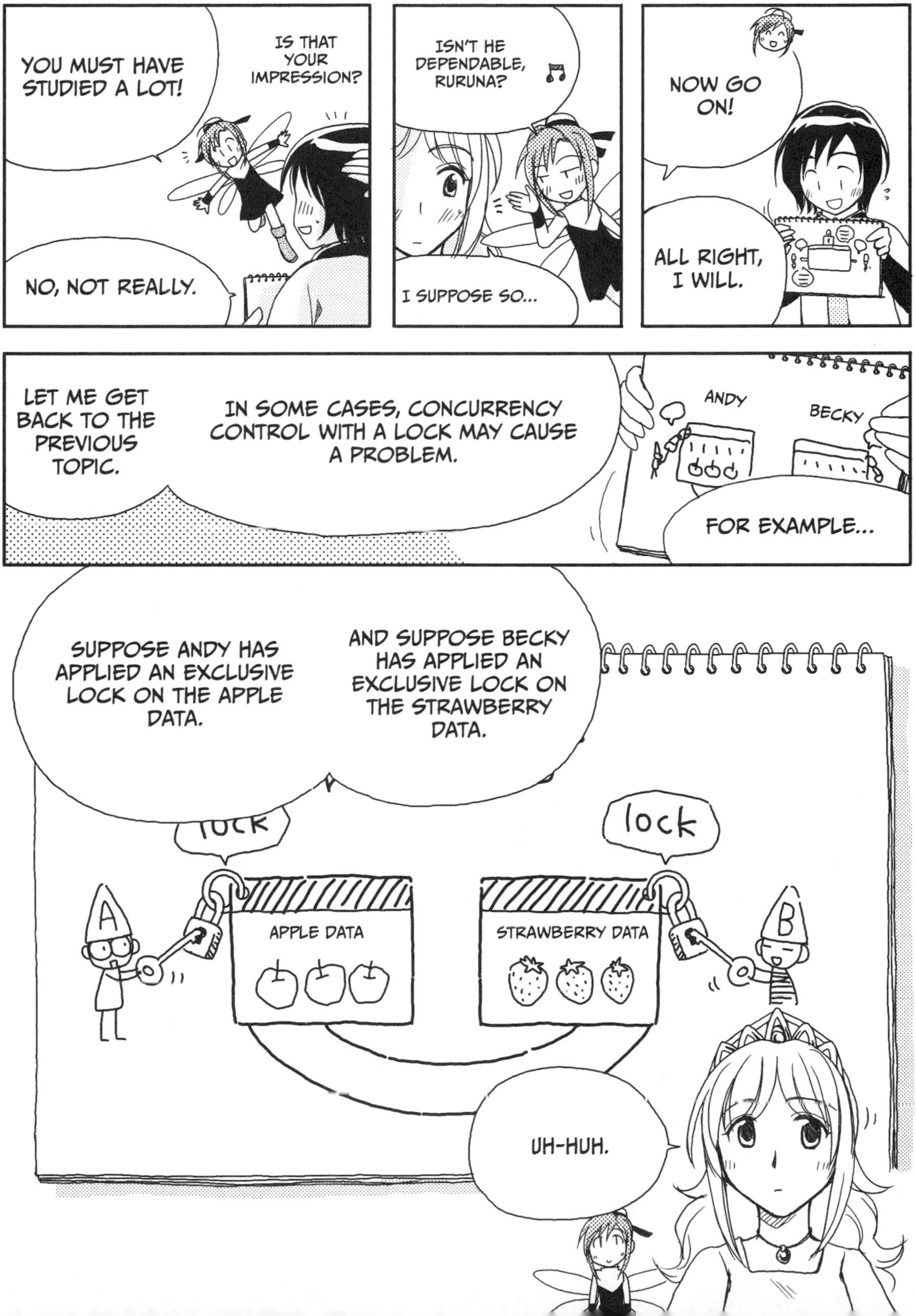
YOU MUST HAVE STUDIED A LOT!
IS THAT YOUR IMPRESSION?
NO, NOT REALLY.
ISN'T HE DEPENDABLE, RURUNA?
I SUPPOSE SO...
NOW GO ON!
ALL RIGHT, I WILL.
LET ME GET BACK TO THE PREVIOUS TOPIC.
IN SOME CASES, CONCURRENCY CONTROL WITH A LOCK MAY CAUSE A PROBLEM.
ANDY
BECKY
FOR EXAMPLE...
SUPPOSE ANDY HAS APPLIED AN EXCLUSIVE LOCK ON THE APPLE DATA.
AND SUPPOSE BECKY HAS APPLIED AN EXCLUSIVE LOCK ON THE STRAWBERRY DATA.
lock
APPLE DATA
STRAWBERRY DATA
A
B
UH-HUH.

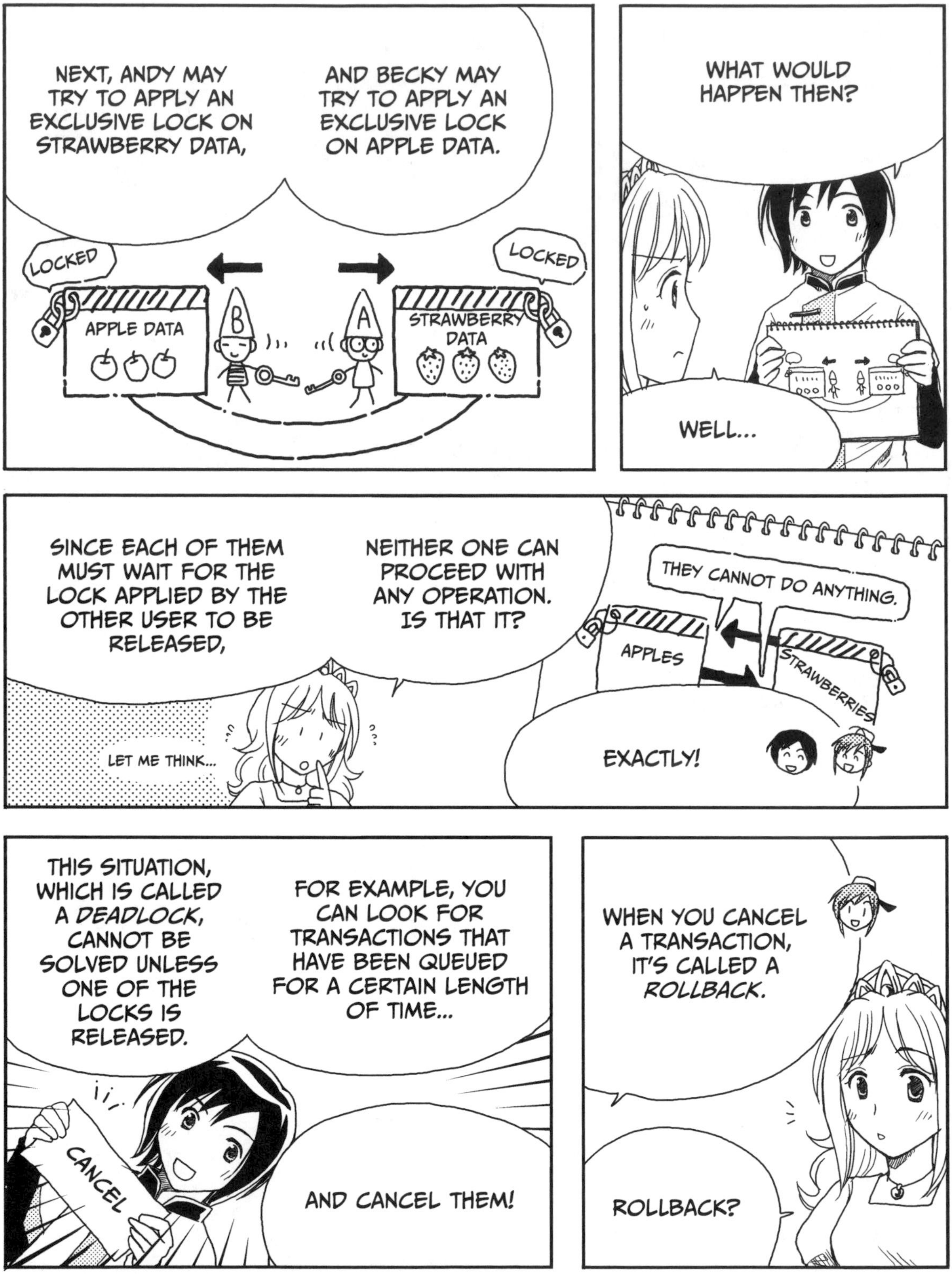
NEXT, ANDY MAY TRY TO APPLY AN EXCLUSIVE LOCK ON STRAWBERRY DATA,
AND BECKY MAY TRY TO APPLY AN EXCLUSIVE LOCK ON APPLE DATA.
LOCKED
LOCKED
APPLE DATA
B
A
STRAWBERRY DATA
WHAT WOULD HAPPEN THEN?
WELL...
SINCE EACH OF THEM MUST WAIT FOR THE LOCK APPLIED BY THE OTHER USER TO BE RELEASED,
NEITHER ONE CAN PROCEED WITH ANY OPERATION. IS THAT IT?
LET ME THINK...
THEY CANNOT DO ANYTHING.
APPLES
STRAWBERRIES
EXACTLY!
THIS SITUATION, WHICH IS CALLED A *DEADLOCK*, CANNOT BE SOLVED UNLESS ONE OF THE LOCKS IS RELEASED.
FOR EXAMPLE, YOU CAN LOOK FOR TRANSACTIONS THAT HAVE BEEN QUEUED FOR A CERTAIN LENGTH OF TIME...
CANCEL
AND CANCEL THEM!
WHEN YOU CANCEL A TRANSACTION, IT'S CALLED A *ROLLBACK*.
ROLLBACK?

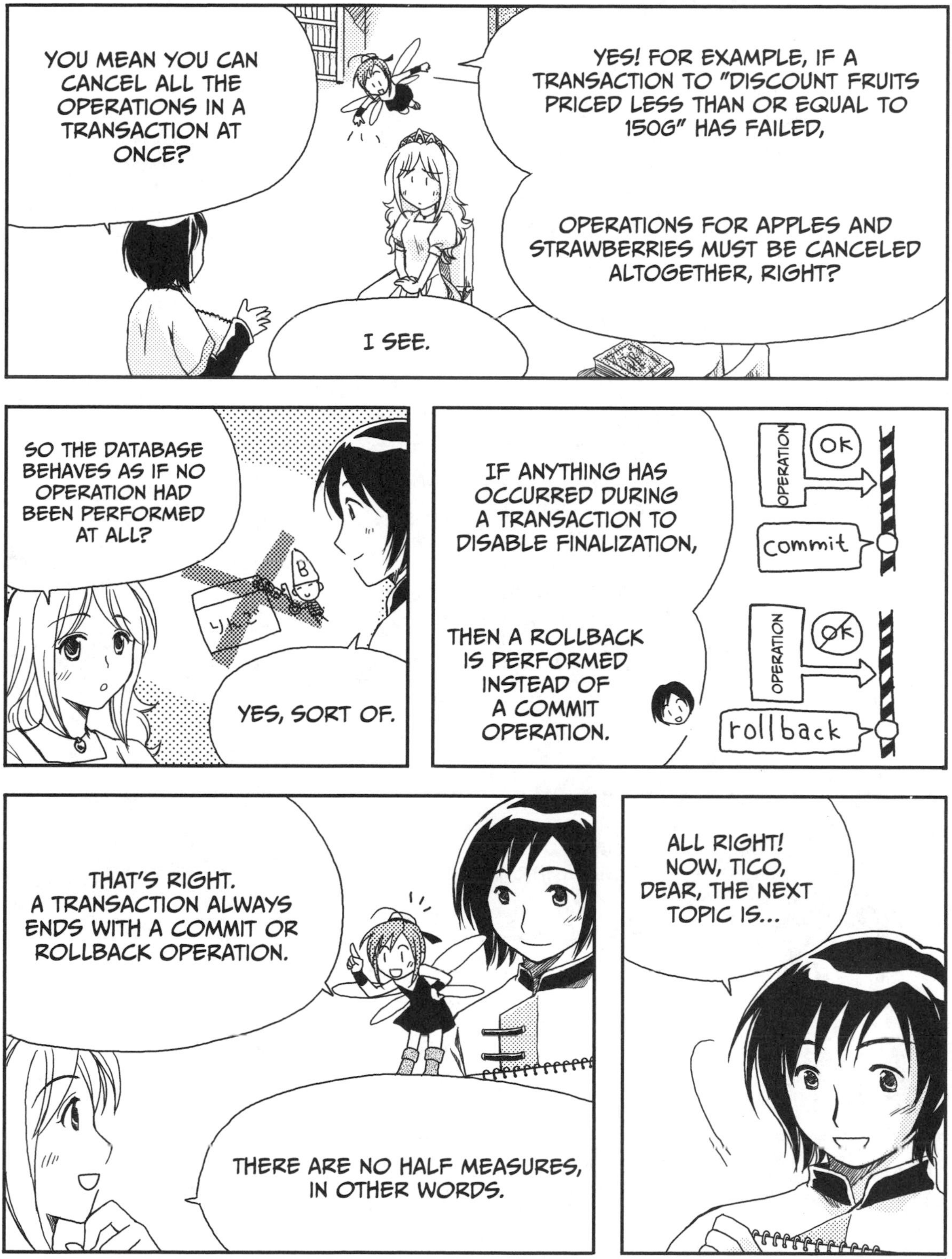
YOU MEAN YOU CAN CANCEL ALL THE OPERATIONS IN A TRANSACTION AT ONCE?
YES! FOR EXAMPLE, IF A TRANSACTION TO "DISCOUNT FRUITS PRICED LESS THAN OR EQUAL TO 150G" HAS FAILED,
OPERATIONS FOR APPLES AND STRAWBERRIES MUST BE CANCELED ALTOGETHER, RIGHT?
I SEE.
SO THE DATABASE BEHAVES AS IF NO OPERATION HAD BEEN PERFORMED AT ALL?
YES, SORT OF.
IF ANYTHING HAS OCCURRED DURING A TRANSACTION TO DISABLE FINALIZATION,
OPERATION
OK
commit
THEN A ROLLBACK IS PERFORMED INSTEAD OF A COMMIT OPERATION.
OPERATION
OK
rollback
THAT'S RIGHT. A TRANSACTION ALWAYS ENDS WITH A COMMIT OR ROLLBACK OPERATION.
THERE ARE NO HALF MEASURES, IN OTHER WORDS.
ALL RIGHT! NOW, TICO, DEAR, THE NEXT TOPIC IS...

Database Security

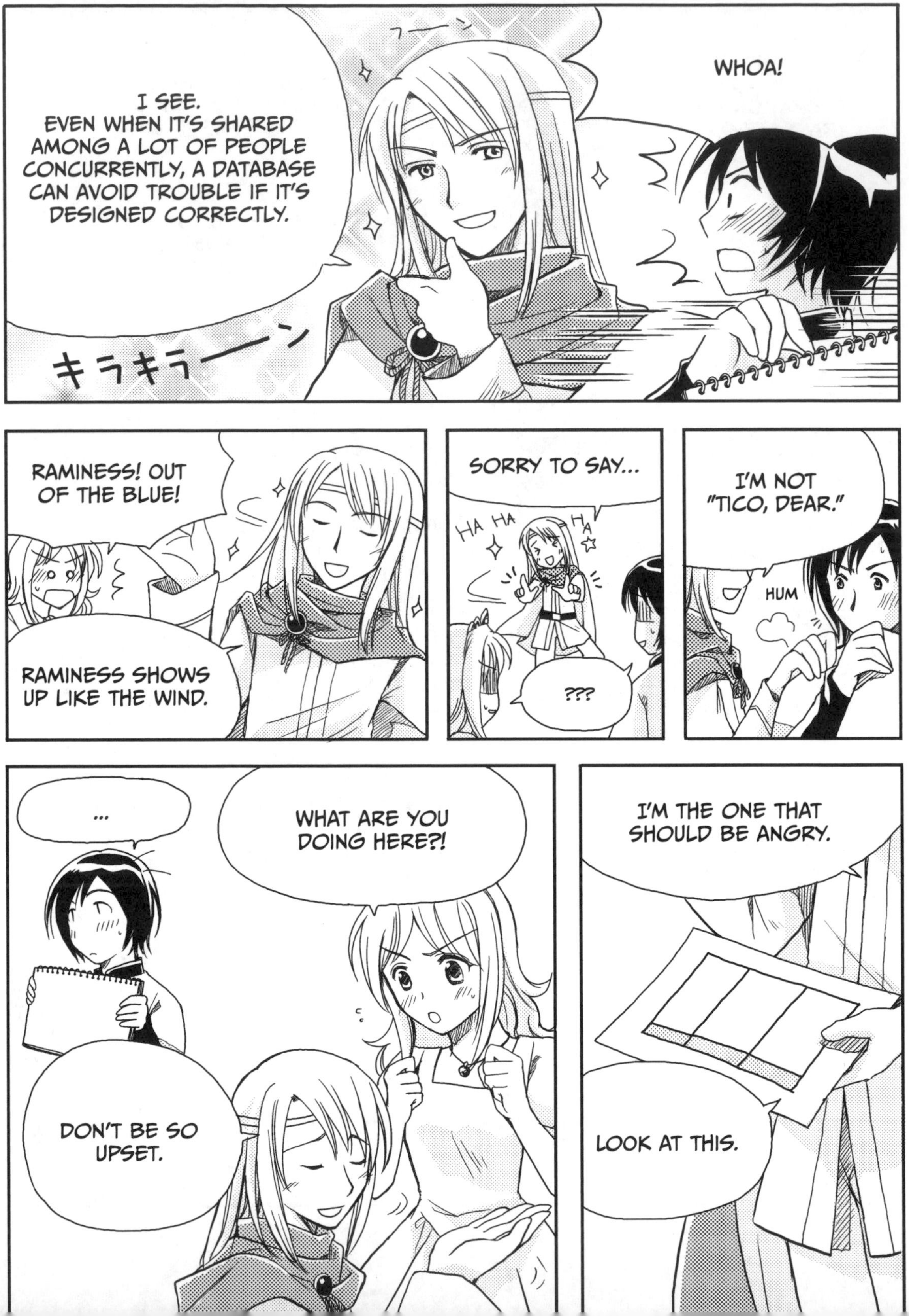
I SEE.
EVEN WHEN IT'S SHARED AMONG A LOT OF PEOPLE CONCURRENTLY, A DATABASE CAN AVOID TROUBLE IF IT'S DESIGNED CORRECTLY.
WHOA!
キラキラーーン
RAMINESS! OUT OF THE BLUE!
RAMINESS SHOWS UP LIKE THE WIND.
SORRY TO SAY...
HA HA HA
???
I'M NOT "TICO, DEAR."
HUM
...
WHAT ARE YOU DOING HERE?!
DON'T BE SO UPSET.
I'M THE ONE THAT SHOULD BE ANGRY.
LOOK AT THIS.

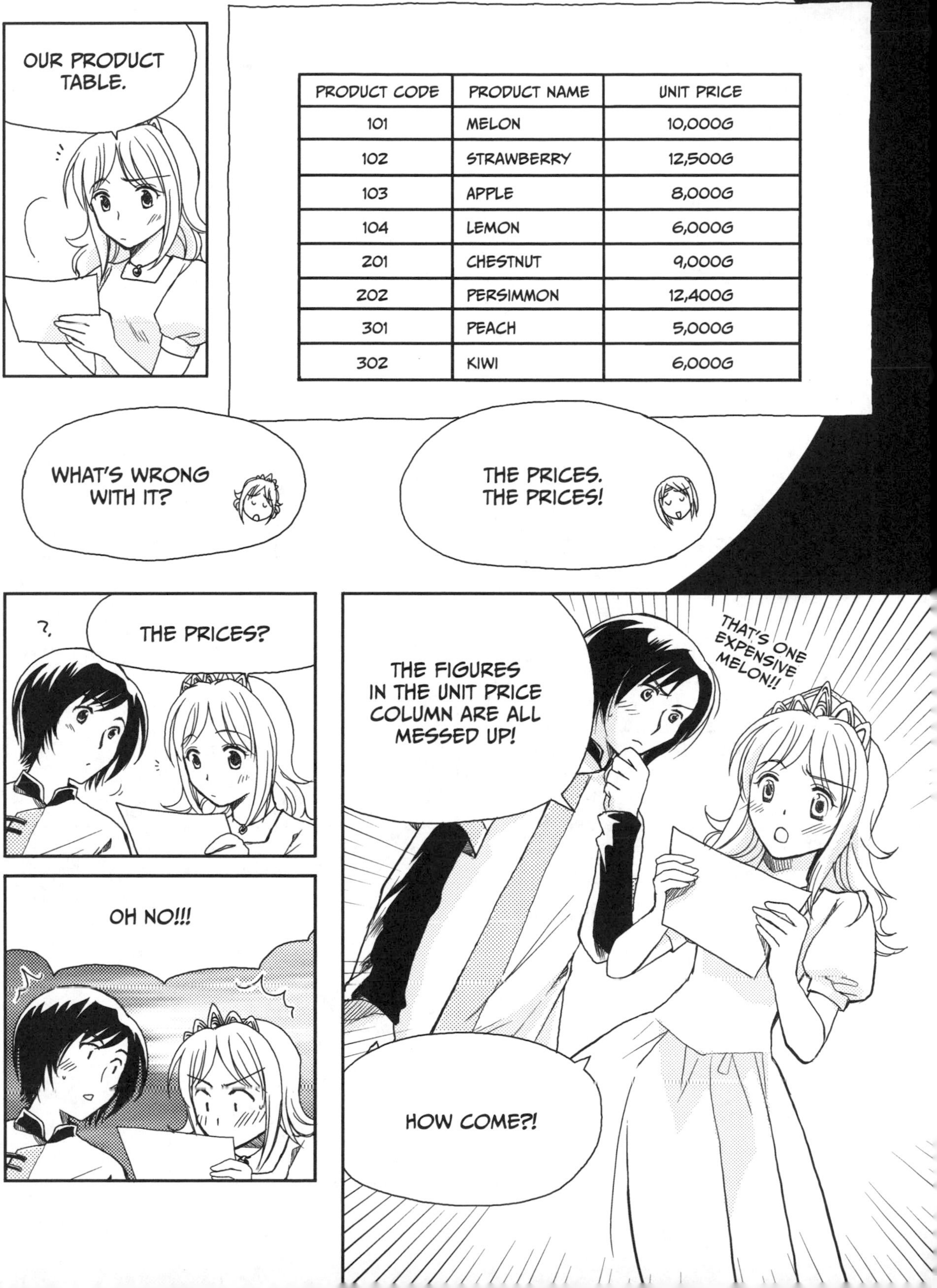
OUR PRODUCT TABLE.

PRODUCT CODE	PRODUCT NAME	UNIT PRICE
101	MELON	10,000G
102	STRAWBERRY	12,500G
103	APPLE	8,000G
104	LEMON	6,000G
201	CHESTNUT	9,000G
202	PERSIMMON	12,400G
301	PEACH	5,000G
302	KIWI	6,000G

WHAT'S WRONG WITH IT?
THE PRICES. THE PRICES!
?
THE PRICES?
OH NO!!!
THE FIGURES IN THE UNIT PRICE COLUMN ARE ALL MESSED UP!
THAT'S ONE EXPENSIVE MELON!!
HOW COME?!

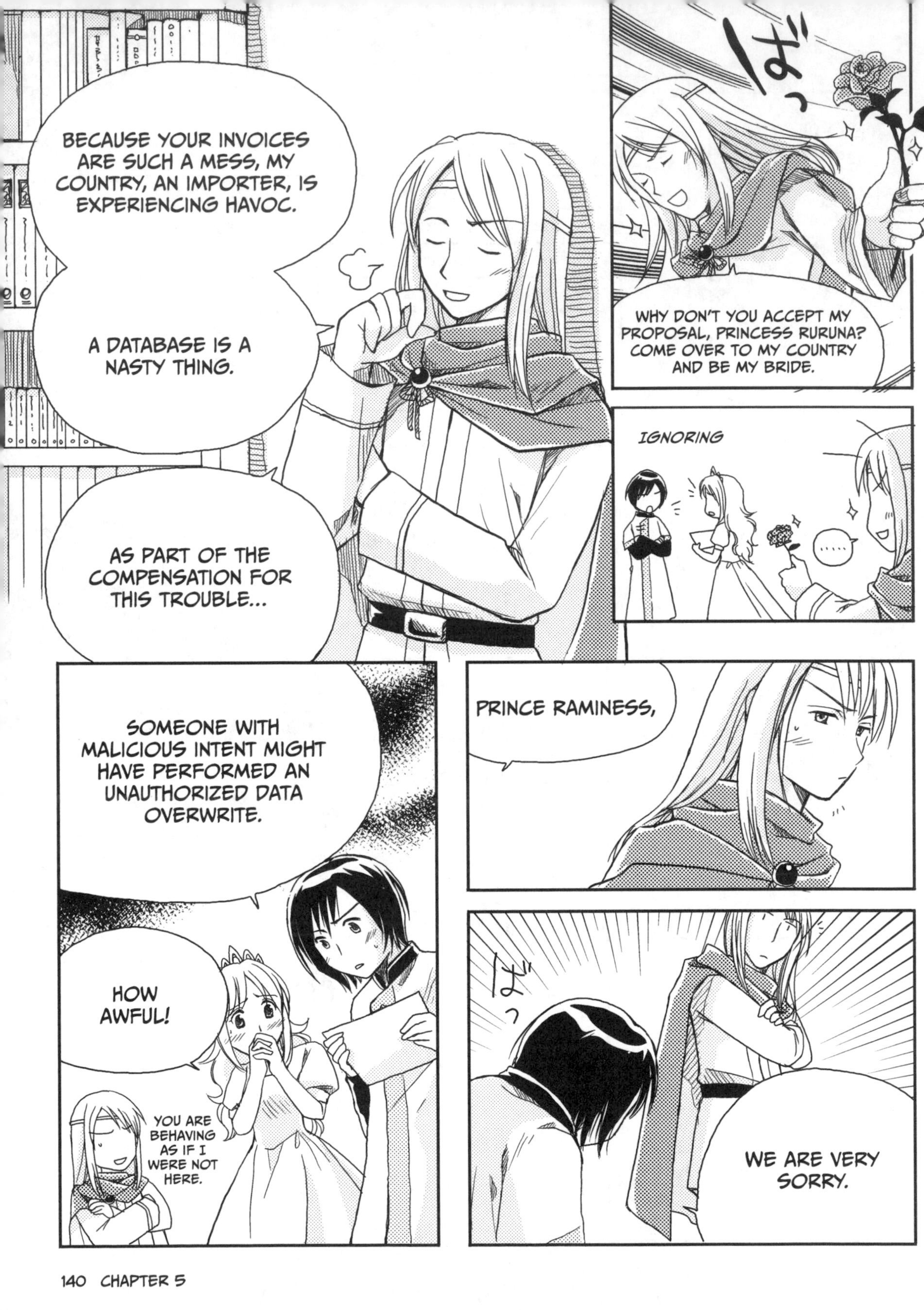
BECAUSE YOUR INVOICES ARE SUCH A MESS, MY COUNTRY, AN IMPORTER, IS EXPERIENCING HAVOC.
A DATABASE IS A NASTY THING.
AS PART OF THE COMPENSATION FOR THIS TROUBLE...
ばっ
WHY DON'T YOU ACCEPT MY PROPOSAL, PRINCESS RURUNA? COME OVER TO MY COUNTRY AND BE MY BRIDE.
IGNORING
.....
SOMEONE WITH MALICIOUS INTENT MIGHT HAVE PERFORMED AN UNAUTHORIZED DATA OVERWRITE.
HOW AWFUL!
YOU ARE BEHAVING AS IF I WERE NOT HERE.
PRINCE RAMINESS,
ばっ
WE ARE VERY SORRY.

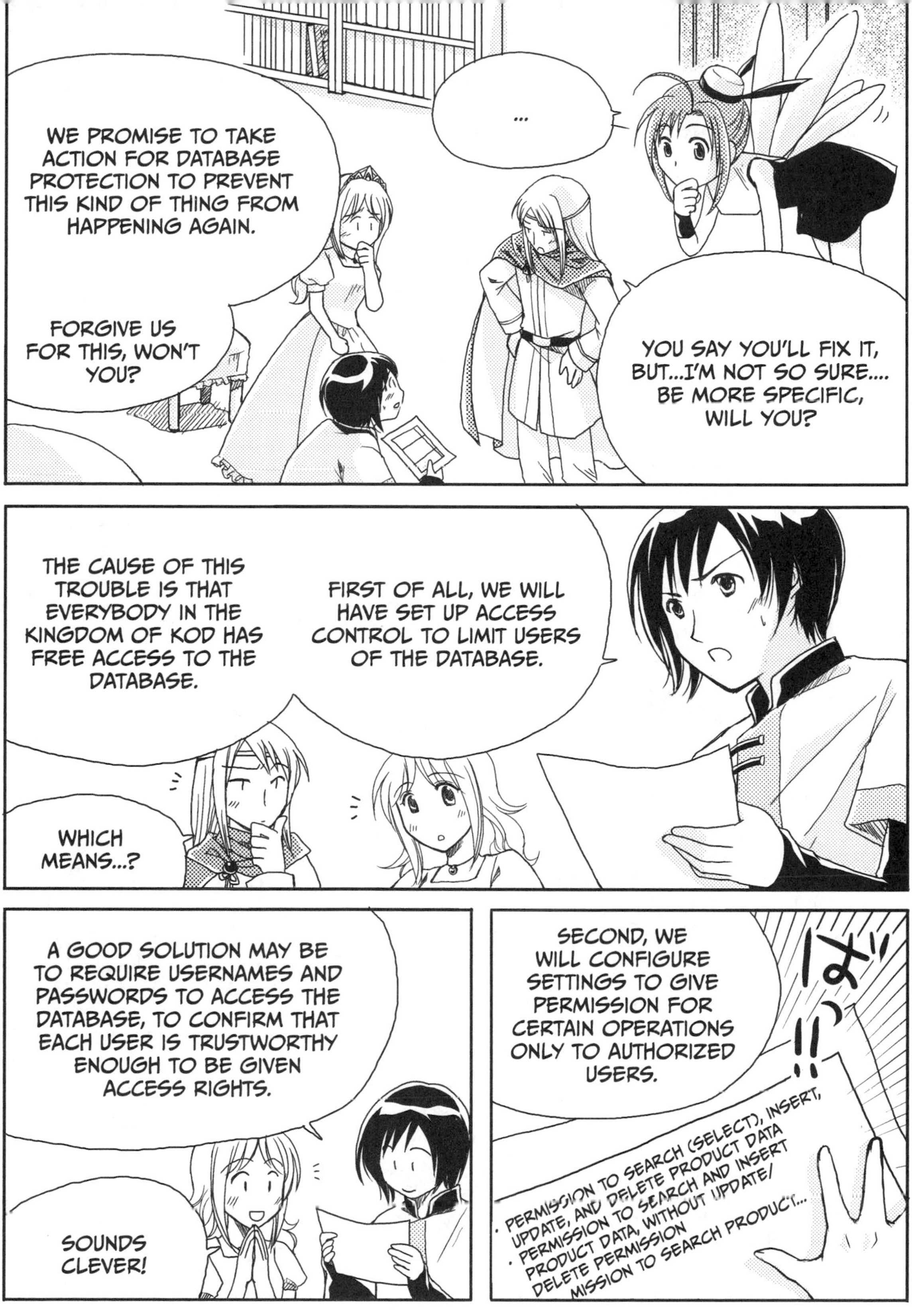
WE PROMISE TO TAKE ACTION FOR DATABASE PROTECTION TO PREVENT THIS KIND OF THING FROM HAPPENING AGAIN.
...
FORGIVE US FOR THIS, WON'T YOU?
YOU SAY YOU'LL FIX IT, BUT...I'M NOT SO SURE.... BE MORE SPECIFIC, WILL YOU?
THE CAUSE OF THIS TROUBLE IS THAT EVERYBODY IN THE KINGDOM OF KOD HAS FREE ACCESS TO THE DATABASE.
FIRST OF ALL, WE WILL HAVE SET UP ACCESS CONTROL TO LIMIT USERS OF THE DATABASE.
WHICH MEANS...?
A GOOD SOLUTION MAY BE TO REQUIRE USERNAMES AND PASSWORDS TO ACCESS THE DATABASE, TO CONFIRM THAT EACH USER IS TRUSTWORTHY ENOUGH TO BE GIVEN ACCESS RIGHTS.
SOUNDS CLEVER!
SECOND, WE WILL CONFIGURE SETTINGS TO GIVE PERMISSION FOR CERTAIN OPERATIONS ONLY TO AUTHORIZED USERS.
ばっ!!
· PERMISSION TO SEARCH (SELECT), INSERT, UPDATE, AND DELETE PRODUCT DATA
· PERMISSION TO SEARCH AND INSERT PRODUCT DATA, WITHOUT UPDATE/ DELETE PERMISSION
MISSION TO SEARCH PRODUCT...

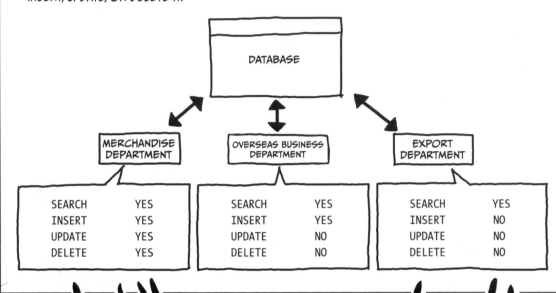

- MERCHANDISE DEPARTMENT PERSONNEL MAY SEARCH, INSERT, UPDATE, AND DELETE PRODUCT DATA.
- OVERSEAS BUSINESS DEPARTMENT PERSONNEL MAY SEARCH AND INSERT PRODUCT DATA, BUT THEY ARE NOT ALLOWED TO UPDATE OR DELETE IT.
- EXPORT DEPARTMENT PERSONNEL MAY SEARCH PRODUCT DATA, BUT THEY ARE NOT ALLOWED TO INSERT, UPDATE, OR DELETE IT.

DATABASE

MERCHANDISE DEPARTMENT		OVERSEAS BUSINESS DEPARTMENT		EXPORT DEPARTMENT	
SEARCH	YES	SEARCH	YES	SEARCH	YES
INSERT	YES	INSERT	YES	INSERT	NO
UPDATE	YES	UPDATE	NO	UPDATE	NO
DELETE	YES	DELETE	NO	DELETE	NO

ばーーーん!!

WE WON'T JUST RESTRICT THE NUMBER OF USERS—WE WILL ALSO SET PERMISSIONS FOR EACH USER WE ALLOW TO ACCESS THE DATABASE.

THIS WAY, PROBLEMS CAN BE AVOIDED AND THE DATABASE CAN STILL BE SHARED.

OH, YEAH... PUTTING THAT ASIDE, WHAT I WANTED TO SAY IS...

THIS IS A GOOD OPPORTUNITY FOR YOU TO CONSIDER MARRIAGE WITH ME, AND...

OH, BUT WAIT...!

SWISH

SPEEDING THINGS UP WITH INDEXING

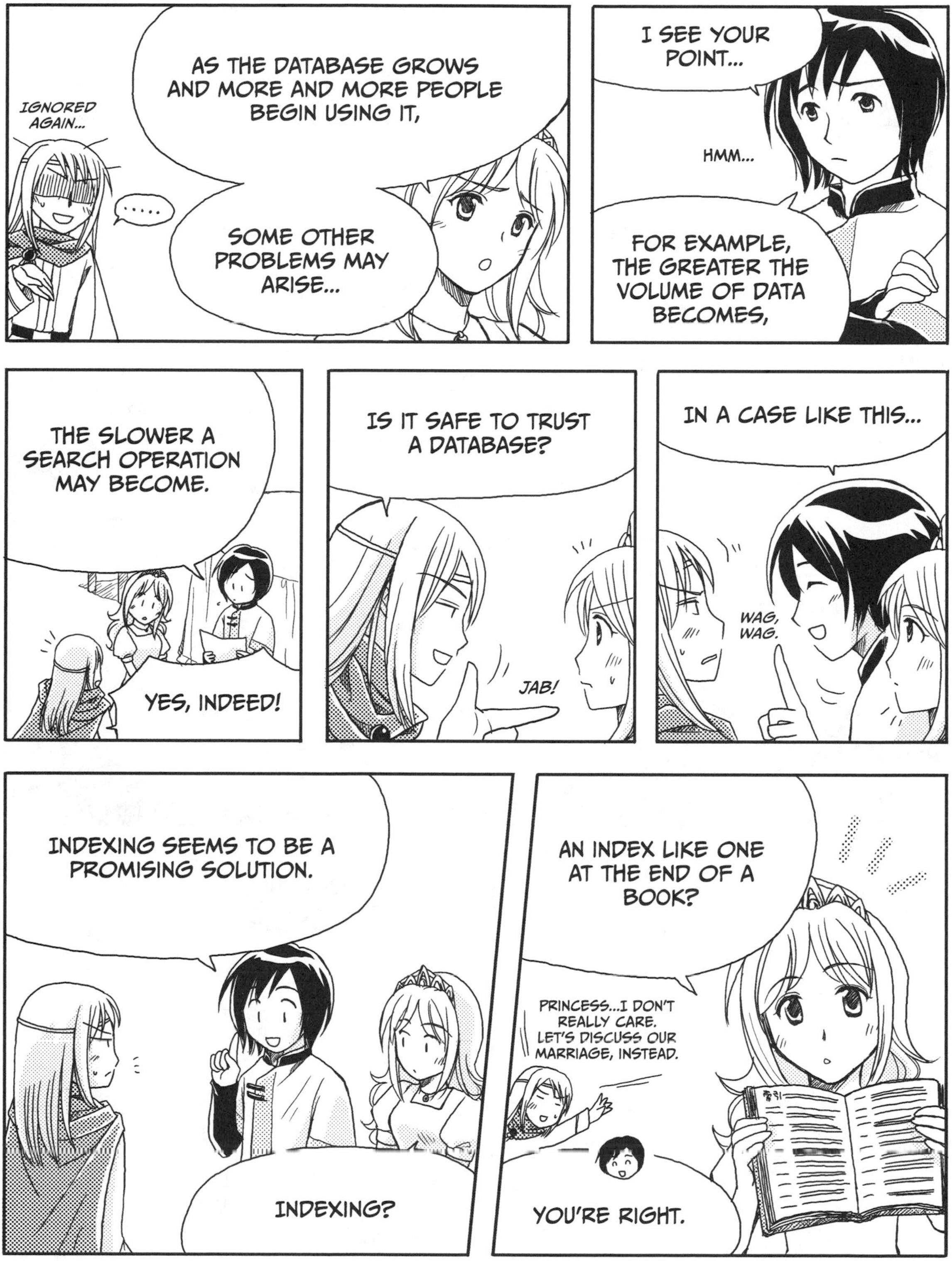
IGNORED AGAIN...
AS THE DATABASE GROWS AND MORE AND MORE PEOPLE BEGIN USING IT,
SOME OTHER PROBLEMS MAY ARISE...
I SEE YOUR POINT...
HMM...
FOR EXAMPLE, THE GREATER THE VOLUME OF DATA BECOMES,
THE SLOWER A SEARCH OPERATION MAY BECOME.
YES, INDEED!
IS IT SAFE TO TRUST A DATABASE?
JAB!
IN A CASE LIKE THIS...
WAG, WAG.
INDEXING SEEMS TO BE A PROMISING SOLUTION.
INDEXING?
AN INDEX LIKE ONE AT THE END OF A BOOK?
PRINCESS...I DON'T REALLY CARE. LET'S DISCUSS OUR MARRIAGE, INSTEAD.
YOU'RE RIGHT.

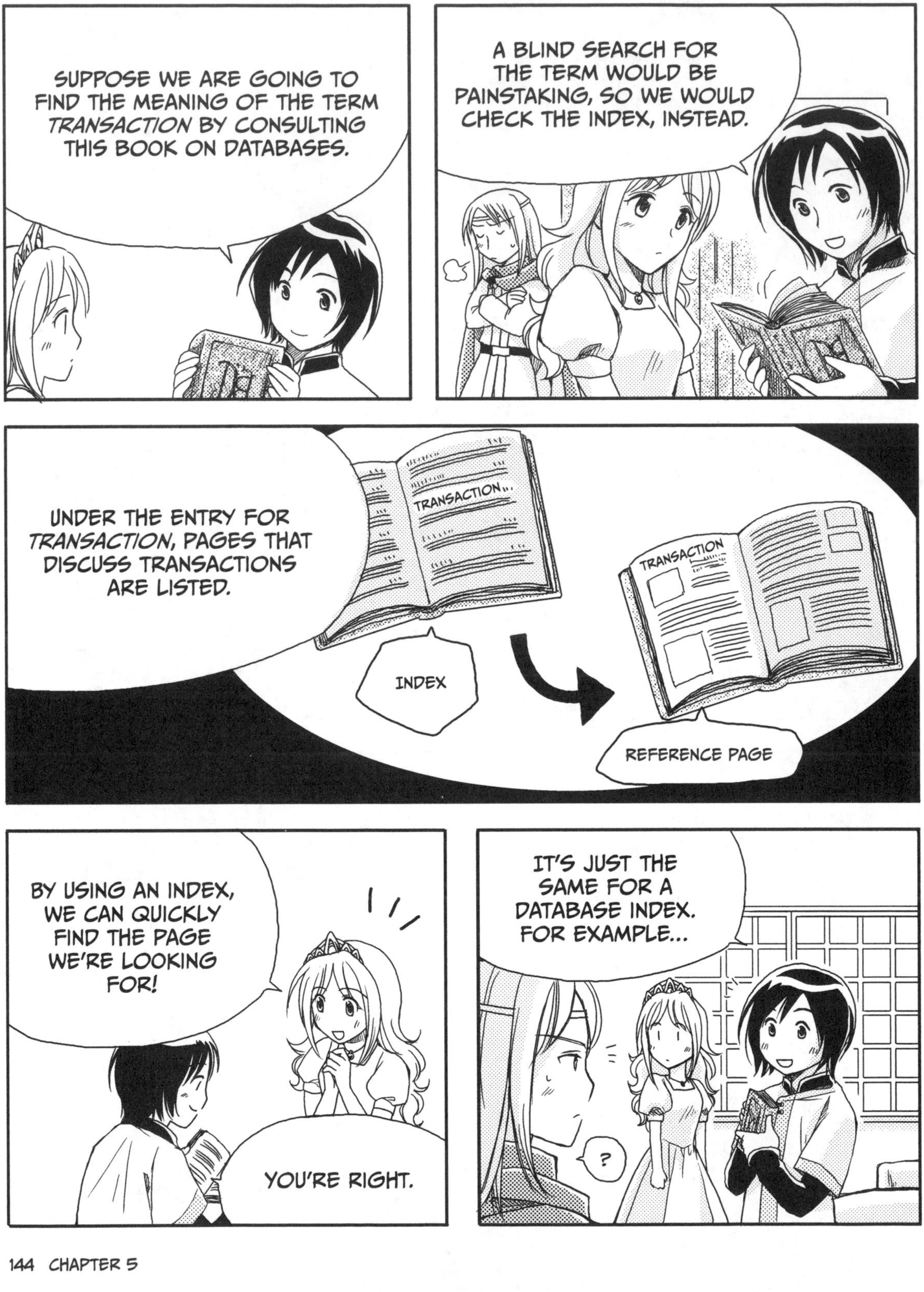
SUPPOSE WE ARE GOING TO FIND THE MEANING OF THE TERM *TRANSACTION* BY CONSULTING THIS BOOK ON DATABASES.
A BLIND SEARCH FOR THE TERM WOULD BE PAINSTAKING, SO WE WOULD CHECK THE INDEX, INSTEAD.
UNDER THE ENTRY FOR *TRANSACTION*, PAGES THAT DISCUSS TRANSACTIONS ARE LISTED.
TRANSACTION
INDEX
TRANSACTION
REFERENCE PAGE
BY USING AN INDEX, WE CAN QUICKLY FIND THE PAGE WE'RE LOOKING FOR!
YOU'RE RIGHT.
IT'S JUST THE SAME FOR A DATABASE INDEX. FOR EXAMPLE...
?

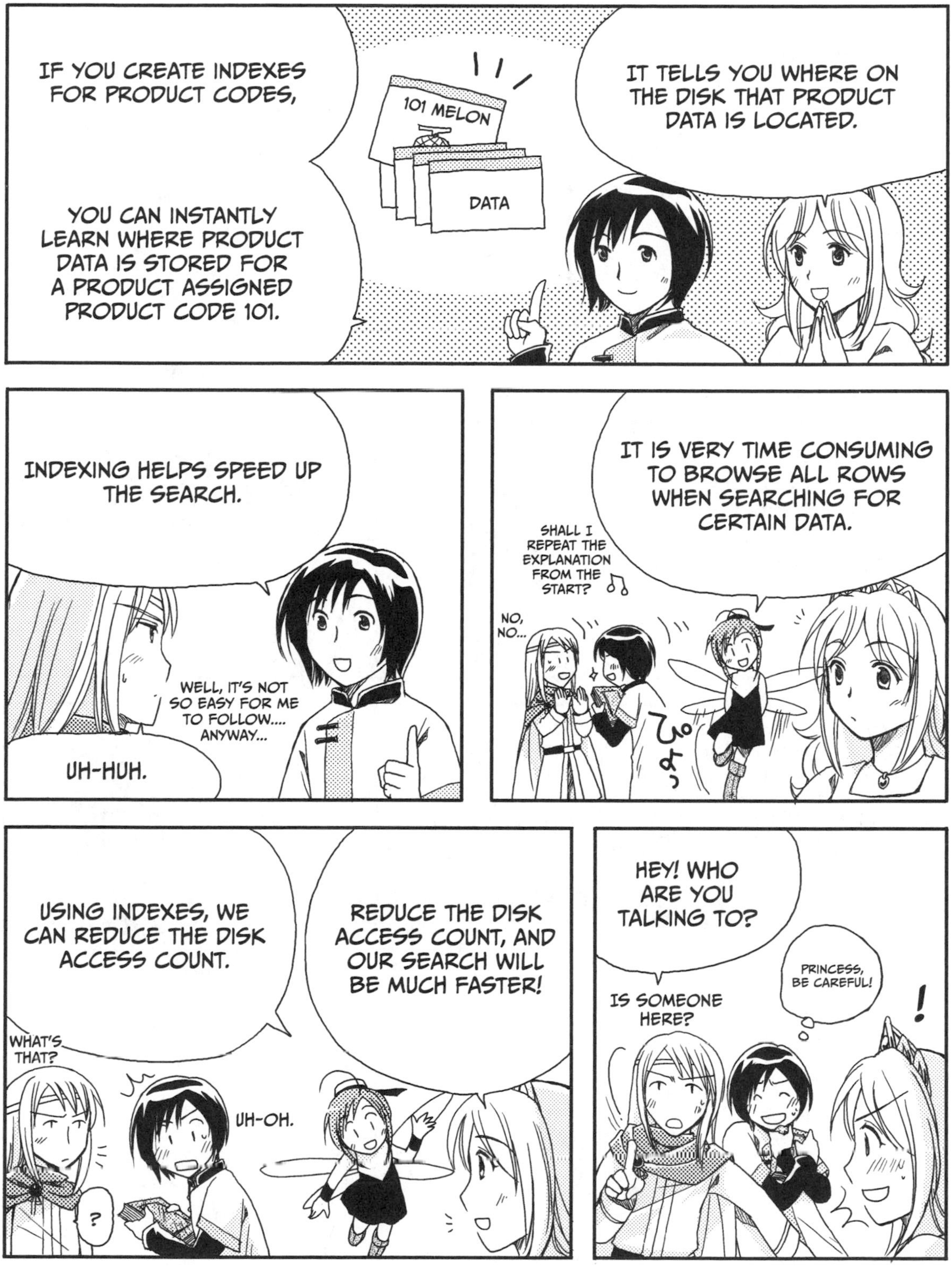
IF YOU CREATE INDEXES FOR PRODUCT CODES,
101 MELON
DATA
YOU CAN INSTANTLY LEARN WHERE PRODUCT DATA IS STORED FOR A PRODUCT ASSIGNED PRODUCT CODE 101.
IT TELLS YOU WHERE ON THE DISK THAT PRODUCT DATA IS LOCATED.
INDEXING HELPS SPEED UP THE SEARCH.
WELL, IT'S NOT SO EASY FOR ME TO FOLLOW.... ANYWAY...
UH-HUH.
IT IS VERY TIME CONSUMING TO BROWSE ALL ROWS WHEN SEARCHING FOR CERTAIN DATA.
SHALL I REPEAT THE EXPLANATION FROM THE START?
NO, NO...
USING INDEXES, WE CAN REDUCE THE DISK ACCESS COUNT.
REDUCE THE DISK ACCESS COUNT, AND OUR SEARCH WILL BE MUCH FASTER!
WHAT'S THAT?
UH-OH.
?
HEY! WHO ARE YOU TALKING TO?
IS SOMEONE HERE?
PRINCESS, BE CAREFUL!
!

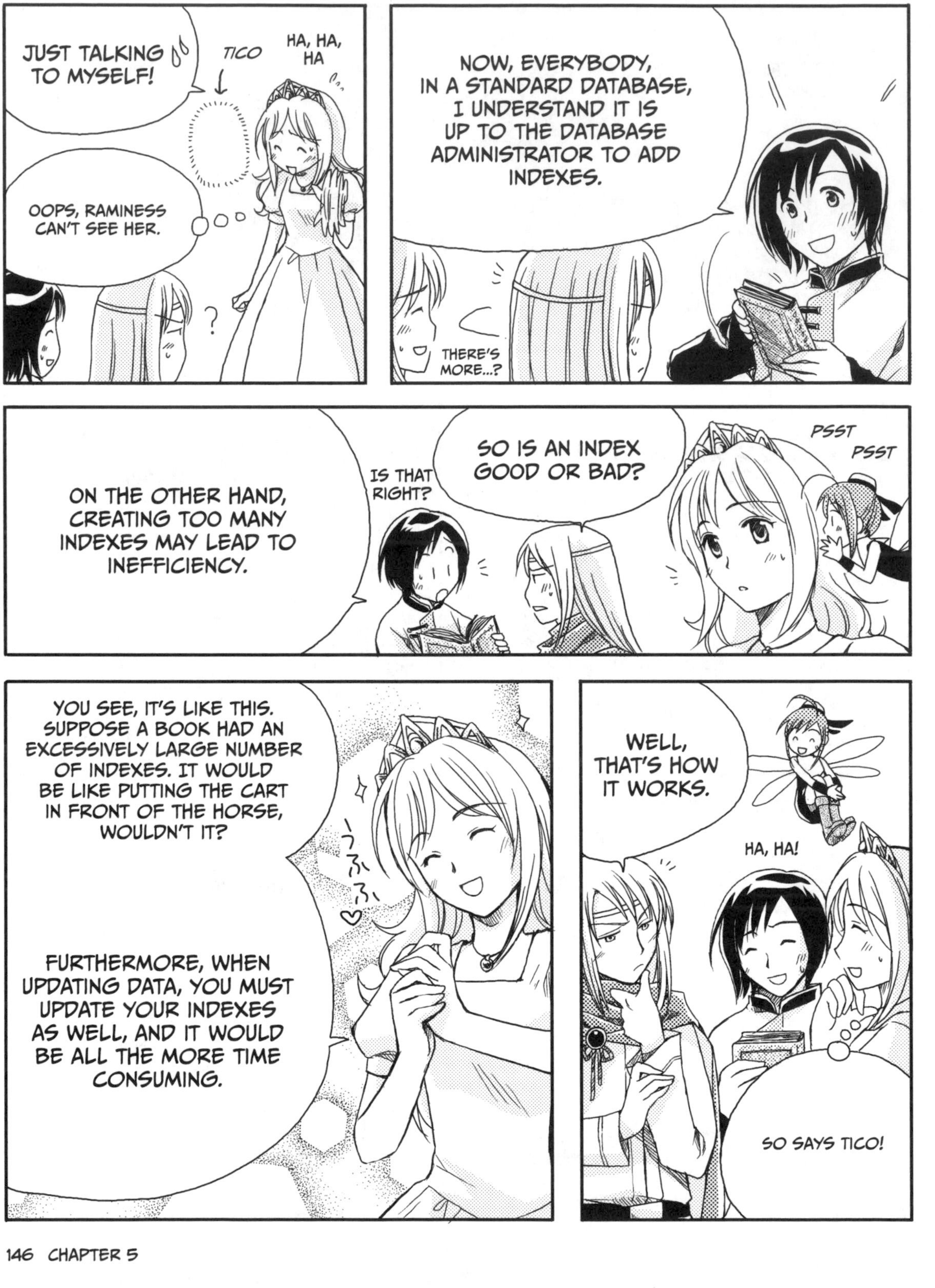
JUST TALKING TO MYSELF!
TICO
HA, HA, HA
OOPS, RAMINESS CAN'T SEE HER.
NOW, EVERYBODY, IN A STANDARD DATABASE, I UNDERSTAND IT IS UP TO THE DATABASE ADMINISTRATOR TO ADD INDEXES.
THERE'S MORE...?
ON THE OTHER HAND, CREATING TOO MANY INDEXES MAY LEAD TO INEFFICIENCY.
IS THAT RIGHT?
SO IS AN INDEX GOOD OR BAD?
PSST
PSST
YOU SEE, IT'S LIKE THIS. SUPPOSE A BOOK HAD AN EXCESSIVELY LARGE NUMBER OF INDEXES. IT WOULD BE LIKE PUTTING THE CART IN FRONT OF THE HORSE, WOULDN'T IT?
うふふ
FURTHERMORE, WHEN UPDATING DATA, YOU MUST UPDATE YOUR INDEXES AS WELL, AND IT WOULD BE ALL THE MORE TIME CONSUMING.
WELL, THAT'S HOW IT WORKS.
HA, HA!
SO SAYS TICO!

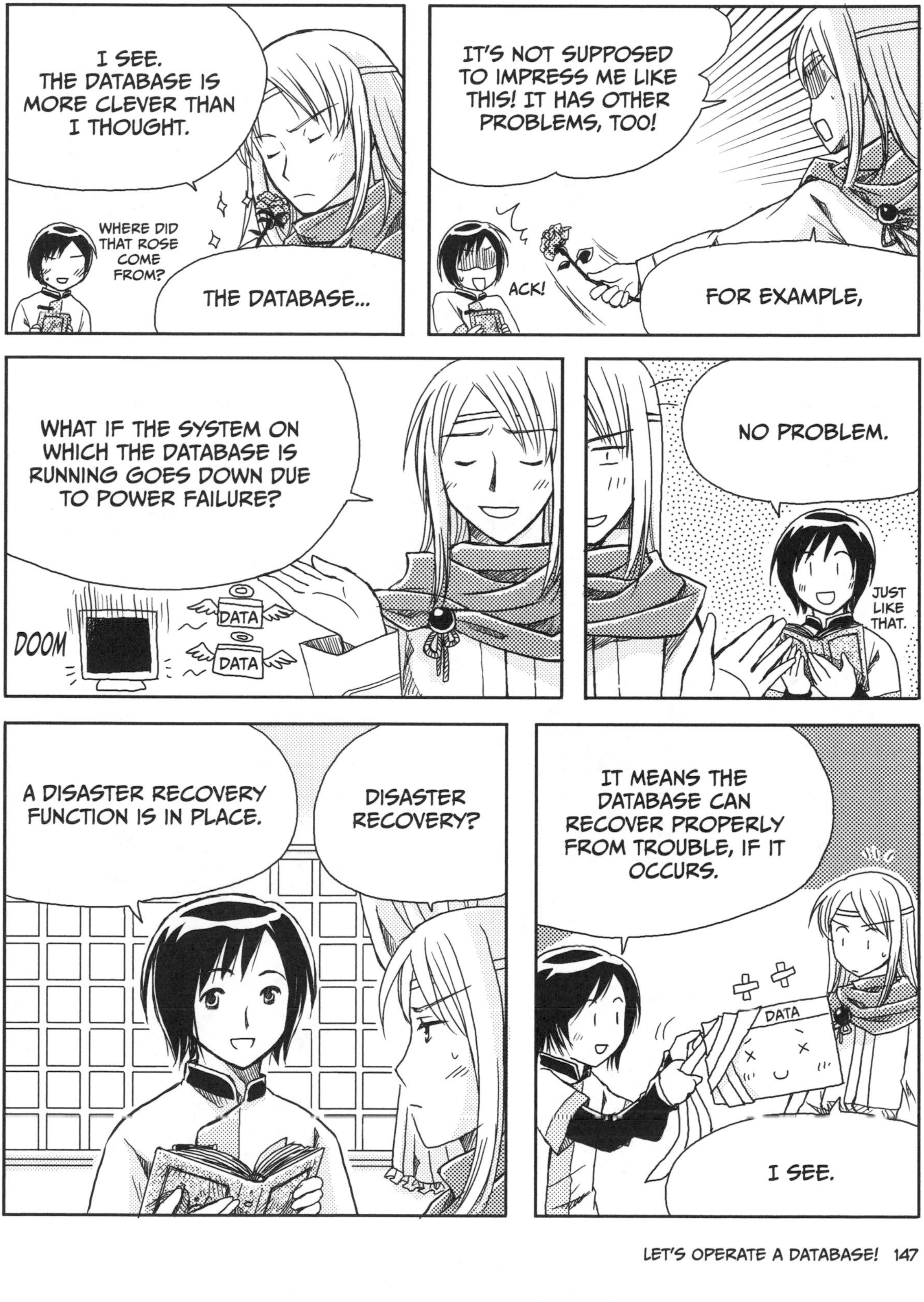
I SEE.
THE DATABASE IS MORE CLEVER THAN I THOUGHT.
WHERE DID THAT ROSE COME FROM?
THE DATABASE...
IT'S NOT SUPPOSED TO IMPRESS ME LIKE THIS! IT HAS OTHER PROBLEMS, TOO!
ACK!
FOR EXAMPLE,
WHAT IF THE SYSTEM ON WHICH THE DATABASE IS RUNNING GOES DOWN DUE TO POWER FAILURE?
DOOM
DATA
DATA
NO PROBLEM.
JUST LIKE THAT.
A DISASTER RECOVERY FUNCTION IS IN PLACE.
DISASTER RECOVERY?
IT MEANS THE DATABASE CAN RECOVER PROPERLY FROM TROUBLE, IF IT OCCURS.
DATA
I SEE.

Disaster Recovery

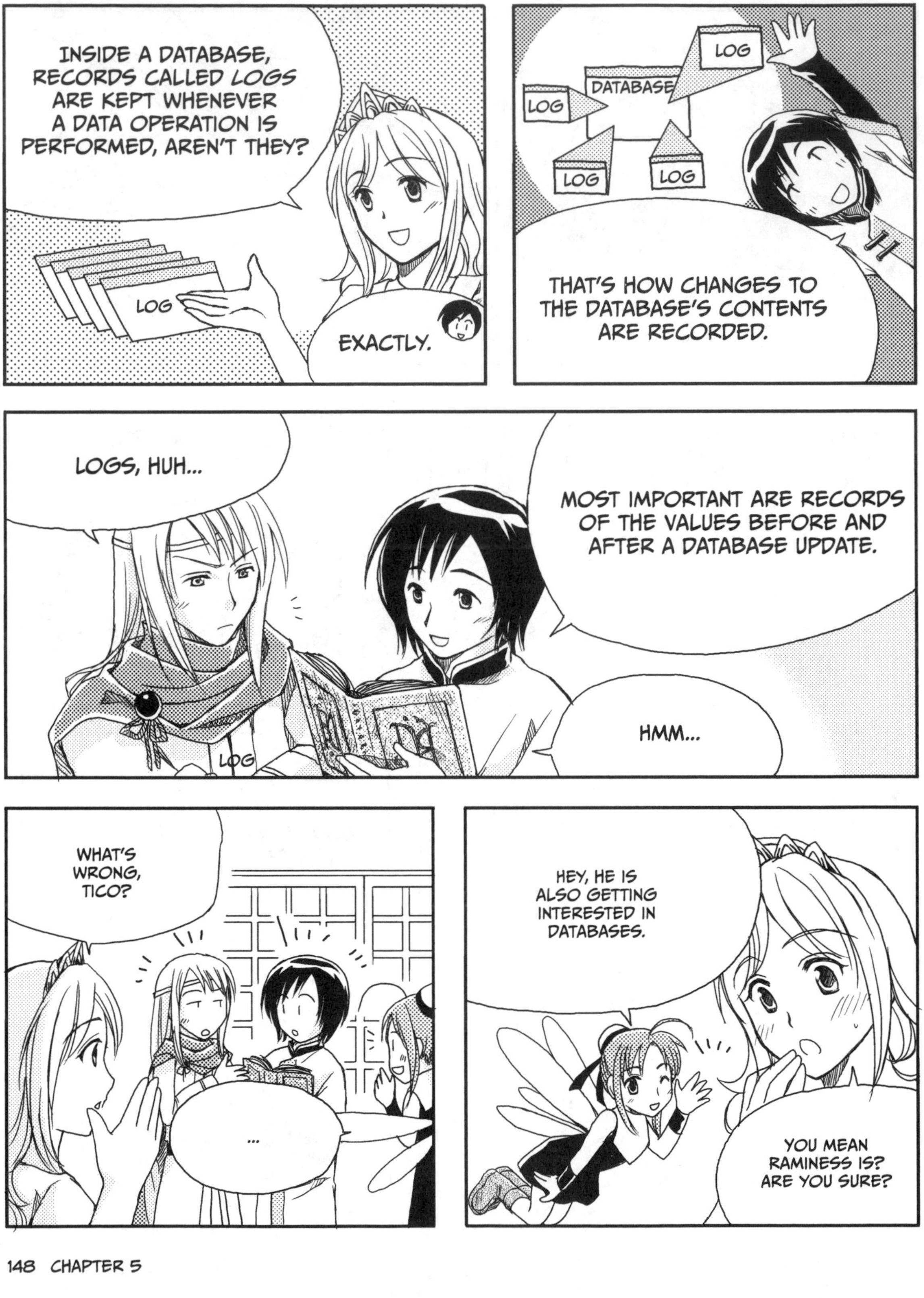

INSIDE A DATABASE, RECORDS CALLED *LOGS* ARE KEPT WHENEVER A DATA OPERATION IS PERFORMED, AREN'T THEY?
LOG
EXACTLY.
LOG
DATABASE
LOG
LOG
LOG
THAT'S HOW CHANGES TO THE DATABASE'S CONTENTS ARE RECORDED.
LOGS, HUH...
MOST IMPORTANT ARE RECORDS OF THE VALUES BEFORE AND AFTER A DATABASE UPDATE.
LOG
HMM...
WHAT'S WRONG, TICO?
...
HEY, HE IS ALSO GETTING INTERESTED IN DATABASES.
YOU MEAN RAMINESS IS? ARE YOU SURE?

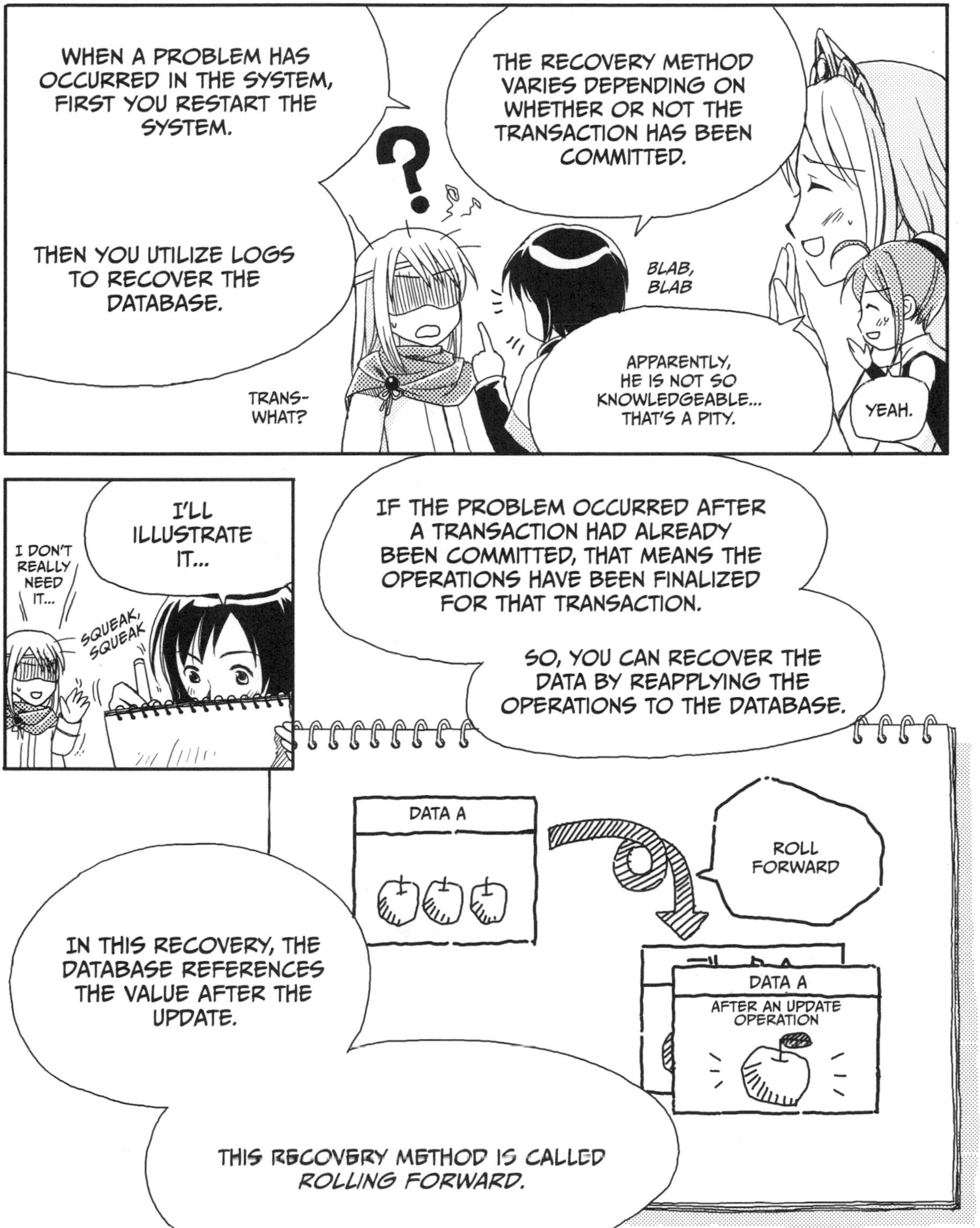
WHEN A PROBLEM HAS OCCURRED IN THE SYSTEM, FIRST YOU RESTART THE SYSTEM.
THEN YOU UTILIZE LOGS TO RECOVER THE DATABASE.
?
THE RECOVERY METHOD VARIES DEPENDING ON WHETHER OR NOT THE TRANSACTION HAS BEEN COMMITTED.
BLAB, BLAB
TRANS-WHAT?
APPARENTLY, HE IS NOT SO KNOWLEDGEABLE... THAT'S A PITY.
YEAH.
I'LL ILLUSTRATE IT...
I DON'T REALLY NEED IT...
SQUEAK, SQUEAK
IF THE PROBLEM OCCURRED AFTER A TRANSACTION HAD ALREADY BEEN COMMITTED, THAT MEANS THE OPERATIONS HAVE BEEN FINALIZED FOR THAT TRANSACTION.
SO, YOU CAN RECOVER THE DATA BY REAPPLYING THE OPERATIONS TO THE DATABASE.
DATA A
ROLL FORWARD
DATA A
AFTER AN UPDATE OPERATION
IN THIS RECOVERY, THE DATABASE REFERENCES THE VALUE AFTER THE UPDATE.
THIS RECOVERY METHOD IS CALLED *ROLLING FORWARD.*

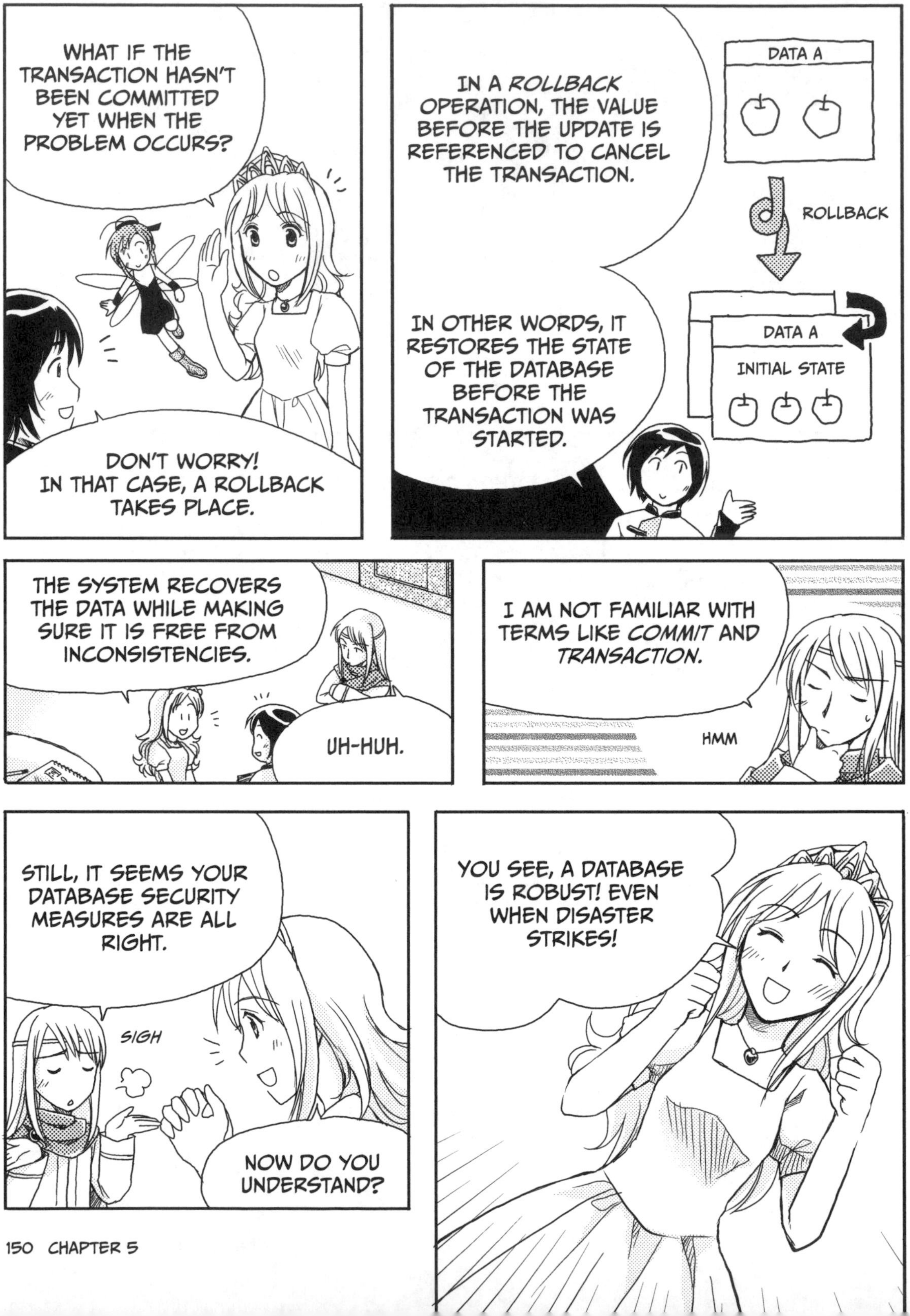

WHAT IF THE TRANSACTION HASN'T BEEN COMMITTED YET WHEN THE PROBLEM OCCURS?
DON'T WORRY! IN THAT CASE, A ROLLBACK TAKES PLACE.
IN A *ROLLBACK* OPERATION, THE VALUE BEFORE THE UPDATE IS REFERENCED TO CANCEL THE TRANSACTION.
DATA A
ROLLBACK
DATA A
INITIAL STATE
IN OTHER WORDS, IT RESTORES THE STATE OF THE DATABASE BEFORE THE TRANSACTION WAS STARTED.
THE SYSTEM RECOVERS THE DATA WHILE MAKING SURE IT IS FREE FROM INCONSISTENCIES.
UH-HUH.
I AM NOT FAMILIAR WITH TERMS LIKE *COMMIT* AND *TRANSACTION*.
HMM
STILL, IT SEEMS YOUR DATABASE SECURITY MEASURES ARE ALL RIGHT.
SIGH
NOW DO YOU UNDERSTAND?
YOU SEE, A DATABASE IS ROBUST! EVEN WHEN DISASTER STRIKES!

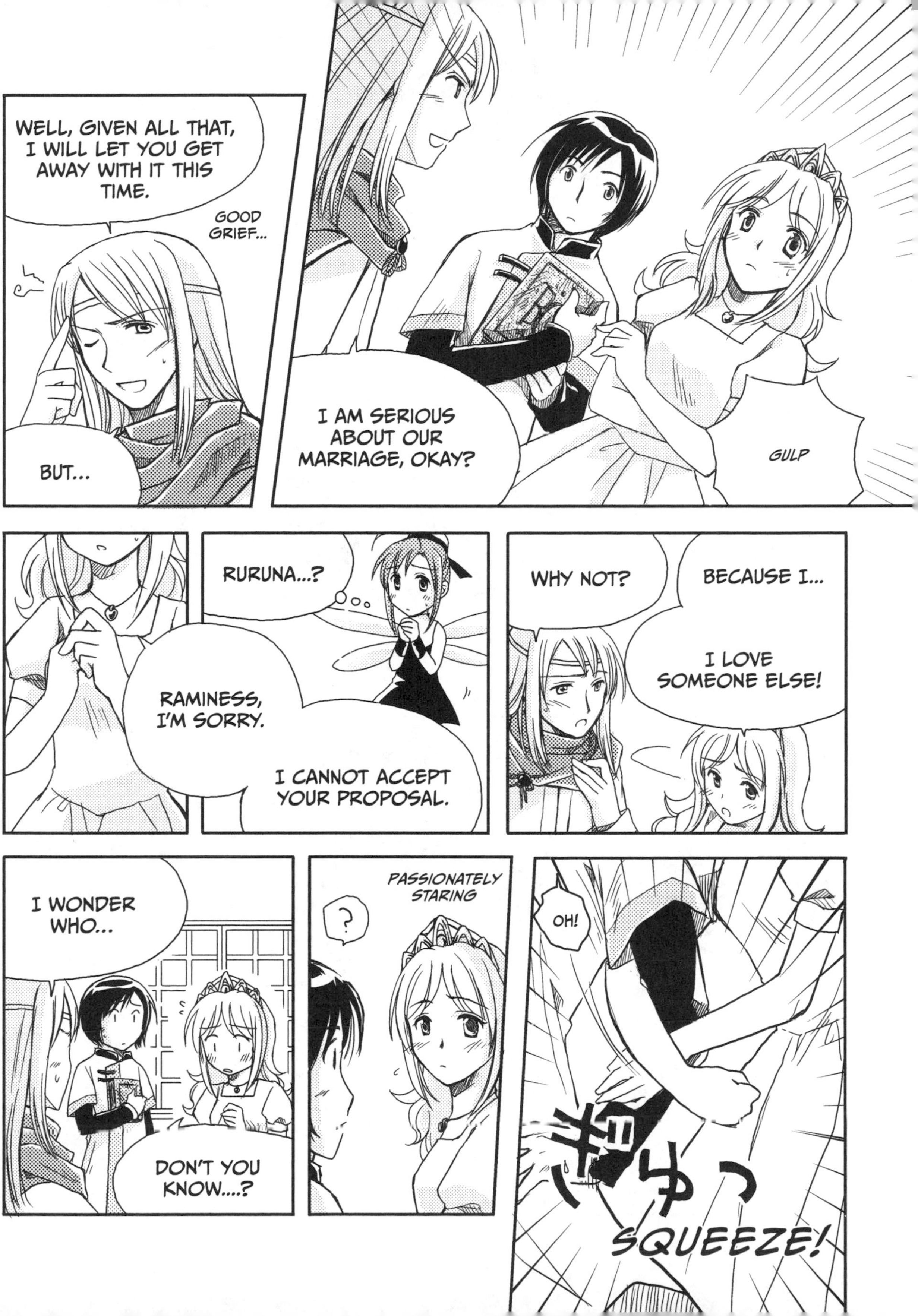
WELL, GIVEN ALL THAT, I WILL LET YOU GET AWAY WITH IT THIS TIME.
GOOD GRIEF...
BUT...
I AM SERIOUS ABOUT OUR MARRIAGE, OKAY?
GULP
RURUNA...?
RAMINESS, I'M SORRY.
I CANNOT ACCEPT YOUR PROPOSAL.
WHY NOT?
BECAUSE I...
I LOVE SOMEONE ELSE!
I WONDER WHO...
DON'T YOU KNOW....?
?
PASSIONATELY STARING
OH!
SQUEEZE!

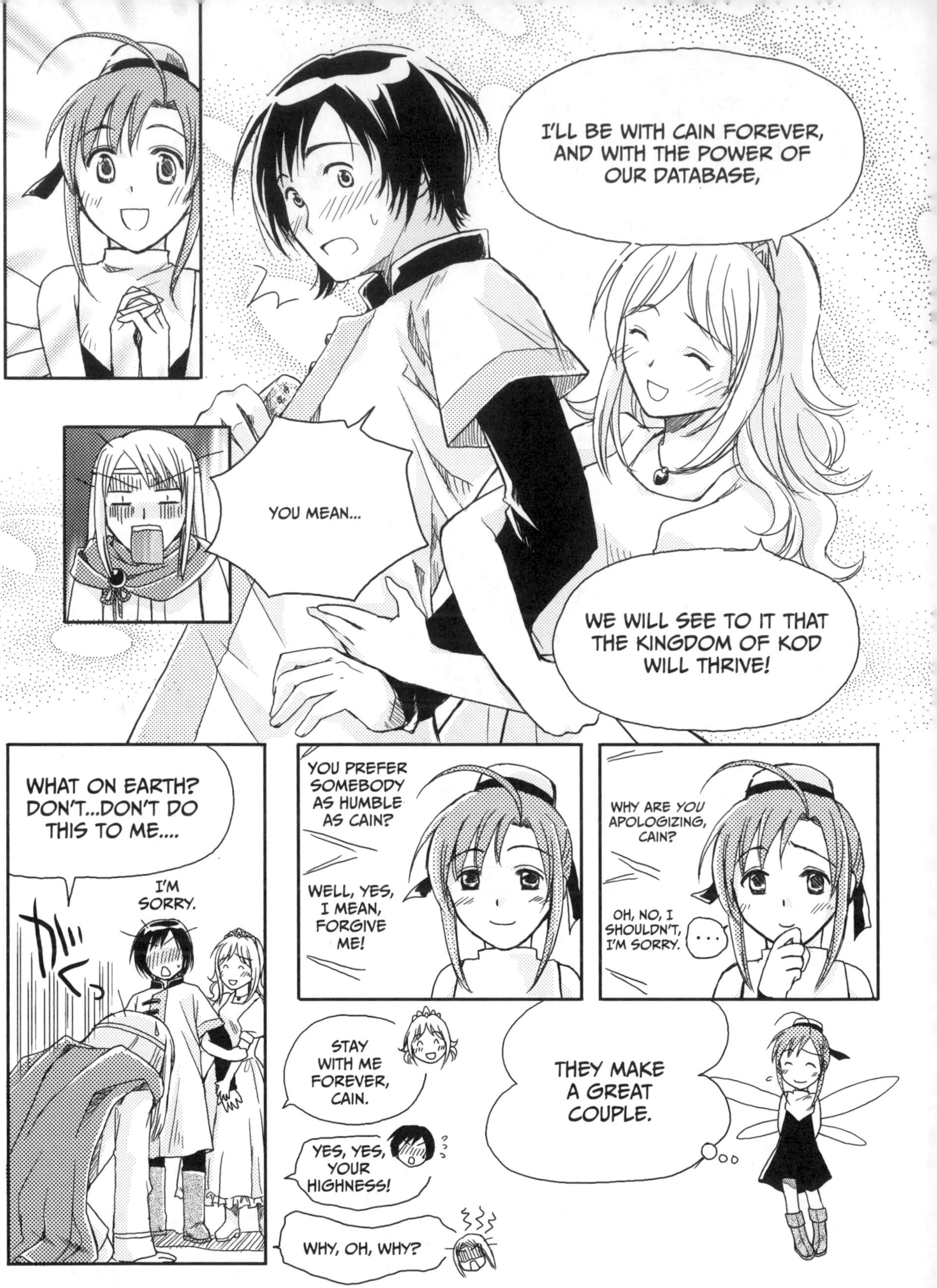
I'LL BE WITH CAIN FOREVER, AND WITH THE POWER OF OUR DATABASE,
YOU MEAN...
WE WILL SEE TO IT THAT THE KINGDOM OF KOD WILL THRIVE!
WHAT ON EARTH? DON'T...DON'T DO THIS TO ME....
I'M SORRY.
YOU PREFER SOMEBODY AS HUMBLE AS CAIN?
WELL, YES, I MEAN, FORGIVE ME!
WHY ARE *YOU* APOLOGIZING, CAIN?
OH, NO, I SHOULDN'T, I'M SORRY.
...
STAY WITH ME FOREVER, CAIN.
YES, YES, YOUR HIGHNESS!
WHY, OH, WHY?
THEY MAKE A GREAT COUPLE.

PROPERTIES OF TRANSACTIONS

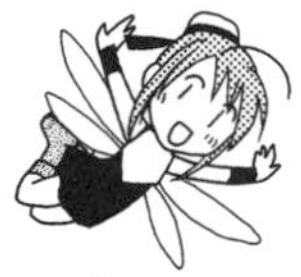

Cain's research showed that users of a database can search for, insert, update, and delete data. A set of successful operations performed by a single user is called a *transaction*.

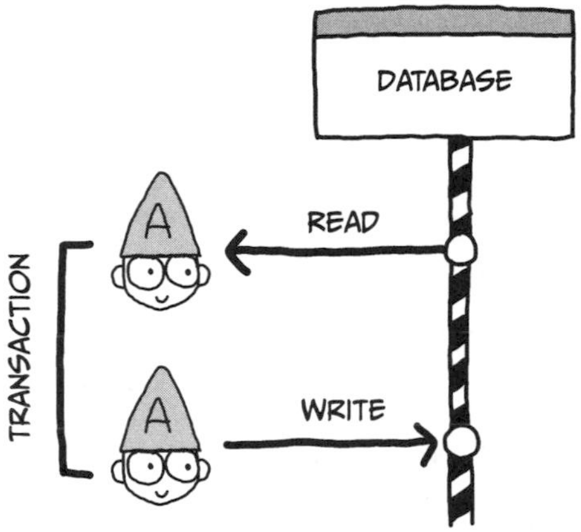

DATABASE
READ
WRITE
A
A
TRANSACTION

When users share a database, it is important to ensure that multiple transactions can be processed without causing conflicting data. It is also important to protect data from inconsistencies in case a failure occurs while a transaction is being processed. To that end, the following table lists the properties required for a transaction, which memorably spell the word *ACID*.

PROPERTIES REQUIRED FOR A TRANSACTION

Property	Stands for	Description
A	Atomicity	A transaction must either end with a commit or rollback operation.
C	Consistency	Processing a transaction never results in loss of consistency of the database.
I	Isolation	Even when transactions are processed concurrently, the results must be the same as for sequential processing.
D	Durability	The contents of a completed transaction should not be affected by failure.

Let's examine each of these properties in depth.

ATOMICITY

The first property required for a transaction, *atomicity*, means that a transaction must end with either a commit or rollback in order to keep a database free of inconsistencies. In short, either all actions of a transaction are completed or all actions are canceled. A *commit* finalizes the operation in the transaction. A *rollback* cancels the operation in the transaction.

DATABASE
A
A
COMMIT
DATABASE
A
A
ROLLBACK

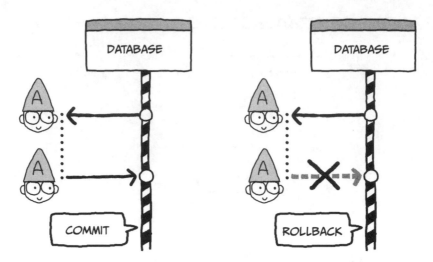

In some cases, a commit or rollback is performed automatically. You can also specify which one should be carried out. For example, you can specify a rollback if an error occurs.

You can use the SQL statements COMMIT and ROLLBACK to perform these operations.

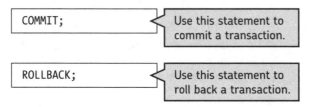

```
COMMIT;
```

Use this statement to commit a transaction.

```
ROLLBACK;
```

Use this statement to roll back a transaction.

QUESTIONS

Answer these questions to see how well you understand atomicity. The answers are on page 167.

Q1

Write an SQL statement that can be used to finalize a transaction.

Q2

Write an SQL statement that can be used to cancel a transaction.

CONSISTENCY

A transaction must not create errors. If the database was consistent before a transaction is processed, then the database must also be consistent after that transaction occurs.

Cain gave the example of Andy and Becky each trying to add 10 apples to an original total of 30 apples. Rather than yielding the correct amount of 50 apples, the database shows a total of 40 apples. This type of error is called a *lost update*.

A
30 APPLES
30 APPLES
30 APPLES
B
+10 APPLES
+10 APPLES
40 APPLES
40 APPLES
40 APPLES?

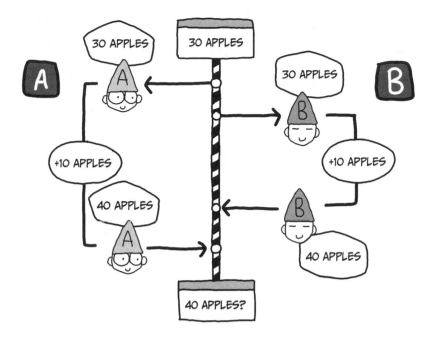

When transactions are processed concurrently, more than one transaction may access the same table or row at the same time, and conflicting data may occur.

Tables and rows subject to operations in a transaction are referred to as *resources*. In a database, transactions should be able to access the same resource concurrently without creating inconsistencies.

ISOLATION

When two or more concurrent transactions yield the same result as if they were performed at separate times, that order of processing is referred to as *serializable*. The *isolation* property requires the schedule to be serializable and protects against errors.

In order to make the order of processing serializable, you need to have control over transactions that are attempted at the same time. The most commonly used method for this purpose is the lock-based control. A *shared lock* is used when reading data, while an *exclusive lock* is used when writing data.

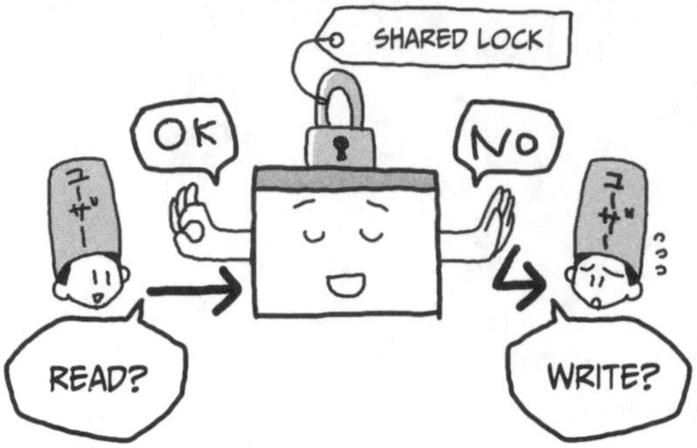
SHARED LOCK
OK
No
READ?
WRITE?

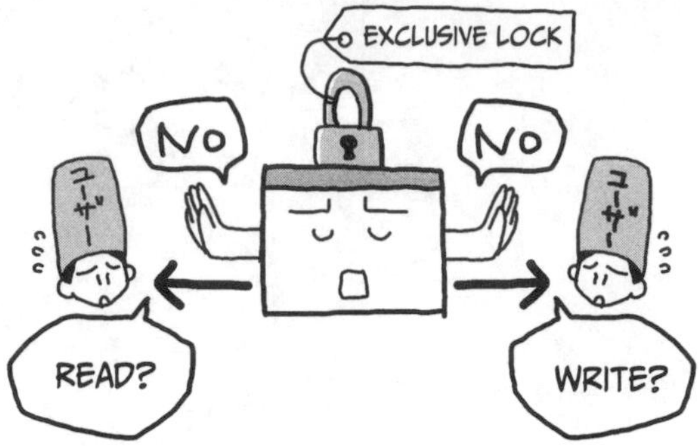
EXCLUSIVE LOCK
No
No
READ?
WRITE?

When a shared lock is in use, another user can apply a shared lock to other transactions, but not an exclusive lock. When an exclusive lock is applied, another user can apply either a shared lock or an exclusive lock to other transactions. The following summarizes the relationship between a shared lock and an exclusive lock.

CO-EXISTENCE RELATIONSHIP BETWEEN LOCK TYPES

	Shared lock	**Exclusive lock**
Shared lock	YES	NO
Exclusive lock	NO	NO

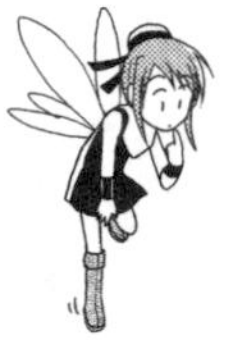

QUESTIONS

Do you understand locks? Answer these questions and check your answers on page 167.

Q3

When Andy has applied a shared lock, can Becky apply a shared lock?

Q4

When Andy has applied an exclusive lock, can Becky apply a shared lock?

Q5

When Andy has applied a shared lock, can Becky apply an exclusive lock?

Q6

When Andy has applied an exclusive lock, can Becky apply an exclusive lock?

TWO-PHASE LOCKING

In order to make sure a schedule is serializable, we need to obey specific rules for setting and releasing locks. One of these rules is *two-phase locking*—for each transaction, two phases should be used: one for setting locks and the other for releasing them.

For example, suppose there are resources A and B, both subject to locking. Transaction ❶ observes the rule of two-phase locking, while transaction ❷ does not. Serialization can only be achieved when each transaction complies with the rule of two-phase locking.

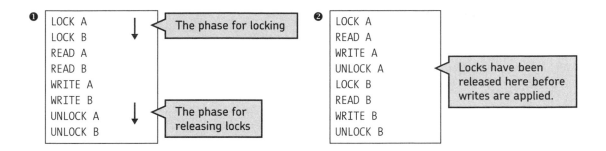

❶

```
LOCK A
LOCK B
READ A
READ B
WRITE A
WRITE B
UNLOCK A
UNLOCK B
```

The phase for locking (LOCK A – LOCK B)

The phase for releasing locks (UNLOCK A – UNLOCK B)

❷

```
LOCK A
READ A
WRITE A
UNLOCK A
LOCK B
READ B
WRITE B
UNLOCK B
```

Locks have been released here before writes are applied. (UNLOCK A)

LOCKING GRANULARITY

There are a number of resources that can be locked. For example, you can lock data in units of tables or units of rows. The extent to which resources are locked is referred to as *granularity*. *Coarse granularity* occurs when many resources are locked at once, and *fine granularity* occurs when few resources are locked.

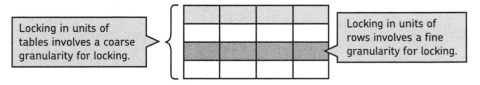

Locking in units of tables involves a coarse granularity for locking.
Locking in units of rows involves a fine granularity for locking.

When granularity is coarse (or high), the number of locks needed per transaction is reduced, making it easier to manage granularity. In turn, this reduces the amount of processing required by the CPU on which the database is operating. On the other hand, as more resources are locked, it tends to take longer to wait for locks used by other transactions to be released. Thus, the number of transactions you can carry out tends to drop when granularity is high.

In contrast, when granularity is fine (or low), a greater number of locks are used in one transaction, resulting in more operations for managing locks. This results in greater processing required by the CPU. However, since fewer resources are locked, you will spend less time waiting for other transactions to release locks. Thus, the number of transactions you can carry out tends to increase.

QUESTIONS

Answer these questions, and check the correct answers on page 168.

Q7

The target resource for locking has been changed from a table to a row. What will happen to the number of transactions you can carry out concurrently?

Q8

The target resource for locking has been changed from a row to a table. What will happen to the number of transactions you can carry out concurrently?

OTHER CONCURRENCY CONTROLS

You can use locking to effectively carry out two or more transactions at the same time. However, using locking comes with the burden of lock management, since *deadlocks*—places where user actions conflict—can occur. Simpler methods for concurrency control can be used when you have a small number of transactions or a high number of read operations. In such cases, the following methods may be used:

Timestamp Control

A label containing the time of access, referred to as a *timestamp*, is assigned to data accessed during a transaction. If another transaction with a later timestamp has already updated the data, the operation will be not permitted. When a read or write operation is not permitted, the transaction is rolled back.

Optimistic Control

This method allows a read operation. When a write operation is attempted, the data is checked to see if any other transactions have occurred. If another transaction has already updated the data, the transaction is rolled back.

LEVELS OF ISOLATION

In a real-world database, you can set the level of transactions that can be processed concurrently. This is referred to as the *isolation level*.

In SQL, the SET TRANSACTION statement can be used to specify the isolation levels of the following transactions:

* READ UNCOMMITTED
* READ COMMITTED
* REPEATABLE READ
* SERIALIZABLE

```
SET TRANSACTION ISOLATION LEVEL READ UNCOMMITTED;
```

Depending on the isolation level setting, any of the following actions may occur.

	Dirty read	Non-repeatable read	Phantom read
READ UNCOMMITTED	Possible	Possible	Possible
READ COMMITTED	Will not occur	Possible	Possible
REPEATABLE READ	Will not occur	Will not occur	Possible
SERIALIZABLE	Will not occur	Will not occur	Will not occur

* A *dirty read* occurs when transaction 2 reads a row before transaction 1 is committed.
* A *non-repeatable read* occurs when a transaction reads the same data twice and gets a different value.
* A *phantom read* occurs when a transaction searches for rows matching a certain condition but finds the wrong rows due to another transaction's changes.

DURABILITY

A database manages important data, so ensuring security and durability in the case of failure is critical. Security is also important for preventing unauthorized users from writing data and causing inconsistencies.

In a database, you can set permissions for who can access the database or tables in it. Cain avoids dangers to the Kingdom's database by enhancing the database's security.

In a relational database, the GRANT statement is used to grant read and write permissions to users. You can use GRANT statements to grant permission for other users to process tables you have created. Setting permissions is an important task for database operation.

```
GRANT SELECT, UPDATE ON product TO Overseas_Business_Department;
```
> This statement grants permission to process data.

You can assign the following privileges (permissions) with SQL statements.

DATABASE PRIVILEGES

Statement	Result
SELECT	Allows user to search for rows in a table.
INSERT	Allows user to insert rows in a table.
UPDATE	Allows user to update rows in a table.
DELETE	Allows user to delete rows in a table.
ALL	Gives user all privileges.

Granting a privilege with WITH GRANT OPTION enables the user to grant privileges to other users. With the statement shown below, the Overseas Business Department can allow other users to search and update the database.

```
GRANT SELECT, UPDATE ON product TO Overseas_Business_Department
WITH GRANT OPTION;
```
> The granted user can grant privileges to other users.

You can also take away a user's privileges. To do this, use the REVOKE statement.

```
REVOKE SELECT, UPDATE ON product FROM
Overseas_Business_Department;
```
> This statement revokes the user's privileges.

Some database products can group a number of privileges and grant them to multiple users at once. Grouping makes privilege management easier.

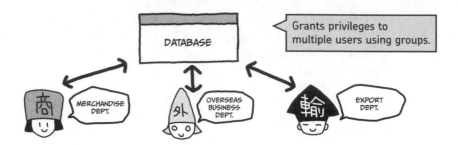

Grants privileges to multiple users using groups.

DATABASE

MERCHANDISE DEPT.

OVERSEAS BUSINESS DEPT.

EXPORT DEPT.

Using views, as described on page 117, enables even more controlled management for enhanced security. First, extract part of a base table to create a view. Setting a privilege for this view means the privilege is also set on the selected portion of data in the view.

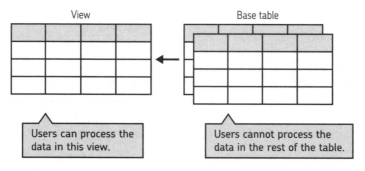

View

Base table

Users can process the data in this view.

Users cannot process the data in the rest of the table.

QUESTIONS

Try these questions on durability. The answers are on page 168.

Q9

Write an SQL statement that allows the Export Department to search for data in the Product Table.

Q10

Create an SQL statement to revoke the privilege to delete data from the Product Table.

Q11

Privileges were set as follows on a Product Table created by the administrator. Enter a YES or NO in each cell of the table below to indicate the presence or absence of the privilege for each department, respectively.

```
GRANT ALL product TO Overseas_Business_Department;
GRANT INSERT, DELETE ON product TO Merchandise_Department;
GRANT UPDATE, DELETE ON product TO Export_Department;
```

	Search	Insert	Update	Delete
Overseas Business Dept.				
Merchandise Dept.				
Export Dept.				

When Disaster Strikes

A database needs to have a mechanism that can protect data in the system in the event of a failure. To ensure durability of transactions, it is mandatory that no failure can create incorrect or faulty data. To protect itself from failure, a database performs various operations, which include creating backup copies and transaction logs.

Types of Failures

Database failure can occur under various circumstances. Possible types of failure include the following:

- Transaction failure
- System failure
- Media failure

Transaction failure occurs when a transaction cannot be completed due to an error in the transaction itself. The transaction is rolled back when this failure occurs.

System failure occurs when the system goes down due to a power failure or other such disruption. In the case of a system failure, disaster recovery takes place after you reboot the system. Generally, transactions that have not yet been committed at the time of failure are rolled back, and those that have already been committed when a failure occurs are rolled forward.

Media failure occurs when the hard disk that contains the database is damaged. In the case of a media failure, disaster recovery is carried out using backup files. Transactions committed after the backup files were created are rolled forward.

Checkpoints

In order to improve the efficiency of a write operation in a database, a *buffer* (a segment of memory used to temporarily hold data) is often used to write data in the short term. The contents of the buffer and the database are synchronized, and then a *checkpoint* is written. When the database writes a checkpoint, it doesn't have to perform any failure recovery for transactions that were committed before the checkpoint. Transactions that weren't committed before the checkpoint must be recovered.

Now, suppose the transactions shown below are being performed at the time a system failure occurs. Which transactions should be rolled back? Which ones should be rolled forward?

Checkpoint
Failure occurrence
Time
T1
Start
T2
Start
Commit
T3
Start
Commit

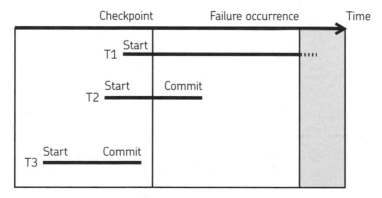

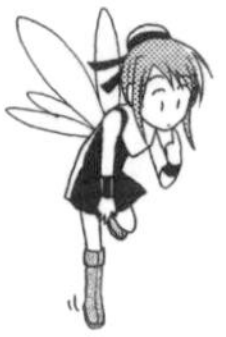

QUESTIONS

Try these questions based on the table on the previous page. The answers are on page 168.

Q12

How should T1 be processed?

Q13

How should T2 be processed?

Q14

How should T3 be processed?

In case of database failure, the recovery mechanisms described above will protect the database against inconsistency. That is why you can be reassured of database integrity when you use it.

INDEXES

A database manages massive amounts of data, so searching for specific data can be very time consuming. But you can use indexes to speed up searches!

Product code	Product name	Unit price	District
101	Melon	800G	South Sea
102	Strawberry	150G	Middle
103	Apple	120G	North Sea
104	Lemon	200G	South Sea
201	Chestnut	100G	North Sea
202	Persimmon	160G	Middle
301	Peach	130G	South Sea
302	Kiwi	200G	South Sea

It is very time consuming to search for each item row by row.

An *index* is a tool that allows you to speedily access the location of the target data. When looking for some data in a large database, searching with indexes promises fast results.

Product code	Product name	Unit price	District
101	Melon	800G	South Sea
102	Strawberry	150G	Middle
103	Apple	120G	North Sea
104	Lemon	200G	South Sea
201	Chestnut	100G	North Sea
202	Persimmon	160G	Middle
301	Peach	130G	South Sea
302	Kiwi	200G	South Sea

The target data location can be accessed quickly by using its index.

Index

Indexing methods include B-tree and hash methods. A *B-tree index* is composed of parent nodes and child nodes, which can have further child nodes. The nodes are arranged in sorted order. Each parent contains information about the minimum and maximum values contained by all of its children. This allows the database to navigate quickly to the desired location, skipping entire sections of the tree that cannot possibly contain the desired value.

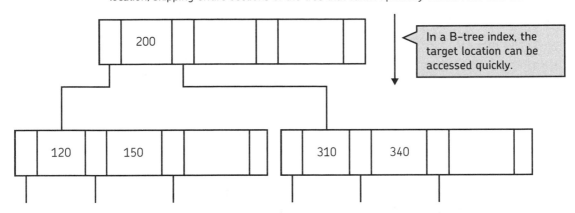

In a B-tree index, the target location can be accessed quickly.

The *hash* index method finds the location of target data by applying a hash function to the key value of the data. The hash acts as a unique fingerprint for a value. The hash index method can perform specific full-match searches, such as a search for *product code 101*. However, it is not designed to search effectively for comparative conditions like *product codes no less than 101* or for fuzzy references like *products with names ending in* n.

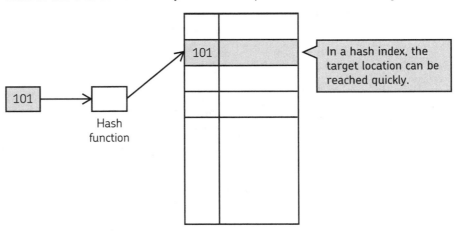

In a hash index, the target location can be reached quickly.

In some cases, using an index may not speed up the search—using an index doesn't save time unless you are looking for only a small portion of the data. Additionally, there are cases where indexes are recreated every time data is updated, resulting in slower processing of an update operation.

QUESTIONS

Try these questions on indexing. The answers are on page 168.

Q15

Which index would be more powerful in a search with an equal sign, a B-tree or hash index?

Q16

Which index would be more powerful in a search with an inequality sign, a B-tree or hash index?

OPTIMIZING A QUERY

When you query a database, the database analyzes the SQL query and considers whether to use an index so it can process the query more quickly. Let's examine the procedure for processing a query.

The database can decide on an optimal order to process a query. Most queries can be processed in several orders with the same results, but with possibly different speeds. For example, suppose there is a query to extract dates of sale and product names for products with a unit price greater than 200G. This query can be seen as consisting of the following steps.

```
SELECT date, product_name
FROM product, sales
WHERE unit_price>=200
AND product.product_code = sales.product_code;
```

1. Join the Product Table and the Sales Table.
2. Select products whose unit price is greater than 200G.
3. Extract columns of dates and product names.

For example, the figure on the left below shows the query processed in order from 1 to 3. The figure on the right shows the query processed in order from 3 to 1. Either way, the queries are equivalent.

SALES TABLE
PRODUCT TABLE
JOIN
SELECTION
PROJECTION

PRODUCT TABLE
SALES TABLE
PROJECTION
PROJECTION
SELECTION
JOIN

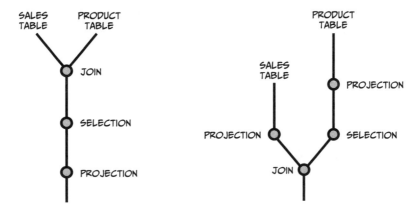

However, when processed from 1 to 3, the same query would generally require a longer processing time, because when the first join is performed, an intermediate table with many rows may be created. On the other hand, the procedure from 3 to 1 requires a shorter processing time, since selection and projection happen first, trimming unwanted data as soon as possible. Thus, the same query may require a different processing time, depending on the order in which projection, selection, and join are performed.

Generally, the database should use the following rules to find the best querying order:

- Execute selection first to reduce the number of rows.
- Execute projection first to reduce the number of columns irrelevant to the result.
- Execute join later.

There are different techniques for executing projection, selection, and join, respectively. For selection, you can use either a full-match search or an index-based search. For join, the following methods are available.

NESTED LOOP

The *nested loop* method compares one row in a table to several rows in another table (see the figure below). For example, one of the values in a row in Table T1 is used to find matching rows in Table T2. If the values are the same, then a joined row is created.

TABLE T1
101
102
103
104
TABLE T2
101
101
102
102
All rows are compared for each row.

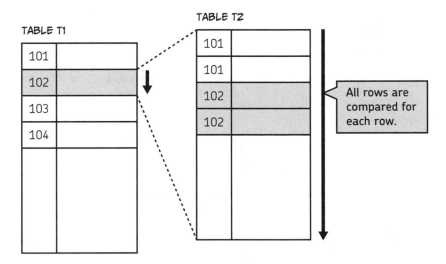

SORT MERGE

The *sort merge* method sorts and then merges rows in multiple tables (see the figure below). First, all or part of Tables T1 and T2 are sorted. Then they are compared starting with the top row, and a joined row is created whenever the same value is found. Since they have already been sorted, processing only needs to be done in one direction, so it will take less time. You should be aware, however, of the time needed for the initial sorting.

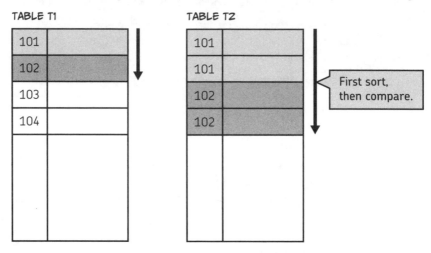

TABLE T1

101	
102	
103	
104	

TABLE T2

101	
101	
102	
102	

First sort, then compare.

HASH

A *hash* divides one of the tables using a hash function and then merges it with a row in another table that has the same hash value. This method effectively selects the row to join.

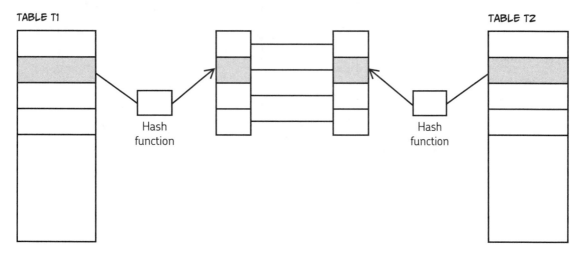

TABLE T1

Hash function

Hash function

TABLE T2

OPTIMIZER

When a query is processed, these different techniques are examined for optimal performance. In a database, the function in charge of optimization of queries is referred to as the *optimizer*. There are two common types.

RULE-BASED PROCESSING

Certain rules are established before any operations are performed. For example, some operations can be combined or reordered in much the same way an algebraic equation can be manipulated and still mean the same thing. The optimizer tries to find the most efficient way to process the query that gives the same results.

COST-BASED PROCESSING

This method tries to estimate the cost of processing the query, based on statistics that the database maintains. Cost-based processing is sometimes more flexible than rule-based processing, but it requires periodical updates of the database's statistics. Managing and analyzing these statistics requires a lot of time.

SUMMARY

- You can set user privileges for a database.
- Locking ensures consistency when a database has multiple users.
- Indexing enables fast searches.
- A database has disaster recovery functions.

ANSWERS

Q1

```
COMMIT;
```

Q2

```
ROLLBACK;
```

Q3 Yes

Q4 No

Q5 No

Q6 No

Q7 Increases

Q8 Decreases

Q9

GRANT SELECT ON product TO Export_Department;

Q10

REVOKE DELETE ON product FROM Overseas_Business_Department;

Q11

	Search	Insert	Update	Delete
Overseas Business Dept.	YES	YES	YES	YES
Merchandise Dept.	NO	YES	NO	YES
Export Dept.	NO	NO	YES	YES

Q12

A rollback is performed since it is not committed at the time of the failure occurrence.

Q13

A roll forward is performed since it has been commited at the time of the failure occurrence.

Q14

No recovery operation is needed since it has been committed at the time of checkpoint.

Q15

Hash

Q16

B-tree

6
DATABASES ARE EVERYWHERE!

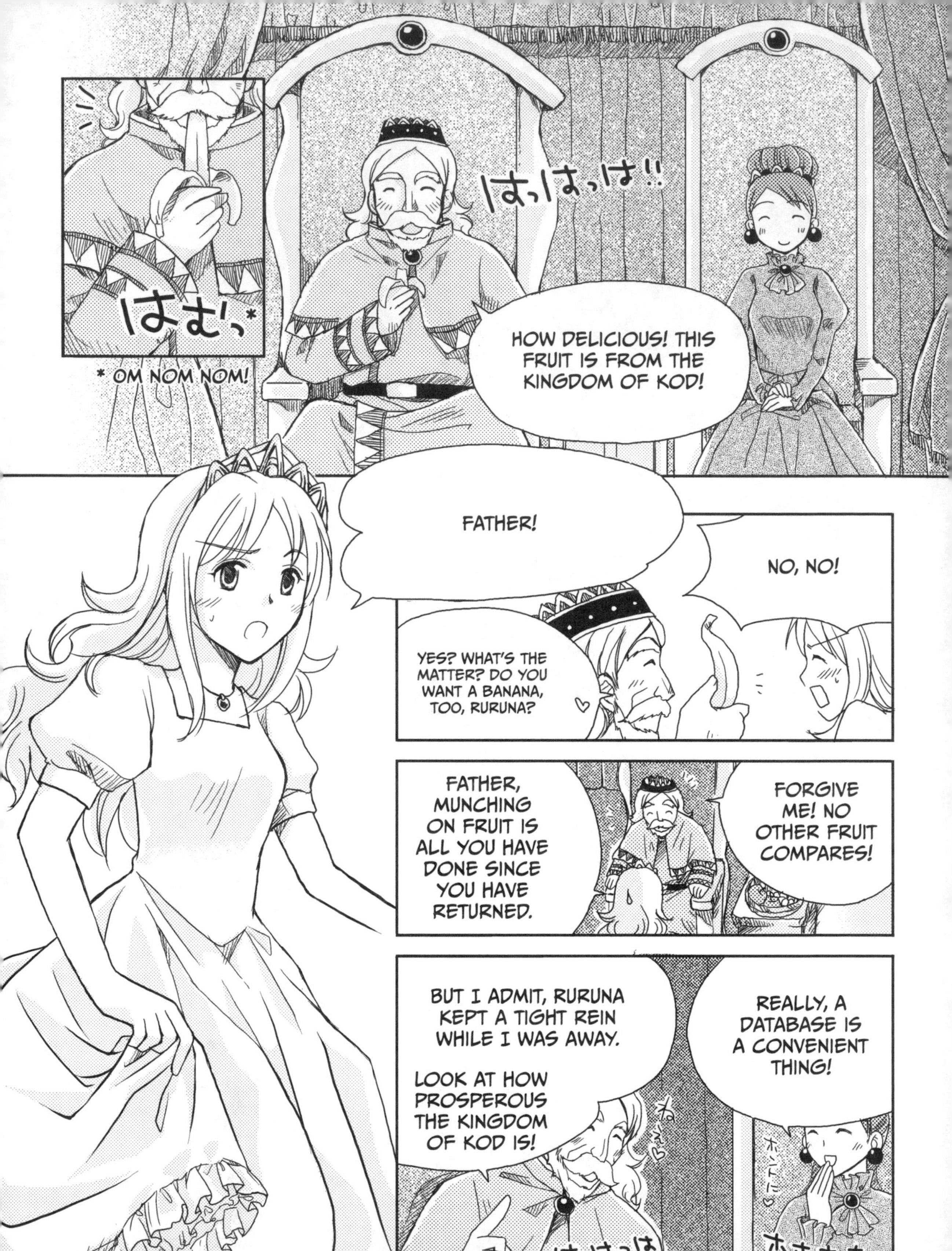
はむっ*
* OM NOM NOM!
はっはっは!!
HOW DELICIOUS! THIS FRUIT IS FROM THE KINGDOM OF KOD!
FATHER!
YES? WHAT'S THE MATTER? DO YOU WANT A BANANA, TOO, RURUNA?
NO, NO!
FATHER, MUNCHING ON FRUIT IS ALL YOU HAVE DONE SINCE YOU HAVE RETURNED.
FORGIVE ME! NO OTHER FRUIT COMPARES!
BUT I ADMIT, RURUNA KEPT A TIGHT REIN WHILE I WAS AWAY.
LOOK AT HOW PROSPEROUS THE KINGDOM OF KOD IS!
ねぇ
はっはっは
REALLY, A DATABASE IS A CONVENIENT THING!
ホントに
ホホホホ

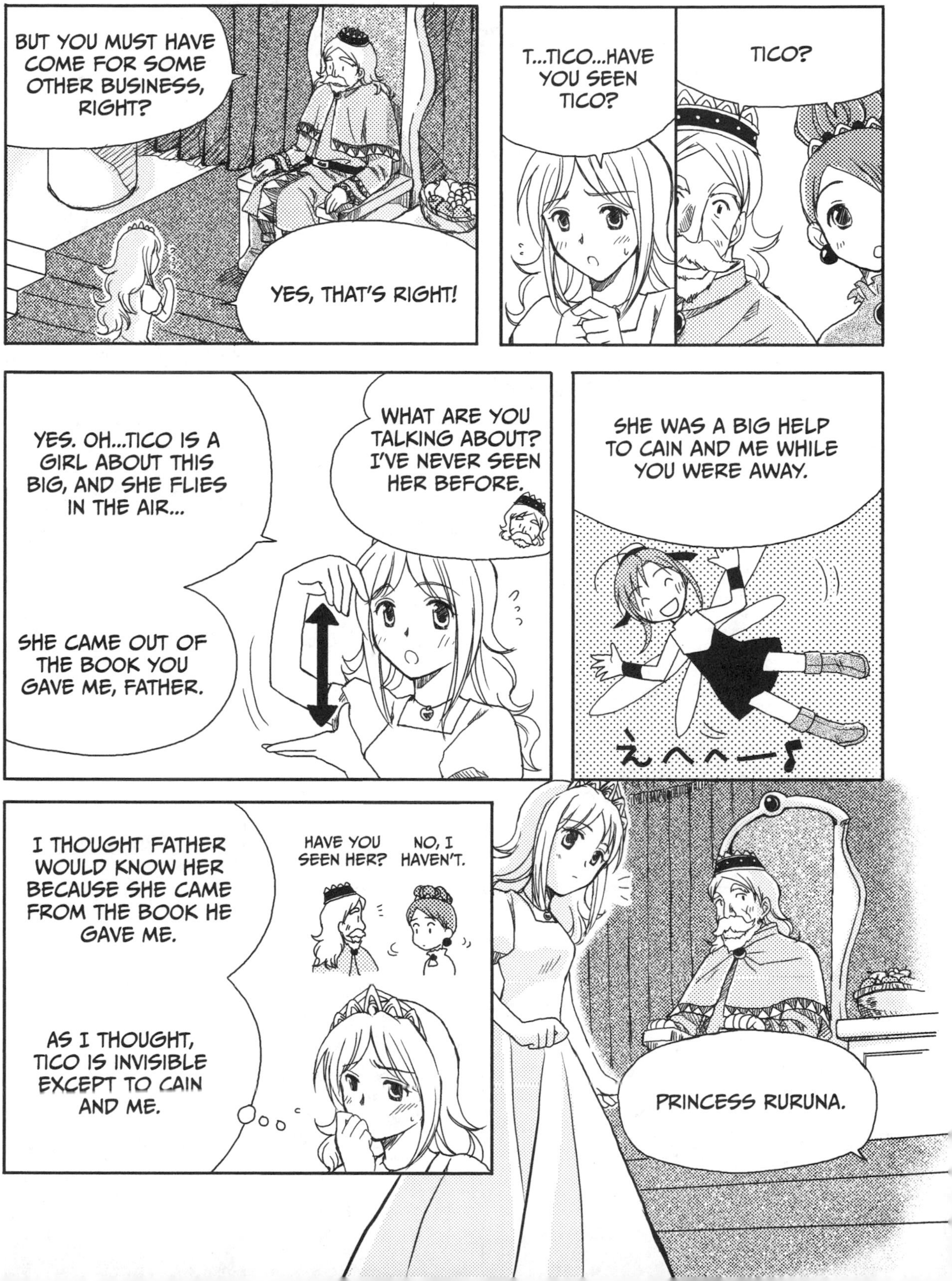
BUT YOU MUST HAVE COME FOR SOME OTHER BUSINESS, RIGHT?
YES, THAT'S RIGHT!
T...TICO...HAVE YOU SEEN TICO?
TICO?
YES. OH...TICO IS A GIRL ABOUT THIS BIG, AND SHE FLIES IN THE AIR...
WHAT ARE YOU TALKING ABOUT? I'VE NEVER SEEN HER BEFORE.
SHE CAME OUT OF THE BOOK YOU GAVE ME, FATHER.
SHE WAS A BIG HELP TO CAIN AND ME WHILE YOU WERE AWAY.
えへへー♪
I THOUGHT FATHER WOULD KNOW HER BECAUSE SHE CAME FROM THE BOOK HE GAVE ME.
HAVE YOU SEEN HER?
NO, I HAVEN'T.
AS I THOUGHT, TICO IS INVISIBLE EXCEPT TO CAIN AND ME.
PRINCESS RURUNA.

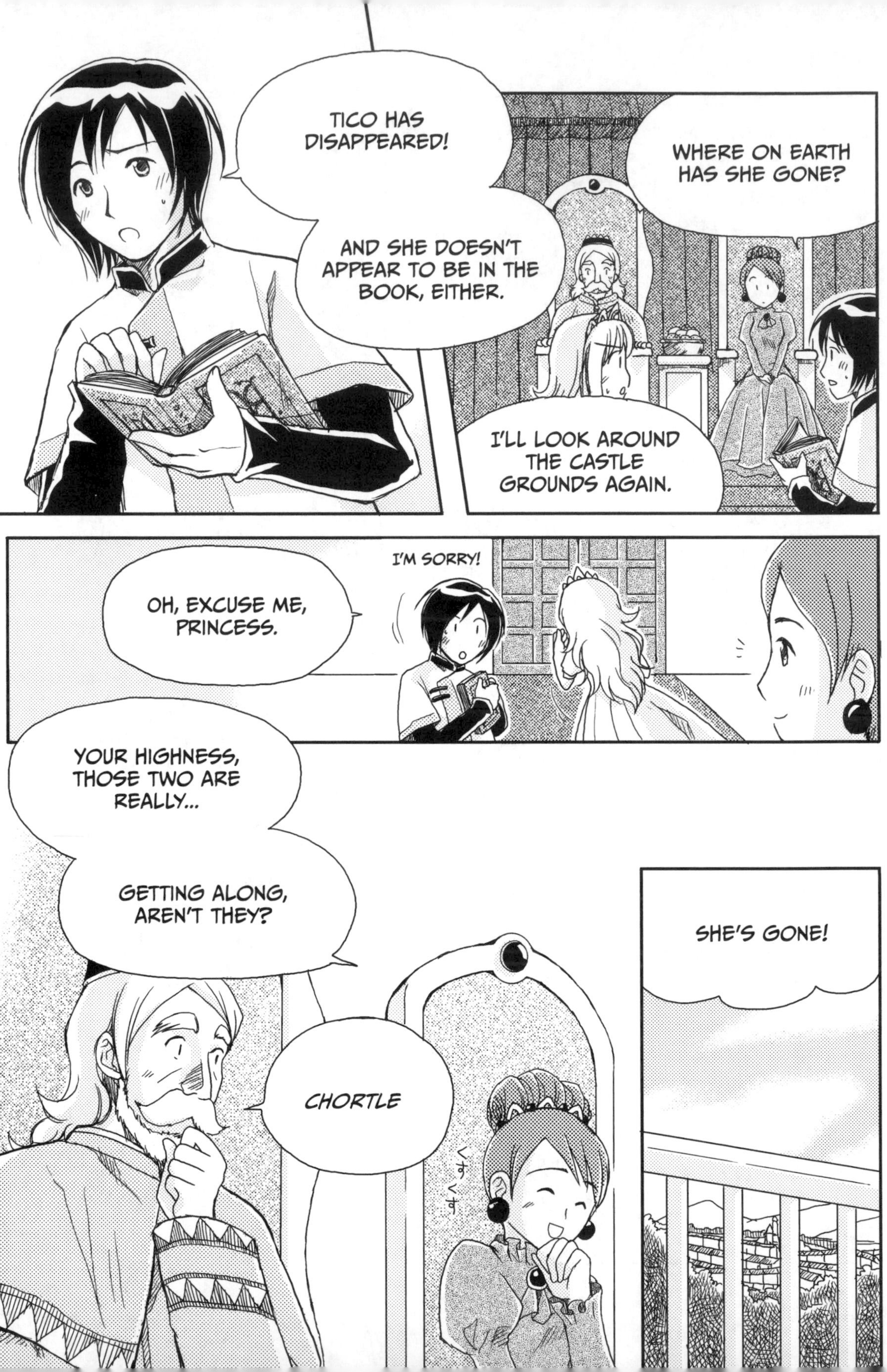
TICO HAS DISAPPEARED!
AND SHE DOESN'T APPEAR TO BE IN THE BOOK, EITHER.
WHERE ON EARTH HAS SHE GONE?
I'LL LOOK AROUND THE CASTLE GROUNDS AGAIN.
OH, EXCUSE ME, PRINCESS.
I'M SORRY!
YOUR HIGHNESS, THOSE TWO ARE REALLY...
GETTING ALONG, AREN'T THEY?
CHORTLE
くすくす
SHE'S GONE!

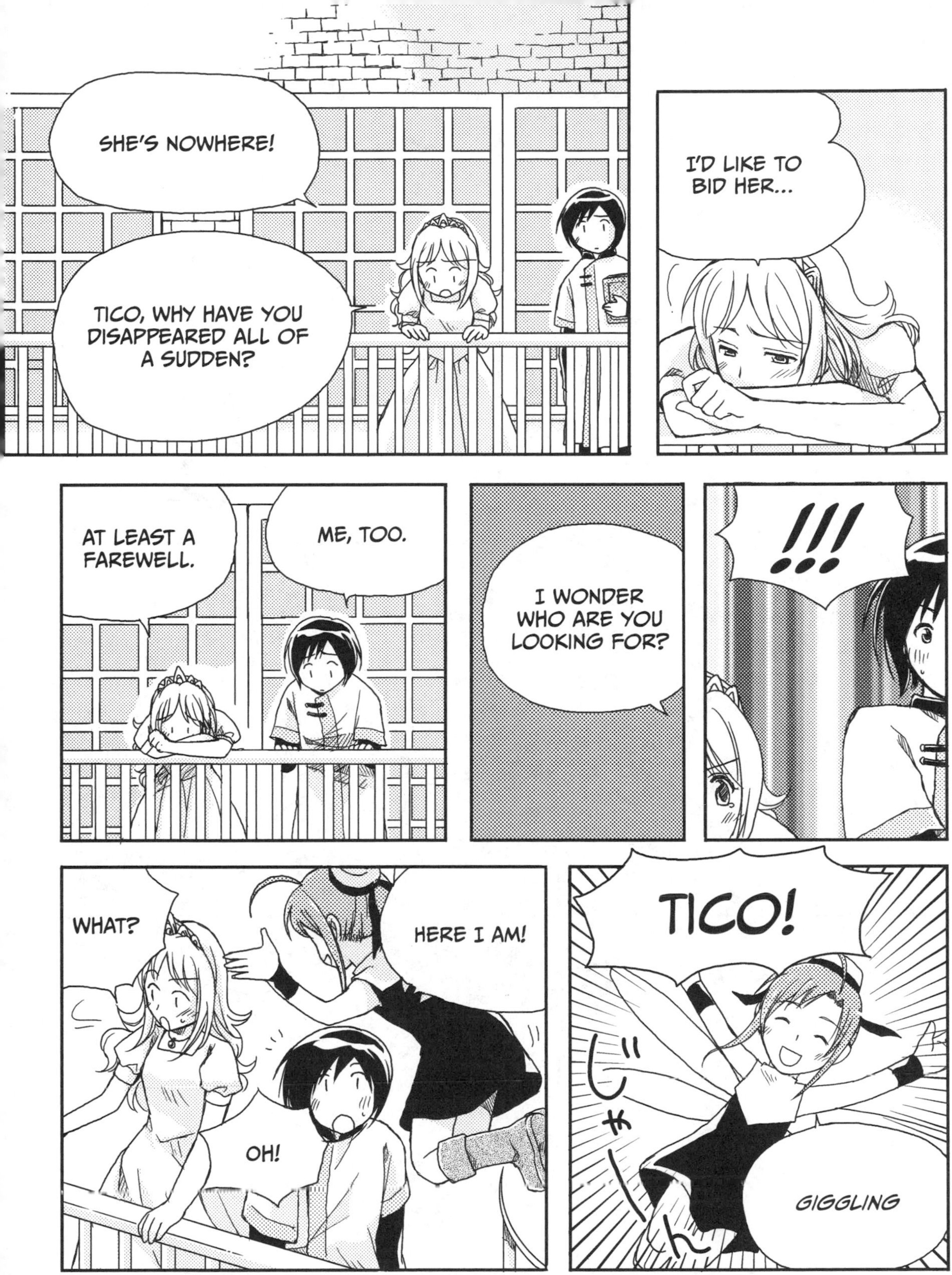
SHE'S NOWHERE!
TICO, WHY HAVE YOU DISAPPEARED ALL OF A SUDDEN?
I'D LIKE TO BID HER...
AT LEAST A FAREWELL.
ME, TOO.
I WONDER WHO ARE YOU LOOKING FOR?
!!!
WHAT?
HERE I AM!
OH!
TICO!
じゃーん
GIGGLING

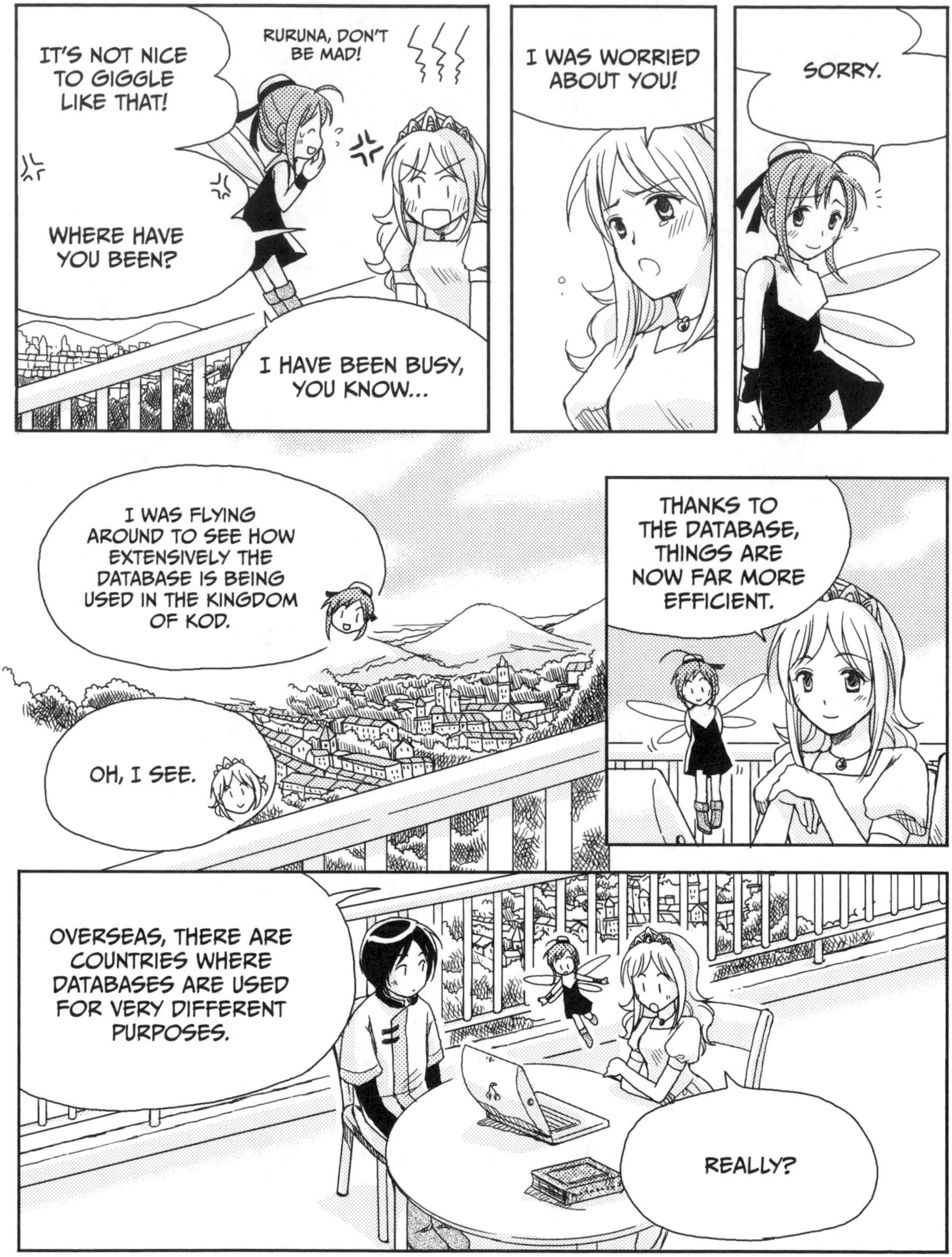

IT'S NOT NICE TO GIGGLE LIKE THAT!
RURUNA, DON'T BE MAD!
WHERE HAVE YOU BEEN?
I HAVE BEEN BUSY, YOU KNOW...
I WAS WORRIED ABOUT YOU!
SORRY.
I WAS FLYING AROUND TO SEE HOW EXTENSIVELY THE DATABASE IS BEING USED IN THE KINGDOM OF KOD.
OH, I SEE.
THANKS TO THE DATABASE, THINGS ARE NOW FAR MORE EFFICIENT.
OVERSEAS, THERE ARE COUNTRIES WHERE DATABASES ARE USED FOR VERY DIFFERENT PURPOSES.
REALLY?

Databases in Use

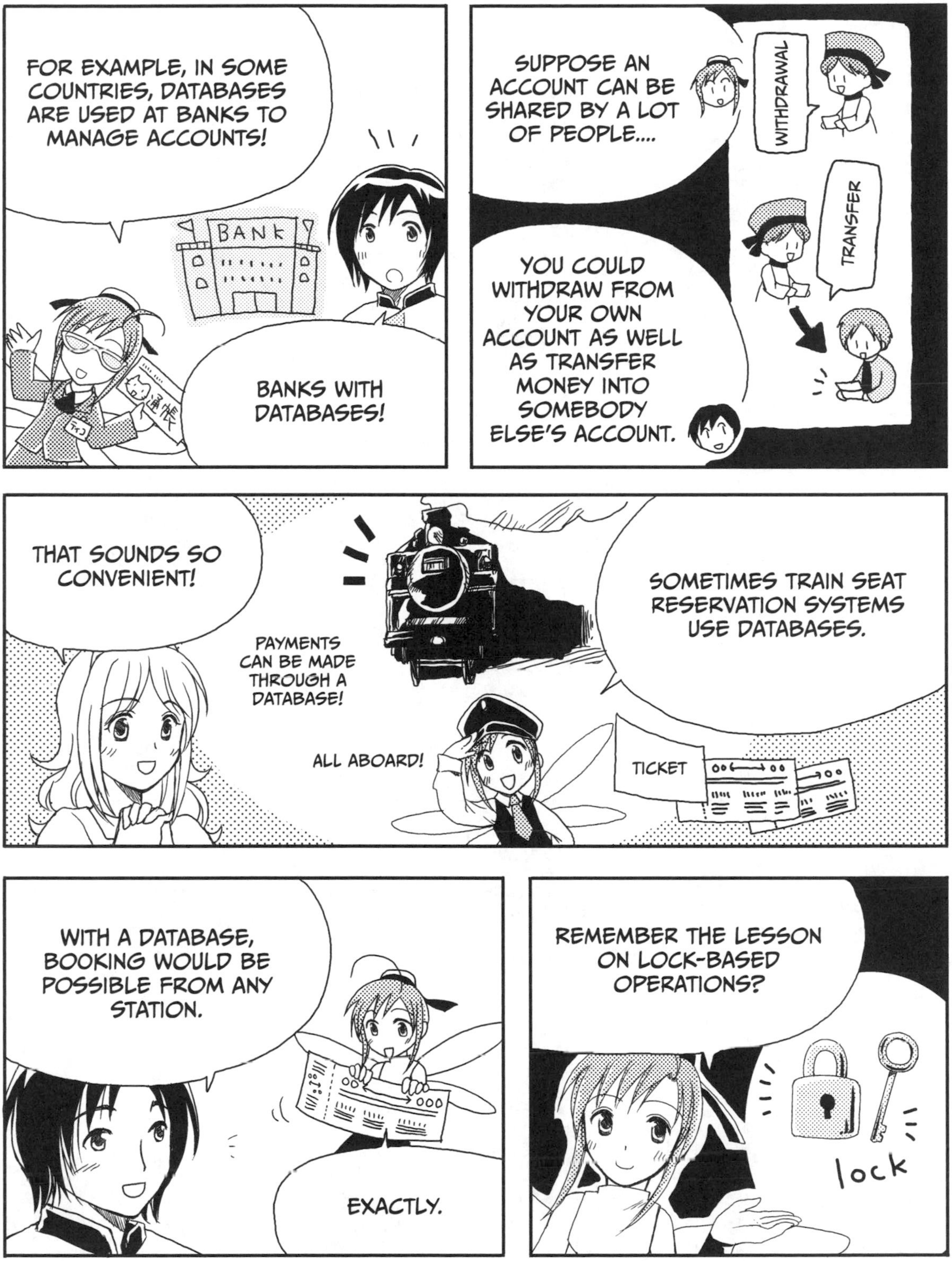

FOR EXAMPLE, IN SOME COUNTRIES, DATABASES ARE USED AT BANKS TO MANAGE ACCOUNTS!
BANK
BANKS WITH DATABASES!
SUPPOSE AN ACCOUNT CAN BE SHARED BY A LOT OF PEOPLE....
WITHDRAWAL
TRANSFER
YOU COULD WITHDRAW FROM YOUR OWN ACCOUNT AS WELL AS TRANSFER MONEY INTO SOMEBODY ELSE'S ACCOUNT.
THAT SOUNDS SO CONVENIENT!
SOMETIMES TRAIN SEAT RESERVATION SYSTEMS USE DATABASES.
PAYMENTS CAN BE MADE THROUGH A DATABASE!
ALL ABOARD!
TICKET
WITH A DATABASE, BOOKING WOULD BE POSSIBLE FROM ANY STATION.
EXACTLY.
REMEMBER THE LESSON ON LOCK-BASED OPERATIONS?
lock

I DO.

THAT'S TRANSACTION CONTROL USING LOCKS, RIGHT?

GOOD OLD ANDY AND BECKY...

YOU'RE RIGHT.

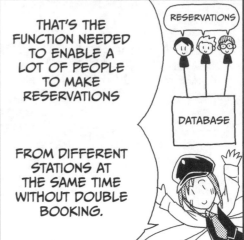

THAT'S THE FUNCTION NEEDED TO ENABLE A LOT OF PEOPLE TO MAKE RESERVATIONS

FROM DIFFERENT STATIONS AT THE SAME TIME WITHOUT DOUBLE BOOKING.

RESERVATIONS

DATABASE

AND SECURITY AND COUNTERMEASURES AGAINST FAILURE ARE ALSO IN PLACE.

DATA-BASE

NO!!

OK!!

MEASURES AGAINST FAILURE

THAT'S RIGHT! BANK DATABASES DEFINITELY NEED THOSE FUNCTIONS.

IT WOULD BE AWFUL IF SOMEONE COULD WITHDRAW MY MONEY AT WILL.

DATABASES ARE ACTIVELY HELPING US EVERYWHERE.

I'D BE FLAT BROKE IF MY ACCOUNT WERE EMPTIED.

YOU CAN SAY THAT AGAIN!

NOT ONLY THAT, DATABASES ARE EVERYWHERE ELSE.

DATABASES AND THE WEB

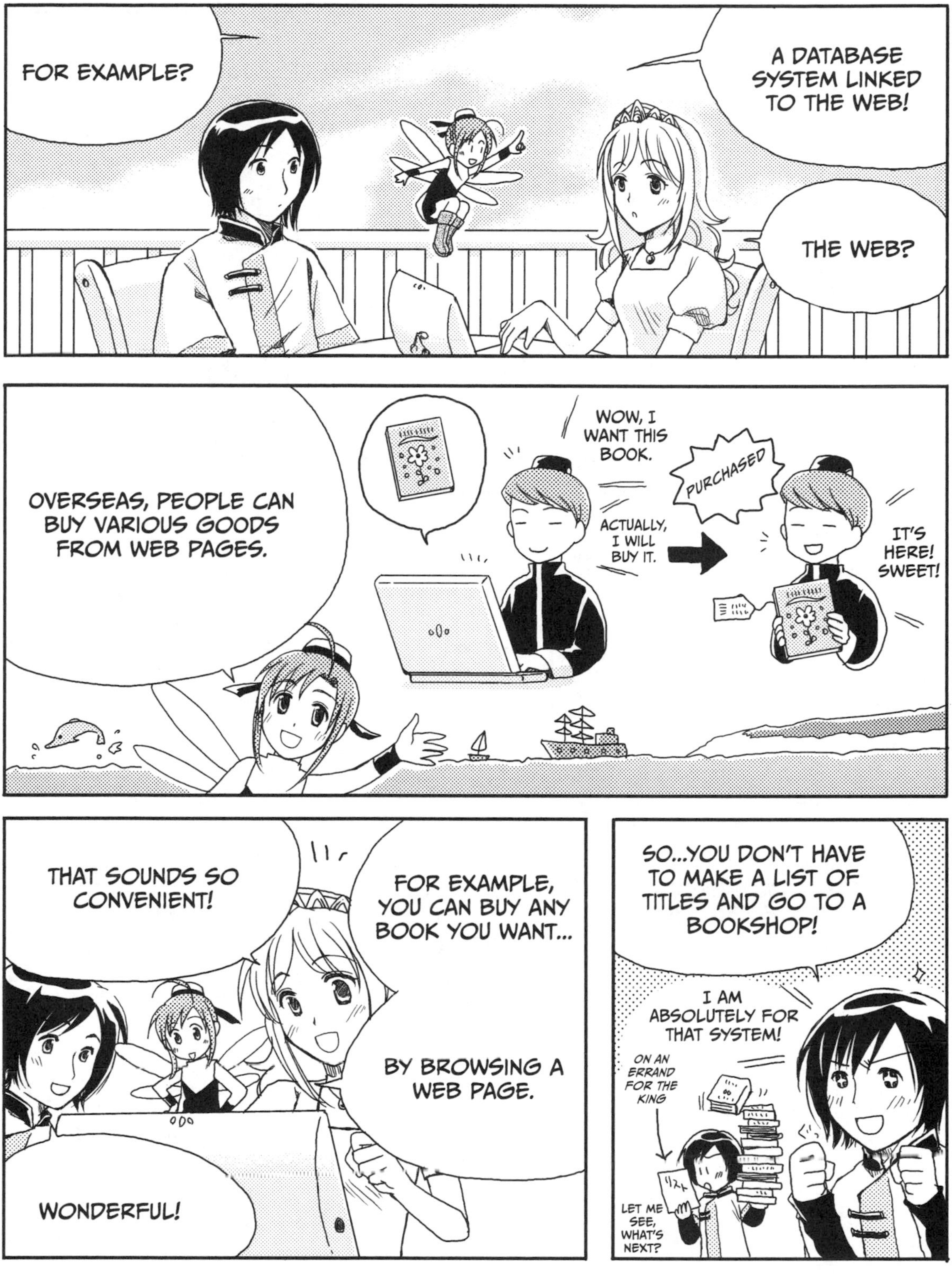
FOR EXAMPLE?
A DATABASE SYSTEM LINKED TO THE WEB!
THE WEB?
OVERSEAS, PEOPLE CAN BUY VARIOUS GOODS FROM WEB PAGES.
WOW, I WANT THIS BOOK.
ACTUALLY, I WILL BUY IT.
PURCHASED
IT'S HERE! SWEET!
THAT SOUNDS SO CONVENIENT!
FOR EXAMPLE, YOU CAN BUY ANY BOOK YOU WANT...
BY BROWSING A WEB PAGE.
WONDERFUL!
SO...YOU DON'T HAVE TO MAKE A LIST OF TITLES AND GO TO A BOOKSHOP!
I AM ABSOLUTELY FOR THAT SYSTEM!
ON AN ERRAND FOR THE KING
リスト
LET ME SEE, WHAT'S NEXT?

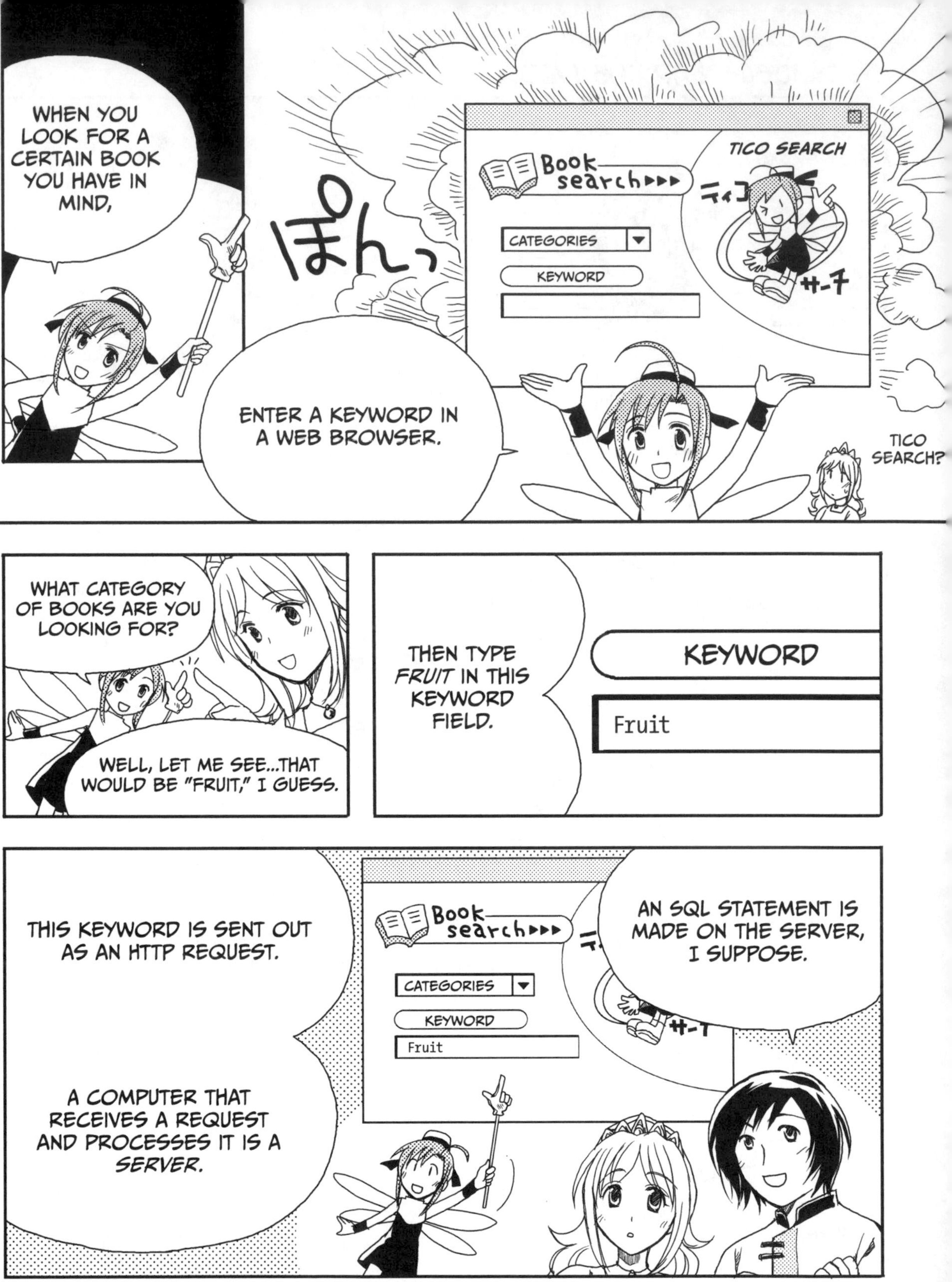

WHEN YOU LOOK FOR A CERTAIN BOOK YOU HAVE IN MIND,
ぽんっ
Book search▸▸▸
TICO SEARCH
ティコ
サーチ
CATEGORIES
KEYWORD
ENTER A KEYWORD IN A WEB BROWSER.
TICO SEARCH?
WHAT CATEGORY OF BOOKS ARE YOU LOOKING FOR?
WELL, LET ME SEE...THAT WOULD BE "FRUIT," I GUESS.
THEN TYPE *FRUIT* IN THIS KEYWORD FIELD.
KEYWORD
Fruit
THIS KEYWORD IS SENT OUT AS AN HTTP REQUEST.
A COMPUTER THAT RECEIVES A REQUEST AND PROCESSES IT IS A *SERVER*.
Book search▸▸▸
CATEGORIES
KEYWORD
Fruit
サーチ
AN SQL STATEMENT IS MADE ON THE SERVER, I SUPPOSE.

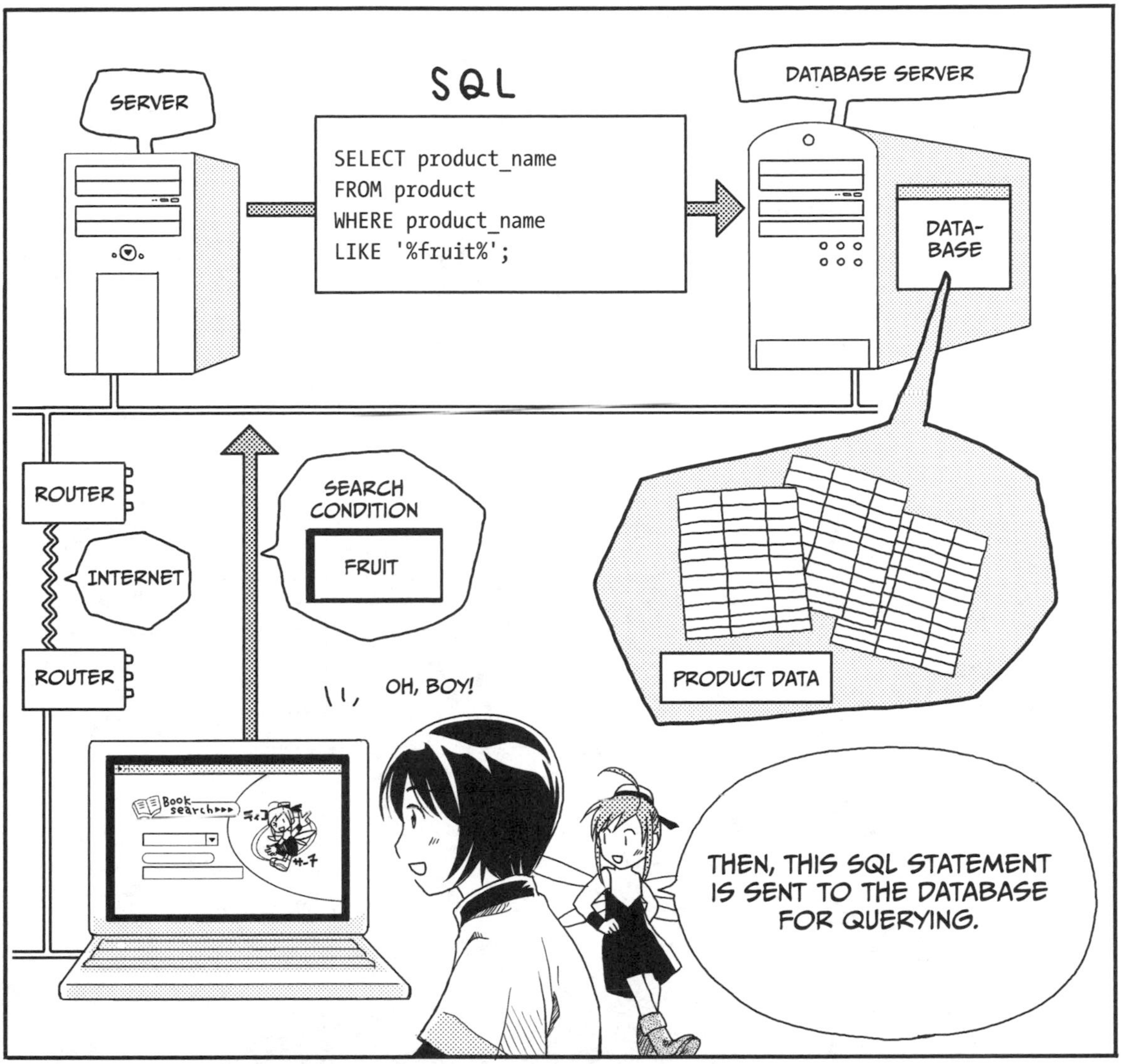
SERVER
SQL
SELECT product_name
FROM product
WHERE product_name
LIKE '%fruit%';
DATABASE SERVER
DATA-
BASE
ROUTER
SEARCH
CONDITION
FRUIT
INTERNET
PRODUCT DATA
ROUTER
OH, BOY!
Book
search
THEN, THIS SQL STATEMENT IS SENT TO THE DATABASE FOR QUERYING.

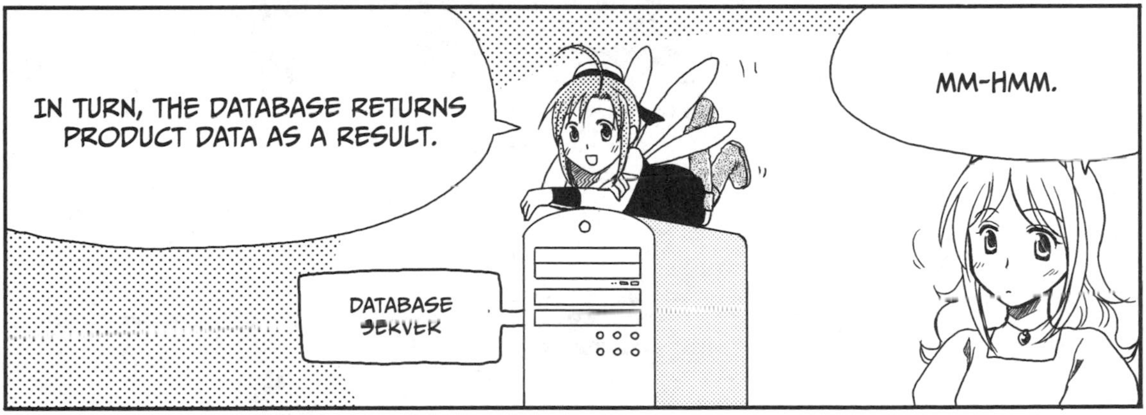
IN TURN, THE DATABASE RETURNS PRODUCT DATA AS A RESULT.
MM-HMM.
DATABASE
SERVER

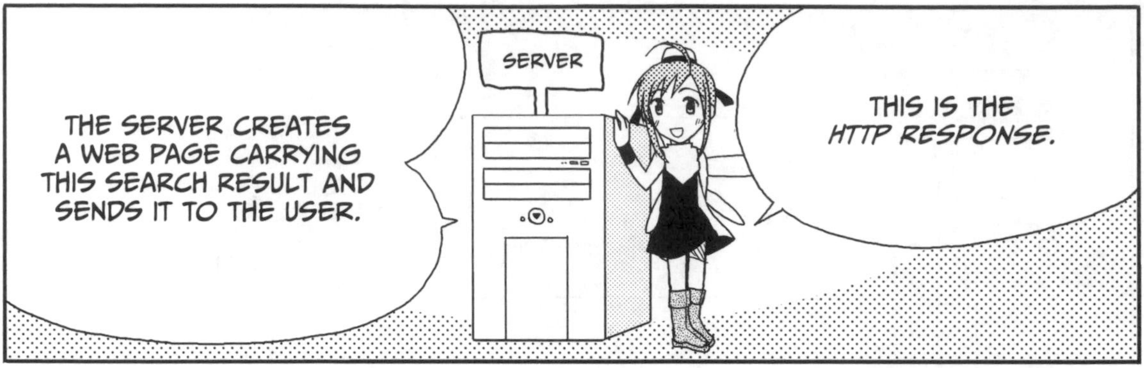
THE SERVER CREATES A WEB PAGE CARRYING THIS SEARCH RESULT AND SENDS IT TO THE USER.
SERVER
THIS IS THE *HTTP RESPONSE.*

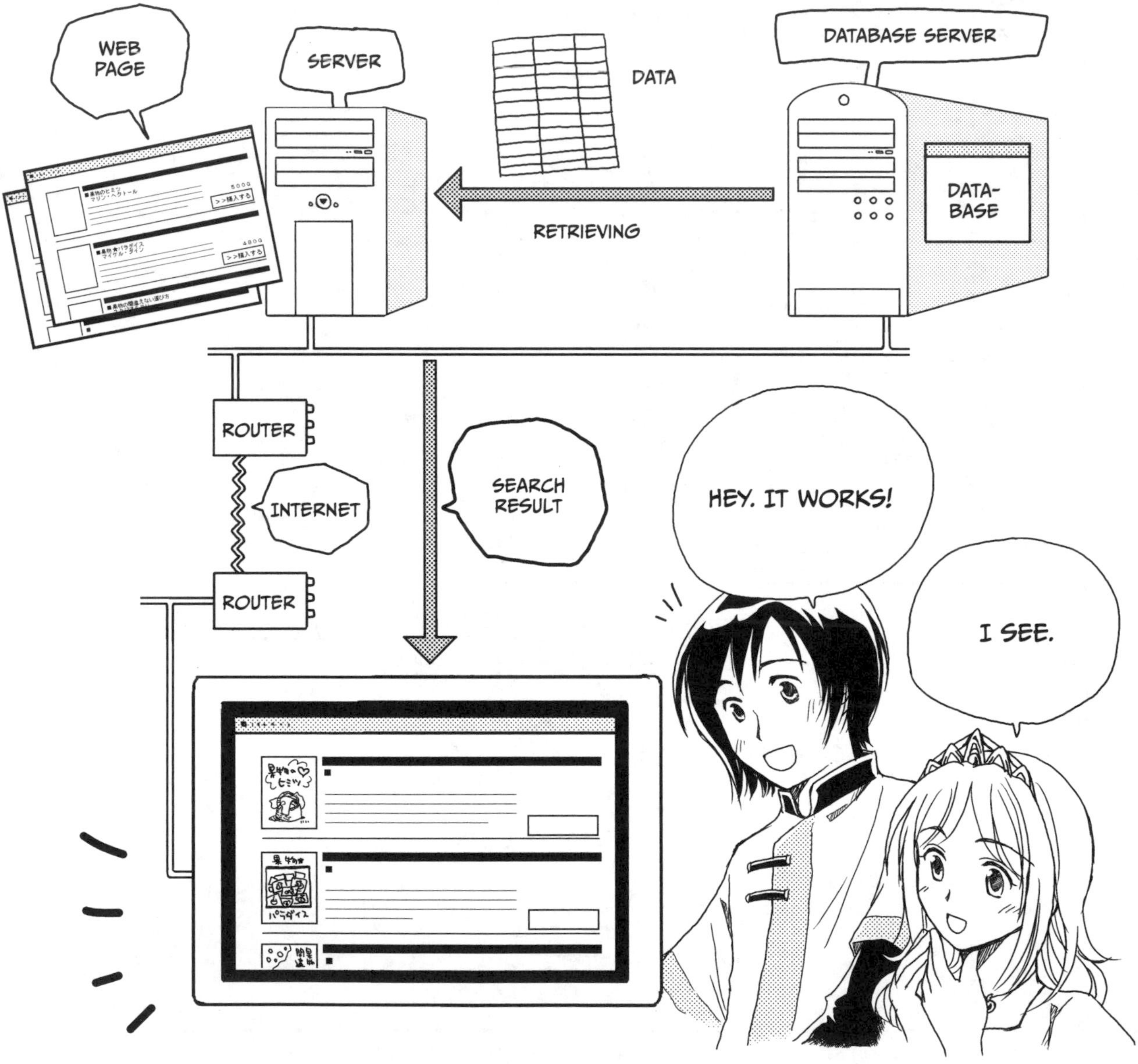
WEB PAGE
SERVER
DATA
DATABASE SERVER
DATA-BASE
RETRIEVING
ROUTER
INTERNET
ROUTER
SEARCH RESULT
HEY. IT WORKS!
I SEE.

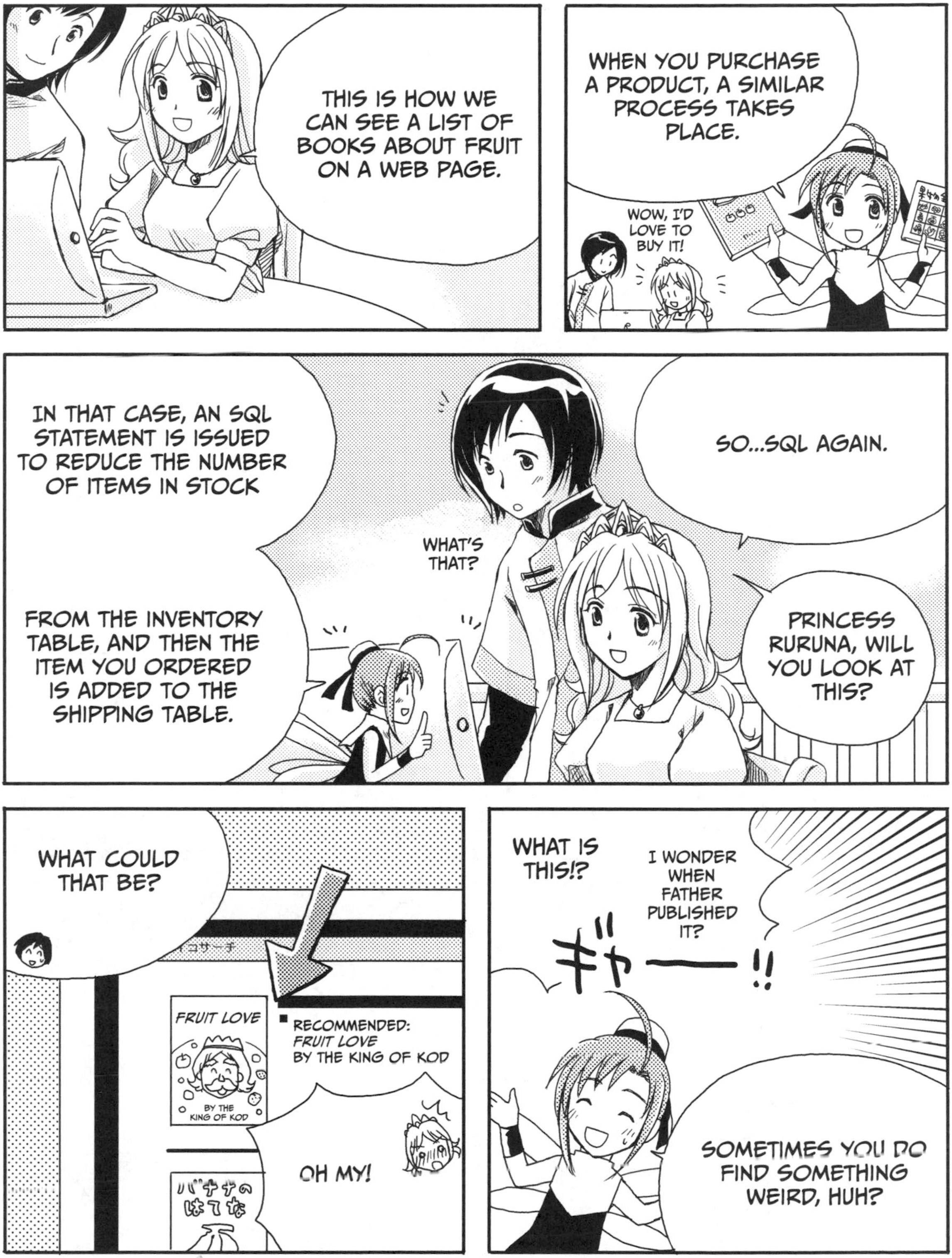
THIS IS HOW WE CAN SEE A LIST OF BOOKS ABOUT FRUIT ON A WEB PAGE.
WHEN YOU PURCHASE A PRODUCT, A SIMILAR PROCESS TAKES PLACE.
WOW, I'D LOVE TO BUY IT!
IN THAT CASE, AN SQL STATEMENT IS ISSUED TO REDUCE THE NUMBER OF ITEMS IN STOCK
SO...SQL AGAIN.
WHAT'S THAT?
FROM THE INVENTORY TABLE, AND THEN THE ITEM YOU ORDERED IS ADDED TO THE SHIPPING TABLE.
PRINCESS RURUNA, WILL YOU LOOK AT THIS?
WHAT COULD THAT BE?
FRUIT LOVE
BY THE KING OF KOD
RECOMMENDED: *FRUIT LOVE* BY THE KING OF KOD
OH MY!
バナナのはてな
WHAT IS THIS!?
I WONDER WHEN FATHER PUBLISHED IT?
ギャーー!!
SOMETIMES YOU DO FIND SOMETHING WEIRD, HUH?

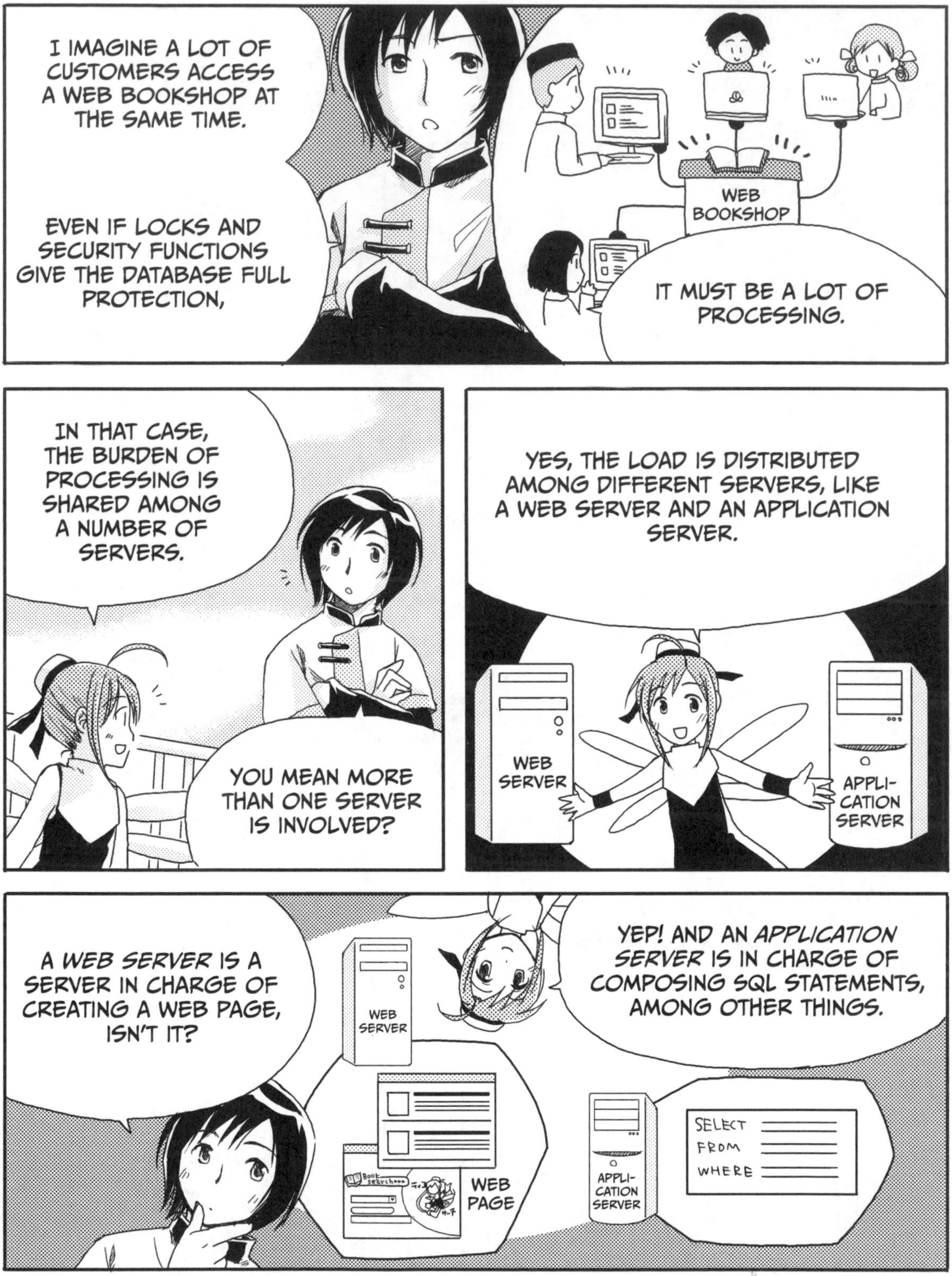
I IMAGINE A LOT OF CUSTOMERS ACCESS A WEB BOOKSHOP AT THE SAME TIME.
EVEN IF LOCKS AND SECURITY FUNCTIONS GIVE THE DATABASE FULL PROTECTION,
WEB BOOKSHOP
IT MUST BE A LOT OF PROCESSING.
IN THAT CASE, THE BURDEN OF PROCESSING IS SHARED AMONG A NUMBER OF SERVERS.
YOU MEAN MORE THAN ONE SERVER IS INVOLVED?
YES, THE LOAD IS DISTRIBUTED AMONG DIFFERENT SERVERS, LIKE A WEB SERVER AND AN APPLICATION SERVER.
WEB SERVER
APPLI-CATION SERVER
A *WEB SERVER* IS A SERVER IN CHARGE OF CREATING A WEB PAGE, ISN'T IT?
WEB SERVER
YEP! AND AN *APPLICATION SERVER* IS IN CHARGE OF COMPOSING SQL STATEMENTS, AMONG OTHER THINGS.
WEB PAGE
APPLI-CATION SERVER
SELECT
FROM
WHERE

DISTRIBUTED DATABASES

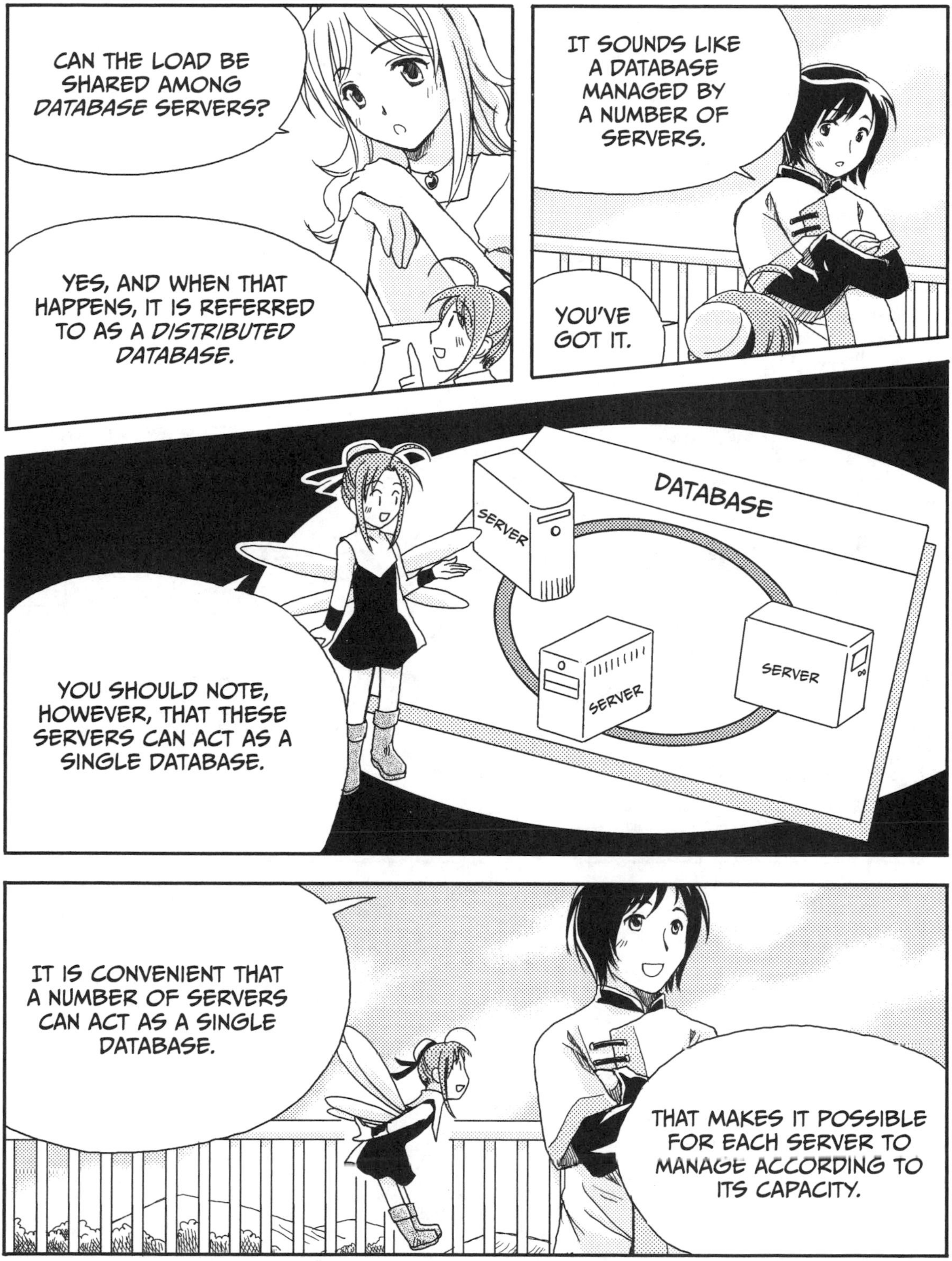
CAN THE LOAD BE SHARED AMONG *DATABASE SERVERS*?
YES, AND WHEN THAT HAPPENS, IT IS REFERRED TO AS A *DISTRIBUTED DATABASE*.
IT SOUNDS LIKE A DATABASE MANAGED BY A NUMBER OF SERVERS.
YOU'VE GOT IT.
DATABASE
SERVER
SERVER
SERVER
YOU SHOULD NOTE, HOWEVER, THAT THESE SERVERS CAN ACT AS A SINGLE DATABASE.
IT IS CONVENIENT THAT A NUMBER OF SERVERS CAN ACT AS A SINGLE DATABASE.
THAT MAKES IT POSSIBLE FOR EACH SERVER TO MANAGE ACCORDING TO ITS CAPACITY.

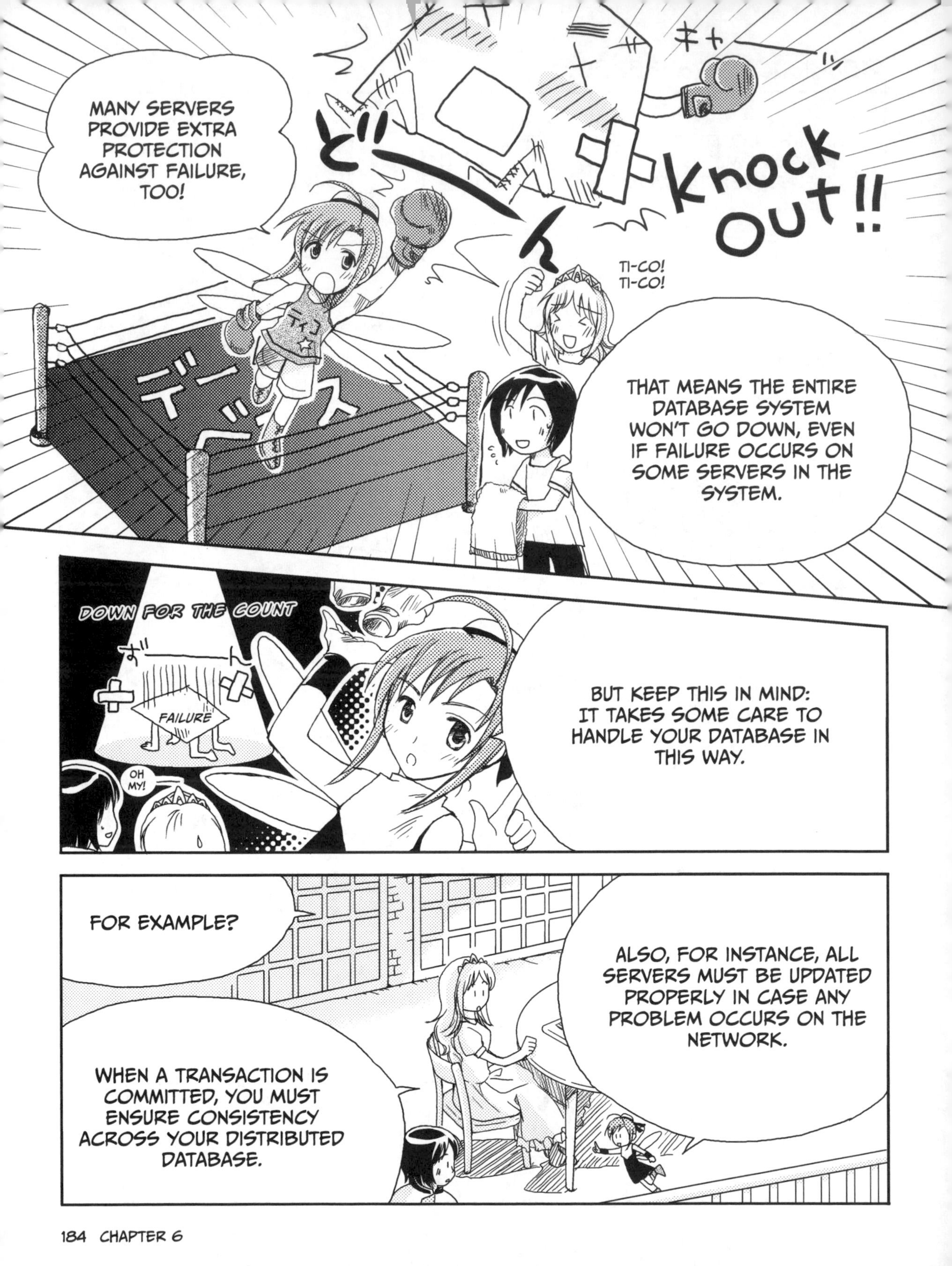
MANY SERVERS PROVIDE EXTRA PROTECTION AGAINST FAILURE, TOO!
Knock Out!!
TI-CO! TI-CO!
THAT MEANS THE ENTIRE DATABASE SYSTEM WON'T GO DOWN, EVEN IF FAILURE OCCURS ON SOME SERVERS IN THE SYSTEM.
DOWN FOR THE COUNT
FAILURE
OH MY!
BUT KEEP THIS IN MIND: IT TAKES SOME CARE TO HANDLE YOUR DATABASE IN THIS WAY.
FOR EXAMPLE?
WHEN A TRANSACTION IS COMMITTED, YOU MUST ENSURE CONSISTENCY ACROSS YOUR DISTRIBUTED DATABASE.
ALSO, FOR INSTANCE, ALL SERVERS MUST BE UPDATED PROPERLY IN CASE ANY PROBLEM OCCURS ON THE NETWORK.

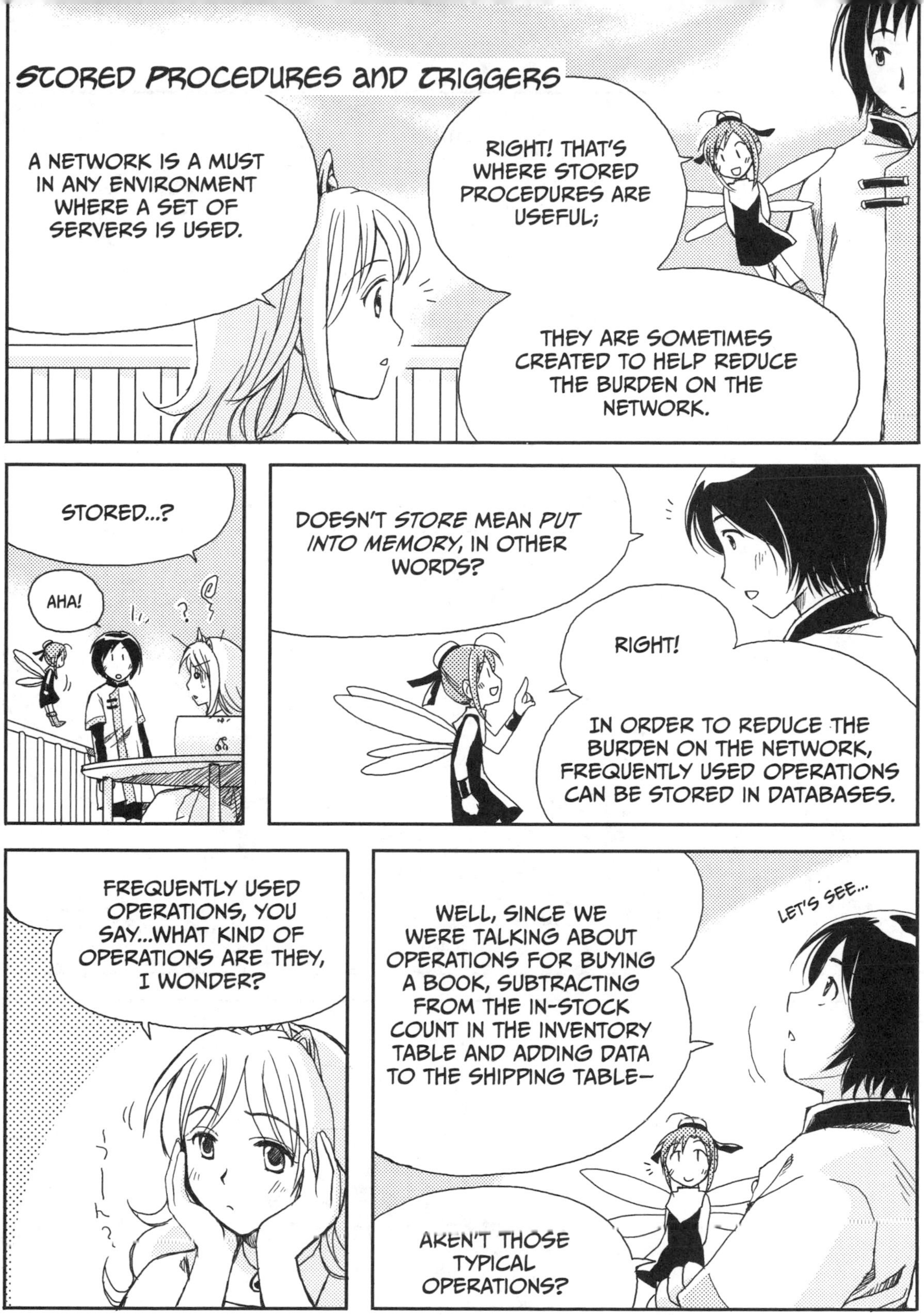
STORED PROCEDURES AND TRIGGERS
A NETWORK IS A MUST IN ANY ENVIRONMENT WHERE A SET OF SERVERS IS USED.
RIGHT! THAT'S WHERE STORED PROCEDURES ARE USEFUL;
THEY ARE SOMETIMES CREATED TO HELP REDUCE THE BURDEN ON THE NETWORK.
STORED...?
AHA!
DOESN'T *STORE* MEAN *PUT INTO MEMORY*, IN OTHER WORDS?
RIGHT!
IN ORDER TO REDUCE THE BURDEN ON THE NETWORK, FREQUENTLY USED OPERATIONS CAN BE STORED IN DATABASES.
FREQUENTLY USED OPERATIONS, YOU SAY...WHAT KIND OF OPERATIONS ARE THEY, I WONDER?
LET'S SEE...
WELL, SINCE WE WERE TALKING ABOUT OPERATIONS FOR BUYING A BOOK, SUBTRACTING FROM THE IN-STOCK COUNT IN THE INVENTORY TABLE AND ADDING DATA TO THE SHIPPING TABLE—
AREN'T THOSE TYPICAL OPERATIONS?

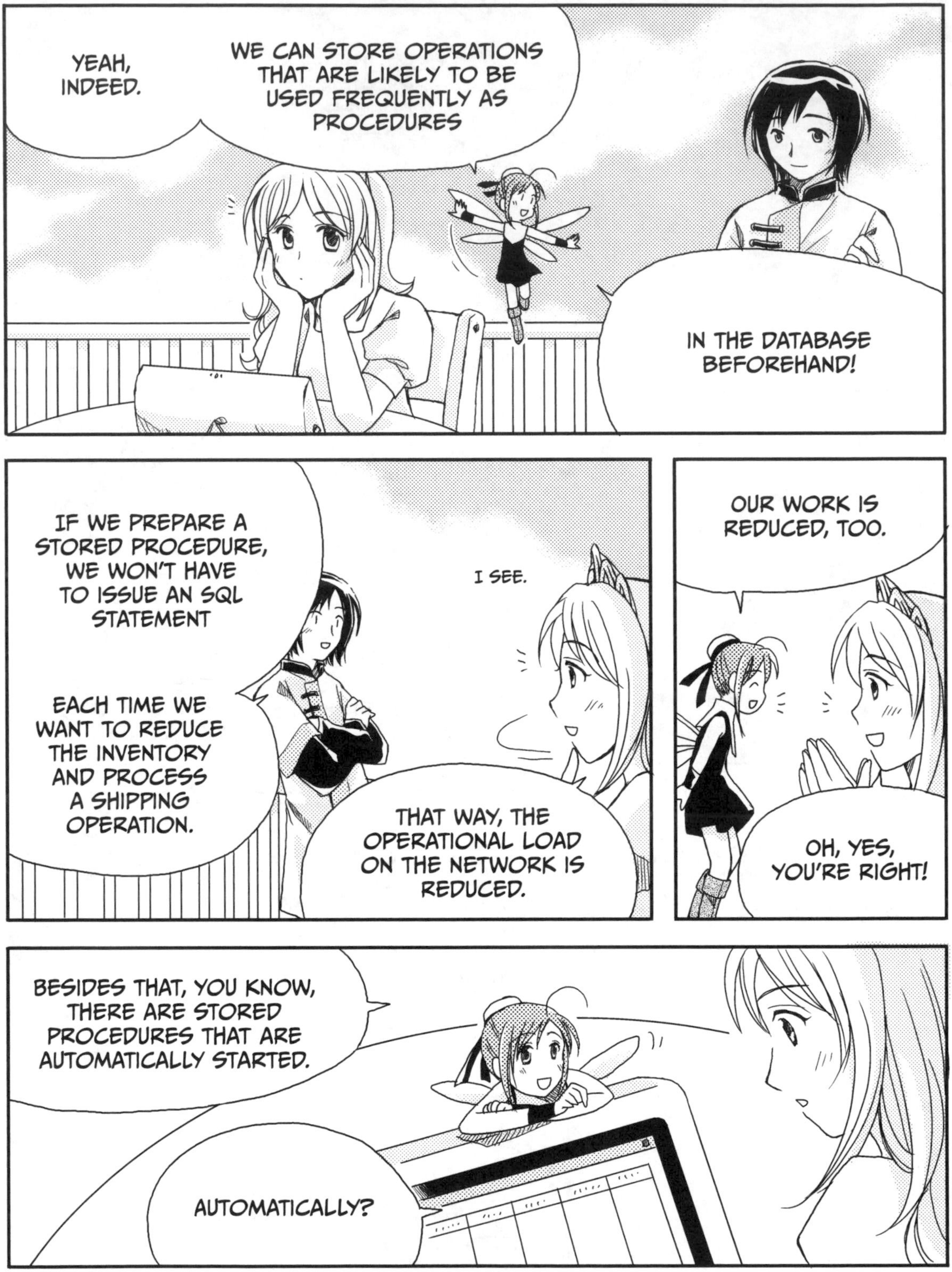
YEAH, INDEED.
WE CAN STORE OPERATIONS THAT ARE LIKELY TO BE USED FREQUENTLY AS PROCEDURES
IN THE DATABASE BEFOREHAND!
IF WE PREPARE A STORED PROCEDURE, WE WON'T HAVE TO ISSUE AN SQL STATEMENT
EACH TIME WE WANT TO REDUCE THE INVENTORY AND PROCESS A SHIPPING OPERATION.
I SEE.
THAT WAY, THE OPERATIONAL LOAD ON THE NETWORK IS REDUCED.
OUR WORK IS REDUCED, TOO.
OH, YES, YOU'RE RIGHT!
BESIDES THAT, YOU KNOW, THERE ARE STORED PROCEDURES THAT ARE AUTOMATICALLY STARTED.
AUTOMATICALLY?

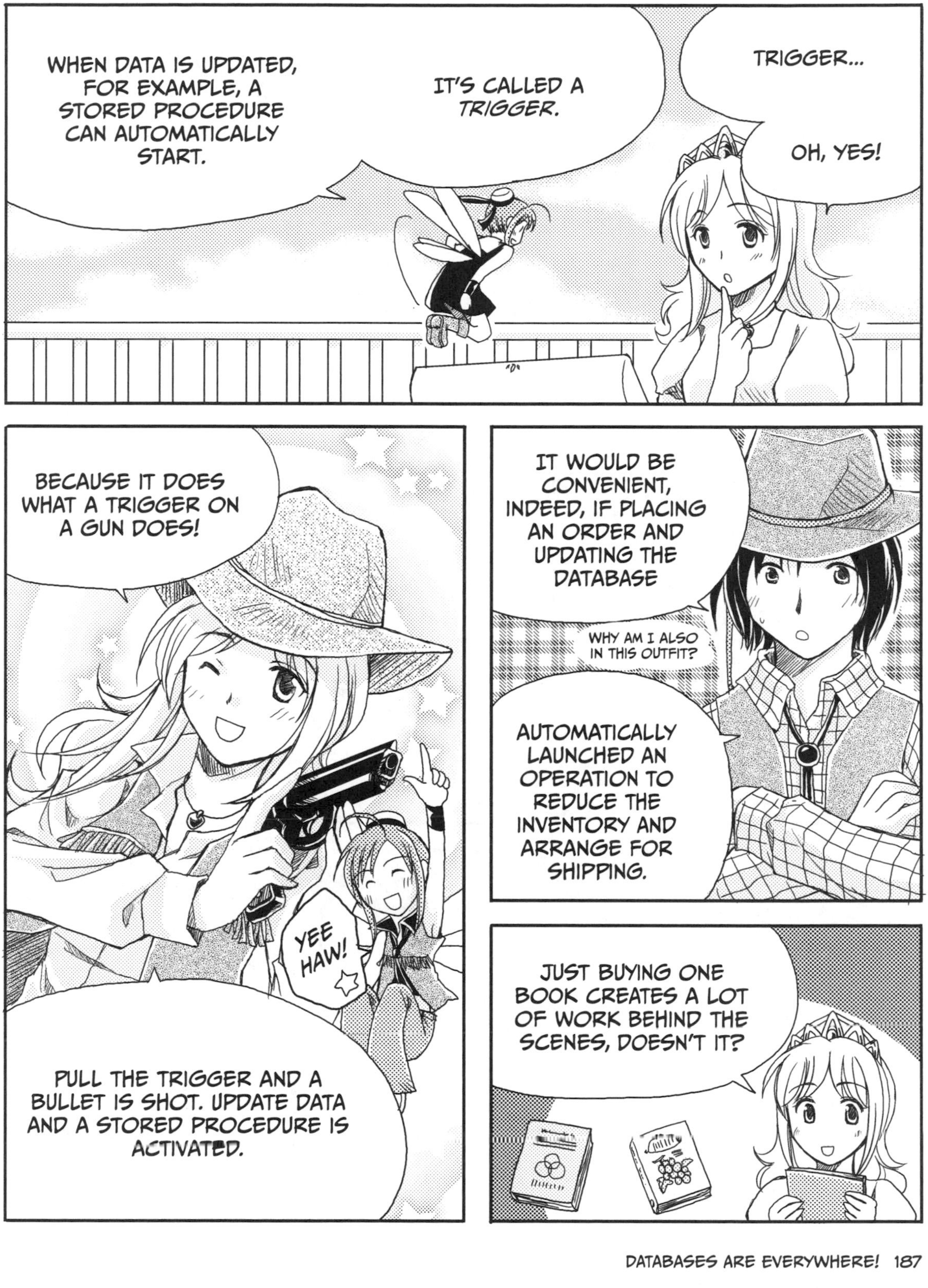
WHEN DATA IS UPDATED, FOR EXAMPLE, A STORED PROCEDURE CAN AUTOMATICALLY START.
IT'S CALLED A *TRIGGER*.
TRIGGER...
OH, YES!
BECAUSE IT DOES WHAT A TRIGGER ON A GUN DOES!
YEE HAW!
PULL THE TRIGGER AND A BULLET IS SHOT. UPDATE DATA AND A STORED PROCEDURE IS ACTIVATED.
IT WOULD BE CONVENIENT, INDEED, IF PLACING AN ORDER AND UPDATING THE DATABASE
WHY AM I ALSO IN THIS OUTFIT?
AUTOMATICALLY LAUNCHED AN OPERATION TO REDUCE THE INVENTORY AND ARRANGE FOR SHIPPING.
JUST BUYING ONE BOOK CREATES A LOT OF WORK BEHIND THE SCENES, DOESN'T IT?

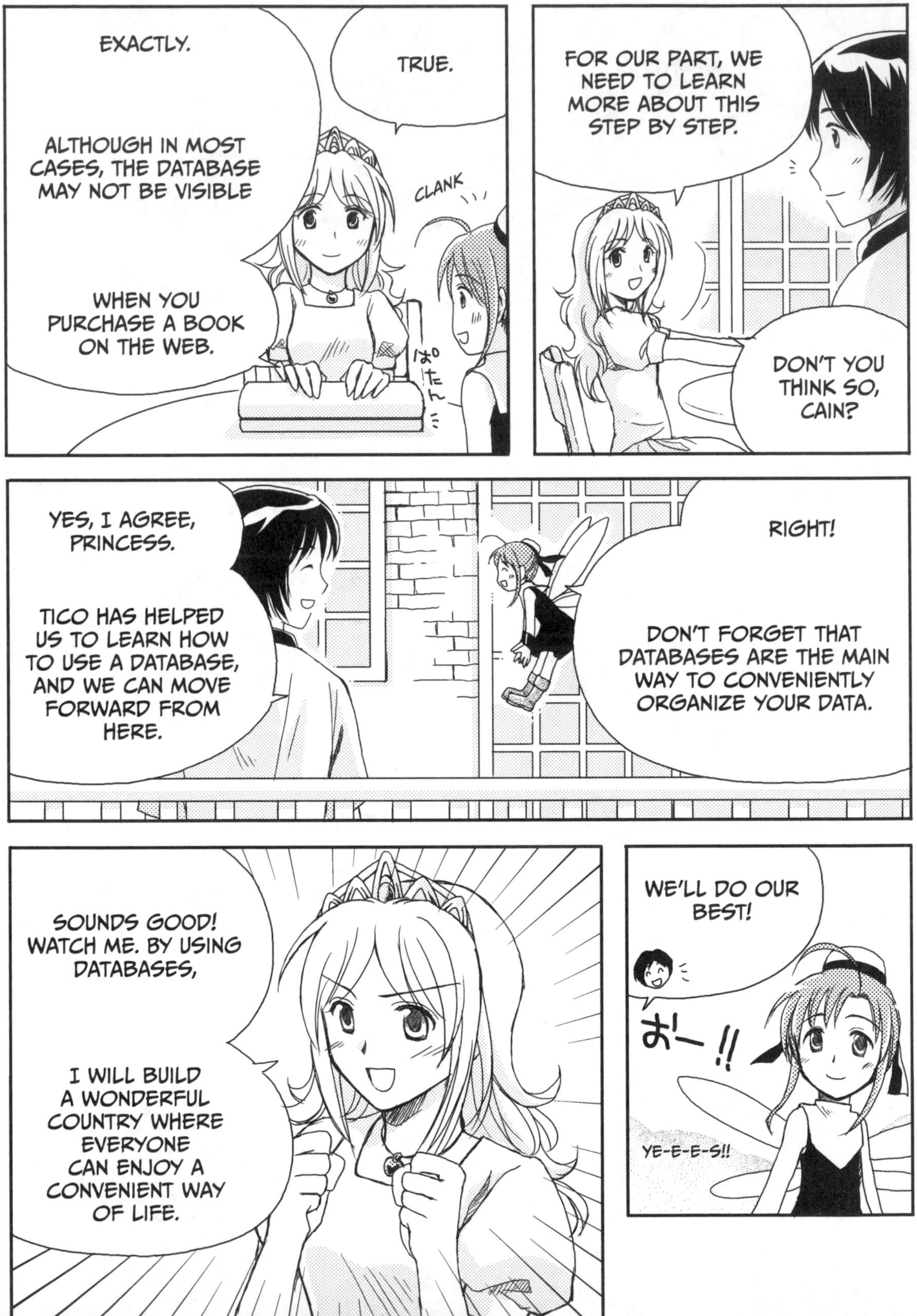
EXACTLY.
TRUE.
ALTHOUGH IN MOST CASES, THE DATABASE MAY NOT BE VISIBLE
CLANK
WHEN YOU PURCHASE A BOOK ON THE WEB.
ぱたん
FOR OUR PART, WE NEED TO LEARN MORE ABOUT THIS STEP BY STEP.
DON'T YOU THINK SO, CAIN?
YES, I AGREE, PRINCESS.
TICO HAS HELPED US TO LEARN HOW TO USE A DATABASE, AND WE CAN MOVE FORWARD FROM HERE.
RIGHT!
DON'T FORGET THAT DATABASES ARE THE MAIN WAY TO CONVENIENTLY ORGANIZE YOUR DATA.
SOUNDS GOOD! WATCH ME. BY USING DATABASES,
I WILL BUILD A WONDERFUL COUNTRY WHERE EVERYONE CAN ENJOY A CONVENIENT WAY OF LIFE.
WE'LL DO OUR BEST!
おー!!
YE-E-E-S!!

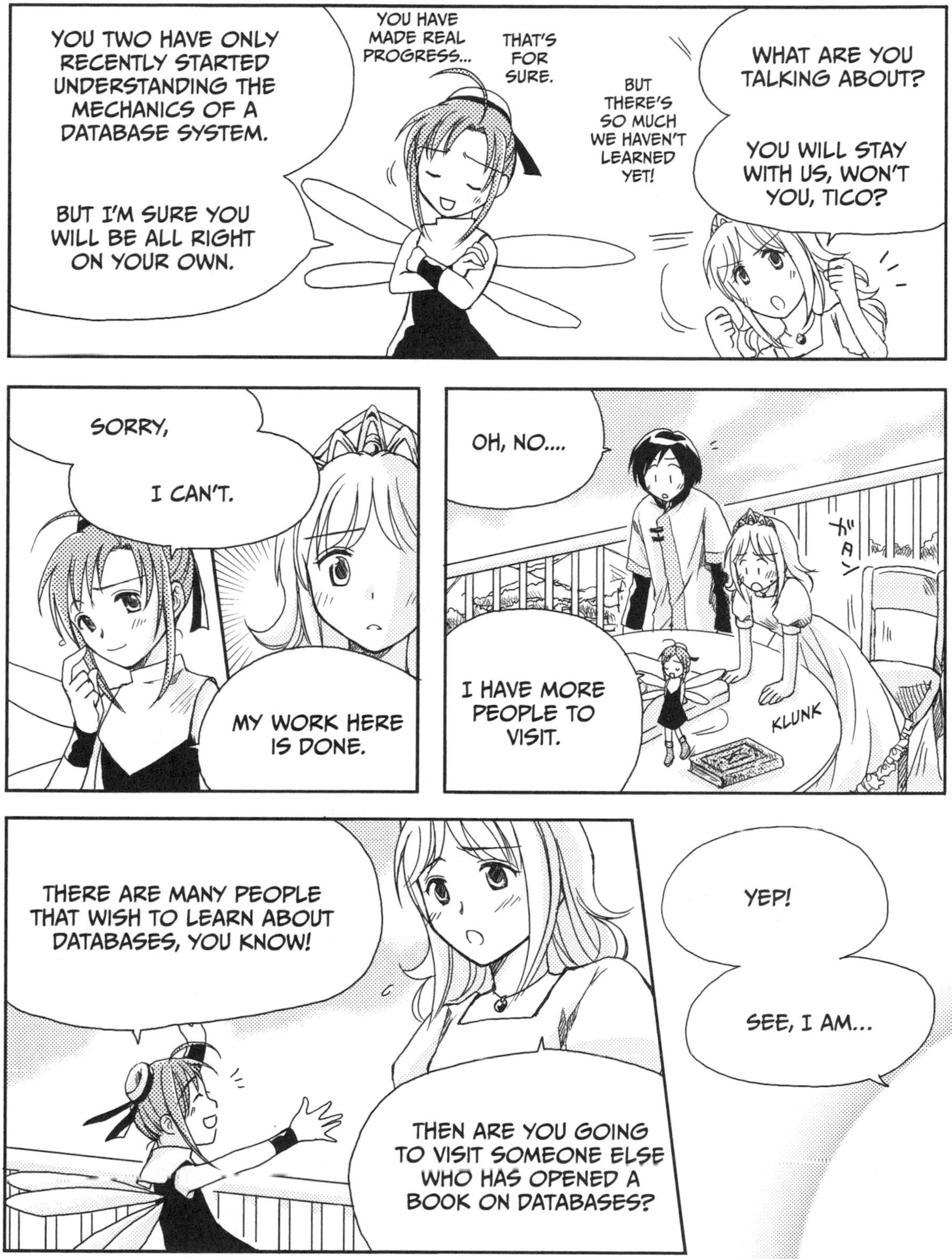
YOU TWO HAVE ONLY RECENTLY STARTED UNDERSTANDING THE MECHANICS OF A DATABASE SYSTEM.
BUT I'M SURE YOU WILL BE ALL RIGHT ON YOUR OWN.
YOU HAVE MADE REAL PROGRESS...
THAT'S FOR SURE.
BUT THERE'S SO MUCH WE HAVEN'T LEARNED YET!
WHAT ARE YOU TALKING ABOUT?
YOU WILL STAY WITH US, WON'T YOU, TICO?
SORRY,
I CAN'T.
MY WORK HERE IS DONE.
OH, NO....
ガタン
I HAVE MORE PEOPLE TO VISIT.
KLUNK
THERE ARE MANY PEOPLE THAT WISH TO LEARN ABOUT DATABASES, YOU KNOW!
THEN ARE YOU GOING TO VISIT SOMEONE ELSE WHO HAS OPENED A BOOK ON DATABASES?
YEP!
SEE, I AM...

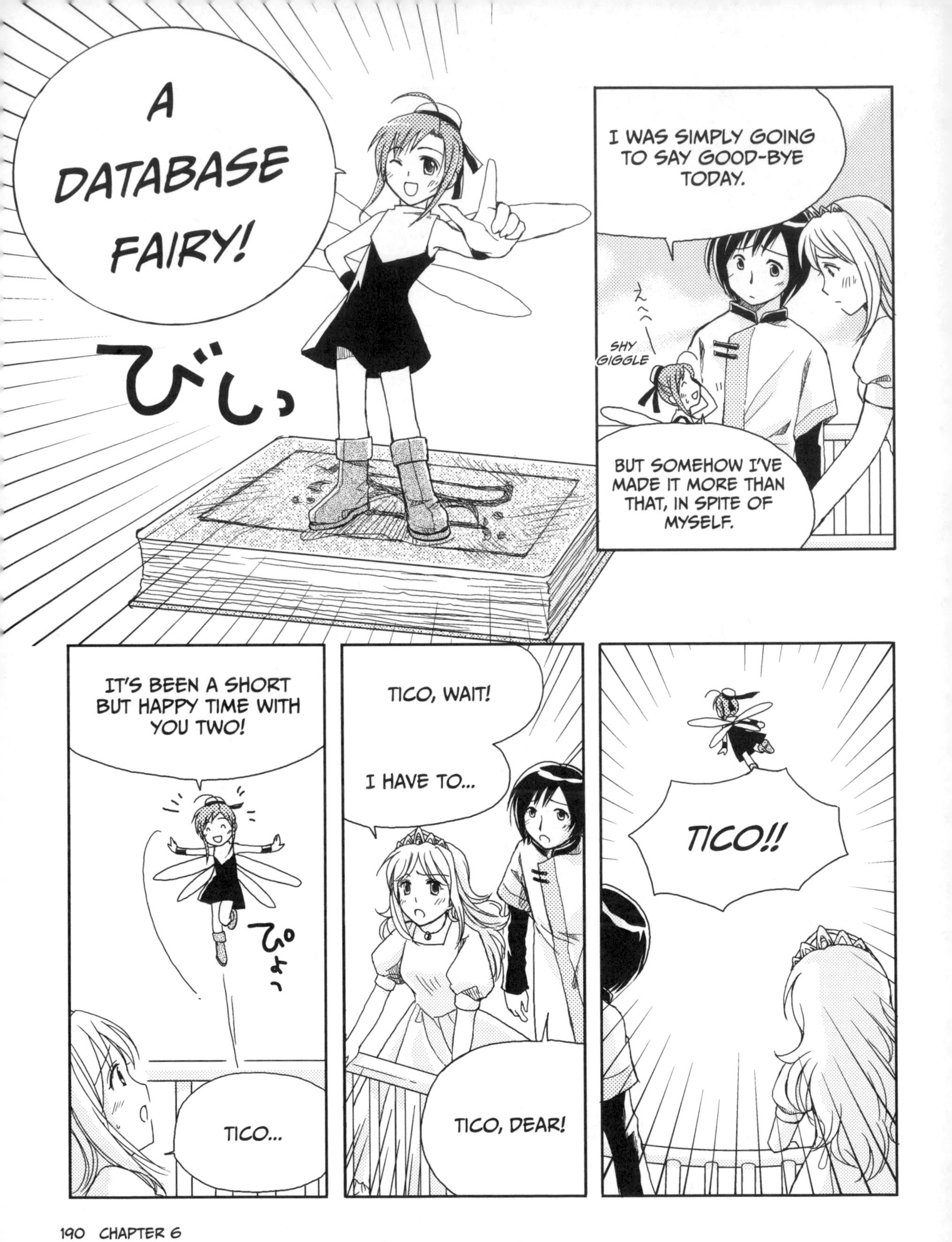
A DATABASE FAIRY!
びしっ
I WAS SIMPLY GOING TO SAY GOOD-BYE TODAY.
えへへ
SHY GIGGLE
BUT SOMEHOW I'VE MADE IT MORE THAN THAT, IN SPITE OF MYSELF.
IT'S BEEN A SHORT BUT HAPPY TIME WITH YOU TWO!
ぴょっ
TICO...
TICO, WAIT!
I HAVE TO...
TICO, DEAR!
TICO!!

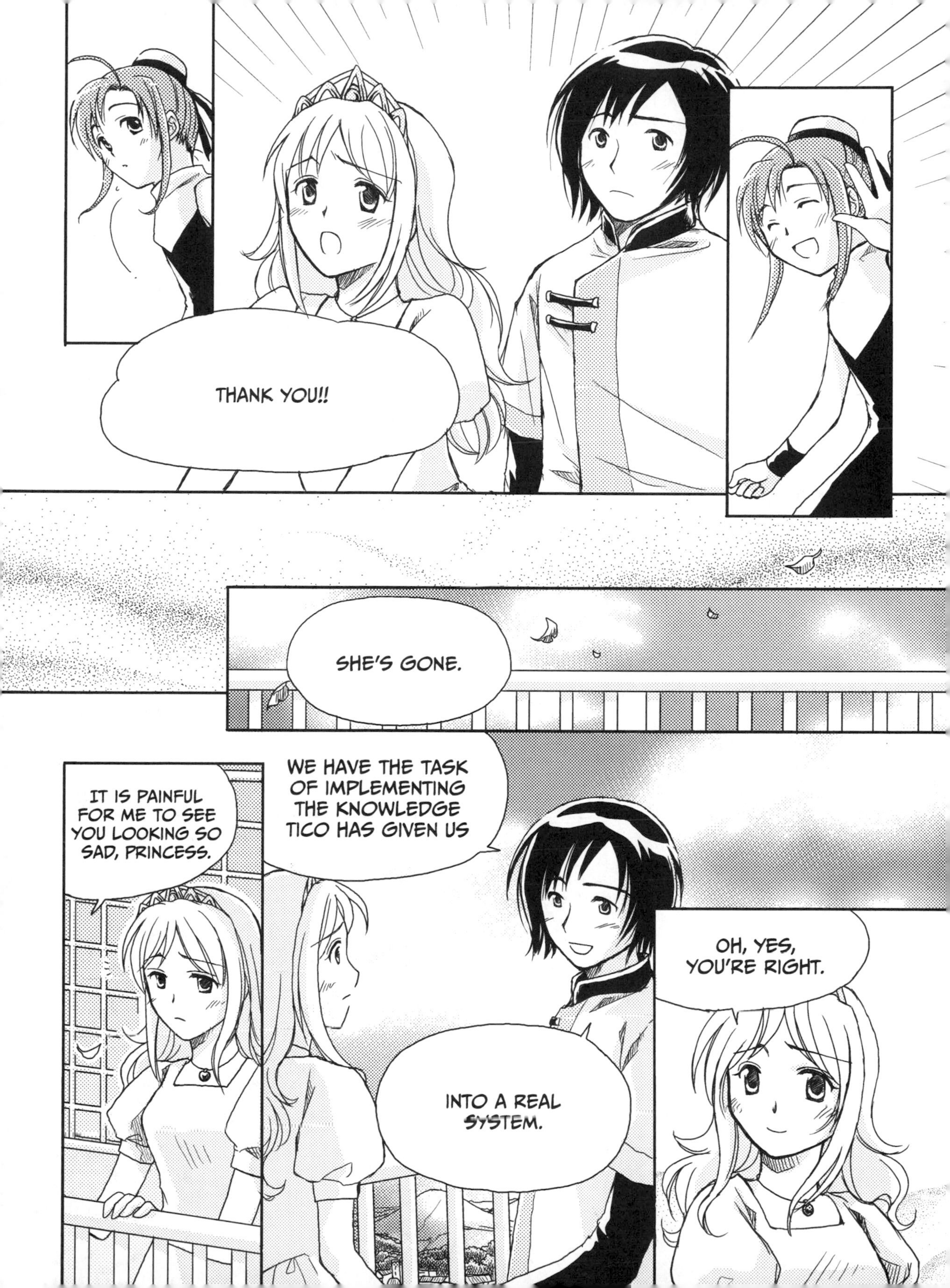
THANK YOU!!
SHE'S GONE.
IT IS PAINFUL FOR ME TO SEE YOU LOOKING SO SAD, PRINCESS.
WE HAVE THE TASK OF IMPLEMENTING THE KNOWLEDGE TICO HAS GIVEN US
INTO A REAL SYSTEM.
OH, YES, YOU'RE RIGHT.

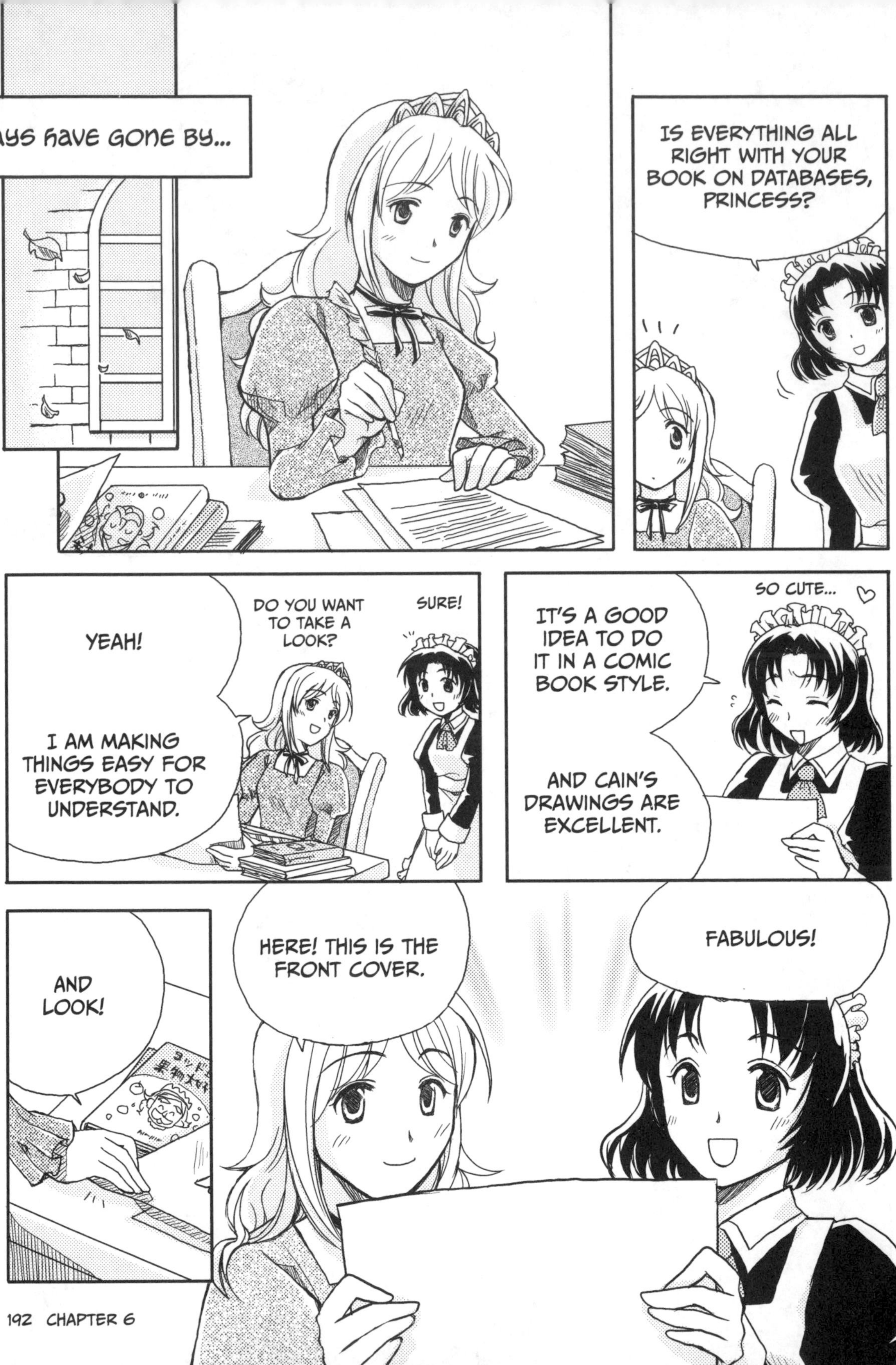
DAYS HAVE GONE BY...
IS EVERYTHING ALL RIGHT WITH YOUR BOOK ON DATABASES, PRINCESS?
YEAH!
DO YOU WANT TO TAKE A LOOK?
SURE!
I AM MAKING THINGS EASY FOR EVERYBODY TO UNDERSTAND.
IT'S A GOOD IDEA TO DO IT IN A COMIC BOOK STYLE.
SO CUTE...
AND CAIN'S DRAWINGS ARE EXCELLENT.
AND LOOK!
HERE! THIS IS THE FRONT COVER.
FABULOUS!

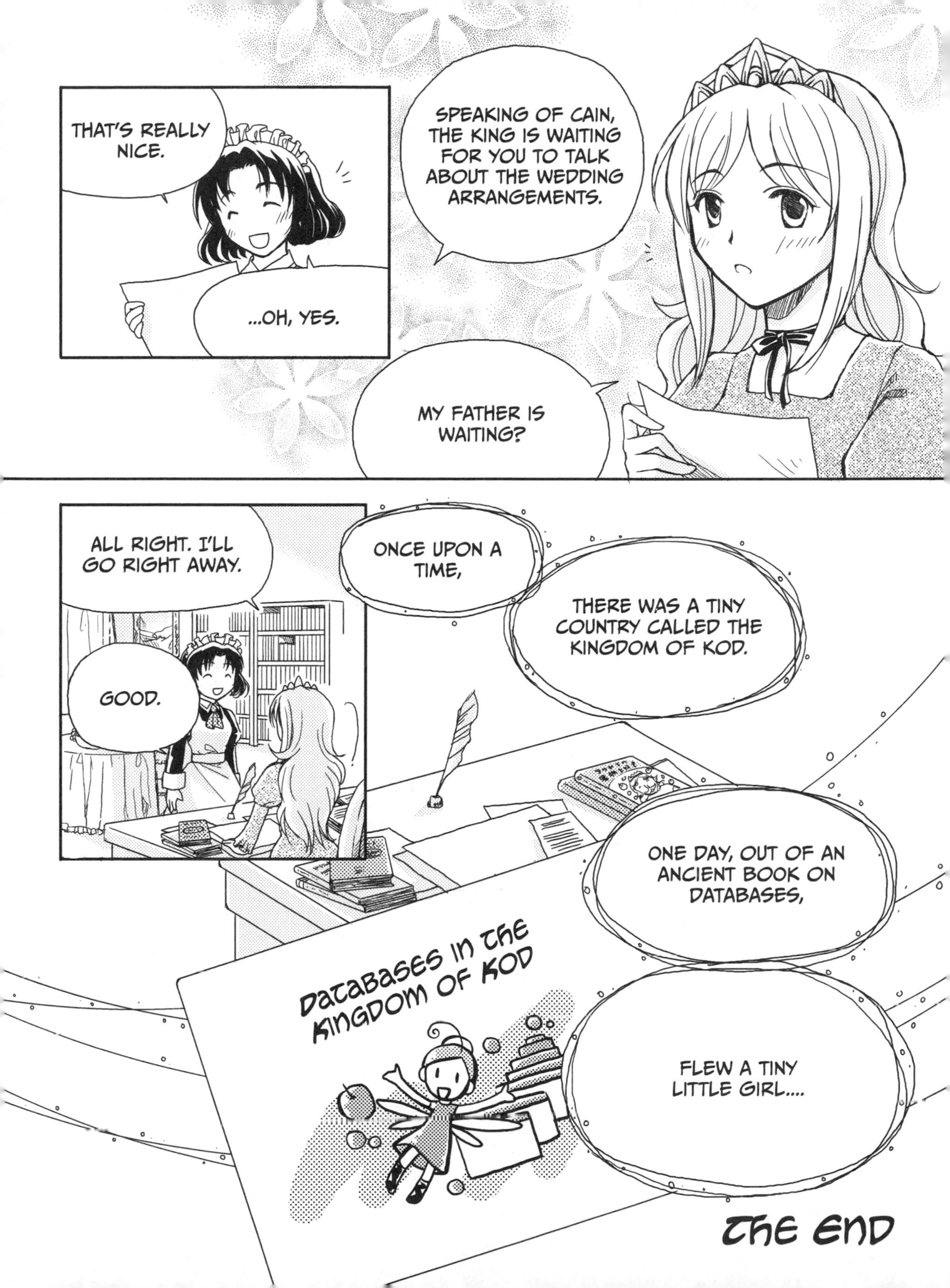
THAT'S REALLY NICE.
...OH, YES.
SPEAKING OF CAIN, THE KING IS WAITING FOR YOU TO TALK ABOUT THE WEDDING ARRANGEMENTS.
MY FATHER IS WAITING?
ALL RIGHT. I'LL GO RIGHT AWAY.
GOOD.
ONCE UPON A TIME,
THERE WAS A TINY COUNTRY CALLED THE KINGDOM OF KOD.
ONE DAY, OUT OF AN ANCIENT BOOK ON DATABASES,
DATABASES IN THE KINGDOM OF KOD
FLEW A TINY LITTLE GIRL....
THE END

DATABASES ON THE WEB

Databases are used for many different purposes, such as train seat reservation systems and bank deposit systems. They are indispensable in daily life and in business operations. As I showed Ruruna and Cain, web-based database systems are popular as well. In a web-based system, the communications protocol used is HyperText Transfer Protocol (HTTP). Server software running on a web server waits for a request from a user. When a user request (HTTP request) is sent, the software answers the request and returns a corresponding web page (HTTP response).

A *web page* consists of text files in HTML format. Other files specified by Uniform Resource Locators (URLs) are embedded within a web page to present information such as images.

WEB CLIENT
WEB SERVER
HTTP REQUEST
HTTP RESPONSE
WEB PAGE

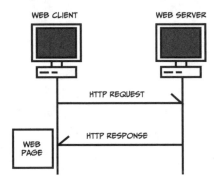

When a database is used with a web page, a database server is added to the system shown above. This system can be configured in three layers and is referred to as a *three-tier client/server system*. A three-tier client/server system consists of a presentation layer, a logic layer, and a data layer.

LOGIC LAYER
DATA LAYER
DATABASE SERVER
ROUTER
INTERNET
ROUTER
PRESENTATION LAYER
CLIENT

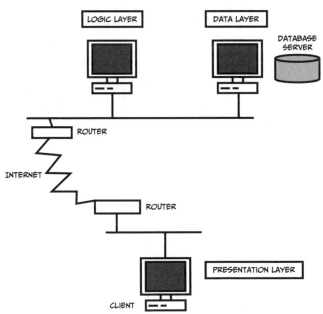

The *presentation layer* receives user input, such as search conditions, that needs to be passed on to the database. The presentation layer also processes query results received from the database so that they can be displayed. A web browser (such as Internet Explorer or Firefox) functions as a presentation tool for the user.

The logic layer performs data processing. This layer is where SQL statements are composed. Processes performed here are written in one or more programming languages. Depending on the contents and load of processes, several servers, such as an application server and a web server, may be used to handle processing.

The data layer processes data on a database server. Search results are returned from the database in response to SQL queries.

Makes queries to the database and processes data
LOGIC LAYER
DATA LAYER
Manages the database
DATABASE SERVER
SERVER
ROUTER
INTERNET
ROUTER
Receives user input and displays results
PRESENTATION LAYER
CLIENT

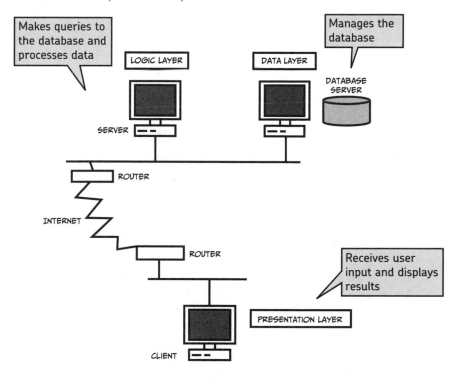

The three-tier client/server configuration is a flexible and simple system. For example, when making additions or modifications to an application, you can separate the portion you want to edit as a logic layer. In the presentation layer, you can use a web browser, eliminating the need for installing a separate software program.

Makes addition and modification of functions easier
LOGIC LAYER
DATA LAYER
DATABASE SERVER
SERVER
ROUTER
INTERNET
ROUTER
A web browser can be used here for operations
PRESENTATION LAYER
CLIENT

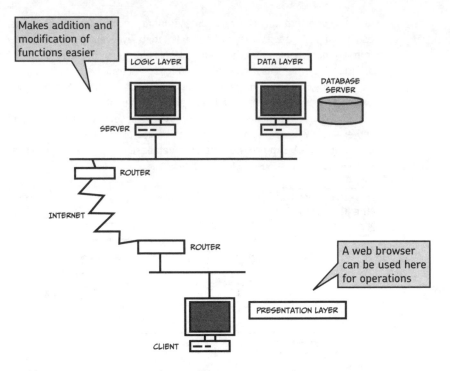

USING STORED PROCEDURES

In a web-based system, too much traffic on the network can be a problem. Fortunately, you can store program logic inside the database server itself as stored procedures.

Storing procedures on the database server helps reduce the load on the network, because it eliminates the need for frequent transfers of SQL queries. In addition, storing procedures also makes it easier to develop applications, since standard processes can be encapsulated into easy-to-use procedures. Actually, stored procedures are just a special kind of a more broad category called *stored programs*. The other two types of stored programs are *stored functions* and *triggers*.

TYPES OF STORED PROGRAMS

Program	**Definition**
Stored procedure	Program that does not return values from the processing procedure
Stored function	Program that returns values from the processing procedure
Trigger	Program that is launched automatically before and after the database operations

QUESTIONS

Can you answer these questions? The correct answers are on page 205.

Q1

In a three-tier client/server system, on which layer does the database operate?

Q2

In a three-tier client/server system, on which layer are user interactions received and results displayed?

What is a Distributed Database?

In a Web-based system, processing is distributed among a database server, a web server, and a web browser, with different tasks assigned to each. This type of distributed system allows for flexible processing and decreases the processing capacity required by each server.

But a database server itself can be distributed among several servers. Distributed database servers can be in different locations or on the same network. Note, however, that a distributed database may be handled as a single database. If the distributed database appears to be a single server, the user doesn't have to worry about data locations or transfers.

A database can be distributed horizontally or vertically, as you'll see.

Horizontal Distribution

Horizontal distribution uses several peer database servers. Each database server can use data from other database servers, and in turn, each one makes itself available to the other database servers. This structure is used for a system of extended databases that operate separately in each department.

A horizontally distributed database is a failure-resistant system by design, since failure on one server will not affect database operation.

SERVER A
SERVER B
Even when a failure occurs on the server in Department A,
ROUTER
ROUTER
other servers continue to operate normally.
SERVER C
SERVER D

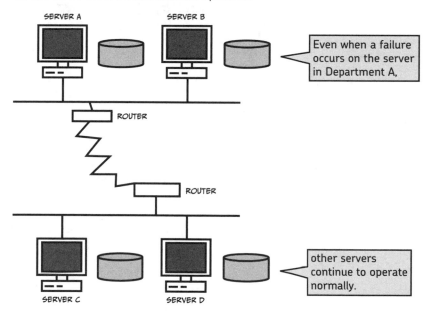

VERTICAL DISTRIBUTION

Vertical distribution assigns different functions to different database servers. One of the servers functions as the main server and performs a key role, while the others are in charge of processing tasks as requested. A vertically distributed database makes it easier to manage the main database server, though this main server will have a heavy load. An example of vertical distribution would include a company-wide main server and individual servers operating in each department.

This server operates the entire server system.
MAIN SERVER
SERVER A
ROUTER
ROUTER
SERVER B
SERVER C

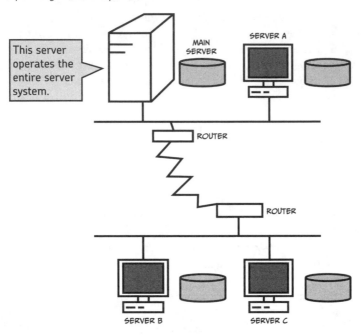

Partitioning Data

In a distributed database, data is spread across servers for storage. You should carefully consider how to divide up the data. Data can be split in the following ways.

HORIZONTAL PARTITIONING

A *horizontal partition* divides data into units of rows. Rows resulting from the split are distributed across servers. This form of partitioning is often used when data can be ordered into groups in such a way that related data, which is often accessed at the same time, is stored on the same server.

REGION A BUSINESS DEPARTMENT
Product name
Unit price
District
Person in charge
REGION B BUSINESS DEPARTMENT

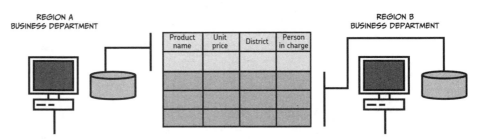

Vertical Partitioning

A *vertical partition* divides data into units of columns. Columns resulting from the split are distributed across servers. For example, a vertical partition can be used to manage and join independent databases belonging to departments like the Merchandise Department, the Overseas Business Department, and the Export Department.

MERCHANDISE DEPARTMENT
Product name
Unit price
District
Person in charge
OVERSEAS BUSINESS DEPARTMENT

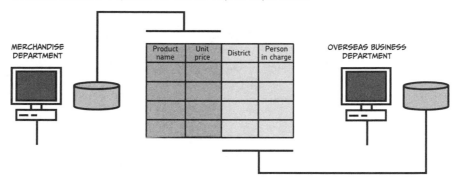

Preventing Inconsistencies with a Two-Phase Commit

Databases on different servers in a distributed database system can be configured to act as a single database in the eyes of users. To achieve this, various steps must be taken to deal with the fact that data is actually distributed across different servers.

First, whenever data is committed, all data on all servers must be updated consistently.

In a distributed database system, the standard commit method may lead to one of the servers being updated while another is not, as shown below. This is a violation of the atomicity property of transactions, as this transaction will not end with either a commit or rollback. This would also cause the database system as a whole to become inconsistent.

USER
SERVER A
SERVER B
UPDATE OPERATION
UPDATE OPERATION
COMMIT
COMMIT

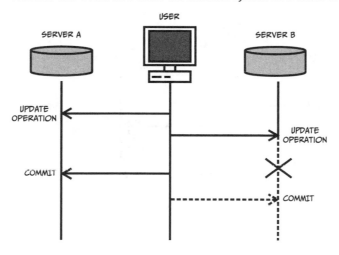

Therefore, a two-phase commit is adopted in a distributed database system. The *two phase commit* creates one commit operation from both the first and the second commit operations.

A two-phase commit operation involves a coordinator and participants. In the first phase of a two-phase commit operation, the coordinator asks the participants if a commit operation is possible. The participants send an OK reply if it is. This preparatory step is referred to as a *prepare*. In the second phase, the coordinator gives the instructions for a commit, and all participants perform a commit accordingly.

COORDINATOR
PARTICIPANT
PARTICIPANT
UPDATE OPERATION
UPDATE OPERATION
SECURE
SECURE
OK
OK
COMMIT
COMMIT

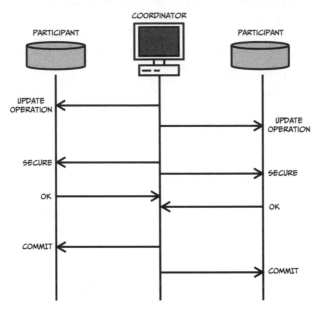

If any one node fails to secure the operation in the two-phase commit, all participants receive a rollback directive. This is how databases on all servers remain consistent with each other.

COORDINATOR
PARTICIPANT
PARTICIPANT
UPDATE OPERATION
UPDATE OPERATION
SECURE
SECURE
OK
OK
ROLLBACK
ROLLBACK

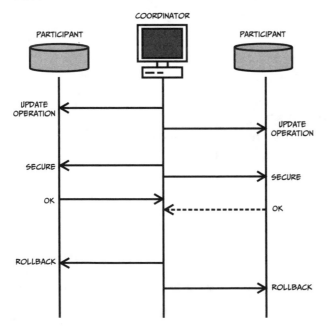

QUESTIONS

Try these questions about two-phase commits. The answers are on page 205.

Q3

In a two-phase commit scheme, what instructions does the coordinator give during the first phase?

Q4

In a two-phase commit scheme, what instructions does the coordinator give during the second phase?

Database Replication

Some distributed databases have a duplicated, or replica, database that reduces the load on the network. This practice is referred to as *replication*. The primary database is referred to as the *master database*, and the copy is called the *replica*. There are several types of replication.

READ-ONLY

A *read-only replica* is created and downloaded from the master database on the main server. To change data, users must connect to the main server.

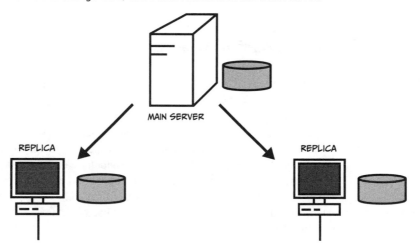

MAIN SERVER

REPLICA

REPLICA

REPLICATION ENABLED FOR ALL SERVERS

In this method, the same master database is shared by all servers. Updates to any of the servers are reflected in all other servers.

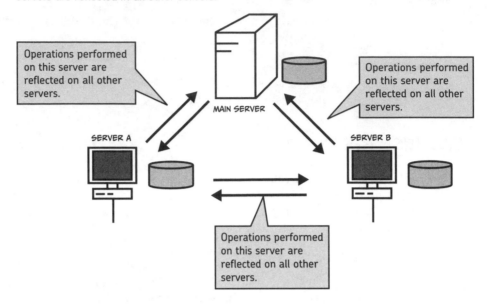

Operations performed on this server are reflected on all other servers.

Operations performed on this server are reflected on all other servers.

MAIN SERVER

SERVER A

SERVER B

Operations performed on this server are reflected on all other servers.

FURTHER APPLICATION OF DATABASES

This final section introduces applied technologies related to databases.

XML

Extensible Markup Language (XML) is becoming increasingly popular as a data storage method. XML represents data by enclosing it in tags. Since these tags can convey information about the data they contain, this language is useful for data storage and retrieval.

XML is useful because its strictly structured grammar makes programmed processes easy. Moreover, XML comes in text files (which are easy to edit) and can communicate with other systems. For these reasons, XML is sometimes used as a data representation method in place of a database.

```
<?xml version="1.0"?>
<products>
  <fruit>
    <product code>101</product code>
    <product name>Melon</product name>
    <unit price>800</unit price>
  </fruit>
  <fruit>
    <product code>102</product code>
    <product name>Strawberry</product name>
    <unit price>150</unit price>
  </fruit>
  <fruit>
    <product code>103</product code>
    <product name>Apple</product name>
    <unit price>120</unit price>
  </fruit>
</products>
```

OBJECT-ORIENTED DATABASES

A relational database stores text data in a table. However, a relational database may be inadequate when handling certain types of data. That's where an object-oriented database (OODB) comes in.

The object-oriented method uses *objects*—sets of data and instructions on how that data should be used. You can hide the data and only expose the operations upon the data in order to handle the object as an independent component. This technique is referred to as *encapsulation*.

In an object-oriented database, each object is represented with an identifier. Sometimes, an object is also called an *instance*.

In an object-oriented database, you can also manage *compound objects*—one object nested within another. This means, for example, that you can store data consisting of an image combined with text as a single object. The object-oriented database allows for flexible management of complex data.

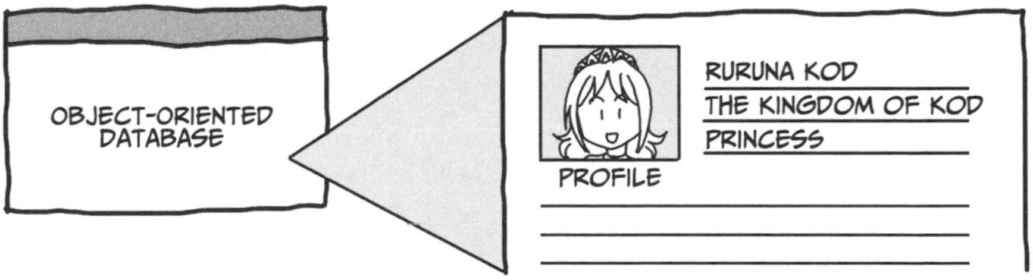
OBJECT-ORIENTED DATABASE
RURUNA KOD
THE KINGDOM OF KOD
PRINCESS
PROFILE

In an object-oriented database, various concepts can ease object-oriented development. The template for objects is referred to as *class*. For example, suppose you have designed an Apple class. Objects (instances) in that class may be Apple A, Apple B, and so on. The Apple class enables the creation of these objects.

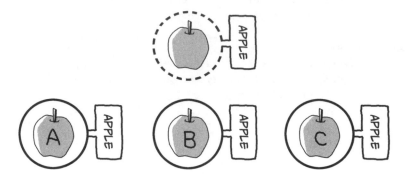

APPLE
A
APPLE
B
APPLE
C
APPLE

In an object-oriented scheme, a class can also have hierarchical relationships. You can create a child class that has the same data and functions of a parent class. This relationship is referred to as *inheritance*. You can also give unique functions to the child class.

For example, class Apple and class Orange may inherit the data and functions from class Fruit, but they also each have their own unique data and functions. In an object-oriented scheme, you can use hierarchical relationships to allow for efficient development.

FRUIT
APPLE
ORANGE
BANANA

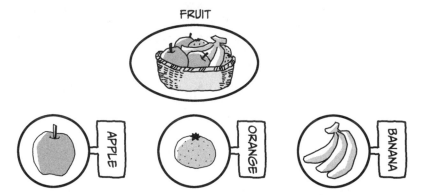

Summary

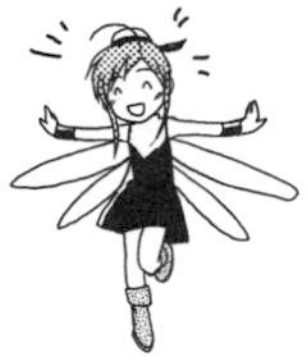

- The three-tier client/server system is a method of Web-based system configuration.
- A database acts as a data layer.
- A distributed database system handles databases that are dispersed.
- A two-phase commit method is used in a distributed database.

Answers

Q1 Data layer

Q2 Presentation layer

Q3 Prepare

Q4 Commit or rollback

Closing Remarks

Have you enjoyed studying databases? You will need to learn even more before you can manage all the aspects of operating a database, but the fundamentals of databases always stay the same. By firmly understanding the basics, you can identify significant data in the real world and design and operate databases. You can acquire advanced database skills by building on your fundamental knowledge. Good luck!

FREQUENTLY USED SQL STATEMENTS

BASIC QUERY

```
SELECT column_name, ...
FROM table_name;
```

CONDITIONAL QUERY

```
SELECT column_name, ...
FROM table_name
WHERE condition;
```

PATTERN MATCHING

```
SELECT column_name, ...
FROM table_name
WHERE column_name LIKE 'pattern';
```

SORTED SEARCH

```
SELECT column_name, ...
FROM table_name
WHERE condition
ORDER BY column_name;
```

AGGREGATING AND GROUPING

```
SELECT column_name, ...
FROM table_name
WHERE condition
GROUP BY column_names_for_grouping
HAVING condition_for_grouped_rows
```

JOINING TABLES

```
SELECT table_name1.column_name, ...
FROM table_name1,table_name2, ...
WHERE table_name1.column_name = table_name2.column_name
```

CREATING A TABLE

```
CREATE TABLE table_name(
column_name1 datatype,
column_name2 datatype,
...
);
```

CREATING A VIEW

```
CREATE VIEW view_name
AS SELECT statement
```

DELETING A REAL TABLE

```
DROP TABLE table_name;
```

DELETING A VIEW

```
DROP VIEW view_name;
```

INSERTING A ROW

```
INSERT INTO table_name(column_name1, ...)
VALUES (value1, ...)
```

UPDATING A ROW

```
UPDATE table_name
SET column_name = value1, ...
WHERE condition;
```

DELETING A ROW

```
DELETE FROM table_name
WHERE condition;
```

REFERENCES

Chen, P.P. 1976. "The Entity-Relationship Model: Toward a Unified View of Data,"
  ACM Transactions on Database Systems 1 (1): 9–36.

Codd, E.F. 1970. "A Relational Model of Data for Large Shared Data Banks,"
  Communications of the ACM, 13 (6): 377–387.

Date, C.J. and Hugh Darwen. 1997. *A Guide to the SQL Standard*, 4th ed. Reading, MA:
  Addison-Wesley.

Masunaga, Yoshifumi. 1990. *Basics of Relational Database*. Tokyo: Ohmsha.

Database Language: SQL, JIS X3005-1-4, 2002.

ISO/IEC 9075, Information Technology—Database Languages—SQL, 1992.

ISO/IEC 9075, Information Technology—Database Languages—SQL, 1995.

ISO/IEC 9075, 1, 2, 3, 4, Information Technology—Database Languages—SQL, 1999.

IT Engineers' Skill Standards—Technical Engineers (Database), Information-Technology
  Promotion Agency, Japan.

INDEX

ABOUT THE AUTHOR

Mana Takahashi is a graduate of the University of Tokyo, Faculty of Economics, in Tokyo, Japan. She is an active technical writer and has published a number of books on topics such as Java, C, XML, Information Engineering, and System Administration.

COLOPHON

The Manga Guide to Databases was laid out in Adobe InDesign. The fonts are CCMeanwhile and Chevin.

The book was printed and bound at Malloy Incorporated in Ann Arbor, Michigan. The paper is Glatfelter Spring Forge 60# Smooth Eggshell, which is certified by the Sustainable Forestry Initiative (SFI).

UPDATES

Visit *http://www.nostarch.com/mg_databases.htm* for updates, errata, and other information.

MORE MANGA GUIDES

Find more Manga Guides at your favorite bookstore, and learn more about the series at *http://www.edumanga.me/*.

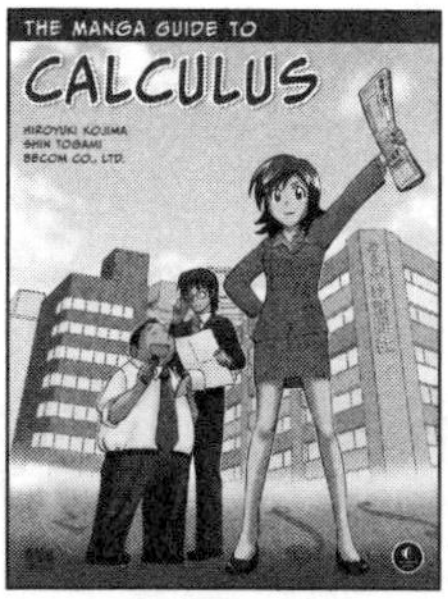
THE MANGA GUIDE TO
CALCULUS

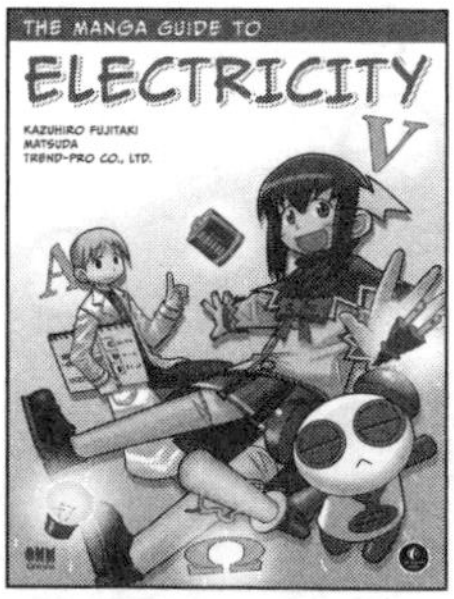
THE MANGA GUIDE TO
ELECTRICITY

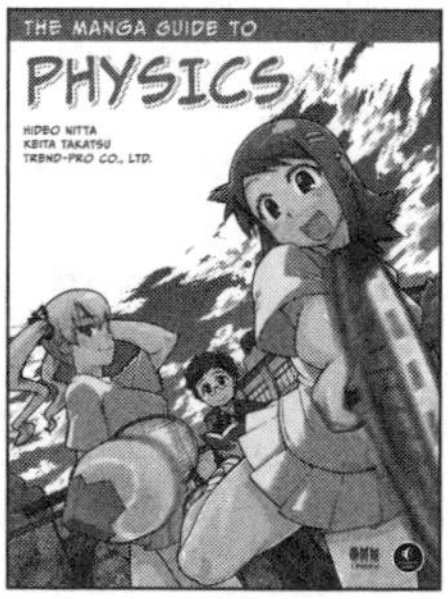
THE MANGA GUIDE TO
PHYSICS

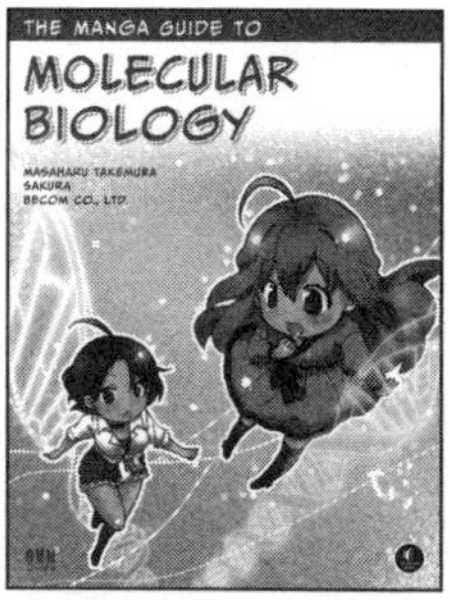
THE MANGA GUIDE TO
MOLECULAR
BIOLOGY